Agentic Coding with Claude Code

The everyday developer's guide to agentic coding with Claude Code

Eden Marco

<packt>

Agentic Coding with Claude Code

Portfolio Director: Ashwin Nair
Relationship Lead: Sneha Shinde
Project Manager: Vishnu Priya R
Content Engineer: Roshan Ravi Kumar
Technical Editor: Rohit Singh
Copy Editor: Safis Editing
Indexer: Hemangini Bari
Proofreader: Roshan Ravi Kumar
Production Designer: Shantanu Zagade
Growth Lead: Priyadarshini Sharma

First published: March 2026

Production reference: 2180626

Published by Packt Publishing Ltd.
Grosvenor House
11 St Paul's Square
Birmingham
B3 1RB, UK.

ISBN 978-1-80602-259-5
`www.packtpub.com`

I would like to dedicate this book to my father, my role model and inspiration.

– Eden Marco

Contributors

About the author

Eden Marco is an LLM specialist at Google Cloud and a LangChain Ambassador with years of experience in software engineering and cloud architecture. He was one of the first engineers at Orca Security, holds a bachelor's degree in computer science from the Technion, and has taught at Reichman University. Eden creates practical, production-ready courses based on real-world experience.

About the reviewers

Pablo Garner is head of IT and AI at Champions (UK) plc, where he leads infrastructure and develops AI-powered internal platforms. With over eight years' experience in IT and computing, he specializes in applied AI, automation, and cloud architecture. He is completing the NVIDIA AI Engineer Level 6 programme, and has contributed to Anthropic's AI safety research program as an external red team researcher. Pablo builds agent-driven systems and shares his work at p4blo.dev, focusing on real-world AI implementation.

I would like to thank the Packt team for the opportunity to contribute as a Technical Reviewer, and my partner Jade and our children Storm and Saint for their support and encouragement.

Iago Cavalcante is a software developer passionate about technology and the impact it creates on people's lives and on businesses. He works with Elixir, React, React Native, Vue.js, and TypeScript, focused on scalability and code quality. Based in Belém, Brazil, he co-founded DevsNorte, a community dedicated to growing the local tech ecosystem. He believes in giving back: the more he shares and learns from others, the more he grows as a professional and person. He collaborates on open source projects and writes technical articles to share knowledge. A proud father of Enzo and husband to Karla, he credits his family as the foundation behind every achievement. He loves exchanging ideas, hearing different perspectives, and continuously learning.

Go Beyond with Practical Learning

If you'd like to go beyond learning the foundational knowledge from a book, you should check out our hands-on workshops that offer clear, live, practical guidance from globally renowned instructors, with the opportunity to get your doubts clarified.

New Workshops are added every fortnight.

Scan the QR code below to check out our upcoming workshops and sign up to receive exclusive offers and discounts.

Table of Contents

Chapter 3: Getting Started with Claude Code – A Tour of Essential Commands 43

Preface

Generative AI and coding agents are rapidly changing how software is built. Tools such as Claude Code, Cursor, and LangChain deep agents are no longer limited to simple prompt-based interactions. They operate across full code bases, integrate with external tools, and execute long-running, multi-step workflows. As these systems become more capable, understanding how they work and how to control them becomes essential.

This book focuses on building a strong and practical understanding of **Claude Code**, agentic workflows, and the underlying concepts that make modern coding agents effective. A central theme throughout the book is context engineering, which explains how agents construct, manage, and use context as they reason and act. As agents grow more complex and tool-driven, proper context handling directly affects performance, cost, reliability, and consistency.

In this book, you will learn how Claude Code interacts with a code base, how to configure it for daily use, and how to extend it using the **Model Context Protocol** (**MCP**). You will explore automation with GitHub Actions, structured planning, multi-agent workflows, subagents, output styles, and agent skills. The book also examines deeper architectural topics, including how deep agents operate and how long-horizon workflows are implemented in practice.

Rather than focusing only on surface-level usage, this book aims to help you understand how these systems are designed and why they behave the way they do. By combining practical examples with deeper architectural insight, the goal is to give you both the skills to use modern coding agents effectively and the understanding needed to adapt as the field continues to evolve.

Who this book is for

This book is for developers and engineers who want to move beyond chat-based AI and build agentic, automated development workflows using Claude Code and MCP. It is intended for application developers with prior software engineering experience who want to integrate context-aware AI agents into their terminal and IDE, automate complex coding tasks, and design scalable multi-agent systems.

It will also benefit AI engineers and generative AI practitioners who work closely with modern development workflows.

To get the most out of this book, you should have experience writing and debugging code in Python or TypeScript, be comfortable working with Git and development environments, and understand core generative AI concepts such as LLMs, RAG, and agents. This is not a beginner-level book and assumes prior software development experience.

What this book covers

Chapter 1, Context Engineering, introduces context engineering and explains why it is critical when building modern AI agents. It covers how context evolves from prompt engineering, how it grows in complex systems, and how poor context handling affects performance and cost. The chapter also examines system prompts and practical context management using Claude code.

Chapter 2, The Gist of Claude Code, provides a practical introduction to Claude Code and explains how it interacts with a code base. It covers project initialization, `CLAUDE.md` files, permissions, and context management. The chapter also introduces MCP, spec-driven design, and begins building the HookHub project used throughout the book.

Chapter 3, Getting Started with Claude Code – A Tour of Essential Commands, focuses on configuring Claude Code for daily use. It covers pricing and authentication, slash commands, user- and project-level configuration, and integration with Cursor. The chapter also explores hooks, checkpointing, custom commands, and the role of the language server protocol.

Chapter 4, Extending Claude Code with MCP Servers and Plugins, explains the Model Context Protocol and how it standardizes integration between AI applications and external tools. It covers MCP architecture, including hosts, clients, and servers, and demonstrates how to configure local and remote MCP servers. The chapter also addresses context management, performance considerations, and plugin-based extensions.

Chapter 5, Automating Your Development Workflow with Claude Code and GitHub, explores the integration between Claude Code and GitHub. It covers repository configuration, pull request and issue automation, and the use of GitHub Actions for workflow execution. The chapter also explains how YAML workflow files define event-driven automation.

Chapter 6, Claude Code Planning and Multi-Agent Workflows, examines structured agentic workflows using planning and coordinated multi-agent execution. It explains how spec-driven development improves predictability and how multiple agents can collaborate within the same codebase.

Chapter 7, Working with Claude Code Subagents, introduces Claude Code subagents and explains how they enable structured and isolated workflows. It covers custom subagent configuration, context flow, and concurrent execution using the Infinite Agentic Loop pattern.

Chapter 8, Creating and Customizing Output Styles, examines how output styles shape Claude Code's responses. It covers creating and scoping custom styles, structured formats such as

YAML, and automating behavior within style definitions. The chapter also explains how to manage roles and session configuration.

Chapter 9, Understanding Agent Skills, explores agent skills as a mechanism for extending AI agent capabilities. It covers foundational concepts, practical usage in Claude Code and LangChain DeepAgent, and the internal context flow when a skill is invoked. The chapter concludes with a real implementation example.

Chapter 10, Using Claude Code Desktop, explains how to use Claude Code within the desktop application. It covers switching between local and cloud modes, running parallel agents with Git worktrees, and coordinating feature branches across environments.

Chapter 11, Understanding Deep Agents, examines deep agents and their role in long-horizon task execution. It defines the characteristics of deep agents and analyzes the LangChain deep agents harness, including its architecture and execution model.

To get the most out of this book

This book assumes prior experience with software development and generative AI concepts. Before you begin, you should be comfortable writing and debugging code in Python or TypeScript, running programs from the terminal, and working with a code base. Basic Git knowledge, such as cloning repositories and committing changes, is expected. You should also understand virtual environments and environment variables.

Familiarity with **large language models** (**LLMs**) and core concepts such as agents, RAG, and ReAct is required. You should have previously interacted with an LLM and built at least a simple agent. This book does not cover beginner-level programming or introductory generative AI topics.

To follow along with the hands-on examples, you will need a working development environment with Node.js and a simple Next.js setup, as introduced in the early chapters. You will also need access to Claude Code, along with the appropriate authentication and pricing configuration. Some chapters require installing and configuring the GitHub CLI, working with GitHub repositories, and using GitHub Actions. Later sections involve configuring MCP servers, both local and remote, and running Claude Code within Cursor and the Claude desktop application.

It is recommended that you follow the examples step by step and experiment with the configurations as they are introduced. The book builds progressively, and several chapters rely on projects and setups established earlier, including the HookHub project.

This book includes examples and screenshots adapted from the author's original course materials, which reference repositories created for instructional purposes.

Note

Disclaimer

This book is an independent publication and is not affiliated with, endorsed by, sponsored by, or officially associated with Anthropic, PBC, or any of its subsidiaries or affiliates. "Claude," "Claude Code," and "Anthropic" are trademarks or registered trademarks of Anthropic, PBC. All other trademarks mentioned herein are the property of their respective owners.

The author is an employee of Google LLC. However, this book is a personal project and does not represent the views, opinions, or official positions of Google LLC, Google Cloud, Alphabet Inc., or any of their subsidiaries or affiliates. This book is not endorsed by, sponsored by, or officially associated with Google in any capacity. "Google," "Google Cloud," and related marks are trademarks of Google LLC.

The content in this book is based solely on the author's personal experience, independent research, and publicly available documentation. The views, opinions, and interpretations expressed are those of the author alone and do not represent the official positions, strategies, or opinions of Anthropic PBC, Google LLC, or any other organization.

While every effort has been made to ensure the accuracy and completeness of the information presented, the author makes no warranties or representations, express or implied, regarding the completeness, accuracy, reliability, or suitability of the content. AI tools and their associated APIs, features, and functionalities evolve rapidly, and information in this book may become outdated after publication.

The author and publisher shall not be held liable for any damages, losses, or consequences arising directly or indirectly from the use of or reliance on the information contained in this book. Readers are encouraged to consult Anthropic's official documentation at `docs.anthropic.com` for the most current and authoritative information.

Download the example code files

This book includes a complete downloadable code bundle containing all the example projects and files used throughout the chapters. We recommend downloading the bundle so you can follow along smoothly and experiment with the examples.

Use the bundle as a practical starting point. Modify it, extend it, and apply what you learn by creating your own variations as you progress through the chapters.

Get the code bundle

If you bought the book directly from Packt:

1. Go to **packtpub.com**
2. Click your **profile picture** and select **Your Orders**
3. Find this book and click **Download Code**

If you bought this book from Amazon or any other channel partner:

1. Go to `packtpub.com/unlock` or scan the following QR code
2. Search for this book
3. Sign up or log in to your free Packt account
4. Upload your proof of purchase and download the code bundle locally

Usage note: You're free to use and modify this code for personal learning and non-commercial projects.

Download the color images

We also provide a PDF file that has color images of the screenshots and diagrams used in this book. You can download it here:`https://packt.link/gbp/9781806022595`.

Conventions used

There are a number of text conventions used throughout this book.

`CodeInText`: Indicates code words in text, database table names, folder names, filenames, file extensions, pathnames, dummy URLs, user input, and X/Twitter handles. For example: "This is done by initializing `CLAUDE.md` files so they can be added to the project context."

A block of code is set as follows:

```
add_context() {
  local context_ref="$1"
```

```
    grep -qxF "$context_ref" "$CLAUDE_MD" || echo "$context_ref" >>
      "$CLAUDE_MD"
}
```

Any command-line input or output is written as follows:

```
npx create-next-app@latest
```

Bold: Indicates a new term, an important word, or words that you see on the screen. For instance, words in menus or dialog boxes appear in the text like this. For example: "Select **Yes** for now, and choose not to be asked again during this session."

> **Note**
>
> Warnings or important notes appear like this.

> **Tip**
>
> Tips and tricks appear like this.

Get in touch

Feedback from our readers is always welcome.

General feedback: If you have questions about any aspect of this book or have any general feedback, please email us at customercare@packt.com and mention the book's title in the subject of your message.

Errata: Although we have taken every care to ensure the accuracy of our content, mistakes do happen. If you have found a mistake in this book, we would be grateful if you reported it to us. Please visit http://www.packt.com/submit-errata, click **Submit Errata**, and fill in the form.

Piracy: If you come across any illegal copies of our works in any form on the internet, we would be grateful if you would provide us with the location address or website name. Please contact us at copyright@packt.com with a link to the material.

If you are interested in becoming an author: If there is a topic that you have expertise in and you are interested in either writing or contributing to a book, please visit.

Share your thoughts

Once you've read *Agentic Coding with Claude Code,* we'd love to hear your thoughts! Scan the QR code below to go straight to the Amazon review page for this book and share your feedback.

`https://packt.link/r/1806022591`

Your review is important to us and the tech community and will help us make sure we're delivering excellent quality content.

Free benefits with your book

This book includes free benefits designed to support your learning and help you apply what you learn effectively. Activate them now for instant access (see the *How to unlock* section for instructions).

Here's a quick overview of what you can instantly unlock with your purchase

Complete Code Bundle

Download the full source code for this book's examples and projects.

DRM-Free PDF Version

Download DRM-free PDF and ePub copies of this book.

7-Day Packt Library Access

Get 7-day unlimited access to 8,000+ books and videos. No credit card required.

Available for first-time Packt+ trial users only.

Next-Gen Reader Access

Read this book on Packt Reader with progress sync, dark mode and note-taking.

How to unlock

Scan the QR code (or go to `packtpub.com/unlock`), search for this book by name, confirm the edition, and then follow the steps on the page.

UNLOCK NOW

Part 1

Foundations of Context Engineering and Claude Code

In *Part 1* of this book, you'll build a clear and practical understanding of context engineering and why it matters when working with modern AI coding agents. We'll examine how the shift from simple prompt engineering to structured context management changes the way agents are designed and used. You'll explore how context is created, how it grows over time, and how poor management affects performance, cost, and reliability.

Alongside the conceptual foundation, you'll begin working directly with Claude Code. Through guided examples, you'll see how it interprets a codebase, constructs working context, and applies that context to real development tasks. By the end of this part, you'll have a grounded understanding of both the theory and day-to-day operation of Claude Code.

This part of the book includes the following chapters:

- *Chapter 1, Context Engineering*
- *Chapter 2, The Gist of Claude Code*
- *Chapter 3, Getting Started with Claude Code – A Tour of Essential Commands*

1

Context Engineering

This chapter introduces context engineering and explains why it has become a critical concept when building and using modern AI agents. While many AI systems are often described as "just prompts wrapped around an LLM," this chapter shows why that view breaks down as agents become more complex, long-running, and tool-driven. You will learn where context comes from, why it keeps growing, and how poor context handling leads to degraded performance, higher costs, hallucinations, and inconsistent behavior.

The goal of this chapter is to give you a clear mental model for context engineering and show how it is applied in practice. We start by explaining how context engineering evolved from prompt engineering, then use Claude Code as a concrete example of how modern agents write, select, compress, and isolate context. Towards the end, we will examine system prompts, why they still matter, and how to design them effectively.

> Note
>
> **Your purchase includes a free PDF copy + code bundle**
>
> Your purchase includes a DRM-free PDF copy of this book, the code bundle, and additional exclusive extras. See the *Free benefits with your book* section in the *Preface* to unlock them instantly and maximize your learning.

The following topics will be covered in this chapter:

- Introduction to context engineering
- Claude Code and its context engineering philosophy
- System prompts and why they matter

> **Note**
>
> This discussion is based on publicly available information, including Anthropic's engineering blog posts and community analysis. It does not represent an official statement from Anthropic.

Introduction to context engineering

In this section, we will go into what context engineering is. Now, if you've been working with AI agents and probably coding agents such as Cursor and Claude Code, or maybe you have even developed AI agents for your companies or for your own use, you probably know that it basically all boils down to a prompt being sent to an LLM and a lot of engineering around it.

There is some truth in calling applications such as Cursor and Claude Code just wrappers around LLMs. However, building really good wrappers requires a lot of deep knowledge and a lot of engineering work. Another term often used for this surrounding system is an *agent harness*. The harness is the orchestration layer around the LLM. It is responsible for managing tool calls, controlling the agent loop, handling errors, enforcing guardrails, and, most importantly, deciding what context is sent to the model at each step.

In practice, most of the real engineering does not live inside the LLM call itself, but around it. The model invocation is often straightforward. What determines whether an agent works reliably is how the surrounding system manages state, tools, memory, and context. This is because calls to LLMs always come with context, and this context comes from various sources and ongoing processes.

For instance, context can come from multiple places:

- It can come from the developer of the application
- It can come from the user
- It can come from previous interactions of the user, tool calls, or other external data

Every day, new sources of context are added, and the amount of context keeps increasing. Sending the correct and relevant context to the LLM is not as simple as we thought it was in the early days.

From prompt engineering to context engineering

In the early days, we believed that prompt engineering was enough. We thought that writing some fancy prompts could fix the problem and give us what we want. The issue, however, is that prompts are static, while context is extremely dynamic.

If context is dynamic, then constructing the correct context requires a dynamic system as well. It is no longer just about writing a static prompt. This is why we are entering the realm of **context engineering**. It is the natural evolution of prompt engineering, but it is a much deeper concept.

Why context matters for agents

We all know the saying "*garbage in, garbage out.*" This is one of the most common reasons why agentic systems do not perform the way they should. They are simply not provided with the right context.

LLMs cannot read our minds. We need to give them the right information. And by the way, it is not always just information or data. Sometimes we need to give them the correct tools so they can fetch other information, take actions, and perform tasks for us.

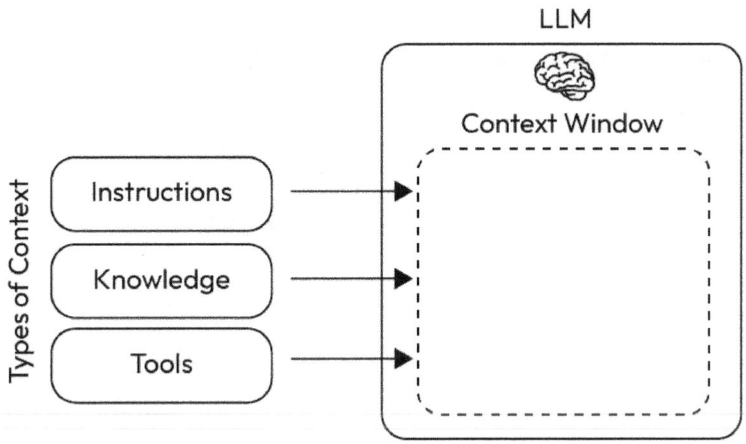

Figure 1.1 – LLM Context Window (Adapted from concepts discussed by LangChain, www.langchain.com)

LLMs are becoming better and better at reasoning. We have tool calling, and we can build AI agents that run tools, invoke them, get outputs, and loop until tasks are completed.

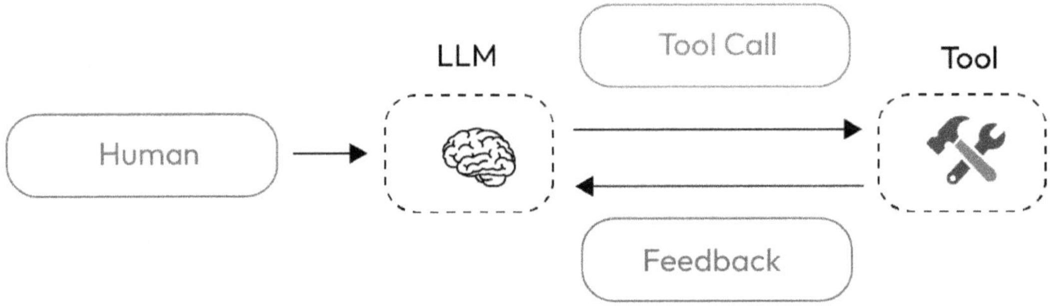

Figure 1.2 – LLM Tool Calling Loop (Adapted from concepts discussed by LangChain, www.langchain.com)

However, when it comes to long-running and complex tasks, we often accumulate feedback from tool calls.

This causes the context window to keep growing, filled with tool call results and intermediate outputs.

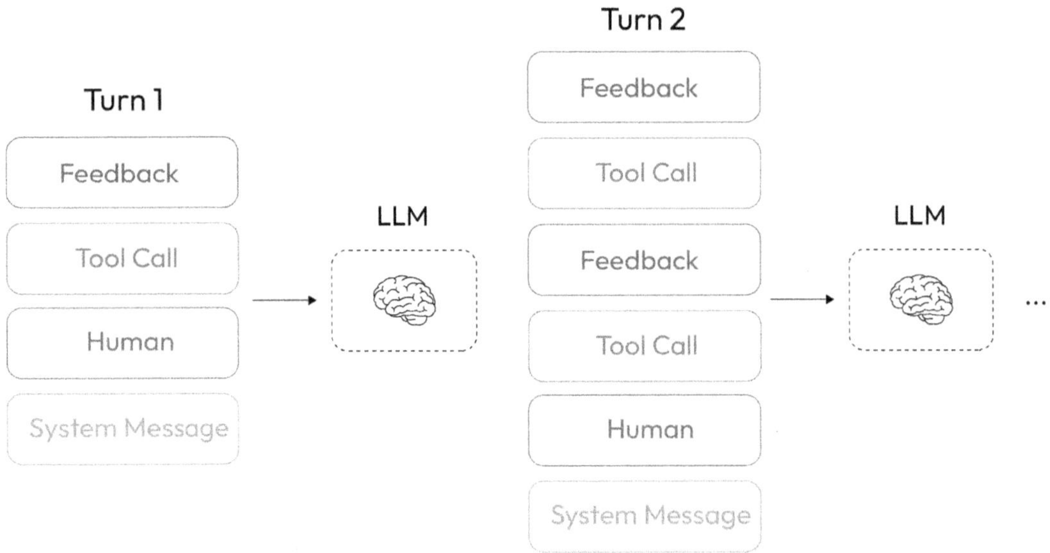

Figure 1.3 – Context Growth Across Multiple Turns (adapted from concepts discussed by LangChain, www.langchain.com)

This leads to several problems:

- The context window can exceed its size limit

- Cost and latency increase
- Agent performance starts to degrade

If nothing is done, this degradation becomes unavoidable. Recent discussions have explored why long contexts fail in practice and how degradation appears gradually as irrelevant or conflicting information accumulates. For a deeper discussion, see this great blog "*How Long Contexts Fail*" by Dan Breunig (`https://www.dbreunig.com/2025/06/22/how-contexts-fail-and-how-to-fix-them.html`). If context is allowed to grow without structure, selection, or control, then various problems will start to appear in agentic systems, such as the following:

- **Context poisoning**: When a hallucination from a tool call or LLM call enters the context and starts affecting future outputs
- **Context confusion**: When unnecessary context influences the response, even though it is not relevant to the task
- **Context clash**: When different parts of the context contradict each other

In the next section, we will discuss techniques for better context engineering. Some of these techniques are implemented by application developers, for example, in tools such as Claude Code. Other techniques are on the user side.

As users of Claude Code, we have a lot of influence over the context that is eventually sent to the LLM and the answers we receive. This means that even non-developers need to understand context engineering if they want better responses from AI systems and AI agents.

Coding agents such as Claude Code are an excellent example of how context engineering techniques are applied on both the developer side and the user side. This is exactly what we will explore in the next section, as well as how to better engineer our context.

Claude Code and its context engineering strategies

In this section, we will talk about Claude Code, its context engineering philosophy, and how Claude Code addresses these challenges. Claude Code applies these context engineering strategies by implementing all four approaches, which are as follows:

- **Write Context**: Persistent memory systems
- **Select Context**: Intelligent context retrieval and injection
- **Compress Context**: Efficient context representation and summarization
- **Isolate Context**: Multi-agent and scoped context management

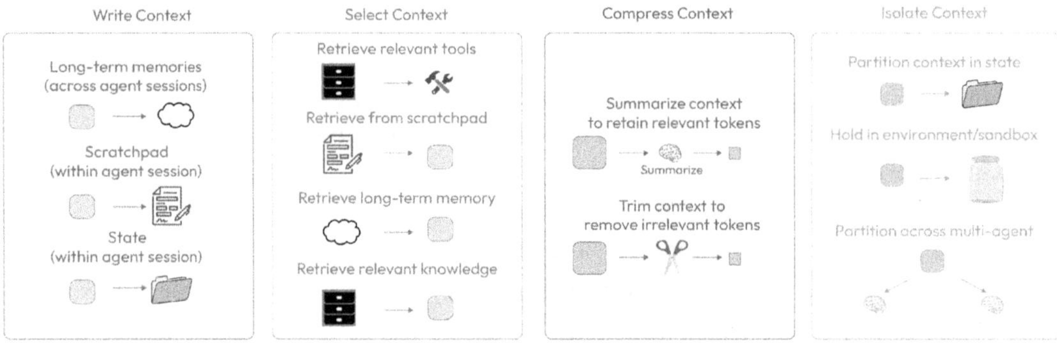

Figure 1.4 – Categories of context engineering (adapted from concepts discussed by LangChain, www.langchain.com)

Let's start with the first one.

Strategy 1: Writing context and persistent memory

The first strategy is **writing context and its persistent memory architecture**. Claude has a multilayered memory system, and Claude Code implements a three-tier memory hierarchy that persists context across sessions while coding with Claude Code.

- We first have the **project memory** (`./CLAUDE.md`). This is a team-shared context for project architecture, standards, or anything related to a specific project. This kind of memory is version-controlled, and it is available to all team members.

```
# Project Context

## Architecture Overview
This is a microservices application using:
- Node.js with Express for API services
- React with TypeScript for frontend
- PostgreSQL with Prisma ORM
- Redis for caching

## Coding Standards
- Use functional components with hooks
- Implement error boundaries for all route components
- Follow RESTful API conventions
- Write unit tests for all business logic
```

- Then we have the **user memory** (`~/.claude/CLAUDE.md`). This is stored in the home directory of the user, in the `claude` directory, in the `CLAUDE.md` file. This contains personal preferences and shortcuts across all projects for that user. It is not committed to GitHub and is user-specific. Every user will have different values here and it persists across all Claude Code sessions.

```
# Personal Development Preferences

## Code Style
- Always use explicit return types in TypeScript
- Prefer const assertions over type annotations
- Use descriptive variable names, avoid abbreviations

## Workflow Shortcuts
- When writing tests, use Jest with React Testing Library
- Always run

 `


 npm

  run lint`

 before commits
- Prefer composition over inheritance
```

- Lastly, we have **dynamic memory imports**. These allow us to import from other memory files using the @ symbol and syntax. This is similar to loading regular context into Claude Code, but this time we can have dedicated memory files with specific information that we can reference inside our memory files.

```
# In any CLAUDE.md file
@path/to/memory/file.md
@./relative/path/context.md
@~/global/user/context.md
```

We can also customize behavior by writing scripts that dynamically update the context based on the Git branch. We can then connect this script to a context-switching hook and build more adaptive workflows.

One important detail to keep in mind is that we should avoid repeatedly appending the same context references to `CLAUDE.md`. If the script simply uses >> on every run, the file will grow indefinitely with duplicate entries. To prevent this, we add a small safeguard that checks whether a context reference already exists before appending it.

Below is an improved version of the script that avoids duplicate imports:

```
# Script to dynamically update context based on git branch
#!/bin/bash
# context-switcher.sh
# Dynamically load relevant context based on user query
# Safe against duplicate imports

CLAUDE_MD="CLAUDE.md"

# Create CLAUDE.md if it doesn't exist
touch "$CLAUDE_MD"

add_context() {
  local context_ref="$1"
  grep -qxF "$context_ref" "$CLAUDE_MD" || echo "$context_ref" >> "$CLAUDE_MD"
}

# --- Branch-based context ---
branch=$(git branch --show-current 2>/dev/null)

case $branch in
  "feature/auth-"*)
    add_context "@./context/auth-system.md"
    ;;
  "feature/payment-"*)
    add_context "@./context/payment-flow.md"
    ;;
  "hotfix/"*)
    add_context "@./context/production-hotfix.md"
    ;;
esac

# --- Query-based context ---
user_input="$1"

if [[ -n "$user_input" ]]; then
  if [[ $user_input == *"database"* || $user_input == *"migration"* ]]; then
```

```
    add_context "@./context/database-context.md"
  elif [[ $user_input == *"API"* || $user_input == *"endpoint"* ]]; then
    add_context "@./context/api-context.md"
  elif [[ $user_input == *"frontend"* || $user_input == *"component"* ]]; then
    add_context "@./context/frontend-context.md"
  fi
fi
```

The key change is the `add_context` helper function. It uses `grep -qxF` to check whether a context reference already exists in `CLAUDE.md`. If it does, nothing is appended. This makes the script idempotent and safe to run on every prompt submission.

We then connect this script to a hook

```
{
  "hooks": {
    "UserPromptSubmit": {
      "command": "./scripts/context-switcher.sh \"$PROMPT\""
      "description": "Dynamically load relevant context based on
        branch and user query"
    }
  }
}
```

With this setup, context switching becomes dynamic but remains stable over time.

Strategy 2: Intelligent context retrieval

The second strategy is **intelligent context retrieval**, usually implemented through dynamic context discovery.

Claude automatically looks through folders to find helpful context files. If we are in a subfolder, it also pulls context from parent folders, but it uses more specific information when it is available. It also prioritizes recently used and frequently accessed information.

This is context engineering at the application level, and Claude Code developers implement this logic. However, users can also add persistent context themselves using the `/memory` command. For example:

```
/memory add Always use descriptive variable names
```

Claude will prompt whether this memory should be stored at the project level or the user level, and it will update the appropriate `CLAUDE.md` file automatically. This allows users to influence future behavior without manually editing context files.

Based on the tool being used, different contexts are propagated to the LLM. For example, when Claude Code is about to edit a file, it automatically remembers things such as checking the existing code style first and looking for existing functions before creating new ones. This is the context that is relevant to the edit tool.

Another example is when Claude Code is about to run a terminal command, it remembers different things, such as checking if there is an existing `npm` script before running commands or making sure the file path exists before executing it.

Strategy 3: Compression of context

The third strategy is **compression of context**, which is about efficient context representation. Claude Code includes built-in compression commands.

- The `/clear` command resets the conversation history for the current context window while keeping the underlying project memory and user memory. It is useful when the running conversation has gone in an unhelpful direction or when you want to start a fresh interaction without losing what the system has already learned about the project.
- The `/compact` command summarizes the existing conversation into a shorter form. Instead of throwing everything away, it keeps the key decisions and important information while dropping minor details. This compressed history uses less of the context window, which reduces cost and latency, and gives the model more room for new inputs.

Strategy 4: Context isolation with subagents

The fourth strategy is context isolation. For this, Claude Code uses sub-agents. Each sub-agent runs in its own isolated context window and does not inherit the full conversation history of the main agent. This strategy is about having different specialist versions of Claude Code for different tasks, each with its own focused knowledge.

Instead of Claude Code trying to do everything at once with all the information, we create specialized sub-agents that act as experts in different areas. We can have the main Claude agent, which acts as a manager and delegates tasks. We can have a code review agent that focuses on code quality and security, a testing agent that focuses on writing and running tests, and a research agent that focuses on finding information and best practices. Here is an example:

```
// Code review agent - focused context
Task(
  description: "Code review",
  prompt: "Review this PR focusing only on security and performance",
  subagent_type: "code-reviewer"
)

// Research agent - broad context
Task(
  description: "Research implementation",
  prompt: "Find best practices for OAuth2 implementation",
  subagent_type: "general-purpose"
)
```

This helps because, without isolation, Claude Code gets confused trying to do everything at once with all the possible information. With isolation, each specialist has a specific knowledge scope and uses it to do their job effectively.

> **Note**
>
> The preceding syntax is illustrative and simplified for demonstration purposes only. Claude Code does not currently use this exact format. In practice, defining subagents requires a YAML configuration with a frontmatter section, which we will cover later in the book.

System prompts and why they matter

In this section, we will discuss system prompts and their importance in context engineering. You have probably read a thousand times on X and LinkedIn that system prompts are important, and that you should work on them, iterate on them, and make them really good. Saying "have a good system prompt" is probably the most generic advice in AI engineering.

There are several public repositories that collect examples of system prompts used by well-known AI agents. These repositories typically aggregate prompts that have been publicly shared or discussed in public sources. Many of the examples focus on coding agents such as Claude Code, Cursor, and Devin, but they may also include prompts from other agent-style systems.

The purpose of referencing these repositories is not to verify the authenticity of every prompt, but to illustrate how large, structured, and carefully engineered system prompts tend to be in practice.

The goal of this section is not to analyze each prompt in detail or explain every technique used. We could have an entire book or course dedicated just to system prompts.

My point here is to show you that system prompts are important. System prompts keep evolving. As LLMs evolve, system prompts evolve with them. A lot of engineering effort goes into curating these prompts and making them better and better. This is an iterative process.

Best practices for crafting system prompts

Let us talk about some best practices when curating and crafting system prompts. It is like giving someone directions.

If we say something such as "go over there," they'll be confused. They won't know where to go. But if we give them a 50-page manual with every possible turn and street, we overwhelm them with information, and they still won't get where they need to go.

So, we want to be clear, we want to be specific, and we want to give just enough information to get them where they need to go. The hard part is finding that sweet spot.

The Goldilocks zone for system prompts

When we write system prompts, we are looking for what Anthropic refers to as the **Goldilocks zone**. Not too vague, not too detailed, but just right.

You can imagine this as a scale. On the far left, we have prompts that are too specific. On the far right, we have prompts that are too vague. What we want is right in the middle.

Figure 1.5 – Goldilocks Zone for System Prompts (Source: Anthropic, "Effective Context Engineering for AI Agents," https://www.anthropic.com/engineering/effective-context-engineering-for-ai-agents)

Let's break this down.

Problem with overly specific prompts

On the far left, we have very specific prompts. The core problem here is that we treat the LLM as a deterministic state machine instead of an intelligent agent. We hardcode logic.

For example, we might say: if the user's intent is incident resolution, ask three follow-up questions. *Why exactly three? What if two are enough? What if we need five?*

We also see exhaustive enumeration, where we try to list every possible escalation scenario. This is impossible to complete and forces the model down predetermined paths that might not match the actual input. It also becomes a maintenance nightmare, because every new edge case requires prompt changes.

At that point, if everything is predetermined, maybe we don't even need an autonomous agent. Maybe a deterministic workflow would be enough.

Problem with overly vague prompts

On the opposite end of the spectrum, we have very vague prompts. The core problem here is that they provide insufficient signal for consistent behavior.

In these prompts, we often see no actionable guidance. For example, consider the following prompt:

You are a bakery assistant. You should attempt to solve customers' issues in a manner consistent with the principles and essence of the company brand. Escalate to a human if needed.

What are those principles?

There is also a false assumption of shared context. The prompt assumes the model knows the company, the brand, and customer service norms, which it does not.

We also see undefined boundaries, such as "escalate to a human if needed." When is it needed? The model has no way to know.

There is no framework or structure for approaching problems systematically. This leads to inconsistent behavior, where different runs produce very different approaches to the same problem. Essentially, the prompt is saying "do the right thing" without defining what "right" actually means.

What a good middle-ground prompt looks like

Now let's look at the middle ground. Consider the following example:

You are a customer support agent for Claude's Bakery.

You specialize in assisting customers with their orders and basic questions about the bakery. Use the tools available to you to resolve issues efficiently and professionally.

You have access to order management systems, product catalogs, and store policies. Your goal is to resolve issues quickly when possible. Start by understanding the complete situation before proposing solutions, and ask follow-up questions if you do not understand.

Response Framework:

1. *Identify the core issue – Look beyond surface complaints to understand what the customer actually needs*
2. *Gather necessary context – Use available tools to verify order details, check inventory, or review policies before responding*
3. *Provide clear resolution – Offer concrete next steps with realistic timelines*
4. *Confirm satisfaction – Ensure the customer understands the resolution and knows how to follow up if needed*

Guidelines:

- *When multiple solutions exist, choose the simplest one that fully addresses the issue*
- *Check the status of an order if a user mentions it before suggesting next steps*
- *Call the human assistance tool*
- *For legal issues, health/allergy emergencies, or situations requiring financial adjustments beyond standard policies, call the human assistance tool*
- *Acknowledge frustration or urgency in the user's tone and respond with appropriate empathy*

You can see the following:

- Here, we start by providing a clear identity and scope. This immediately establishes boundaries. It's customer support, not marketing or sales. It covers orders and basic questions, not complex business operations.
- We also empower rather than constrain. Instead of prescribing exactly which tool to use in every situation, we define a goal, such as efficient and professional resolution. The heuristic here is that we trust the agent to select appropriate tools when needed.
- We also provide a reasoning framework instead of a flowchart. A four-step response framework is being followed here: identify the core issue, gather necessary context, provide a clear resolution, and confirm customer satisfaction. This kind of framework should work across various scenarios, not rigid branching logic.
- Lastly, we have also established clear boundaries and principles. For example, if there are multiple solutions, choose the simplest one. This is a heuristic, not a rule, and it's similar to a greedy approach in computer science.

The overly specific prompt tries to do the LLM's thinking for it and breaks down when situations don't match the script. The vague prompt doesn't give the LLM enough to work with.

The middle prompt takes advantage of what modern LLMs are really good at: recognizing patterns and applying general principles to specific situations. It handles new situations well because it teaches principles instead of rules. It is efficient because it doesn't waste words. Each guideline covers many scenarios. The principles are compressed, and there are no overlapping or contradictory instructions.

Summary

In this chapter, we introduced context engineering and explained why it is essential for building reliable and scalable AI agents. We examined how context differs from static prompts, where it comes from, and why unmanaged context leads to problems such as performance degradation, hallucinations, and inconsistent behavior. Using Claude Code as a practical example, we explored four core context engineering strategies: writing context through persistent memory, selecting relevant context dynamically, compressing context to keep it manageable, and isolating context using specialized sub-agents. We also discussed the role of system prompts, showing how effective prompts strike a balance between being too rigid and too vague. By now, you should have an idea of how modern AI agents manage context and how both developers and users can influence their behavior. In the next chapter, we will build on this foundation and begin working with more advanced agentic workflows, using the HookHub project to explore how Claude Code coordinates tasks, manages context, and operates beyond simple single-step interactions.

In the next chapter, we will look into Claude Code and how it interacts with a codebase.

Get this book's PDF copy, code bundle, and more

Scan the QR code (or go to `packtpub.com/unlock`). Search for this book by name, confirm the edition, and then follow the steps on the page.

UNLOCK NOW

Note: Have your invoice handy. Purchases made directly from the Packt website don't require an invoice.

2

The Gist of Claude Code

This chapter should help you get comfortable with Claude Code by walking through how it actually works in practice. Instead of jumping straight into advanced features, we start by building an understanding of the system itself, the terminology it uses, and the way it interacts with a code base. Along the way, you will see how Claude Code observes a project, builds context, and uses that context to assist with coding tasks.

We start by setting up a simple Next.js project and integrating it with Claude Code. This gives us a practical way to explore concepts like `CLAUDE.md` files, the permission system, and why being deliberate about context matters. We also look at how Claude Code can be extended using external tools through the **Model Context Protocol (MCP)**, and what that enables in day-to-day workflows.

The chapter also introduces spec-driven design as a way to guide Claude's behavior before any code is written. By creating and referencing a specification, we can influence the quality and consistency of the results we get back. As part of this process, we start building a project called HookHub. The HookHub project you build here will stay with us throughout the book and act as a shared reference point as we move into more advanced agentic workflows later on.

The following topics will be covered in this chapter:

- Setting up the Next.js project
- Connecting Playwright MCP to Claude Code
- Using spec-driven design
- Implementing the main page using spec-driven design

All right. Let's get to it!

Note

Installing Claude Code

Before proceeding, ensure that Claude Code is installed on your machine.

Claude Code now provides a native installer that detects your operating system and installs the appropriate version automatically. Follow the official installation guide:

`https://code.claude.com/docs/en/setup#native-install-recommended`

The installer handles setup and updates based on your machine type. Once installation is complete, you can verify it by running:

```
claude --version
```

After confirming Claude Code is installed correctly, continue with the Next.js setup below.

All terminal commands in this chapter are demonstrated on macOS. If you are using Windows, you should run these commands inside **WSL (Windows Subsystem for Linux)** or an equivalent Unix-like shell environment. This ensures that commands such as `npx`, `npm`, `claude`, and other CLI tools behave as shown in the examples.

Setting up the Next.js project

In this section, we will set up the Next.js project manually. Although Claude could have been prompted to create the Next.js project, I am doing this manually due to local permission issues and configurations that need to be handled beforehand. For those who prefer, Claude is fully capable of running these Bash commands when given the correct syntax.

We begin by setting up a Next.js project. You can follow the official Next.js installation guide (`https://nextjs.org/docs/app/getting-started/installation`) or paste the following command:

```
npx create-next-app@latest
```

As you can see from the following screenshot, we are in the **project/HookHub** branch.

Figure 2.1 – project/hookhub branch

We paste the command and scaffold the Next.js project. You will get an option to proceed as shown:

```
edenmarco@Edens-MacBook-Pro-2 claude-code-crash-course % npx create-next-
app@latest
Need to install the following packages:
create-next-app@15.4.6
Ok to proceed? (y)
```

After pasting the command, you may encounter an error. This occurs because the current user does not have the required permissions to install packages globally on the system.

There are two ways to resolve this. One option is to run the command with `sudo`. Another option is to adjust `npm` permissions so that the installation can proceed without elevated privileges. For simplicity, we rerun the command with `sudo`, which grants the necessary permissions.

Once executed with the correct permissions, the Next.js project scaffolding proceeds successfully. You will be prompted to confirm the configuration options. Select the default options and continue. The dependencies are then installed, and the boilerplate code for the Next.js project is generated.

After installation is completed, navigate into the newly created project directory:

```
cd hookhub
```

Now start the development server:

```
npm run dev
```

If you attempt to run the server from the wrong directory, the command will fail. Ensure that you are inside the project directory before running it.

Once the server starts successfully, open `http://localhost:3000` in your browser. You should see the default Next.js boilerplate application.

At this point, the Next.js project is running locally and ready to be integrated with Claude Code. After running the command again, we create the project hookhub. Select **Yes** for the prompts and install all the required dependencies. Once the setup is complete, you will be able to see the boilerplate code for the Next.js project.

Running and verifying the application

Once everything is set up, we navigate into the hookhub directory and run the project using `npm run dev`.

The Next.js application is now running. Open `localhost:3000` and you will see the standard Next.js boilerplate application as shown:

Figure 2.2 – Default Next.js application running on localhost:3000

Initializing Claude code

Before making further changes, return to Claude Code and provide it with the context of the project. This is done by initializing `CLAUDE.md` files so that they can be added to the project context.

Claude Code is opened through the Cursor integration. I personally prefer positioning Claude Code centrally and the code editor on the right, as shown. This setup allows Claude Code to act as the primary driver.

Figure 2.3 – Claude Code opened via Cursor Integration

The first step when initializing a project with Claude Code is to run the `/init` command. This applies whether the project is new or already contains many files. When `/init` is executed, Claude scans the files, checks their content, and begins generating reflections on the code base.

Claude identifies the tech stack, main content, and directory structure. All of this information is captured in a `CLAUDE.md` file, which will be explored later in the book. These Markdown files will eventually be distributed across the project to support context engineering. The purpose of these files is to send high-quality context to the LLM with every request. This makes it easier for the LLM to generate accurate and useful code.

While Claude runs, its status shows that it is **Booping**.

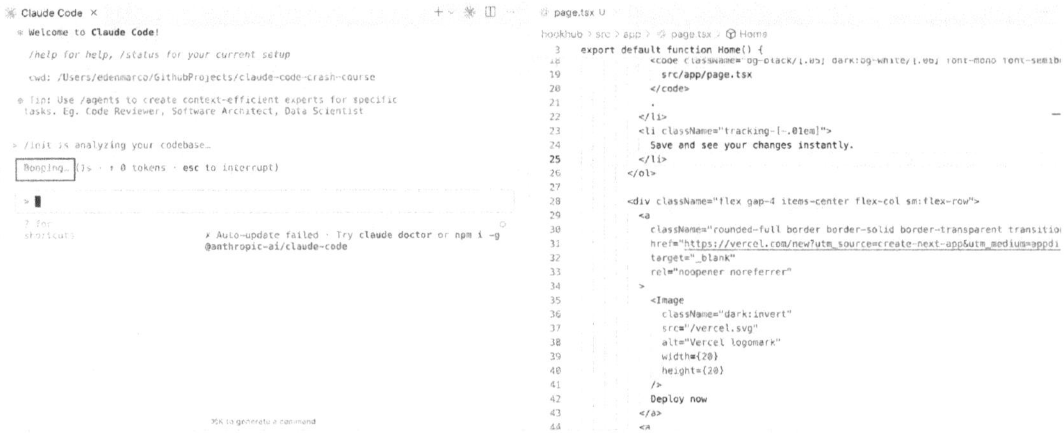

Figure 2.4 – Booping in Cursor Integration

In this context, Claude is analyzing the repository, exploring the directory structure, and reading file contents. After that, a task will be created to analyze the codebase structure, and a series of batch commands will be executed to list and read files.

Please keep in mind that this process can take longer for larger projects. Once it is done, Claude prepares to create the `CLAUDE.md` file based on the information it has gathered and will generate the following:

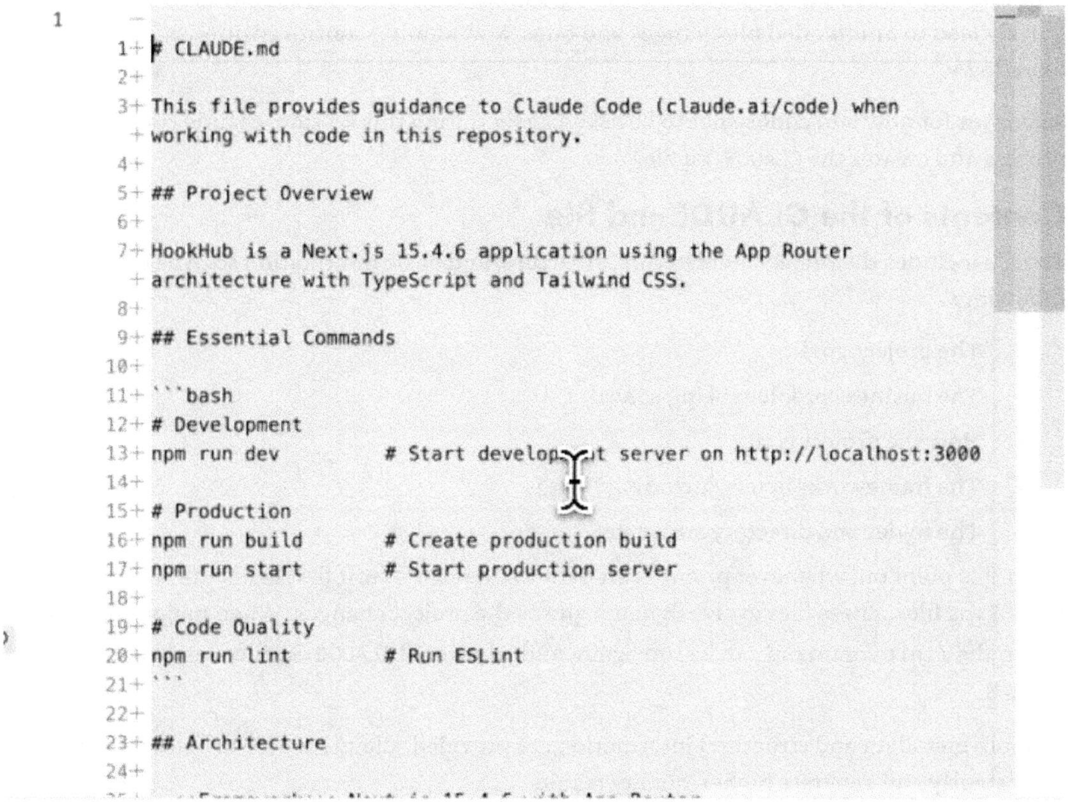

Figure 2.5 – Generated CLAUDE.md file with project overview and commands

As you can see, a `CLAUDE.md` file has been created, containing the project structure and related details.

To save the file, Claude requests permission. We can either allow it to write the file and continue editing without further prompts or deny the change if we want to modify or discard it. This permission system applies to every new file or edit.

```
Opened changes in Cursor
Save file to continue...

Do you want to make this edit to CLAUDE.md?
1. Yes
2. Yes, and don't ask again this session (shift+tab)
3. No, and tell Claude what to do differently (esc)
```

This is an important part of practicing safe agentic coding. Allowing unrestricted access can quickly lead to unintended file changes and bugs. Maintaining control ensures safer workflows.

Select **Yes** for now and choose not to be asked again during this session. Claude completes the process and creates the `CLAUDE.md` file.

Contents of the CLAUDE.md file

The file includes the project architecture, structure, and basic information such as the following:

- The project goal
- The business problem being solved
- How the project is run
- The frameworks in use, including Next.js
- The folder and directory structure

From this point on, whenever prompts are sent to Claude Code, it first loads the relevant `CLAUDE.md` files. These files evolve dynamically as the project changes. When major updates occur, the `/init` command can be run again, and additional `CLAUDE.md` files can be added as needed.

As more metadata and structural information are provided, Claude is able to behave more consistently and generate higher-quality results.

Claude Code now provides a dedicated installer, which handles setup and updates automatically. If issues occur, rerunning the installer typically resolves them.

After exiting the current session and restarting, a new command called `security review` becomes available. This command introduces a sub-agent designed to assist with security reviews and penetration testing against common vulnerabilities. It analyzes your codebase and flags common issues such as insecure patterns, misconfigurations, and vulnerabilities aligned with OWASP Top 10 risks.

Sub-agents will be covered in depth in *Chapter 3*.

Connecting Playwright MCP to Claude Code

We begin by searching in Google for Playwright MCP. For those who do not know, Playwright is a browser automation tool that can be connected to Claude Code using the Model Context Protocol (MCP). If you do not know what MCP is, do not worry, it is covered in depth in the book. There is also an entire chapter dedicated only to MCP.

You can think of MCP as external capabilities that we can equip Claude Code with. In this repository, there are instructions for how to connect Claude Code to the Playwright MCP. Scroll and find the following command:

```
claude mcp add playwright npx @playwright/mcp@latest
```

Copy the command and paste it into the terminal. At this point, we are using the Claude Code **command-line interface** (**CLI**).

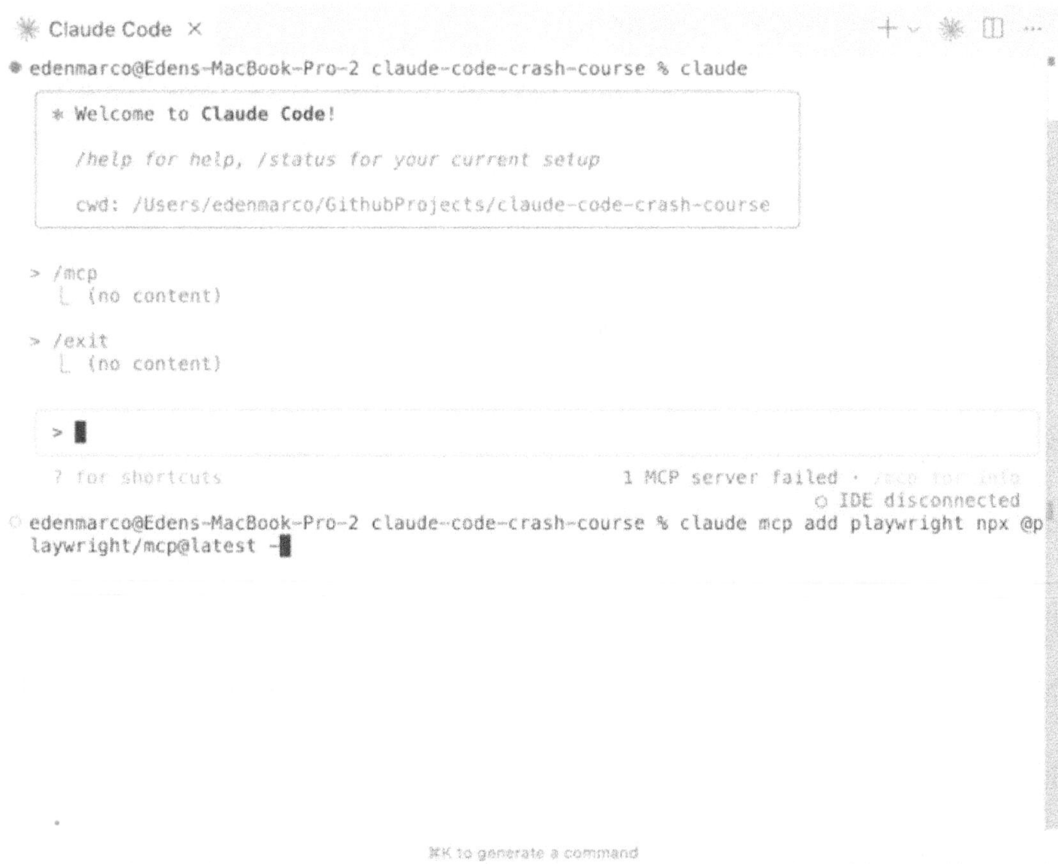

Figure 2.6 – Running Claude Code CLI in the terminal

In the terminal, we enter the command as shown in the following:

```
edenmarco@Edens-MacBook-Pro-2 claude-code-crash-course % claude mcp add playwright
npx @playwright/mcp@latest -s user
```

As you can see, we specified the MCP name as `playwright` and used `npx @playwright/mcp@latest`, which is where Claude Code pulls the repository and runs the code. The code being run is the Playwright MCP, and this is what gives Claude Code the extra capability of browser automation.

We also added the `-s user` flag. This ensures the MCP works for every instance of Claude Code we open because it is applied at the user scope. By doing this, we are taking advantage of Claude Code's hierarchy system, which will be covered in depth in later sections.

Verifying the MCP connection

Now, we open Claude again and enter `/mcp`. After pressing *Enter*, we should see all the MCP servers connected to Claude Code.

```
Manage MCP servers

  1. context7     ✓ connected · Enter to view details
❯ 2. playwright   ✓ connected · Enter to view details

MCP Config locations (by scope):
 • User config (available in all your projects):
   • /Users/edenmarco/.claude.json
 • Project config (shared via .mcp.json):
   • /Users/edenmarco/GithubProjects/claude-code-crash-course/.mcp.json (file does
   not exist)
 • Local config (private to you in this project):
   • /Users/edenmarco/.claude.json [project:
   /Users/edenmarco/GithubProjects/claude-code-crash-course]

For help configuring MCP servers, see:
https://docs.anthropic.com/en/docs/claude-code/mcp
```

Figure 2.7 – Verifying MCP Server Connections in Claude Code

We can see the **playwright** MCP, and we can also see another MCP called **context7**, which was configured earlier. This is another useful MCP that will be discussed later.

Using Playwright MCP to pen a browser

To verify the Playwright MCP integration, we enter `open browser` in Claude Code and add `cnn.com`. At this point, we encounter the permission system again, similar to the one shown:

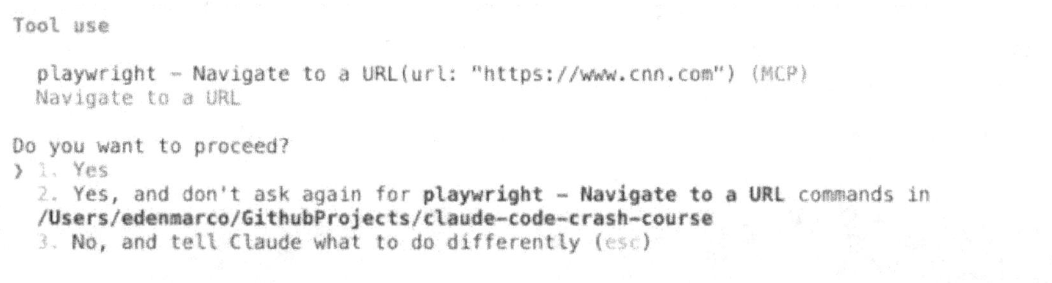

Figure 2.8 – Playwright MCP Permission Prompt to Open a Browser

Claude Code prompts us with a tool use request, asking whether it can run the Playwright tool to navigate to the URL `cnn.com`.

This is an external tool that has been connected to Claude Code, not a built-in tool. A built-in tool would be something like editing a file, creating a file, or deleting a file. As before, select **Yes**, and choose not to be asked again for this specific tool.

A browser opens, and we are now on `cnn.com`. Claude Code has used the Playwright MCP for browser automation and opened the site.

This becomes useful when we want to test a user interface or perform UI automation.

Using cursor rules as additional context

Next, open a browser and search for `cursor directory`, or navigate directly to `https://cursor.directory/`. The Cursor directory is a place where useful Cursor rules can be found. These rules allow additional context to be provided to Cursor through Markdown files, such as personas for the AI coding assistant—for example, making it behave like a senior developer specialized in a specific field.

These Cursor rules also work with Claude Code. To see this in practice, look for a Cursor rule for Next.js, select one, and copy it as shown.

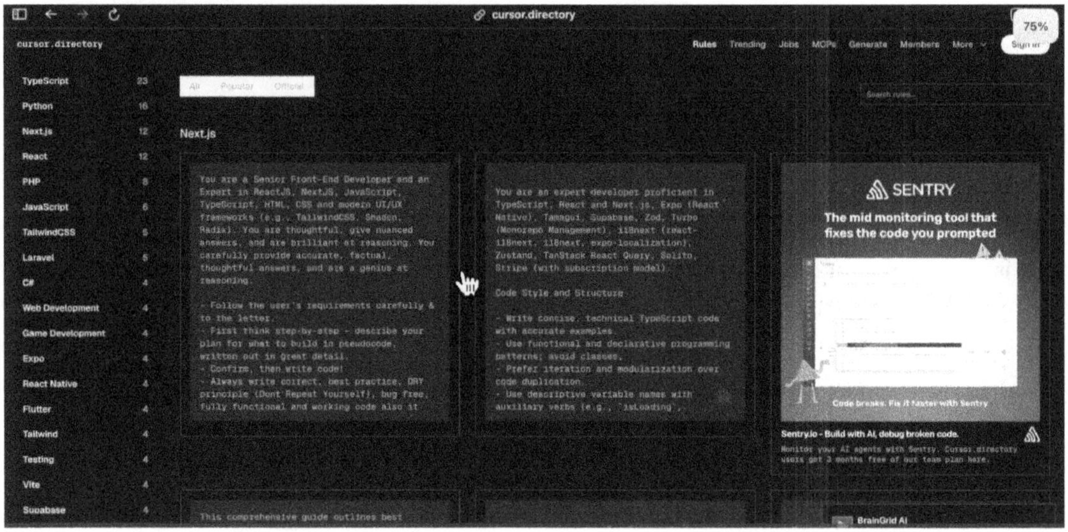

Figure 2.9 – Browsing Cursor Directory for Next.js Rules

Creating a frontend memory context

We return to Cursor and add this to a `CLAUDE.md` file. We already have the `CLAUDE.md` file that Claude created previously. We also have a broader memory system in which we can provide Claude with extra context.

In this case, we want to give it the Cursor rule and the persona of someone who knows Next.js very well, with the goal of producing better results. We first create a directory called `memory`, then create a subdirectory called `frontend`. Inside it, we create a file named `CLAUDE.md` and paste in the Cursor rule that you copied previously.

> **Note**
>
> The memory file mentioned will not be automatically loaded by Claude. This is intentional. Claude only auto-loads certain `CLAUDE.md` files by default. In this chapter, we are setting up the memory structure first. In *Chapter 3*, we will configure when and how these memory files are loaded so they influence responses.

The rule that I copied contains content such as: *"You are a senior frontend developer and an expert in React, Next.js, JavaScript, TypeScript, HTML, CSS..."* and so on. In effect, we are giving Claude Code a more focused persona aligned with the tech stack we are using.

In the previous `CLAUDE.md` file, we told it that we are using a Next.js tech stack. In this `CLAUDE.md` file, we are giving it a persona.

At this point, it is clear that context is important for LLMs. So, we ask Claude the following question:

```
What are you expert in?
```

You might expect it to recite that it is an expert in frontend engineering, Next.js, TypeScript, and everything written in the `CLAUDE.md`. However, the response may be surprising.

The answer comes back as a generic statement:

```
> what r u expert in?

● I'm an expert AI assistant specialized in software engineering and coding tasks. I
  can help with:

  - Full-stack development - Frontend (React, Vue, Angular), Backend (Node.js,
  Python, Go, Rust, etc.)
  - Debugging and troubleshooting - Finding and fixing bugs, performance issues,
  type errors
  - Code refactoring - Improving code structure, readability, and maintainability
  - Building features - Implementing new functionality from scratch or extending
  existing code
  - Testing - Writing unit tests, integration tests, debugging test failures
  - DevOps - CI/CD, Docker, deployment configurations, build processes
  - Database work - SQL, NoSQL, migrations, query optimization
  - API development - REST, GraphQL, WebSockets
  - Security analysis - Defensive security, vulnerability detection, security best
  practices
  - Code reviews - Analyzing code quality, suggesting improvements
  - Documentation - When requested, creating technical docs and API documentation

  I have access to your file system and can read, write, and execute code directly.
  I also have web browsing capabilities and can fetch up-to-date library
  documentation through Context7.
```

Figure 2.10 – Generic Claude Response Without Loaded Project Context

As you can see, it says "expert AI assistant specialized in software engineering and coding tasks," without anything specific to Next.js or frontend. This makes it seem like the file is not working.

However, this is by design. Claude has a system of automatically loading `CLAUDE.md` files, and this will be covered in depth in *Chapter 3*. There are also other files, called memory files, that are not automatically loaded.

Instead, we can explicitly tell Claude when to load them, depending on context. This opens the door to context engineering, which will be explored in the book.

The idea is that we can configure Claude to load the frontend context only when needed. For example, we can load it when designing or building the UI, when working only on TypeScript files, when working in specific directories, or when the request is clearly related to frontend work.

This gives us the freedom to customize Claude's behavior according to our needs. This will be demonstrated in the book, and one hint is that hooks can be used for this. We can reference context from other files, and there are several ways to work with memory, which will be covered in depth later in the book.

Using spec-driven design

In this section, instead of vibe coding the application, we use something called **spec-driven design**. This will be elaborated on later in the book, but the general idea is to create a spec file describing the application, the use case or business use case, and possibly some nonfunctional requirements.

The spec file that we create should tell Claude to reference the spec file when it is going to code. This helps optimize the context window and improves the results we get.

To begin, we press *Shift* + *Tab* and switch to **plan mode** in Claude Code. Plan mode is designed for tasks like this, where we want to do read-only work, conduct some research, and plan what Claude is going to do.

I have added the following prompt, in which I ask Claude to help write a spec file for a project called HookHub.

```
I want you to help me write a spec file for a project I am building. It's called
"hookhub". It's a place where cool open source Claude hooks are displayed and
browsed. Search on Claude hooks and write an initial spec for this. Remember it's
an MVP ATM and we need only the functionality of displaying the hooks. Hooks are
found in GitHub repositories, they have name, category, description and link to
repo. The main page should display the hooks in a grid-like view.
```

As shown in the prompt, I have

- Described `HookHub` as a place where open-source Claude hooks are displayed and browsed
- Asked Claude to `search for Claude hooks` and write an initial specification
- Clarified that this is an `MVP`, with functionality limited to displaying hooks
- Specified that hooks are found in `Git repositories` and include a name, category, description, and a link to the repository
- Stated that the `main page should display the hooks in a grid view`

This is the full prompt. There is nothing fancy here, and no prompt engineering is applied.

Once we submit the prompt, Claude only uses read-only tools. No writing or editing occurs at this stage.

> **Note**
>
> Since we are working in plan mode, we also need to select the model before pasting the prompt. Most of the time, when using plan mode, we prefer heavier models with deep reasoning capabilities. To control which model is used, we run the `/models` command and ensure that the latest version of Opus is selected. At the time of writing, this is the most advanced model available for deep reasoning. When the prompt is pasted, we only see a representation of the text rather than the actual text.

Claude begins by researching Claude hooks. It calls the web search tool with queries related to open-source Claude Code hooks and requests permission to fetch documentation from Anthropic, which we approve before proceeding.

After the research step is completed, Claude presents a plan similar to the following:

```
Ready to code?

Here is Claude's plan:

  Plan for HookHub MVP Specification

  I'll create a comprehensive specification document for HookHub that includes:

  1. Project Overview - Clear definition of what HookHub is and its purpose
  2. MVP Scope - Focus on displaying hooks only (no submission/editing features
  yet)
  3. Data Model - Structure for hook information (name, category, description, repo
   link)
  4. UI/UX Requirements - Grid layout for browsing hooks
  5. Technical Architecture - Simple tech stack recommendations
  6. User Stories - Basic user interactions for MVP
  7. Future Considerations - Potential features for post-MVP

  The spec will be written in Markdown format and saved as hookhub/SPEC.md

Would you like to proceed?

> 1. Yes, and auto-accept edits
  2. Yes, and manually approve edits
  3. No, keep planning
```

Figure 2.11 – Claude's Proposed Plan for HookHub MVP Specification

The plan includes the following:

- Creating a specification that covers the project overview
- MVP scope
- Data model for a Claude Code hook
- UI and UX requirements
- Technical architecture
- User stories
- Future considerations

At this point, we approve the plan. Claude then moves to write mode and requests to write the file to `hookhub/SPEC.md`. Decline and instruct Claude to write the spec under a spec directory and name the file `CLAUDE.md`.

```
I want you to write it into a spec directory and make this a CLAUDE.md file
```

Claude responds again and prepares to write the file under `spec/CLAUDE.md`. Approve this and allow the edit.

Claude will provide a to-do list for the first time. Claude begins iterating through the tasks and requests. We approve the actions as prompted.

Claude creates the spec directory and generates the `CLAUDE.md` file. We will go into much more detail about to-dos later in the book, but it is important to note that they play a major role in the quality of the results. This is one of the reasons Claude Code works well as a coding agent. Specifically, Claude Code behaves as a deep agent that can handle long-running, multi-step tasks that require significant reasoning. Deep agents and how Claude fits into this category will be covered later in the book.

Reviewing the generated spec

Once the process is completed, we now have a new `CLAUDE.md` file.

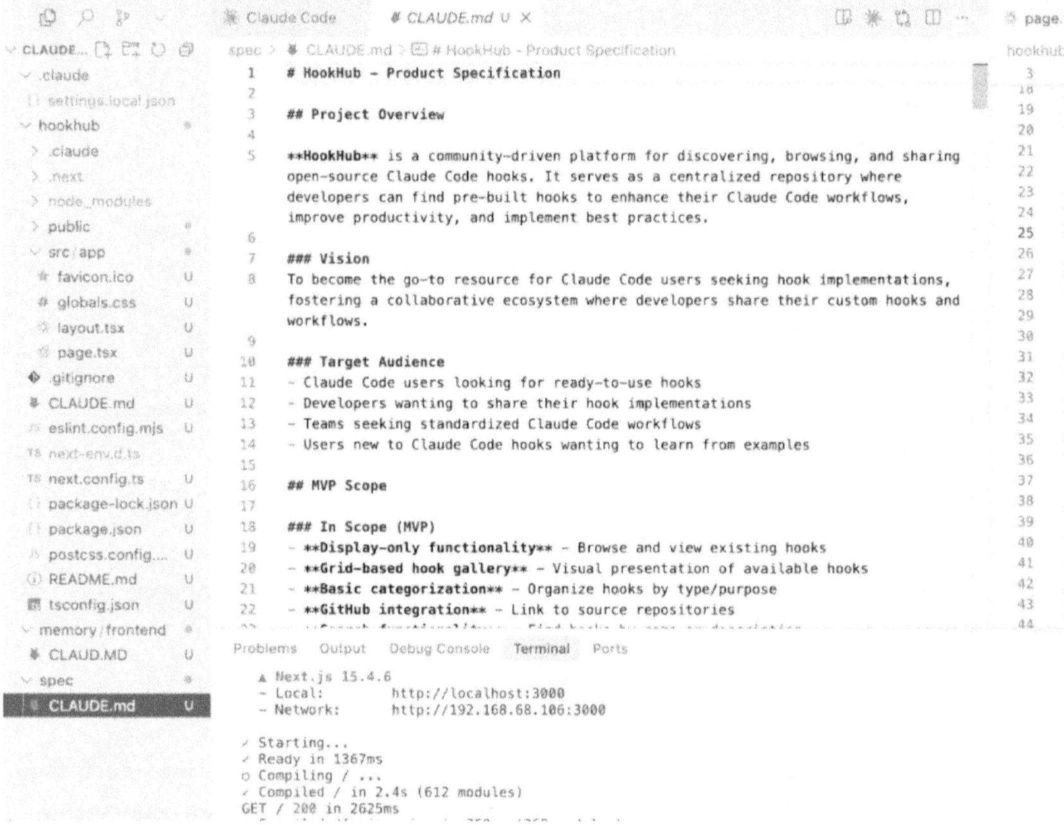

Figure 2.12 – HookHub Product Specification in CLAUDE.md

The file includes the project overview, vision, and a large amount of information that will help Claude during implementation.

The spec provides useful context, such as hook categories, hook object structure, and how the application should look. It also includes the steps required to build the project. This document will be added to the repository and will help Claude produce better results during implementation.

With this, you should have an idea of how using an LLM to help generate a spec is a common pattern. Other advanced patterns will be covered later in the book.

Finally, move the `spec` directory under the `memory` directory.

At this point, your structure should look like this:

```
memory/
├── frontend/
│   └── CLAUDE.md
└── spec/
    └── CLAUDE.md
```

This allows all long-term context to live in one place and be reused whenever it is needed.

Implementing the main page using the SPEC

Before we implement anything, we switch the model and use **Sonnet**. In the prompt, we write the following:

```
Can you please help me implement the main page grid as specified in the spec file?
```

We then use the `@` symbol to tag the spec file. The spec file we have is `spec/CLAUDE.md`. We will need to tag the file to attach it to the context.

> **Note**
>
> Every time we make a prompt, get a result, and then make another prompt, we keep filling the context. Over time, this results in many back-and-forth iterations between us and Claude.
>
> If we continue using the same session without doing anything about it, we eventually fill the context window. When that happens, results start to get worse.
>
> There are a couple of ways to handle this. There are custom commands, which will be covered later in the book, that help clear or summarize the context window while keeping the useful parts. For now, we use a simple, naive technique. Claude Code also provides built-in commands such as `/clear` and `/compact` for managing the context window without restarting the session. These were introduced earlier, and we will revisit them later. For now, restarting gives us a clean slate in the most straightforward way.
>
> We exit the current Claude Code session by running `/exit`. After that, we open Claude again, navigate into the HookHub Next.js project, and open it from there. At this point, the context is fresh and empty.
>
> We write the prompt again: *Can you please implement the main page, a grid of the hooks, as specified in the spec file?*

This time, we notice that the file reference cannot be found. The reason is that Claude Code was opened within the HookHub directory, but the memory directory is still at the root of the project.

To fix this, we move the memory directory up in the hierarchy so that it sits under hookhub. Once this is done, the file reference works as expected. After this move, the memory directory is no longer at the crash course root level. It now lives inside the HookHub project directory.

Running the implementation

We write the prompt again to implement the grid according to the spec file. Claude now begins doing the heavy lifting. It creates a to-do list and starts implementing each task in the list.

A request will appear to approve file writes, such as creating the Hooks.ts file. Once approved, the implementation will continue and will take some time to complete.

Once the implementation is completed, the hook card component is created, and Claude continues running through the remaining steps. It then runs linting to catch potential errors. Once that finishes, we see a summary of what was implemented, including the card components, the hero section, the header, and other related pieces.

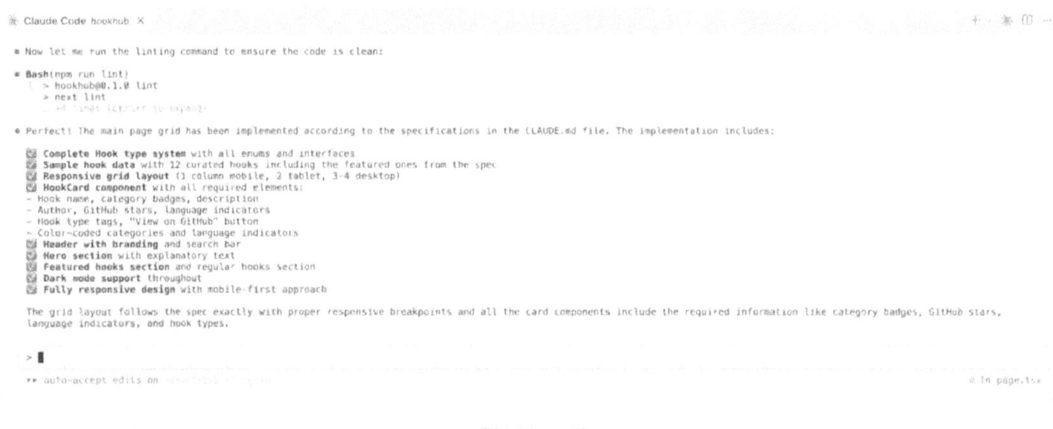

Figure 2.13 – Claude Implementation Summary After Code Generation

Refresh the application in the browser and you will see a grid of Claude Code hook cards.

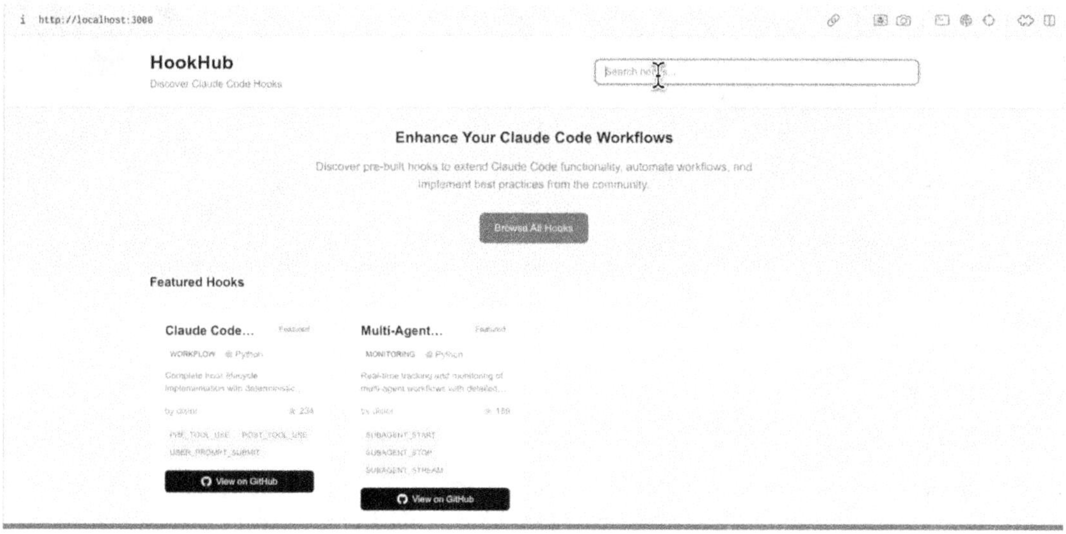

Figure 2.14 – Basic Next.js application

This is a basic Next.js application. While some features, such as search, are not yet implemented, others are already in place. Overall, it provides a solid skeleton that we can continue building on.

Later in the book, we will explore advanced agentic workflows for AI coding. This includes spinning up multiple sub-agents dynamically, iterating on UI components, and using meta-prompting. This project will serve as the foundation for those experiments.

At this point, we commit the code to the repository so it can be shared. We run `git status`, add all files, and confirm that there are no secrets or environment variables included.

We then commit the changes with a message such as *initial project* and push them to the repository.

From the repository, you can navigate to the `project/hookhub` branch, review the files, and pull the exact code from this commit. A command is also provided so you can clone the repository and get everything set up locally. To access the repository link, follow the steps in the *Download the example code files* section in the *Preface*.

After completing all the steps in this chapter, your HookHub project should have the following structure:

```
hookhub/
  ├── app/
  ├── components/
```

```
├── memory/
│   ├── frontend/
│   │   └── CLAUDE.md
│   └── spec/
│       └── CLAUDE.md
├── package.json
├── next.config.js
└── ...
```

If your structure matches this, you are correctly set up for the next chapter.

Summary

In this chapter, we established a practical foundation for working with Claude Code by moving through each step of the setup and workflow. Rather than jumping straight into advanced features, we focused on understanding how Claude Code observes a project, builds context through `CLAUDE.md` files, and relies on explicit permissions to operate safely. This groundwork is essential because the quality of results you get from Claude Code depends directly on the quality of context, structure, and control you provide.

We also saw how Claude Code can be extended beyond its built-in capabilities using MCPs, how external tools like Playwright fit into the workflow, and why spec-driven design helps produce more consistent and predictable outcomes. The HookHub project created here is not just an example, it is a working baseline that will be reused as we explore more advanced agentic workflows later in the book. Every concept introduced in this chapter is something we will build on, rather than revisit from scratch.

In the next chapter, we will cover pricing and authentication, slash commands, user and project level configuration, and integration with Cursor.

Get this book's PDF copy, code bundle, and more

Scan the QR code (or go to `packtpub.com/unlock`). Search for this book by name, confirm the edition, and then follow the steps on the page.

UNLOCK NOW

Note: Have your invoice handy. Purchases made directly from the Packt website don't require an invoice.

3

Getting Started with Claude Code – A Tour of Essential Commands

In this chapter, we will move from getting started with Claude Code to configuring it for day-to-day use. The goal is to help you get comfortable with how Claude Code behaves in practice, how you control it inside a session, and how you set it up so it stays consistent across projects.

We will briefly cover pricing and authentication so you can choose the right setup before you begin. After that, we focus on the parts you will use constantly: slash commands for managing sessions and context, configuration at the user and project level, and running Claude Code directly inside IDEs like Cursor. We then build on those foundations with the features that make longer workflows more secure and reliable, including hooks for automation, memory through `CLAUDE.md` files, rewind through checkpointing, and custom slash commands (skills) for repeatable, well-scoped workflows.

> **Note**
>
> Skills can be invoked manually using the `/skill-name` syntax, which is why older documentation sometimes refers to them as *skills*. Internally, they are now unified under the **Skills** system.

The following topics will be covered in this chapter:

- Pricing and plans for Claude Code
- Controlling Claude Code with slash commands

- Using hooks in Claude Code
- Understanding memory in Claude Code
- Rewind feature in Claude Code
- Skills in Claude Code

Pricing and plans for Claude Code

In this section, we will discuss the pricing options and the different plans available for operating and consuming Claude Code. We start with authentication because the way you authenticate also determines how you are billed for token usage.

> **Note**
>
> Pricing and plan details mentioned in this section are accurate at the time of writing. Because subscription tiers, usage limits, and billing policies may change, always refer to the official Claude pricing page for the most up-to-date information: `https://claude.com/pricing`

Figure 3.1 – Claude Code authentication options screen

Claude Code provides three main ways to authenticate and pay for the tokens you use.

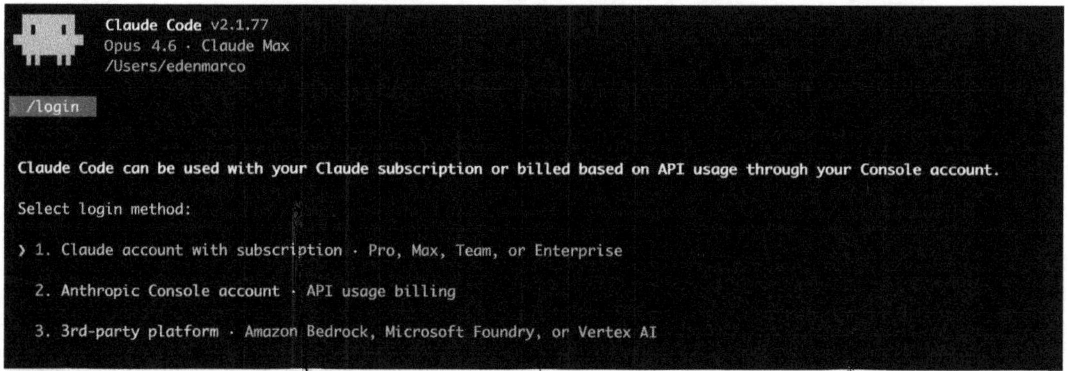

Figure 3.2 – Login methods for Claude Code subscription and API billing

Option 1: Using an Anthropic API key

One option is to authenticate using an Anthropic API key. This uses a pay-as-you-go billing model, where usage is tracked through the Anthropic console. This option is useful for users who prefer usage-based billing or who want to evaluate Claude Code before committing to a subscription.

When using the Anthropic API key method while following this book, usage will vary depending on how frequently Claude Code is invoked and which models are used.

If you follow this option, select the API key authentication method and authorize Claude Code through your Anthropic organization. Claude Code then generates an API key and configures it automatically in the terminal. Once complete, Claude Code operates using the pay-as-you-go model.

Points to keep in mind when using Anthropic API

When using an API key, it is important to monitor token consumption. This can be done directly inside Claude Code using the `/cost` command. This command is available only when Claude Code is authenticated using an Anthropic API key. It displays the number of tokens consumed and their distribution.

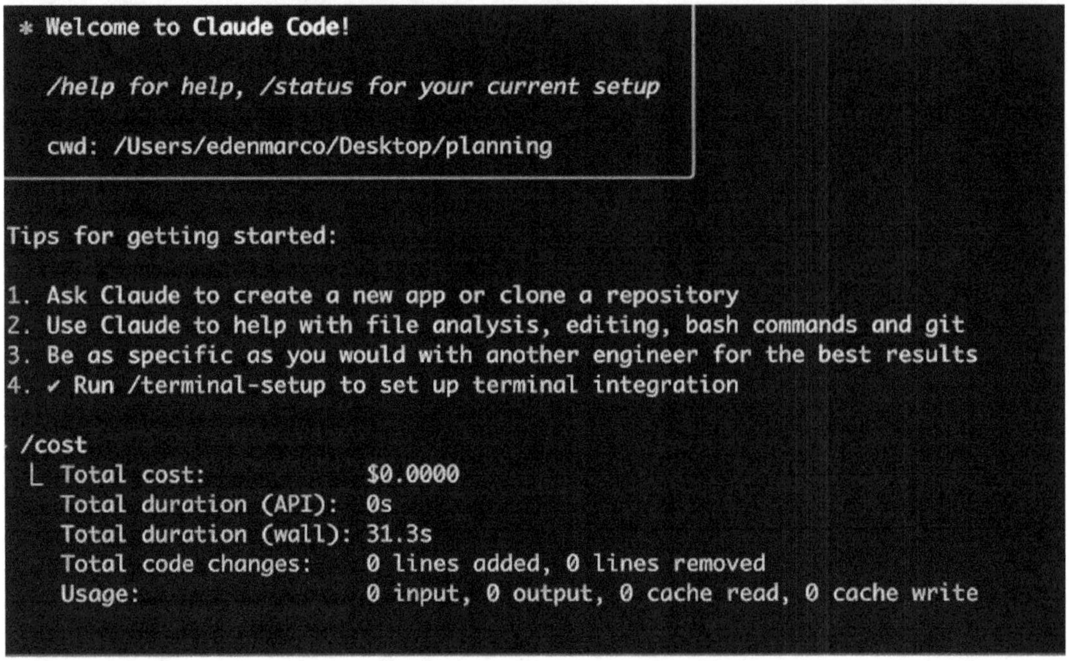

Figure 3.3 – Monitoring Token Usage with the /cost Command

The same information is also available through the Anthropic console. The cost is zero because no tokens have been used yet. Just type anything, and then once you receive the output, type `/cost` again.

```
Tips for getting started:

1. Ask Claude to create a new app or clone a repository
2. Use Claude to help with file analysis, editing, bash commands and git
3. Be as specific as you would with another engineer for the best results
4. ✓ Run /terminal-setup to set up terminal integration

> /cost
  ⎿ Total cost:            $0.0000
    Total duration (API):  0s
    Total duration (wall): 31.3s
    Total code changes:    0 lines added, 0 lines removed
    Usage:                 0 input, 0 output, 0 cache read, 0 cache write

> hello!

● Hello! How can I help you today?

> /cost
  ⎿ Total cost:            $0.2873
    Total duration (API):  3.9s
    Total duration (wall): 40.3s
    Total code changes:    0 lines added, 0 lines removed
    Usage by model:
        claude-3-5-haiku:  87 input, 27 output, 0 cache read, 0 cache write
             claude-opus:  3 input, 13 output, 0 cache read, 15.3k cache write
```

Figure 3.4 – Updated Token Usage after Running a Prompt

Please remember that pricing varies depending on the model being used. For example, using Opus results in higher token costs compared to other models.

Important considerations when using an API key

Using an API key requires caution. There is a risk of accidentally exposing the key, which could allow others to consume tokens at your expense. In extreme cases, this can result in unexpectedly high charges.

In addition, this book involves working with agents, sub-agents, and orchestration patterns, all of which can consume a large number of tokens. If something is misconfigured, it is possible to trigger many agents simultaneously, significantly increasing costs.

One way to mitigate this risk is to set spending limits in the Anthropic console. Anthropic allows you to define usage limits for your account, after which requests are no longer served. For details on configuring these limits, refer to the Anthropic settings page (`https://platform.claude.com/settings/limits`).

Option 2: Using a Claude subscription

If you followed the setup in *Chapter 2*, you are using Option 2, which authenticates through a Claude subscription. We will be using this option throughout this book, which is authenticating through a Claude subscription. With this approach, you connect your existing Claude subscription directly to Claude Code. This provides seamless integration with predictable monthly billing.

Claude currently offers the following subscription tiers:

- Free – $0/month (does not include access to Claude Code)
- Pro – $20/month
- Max 5x – $100/month
- Max 20x – $200/month

Claude Code access is available starting from the Pro plan and above.

In this book, I use the Max 5x plan, which provides higher usage limits than Pro while remaining cost-effective for regular development workflows.

Now, unlike the previous option, with a subscription plan, cost monitoring behaves differently. Since Claude Code usage is included in the subscription, there is no need to track token-level costs using `/cost`. Pricing is fixed, although usage limits still apply depending on the plan.

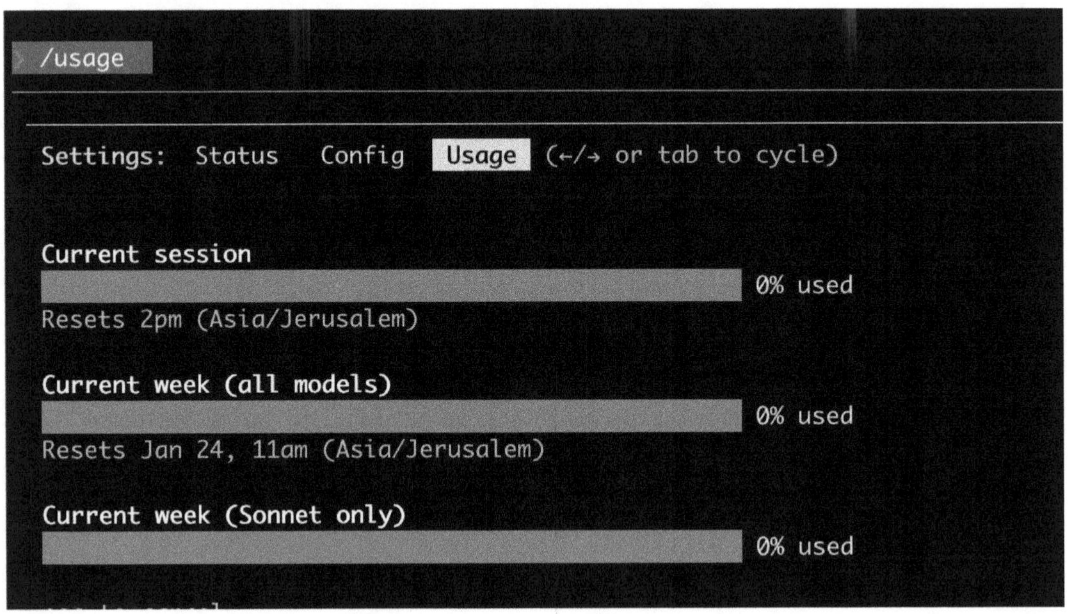

Figure 3.5 – Viewing Subscription Usage with the /usage command

Available models under this option

Using the `/models` command shows which models are available. Claude Code currently supports Opus, Sonnet, and Haiku:

- **Claude Opus**: Claude Opus is the most capable model and is well suited for complex tasks and deep reasoning. It has a context window of 200K tokens and is typically used for deep planning or research tasks. Because of its higher cost, Opus is generally not used for writing large amounts of code.
- **Claude Sonnet**: Claude Sonnet provides a balance between intelligence, speed, and cost. It also has a 200K token context window and is the primary model used for code generation throughout this course. Because of its balance, Sonnet performs most of the heavy lifting when writing and modifying code.
- **Claude Haiku**: The fastest and most lightweight model. It is well suited for simple tasks, quick iterations, and lower-latency workflows where speed is more important than deep reasoning.

> Note
>
> The models themselves are hosted and served by Anthropic. For enterprise environments, they can also be accessed through supported third-party cloud providers such as AWS Bedrock, Google Cloud Vertex AI, or Microsoft Azure. This setup is typically used by organizations that require centralized billing, cloud-specific compliance controls, regional deployment options, or governance through existing cloud infrastructure.

Subscription plans and pricing

Claude offers several subscription tiers.

- Free plan
- Pro plan
- Max 5x plan
- Max 20x plan

Rate limits were introduced to prevent misuse, such as sharing credentials or abusing the system. These limits apply across Pro and Max plans.

For most users, especially hobbyists, starting with the Pro plan is recommended. Upgrading to the Max plan makes sense only when higher usage becomes necessary.

Exact usage limits can be difficult to quantify, and this is not unique to Claude Code. Pricing for AI coding agents is an ongoing challenge across the industry. Changes in pricing models have led to frustration in the developer community, and this remains an evolving area.

This section was intended to clarify the available pricing options and help you understand how billing works when using Claude Code so you can choose the approach that best fits your needs.

> Note
>
> **Option 3: Using a third-party cloud provider**
>
> Claude Code can also be authenticated through supported third-party cloud platforms such as Amazon Bedrock, Microsoft Azure AI, or Google Cloud Vertex AI. In this case, billing and usage are managed through the selected cloud provider rather than through a Claude subscription or an Anthropic API key. For details on supported third-party integrations, refer to the official documentation: `https://code.claude.com/docs/en/third-party-integrations`

Controlling Claude Code with slash commands

Slash commands are the primary way to control Claude Code features and settings within the Claude Code chat. When we type /, Claude Code shows a list of available commands, as shown here:

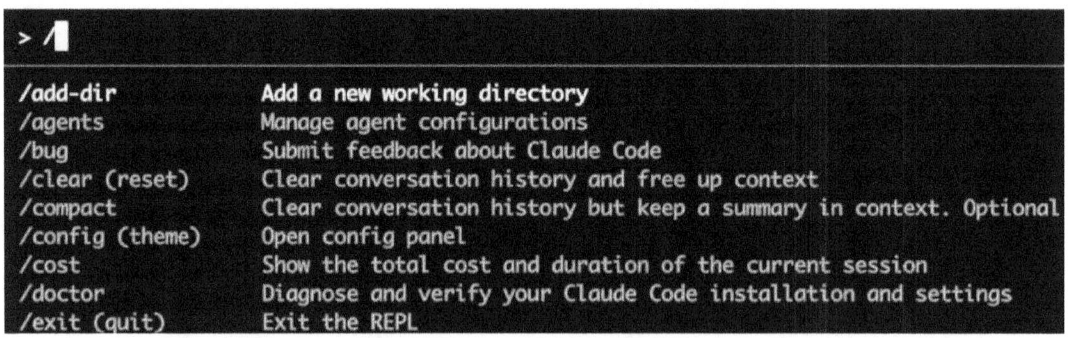

Figure 3.6 – Listing available slash commands in Claude Code

When we chat a lot with Claude Code, the conversation can get very long, which can slow things down and cause context rot, which will be discussed later in the book. It can also cost more money or even confuse Claude if it has too much to remember.

To handle this, there are two commands

- `/clear`, which erases everything and starts fresh, like a clean slate
- `/compact`, which creates a short summary of what is important, keeps the key information, and removes extra detail

Using `/clear` and `/compact` helps Claude stay focused and work better over time. This is context engineering in action (see *Chapter 1*).

Let us start the session from zero. For that, we need to run `/clear`.

Another command worth noting is `/agents`, which helps manage specialized sub-agents. **Sub-agents** can be thought of as expert assistants created for specific tasks, such as a code reviewer, debugger, or architect.

They operate with their own context and tools, and they are used as part of multi-agent workflows. Sub-agents and these workflows will be covered in a hands-on section later.

Next, we have the `/config` command. The `/config` command opens the configuration panel for Claude Code, where settings and preferences are shown. Once you run this command, you will see the settings as shown here:

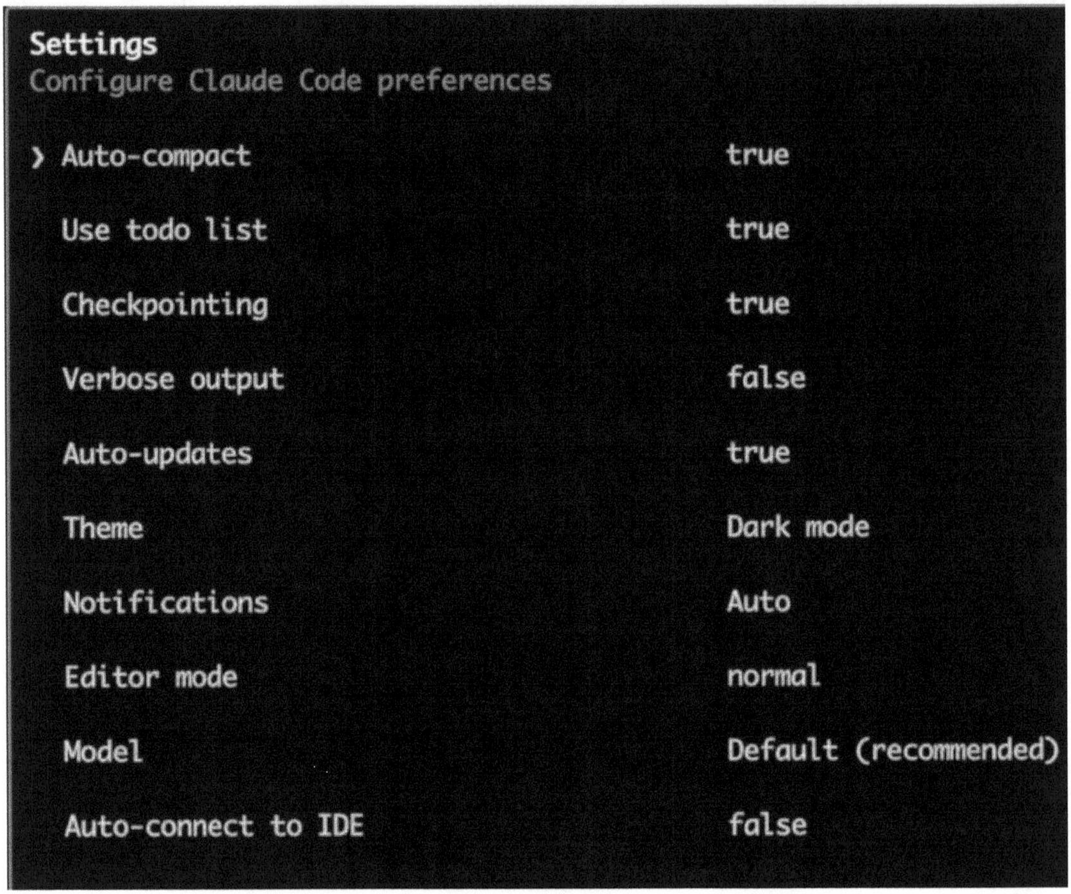

Figure 3.7 – Claude Code settings panel with configuration options

For example, we can see that **Auto-compact** is enabled. This means Claude will automatically run `/compact` when it detects that the conversation is approaching token limits or when it decides it is a good point to compact the context. There are also settings such as using to-do lists, checkpointing, and other options. We will not go through all of them here; the complete and up-to-date list of settings is available in the official Claude Code documentation (`https://code.claude.com/docs/en/settings`).

Beyond the individual options themselves, what matters is how these settings are organized and applied. Claude Code provides a granular configuration system:

- User-wide settings, stored in the home directory under `.claude/settings`, apply globally to every Claude Code instance

- Project-specific settings, stored in `.claude/settings.json` within a project directory, apply only to that project and can be shared with a team
- Local settings, allowing personal tweaks without affecting shared project settings

This structure makes it possible to maintain global defaults, apply project-level guidelines, and still keep individual preferences. Throughout the book, the settings shown can be configured through these settings files based on personal and team needs.

Finally, we look at `/cost`. Since this setup uses a Claude Pro subscription, cost monitoring is not shown here because the subscription includes Claude Code usage. The `/cost` command becomes more relevant when you use an Anthropic API key.

Integrating Claude Code with the IDE

Before wrapping up this section, let us see how to integrate Claude Code with an IDE. In this example, we will integrate it with the Cursor IDE. Open the slash menu and select **IDE** to integrate Claude Code into Cursor. This will install the Claude Code extension directly in the IDE.

Once installed, we can see the Claude Code extension inside Cursor.

Figure 3.8 – Claude Code extension inside the Cursor editor

You will notice the Claude Code icon in the top-right corner. This is how most developers use Claude Code in practice. Claude Code is typically opened through the Cursor extension, so it runs directly inside the IDE. This allows us to work within the editor, view diffs more clearly, and keep everything in one place. We will use this setup throughout the book.

> **Note**
>
> We also have the `/mcp` command, which is used to manage MCP servers. With this command, we can add, remove, and list all configured MCP servers.
>
> At this point, no MCP servers are configured. MCP servers provide additional functionality that can be added to Claude Code. They may come from verified vendors or be open source, and they effectively extend Claude Code with extra tools and capabilities.

> MCP is a deep topic on its own. Throughout this book, we will be integrating and using MCP servers as part of our workflows. For now, it is assumed that you are familiar with the basic idea of MCP servers.

Using hooks in Claude Code

Hooks are a powerful feature in Claude Code. They are automatic logic that runs at specific points during Claude Code's workflow.

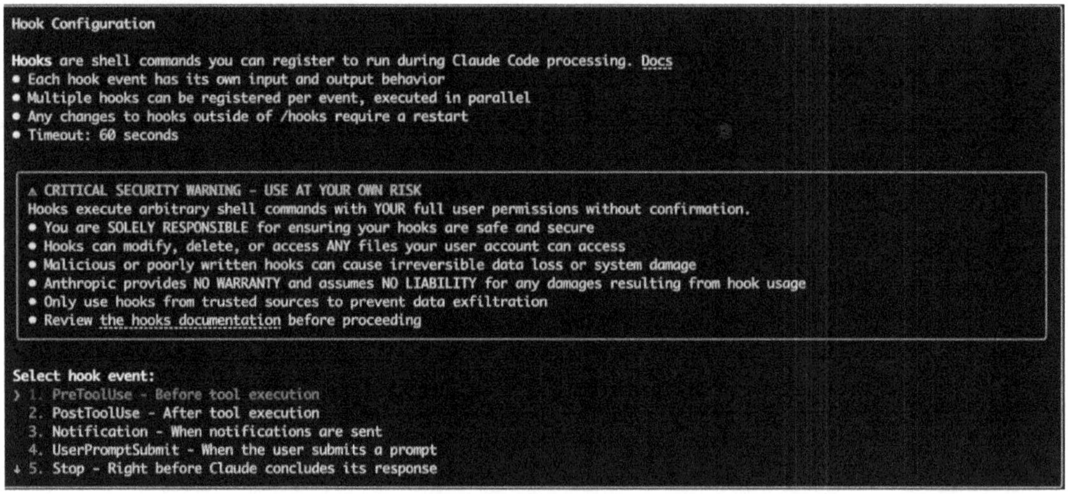

Figure 3.9 – Hook configuration and security warning in Claude Code

For example, hooks can run before or after a tool is used, or when Claude finishes working. They help automate tasks such as formatting code, running tests, or blocking unsafe edits. By doing this, hooks ensure that these actions happen consistently without manual intervention.

> **Note**
>
> Hooks are a key part of building reliable workflows, and we will spend a significant amount of time working with them hands-on later in the book. To give a brief preview, hooks can also be used to trigger Claude's sub-agents. Each sub-agent runs with its own context and its own set of tools, which opens the door to more complex and powerful workflows.

Creating a notification hook

Let us now configure our first hook. In this section, we will build a simple notification hook that plays a sound whenever Claude finishes producing output.

All the related code can be found in the repository under `project/hooks-notification`. Before proceeding, clone the repository and check out the `project/hooks-notification` branch.

Initializing the environment

Follow these steps:

1. Ensure that the repository contains all required artifacts, including the sound file. Remove everything except the audio recording so that the setup starts from scratch.
2. Initialize the Python environment for the hook. Since the hook is a Python script, initialize a Python environment and install dependencies. Initialize the environment using `uv`. Run the following:

   > **Note**
   >
   > This example uses `uv`, a fast Python package and environment manager by Astral. If you do not have `uv` installed, follow the installation instructions in the official documentation: `https://docs.astral.sh/uv/`.

   ```
   uv init
   ```

   This creates a virtual environment and a main file.
3. Rename and run the main file. Rename the main file to `play_sound.py`, then run the following:

   ```
   uv run play_sound.py
   ```

   This confirms that the environment is set up correctly.
4. Reopen Claude Code and verify that the hook does not exist yet. Run a prompt and confirm that a response is produced but no sound is played.
5. Tell Claude Code to write the hook script. Use the following prompt.

   ```
   I want you to please write a python script that is going to play the sound
   @ulala.wav, every time the script runs.
   ```

Ask Claude to write a Python script that plays the recorded sound every time it runs.

> **Note**
>
> **Customizing the notification sound**
>
> The hook does not depend on a specific sound file. It simply plays whichever file the script points to. The examples in this section reference `@ulala.wav`, but you can replace this with any audio file you prefer.
>
> If you choose a different file, place it in the project (for example, under a `hooks/` or `assets/` folder) and update the script to use the new filename or path.

Review the proposed changes.

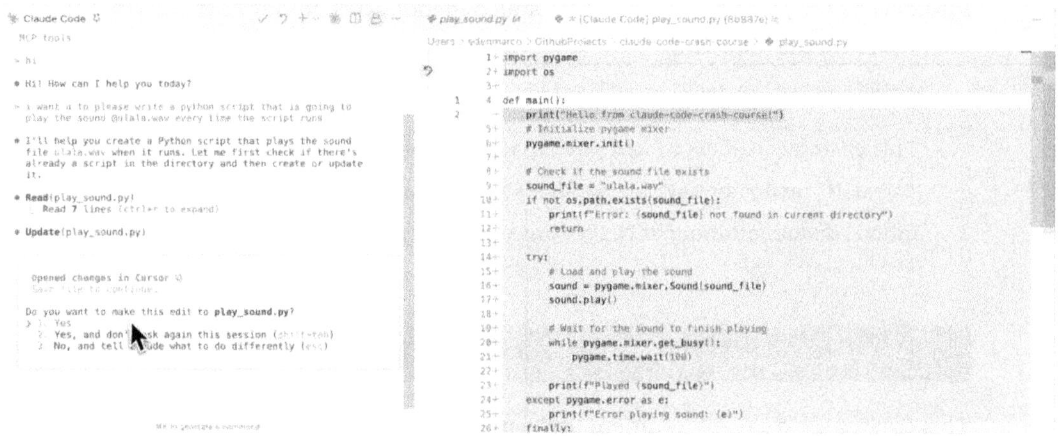

Figure 3.10 – Reviewing and approving hook file changes in diff view

6. Claude shows a `diff` view, highlighting added and removed lines, and asks for permission to edit `play_sound.py`. Approve the file edit:

```
Choose one of the approval options:
1. Approve once
2. Approve for the rest of the session
3. Reject and provide different instructions
```

Approving for the session updates local settings so Claude does not ask again for this file. This permission step is a security measure because Claude Code modifies files directly.

7. Install the required dependencies. The script uses pygame to play audio. Install it by running the following:

```
uv add pygame
```

8. Test the script. Run the script again to confirm that the sound plays correctly by running the following command:

```
Uv run play_sound.py
```

9. Open the hooks configuration to register the script as an automated action. Open the slash menu, type /hooks, and add a new hook from the list provided.

   - **PreToolUse** – Before tool execution
   - **PostToolUse** – After tool execution
   - **Notification** – When notifications are sent
   - **UserPromptSubmit** – When the user submits a prompt
   - **Stop** – Right before Claude concludes its response

   This step is required so Claude Code knows when and how to automatically run the script instead of requiring it to be executed manually each time.

10. Select the hook event. Choose the **Stop** event, which triggers just before Claude finishes its response. This ensures that the script runs immediately after output is generated, making it suitable for notification-style hooks. Other events exist, but this one matches our requirements for now.

11. Configure the hook command. Set the command to the following:

```
uv run play_sound.py
```

If it is inside a folder like hooks/:

```
your/path/to/play_sound.py
```

This ensures the script runs inside the virtual environment. Select the project scope so that the hook applies only to this project.

12. Review the generated configuration. A `.claude` directory is created containing a settings file with the hook configuration stored as JSON:

```
{
  "hooks": {
    "Stop": [
      {
        "matcher": "",
        "hooks": [
          {
            "type": "command",
            "command": "uv run
              /Users/edenmarco/GithubProjects/
                claude-code-crash-course/play_sound.py"
          }
        ]
      }
    ]
  }
}
```

    The empty `"matcher": ""` field means the hook applies to all matching events of that type. In this case, it triggers on every Stop event without additional filtering.

    The configuration specifies the event type, the optional matcher, and the command to run when Claude finishes outputting.

13. Reload Claude Code. Exit Claude Code and reopen it so the new settings are loaded.
14. Verify the hook. Enter any prompt and confirm that the sound plays every time Claude completes its response. This confirms that the hook is working as expected.

At this point, the hook is fully configured. Open Claude Code inside Cursor and enter any prompt:

```
hello how are you?
```

Once Claude finishes responding, the notification sound should play automatically.

This confirms that

- The Python environment is correctly initialized

- The script executes successfully
- The hook is registered and triggered on the Stop event

If no sound plays, revisit the hook configuration and ensure that the command path is correct.

Note

Notes on hooks and extensibility

This hook does not receive any arguments, but hooks can be configured to receive contextual information. This may include user input, tool calls, or other runtime details. Hooks are best organized inside a dedicated hooks directory, as they function like reusable utilities.

Hooks can also produce outputs that influence what Claude Code does next. They can block actions, modify behavior, or even trigger sub-agents. More advanced hook usage will be covered later in the book. This example serves as a simple introduction.

Skills continue to work as described earlier. Internally, commands have been unified under the concept of skills. Existing `.claude/commands/` files remain fully supported, and equivalent skill definitions under `.claude/skills/` behave the same way. Skills add optional structure, support files, and more control over when and how Claude is invoked. More on skills will be covered in *Chapter 9*.

Before moving on, it is worth noting that hooks are one of several mechanisms Claude Code provides for extending behavior. While hooks operate at specific execution points, other features focus on controlling context and persistence, which we explore next through the memory system.

Tip

Keep production hooks lightweight. Hooks run automatically and can execute frequently, so heavy scripts may introduce unnecessary latency. For simple notifications, a minimal system command such as `afplay sound.wav` (macOS) or `aplay sound.wav` (Linux) is often faster than loading a full Python runtime with external dependencies. If possible, prefer lightweight commands for high-frequency hooks.

Understanding memory in Claude Code

In Claude Code, memory refers to a system that allows the AI to retain and reuse important information, such as settings, rules, and contextual details, across coding sessions. The purpose of memory is to improve workflow efficiency and maintain consistency over time.

Memory is primarily managed through special files called `CLAUDE.md` files. These files store instructions and preferences that Claude Code loads at the start of each session and uses to guide its behavior throughout the interaction.

Types of memory

Memory in Claude Code is granular and can be defined at different levels:

- **User memory**: User-level memory is stored in the user's home directory at `~/.claude/CLAUDE.md`. This file typically contains personal preferences that apply across all projects. Examples include coding style preferences, frequently used workflows, shortcuts, and other habits that should remain consistent regardless of the project
- **Project memory**: Project-level memory is stored as a `./CLAUDE.md` file within a project directory. This memory typically contains team-shared rules and project-specific context, such as coding standards, architectural decisions, and common workflows that apply only to that project
- **Managed policy (organization-level memory)**: Organization-wide instructions managed by IT or DevOps teams. These are stored in system-level paths (for example, `/Library/Application Support/ClaudeCode/CLAUDE.md` on macOS, `/etc/claude-code/CLAUDE.md` on Linux/WSL, or `C:\Program Files\ClaudeCode\CLAUDE.md` on Windows). This memory is used for company-wide coding standards, security policies, and compliance requirements, and it applies to all users within the organization.

How does Claude Code read memory?

Claude Code loads memory using a hierarchical and layered approach. Starting from the current working directory, it recursively searches upward through parent directories to locate relevant memory files. All applicable memory files that are discovered are loaded into the session and combined to form the working context.

This design allows Claude Code to support layered configuration. Global preferences can coexist with project-level rules, and more specific instructions override broader defaults when conflicts occur.

The Claude Code memory hierarchy

Claude Code organizes memory into multiple levels, each serving a distinct purpose. Higher levels take precedence and cannot be overridden by lower ones:

- **Level 1 – Managed Policy (Highest Priority)**: Organization-wide rules managed by IT or DevOps teams
  - **Location**: System-managed path (for example, `/Library/Application Support/ClaudeCode/CLAUDE.md` on macOS)
  - **Scope**: Entire organization
  - **Override behavior**: Cannot be overridden
- **Level 2 – User Memory**: This file captures personal preferences that apply across all projects:
  - **Location**: `~/.claude/CLAUDE.md`
  - **Scope**: Personal only
- **Level 3 – Project Memory**: This file defines shared rules and conventions for a project:
  - **Location**: `./CLAUDE.md` or `./.claude/CLAUDE.md`
  - **Scope**: Shared across the team and committed to version control
- **Level 4 – Project Rules**: For larger projects, memory can be broken into topic-specific rule files:
  - **Location**: `./.claude/rules/*.md`
  - **Scope**: Shared across the team and committed to version control
- **Level 5 – Project Local Memory**: Allows personal overrides for a specific project:
  - **Location**: `./CLAUDE.local.md`
  - **Scope**: Personal only and automatically ignored by Git

When conflicts occur at the same level, more specific files (those closer to the current working directory) take precedence.

How upward discovery works

When Claude Code is launched, it begins searching for memory files from the current working directory and continues upward toward the file system root.

For example, take the following directory structure:

```
/Users/edenmarco/
├── .claude/
```

```
│   └── CLAUDE.md
└── Desktop/
    └── my-company/
        ├── CLAUDE.md
        └── frontend/
            └── CLAUDE.md
```

Let's say Claude Code is started from the following:

```
/Users/edenmarco/Desktop/my-company/frontend/
```

The following memory files are loaded into the session:

```
frontend/CLAUDE.md (current directory)

my-company/CLAUDE.md (parent directory)

~/.claude/CLAUDE.md (user-level memory)
```

All three files are combined to form an effective context.

Lazy loading of nested memory files

Memory files located below the current working directory are not loaded immediately. These files are loaded lazily only when Claude Code accesses files within those subdirectories.

For example, if Claude Code is started in the project root, a memory file inside a `backend/` directory is not loaded until Claude Code begins working with files in that directory.

Adding and editing memory in Claude Code

Adding memory can be done using the hashtag (#) character, which prompts Claude Code to store the information in the appropriate memory file. For more substantial changes, the `/memory` command can be used to open the memory file directly in the code editor.

A recommended best practice is to keep memory files concise and specific. Overloading memory with vague or excessive information can waste tokens, introduce confusion, and reduce the quality of results.

Using memory reduces the need for repetitive instructions and helps ensure consistent output across sessions. It makes interactions more efficient and focused, while preserving important context over time.

If you have worked with Cursor before, this concept is similar to Cursor rules.

Initializing memory with /init

Claude Code also provides the `/init` command, which initializes a new `CLAUDE.md` file based on the existing code base. When run, Claude reviews the files in the project and generates a `CLAUDE.md` file containing relevant contextual information to support future interactions.

While this section focuses primarily on concepts rather than hands-on examples, practical usage will be demonstrated shortly. The upcoming sections will show these ideas in action, making it easier to see how memory works in real workflows.

Hands-on example: Using memory with an existing project

To further illustrate how memory works in practice, I use an existing repository created for a LangChain project. This project was created to scrape information from LinkedIn and the X platform and use it to generate an icebreaker. More details on icebreakers can be found at `https://github.com/emarco177/IceBreaker`. It is a practical example built with LangChain agents and works well for demonstrating Claude Code's capabilities.

We begin by cloning the repository into a new directory and opening it in Cursor. For this example, I have named the directory `tmp3`. Once it is opened, we can see the full project structure. This is a Python project built using the LangChain stack.

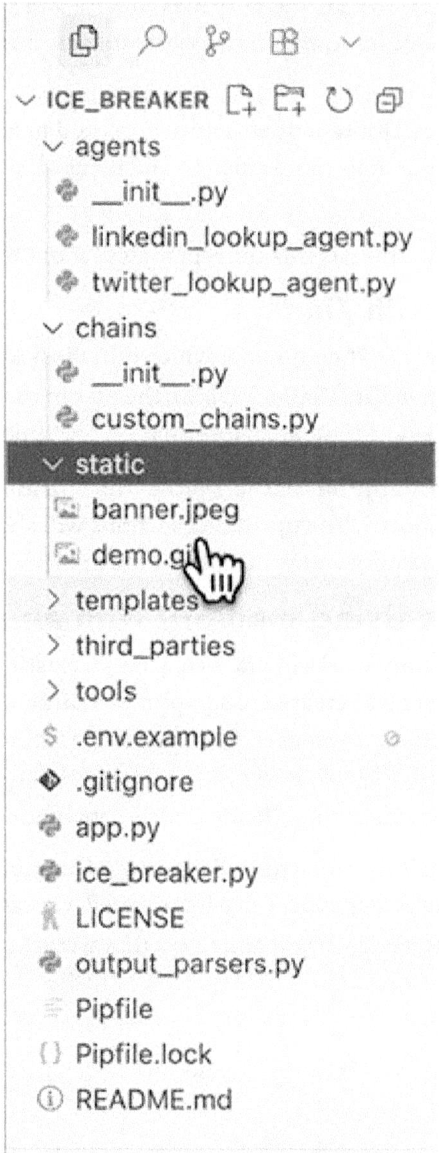

Figure 3.11 – Cloned IceBreaker repository opened in Cursor

We then open Claude Code and pin it in the interface. When prompted, we approve Claude Code's request to access and analyze the project files.

The first step is to create a `CLAUDE.md` file for the project file by running the `/init` command. Running the initialization process causes Claude to scan all the files in the repository. It identifies the tech stack, installed packages, required environment variables, and overall structure. Based on this analysis, Claude generates a `CLAUDE.md` file that captures this information as project memory.

Figure 3.12 – Claude scanning repository files to generate CLAUDE.md

During this process, Claude lists directories, searches through files, and performs a quick analysis using pattern matching and content inspection. After reading the files, it will produce a suggested `CLAUDE.md` file.

CLAUDE.md ×

C: > Users > [redacted] > Desktop > IceBreaker-main > IceBreaker-main > CLAUDE.md > # CLAUDE.md

```
# CLAUDE.md
## Development Commands

### Code Quality Tools
```bash
# Format code with Black
pipenv run black .

# Sort imports with isort
pipenv run isort .

# Lint code with pylint
pipenv run pylint [module_name]
```

Testing
```bash
# Note: No test files currently exist, but the README mentions pytest
pipenv run pytest .
```

Architecture & Key Components

Core Pipeline Flow
1. **Web Interface** (`app.py`): Flask server handling UI and API endpoints
2. **Main Logic** (`ice_breaker.py`): Orchestrates the entire ice breaker generation pipeline
3. **Agent System**: Profile lookup agents for LinkedIn and Twitter discovery
4. **Data Extraction**: Third-party integrations for scraping social media data
5. **AI Processing**: LangChain chains for generating summaries, interests, and ice breakers
6. **Output Parsing**: Structured response formatting using Pydantic models

Key Modules
```

Figure 3.13 – Generated CLAUDE.md file with project overview and architecture details

The generated file includes details such as how to install dependencies using `pip`, how to run the project, and an overview of the main components, including scraping, summarization, and agent logic. Once approved, this file will become part of the project's memory.

From this point on, every prompt sent to Claude will include the contents of this `CLAUDE.md` file as part of the context.

Verifying project memory

To confirm that the memory is working, we first reset the conversation to eliminate any influence from prior chat history. Use the `/clear` command, then ask the question again. For instance, I have asked Claude about the tech stack used in the project:

```
What stack am I using for this project?
```

The following should be the output:

```
Based on the codebase analysis, your project uses this tech stack:

Backend Framework: Flask (Python web framework)
AI/LLM Framework: LangChain with OpenAI GPT models (GPT-4o-mini for agents,
GPT-3.5-turbo for content generation)
Data Sources: Scraping (LinkedIn), Twitter API, Tavily (web search)
Package Management: Pipenv
Code Quality: Black (formatting), isort (import sorting), pylint (linting)
Testing: pytest
Output Parsing: Pydantic models
Frontend: HTML templates with Flask templating
Environment: Python 3.10+
The core architecture is a LangChain-powered AI pipeline that combines social
media data scraping with LLM-based content generation.
```

Claude has provided an accurate response without needing to invoke any tools. This information was inferred earlier when Claude analyzed the files during initialization.

With this, we can confirm that Claude is relying on stored memory rather than the chat history.

Adding and using memory entries

Let us now see how to add new memory entries. At this point, if we ask a question such as *What do I like to eat?*, Claude generates a response similar to the following:

```
> what do i like to eat?

I don't have any information about what you like to eat. I can only see your
codebase files and project structure, but there's no personal information about
your food preferences in this ice breaker application repository.
```

```
If you'd like to share what you like to eat, I'd be happy to help with any related
coding tasks!
```

To enable Claude to answer this question, we add a memory entry using the hashtag syntax. In this case, we state that we like to eat pizza and store the entry in the project memory:

```
# I like to eat pizza
```

With this information added, after clearing the conversation and asking the same question again, Claude will now be able to answer correctly using the stored memory:

```
> what do i like to eat?
Pizza
```

If we want to add another memory entry, we repeat the same process and add a new entry stating a preference for hamburgers. This time, the entry is stored in user memory, which lives in `~/.claude/CLAUDE.md`. Clear the conversation and try asking the same question again. Claude will correctly recall both preferences:

```
> what do i like to eat?
Based on your CLAUDE.md files, you like to eat both Hamburger (from your global
preferences) and Pizza (from your project-specific memory).
```

The same approach can be used for other kinds of persistent information, such as preferred coding styles, commonly used tools, or recurring workflow conventions that we want Claude to remember across projects and sessions.

Working with multiple memory files

As projects grow, a single `CLAUDE.md` file can become large and difficult to manage. Claude Code supports using multiple `CLAUDE.md` files distributed across a repository. Claude recursively traverses the directory structure and loads all relevant memory files into the context.

This allows memory to be organized in a structured way. For example, server-side context can live in one area, frontend context in another, and DevOps or Claude-specific rules elsewhere. This approach makes memory easier to maintain and more targeted.

When combined with hooks, this setup enables more advanced behavior. For instance, different memory files can be attached depending on the type of work being done. A context-switching hook can attach database-related memory when working with database code, frontend context when working on UI components, or API-related memory when handling backend logic.

This level of control allows memory to be tailored dynamically based on user input and workflow needs, opening the door to more advanced and flexible context management patterns.

Rewind feature in Claude Code

In this section, we will explore Claude Code's checkpointing and rewind feature, which allows you to safely undo changes made during a coding session. Claude Code automatically tracks file modifications created by each prompt, making it possible to roll back unwanted edits when needed.

To trigger a rewind, press *Esc* twice or use the `/rewind` command.

Benefits and importance of the rewind feature

The value of this feature is straightforward:

- It provides a safety net when experimenting with larger or more ambitious changes
- It allows alternative implementations to be explored without losing working code
- It makes recovery from mistakes fast and predictable
- It reduces the cost of correcting AI-generated errors by making undo operations easy
- It increases user confidence when working with AI-assisted coding
- It encourages wider adoption by lowering the perceived risk of using AI tools
- It is closely related to the **Cost of AI Recovery (CAIR)** metric (`https://www.blog.langchain.com/the-hidden-metric-that-determines-ai-product-success/`), which measures how easily users can recover from AI errors and is revisited later in the course

The rewind feature was introduced several months after Claude Code was initially released.

```
2025
│
├─ Feb 24 ──────────────────────── Claude Code (Research Preview)
│                                   │
│                                   │
├─ May 22 ──────────────────────── Claude Code (General Availability)
│                                   │
│                                   │
│                                   │
└─ Sep 29 ──────────────────────── Checkpointing/Rewind Feature Added
                                     (Claude Code v2.0.0 + Sonnet 4.5)
                                    "Most Requested Feature"
```

Figure 3.14 – Timeline of Claude Code releases and the rewind feature introduction

The rewind feature was heavily requested by the community, and several open source tools attempted to provide similar functionality before it became a native capability. Today, rewind is built directly into Claude Code and is intuitive enough that very little explanation is required. To understand how the rewind feature appears and behaves in practice, let us briefly review the interface context in which it is used.

Using rewind in practice

At the time of writing this book, Claude Code is running version 2.1. The interface includes several recent updates, including visual refinements and the use of Sonnet 4.5, which is Anthropic's latest model optimized for coding tasks. You will also notice a custom status line at the bottom of the interface. This is a user-defined customization and will be covered later in the book.

To demonstrate the rewind feature, we begin with a simple Next.js example:

1. Ask Claude Code a question, such as the following:

   ```
   How do I bootstrap a Next.js project?
   ```

   The prompt is executed locally. Once the setup is complete, run the application using `npm run dev` and open it in the browser. As expected, this will produce the standard Next.js boilerplate application.

2. We then intentionally apply a short sequence of incremental changes to the code base. The goal here is not to evaluate the quality of the user interface, but to simulate a

realistic development workflow in which changes may later need to be undone. In my example, I will be doing the following:

1. First, prompt Claude Code to create a landing page for HooksHub with a visually distinct style
2. Next, prompt Claude Code to add an FAQ section
3. Finally, prompt Claude Code to add a footer section

Figure 3.15 – HooksHub landing page generated with Claude Code

Each prompt results in file edits that are visible through the `diff` view, and each change is immediately reflected in the running application.

After the footer is added, it becomes clear that although the feature works, the result is heavier and more visually dominant than desired. This is a natural point at which undoing the change is preferable to manually editing the code or issuing corrective prompts.

3. To revert changes, invoke the rewind feature using the `/rewind` command. This opens a timeline of the current session, showing all prompts issued so far and indicating which prompts resulted in file modifications.

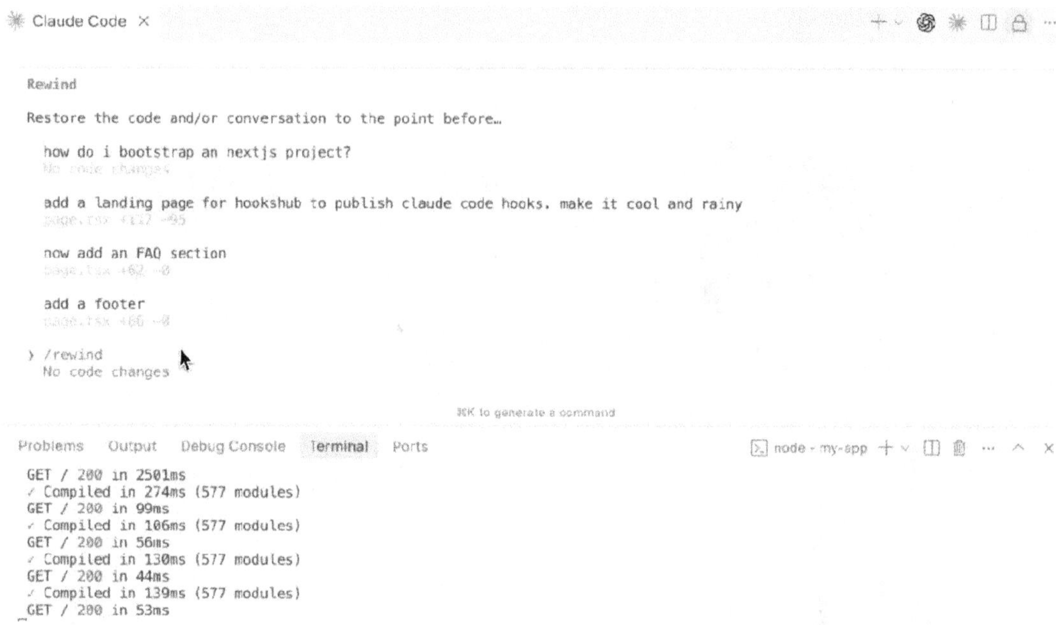

Figure 3.16 – Using the /rewind command to view session history and file changes

Prompts that only generate explanations appear without associated file changes, while prompts that modify files clearly display the affected files and lines.

4. Select the last prompt you added for your example. In this case, select the prompt that added the footer. Three options will be presented to you:
   - **Restore code and conversation**, which resets both the files and the chat context to that point
   - **Restore conversation**, leaving file changes intact
   - **Restore code**, leaving the conversation history unchanged

   In practice, restoring both code and conversation is the most common choice, as it returns the project to a clean and consistent state. Restoring only the code is useful when you want to preserve the conversational context while reworking an implementation.

5. To illustrate this, restore only the code changes associated with the footer. The footer is immediately removed from the application. This works because Claude Code automatically creates a checkpoint before applying any file edits.

Each prompt that results in code changes creates a new checkpoint. These checkpoints persist across sessions and are retained for up to 30 days, providing a safety net for experimentation and iteration.

Because the conversation history is still present, a follow-up prompt such as `create a footer, make it minimalistic` can now be issued. Claude Code correctly resolves the reference using the existing context and generates a lighter implementation. Refreshing the application confirms that the updated footer better matches the intended design.

While rewind is powerful, it does have limitations:

- Bash commands executed by Claude Code are not tracked and cannot be reverted
- Manual edits made outside of Claude Code are not captured by checkpoints
- Rewind does not replace version control systems such as Git
- Checkpoints should be thought of as local, short-term undo functionality rather than a permanent history

Used correctly, rewind significantly reduces the cost of experimentation. It encourages exploration, lowers the risk of making changes, and makes iterative development with Claude Code both safer and more productive.

Custom slash commands in Claude Code (powered by Skills)

In this section, we will review how to create custom slash commands in Claude Code. This feature is powerful because it gives developers a high degree of flexibility in how Claude Code can be customized and extended. We will create a custom slash command by defining a skill that creates Git commit messages. More advanced skills will be covered in *Chapter 7*.

Creating a skill

We will begin with a clean project and switch to the `custom-commands` branch. To create a skill, first create a `.claude` directory in your project (if it does not already exist). Inside it, create a `skills` directory.

1. Each skill is defined as its own directory:

   ```
   .claude/skills/commit-code/
   ```

2. Inside that directory, create a required file named

   ```
   SKILL.md
   ```

   Skills are defined as Markdown files. Metadata is declared using YAML frontmatter at the top of `SKILL.md`, enclosed between `---` delimiters. The body of the file contains the actual prompt, written in Markdown.

3. Add a title to the file. This title appears in the slash command menu.
4. Write the command prompt:

   ```
   Review the files that have changed, and create a commit with a commit
   message summarizing the changes made. Always try to give short and concise
   messages that convey the business logic.
   ```

   I have asked Claude Code to review the files that have changed and to create a commit with a concise commit message summarizing the business logic of the changes.

Although the prompt itself is short, Claude Code is able to infer and perform multiple operations. It can inspect changed files using Git commands, review diffs, and create a commit. This demonstrates how a single skill can encapsulate a sequence of actions.

Executing the skill

To test the command, open Claude Code and type `/`. The new `commit-code` command should appear in the list. Executing it will cause Claude Code to run the prompt defined in the Markdown file.

Claude Code will also detect untracked files in the `.claude` directory and ask whether they should be added. Any approved decision will be stored in `settings.local`. Claude will then propose a commit message based on the detected changes and display the corresponding Git commands.

But what if the generated commit message is not descriptive enough? Instead of proceeding, we stop and improve the skill.

Improving the skill with $ARGUMENTS

Head to the initial prompt added at the start and update the command prompt. In my example, I am asking Claude Code to accept user-provided hints by introducing an `$ARGUMENTS` placeholder.

> **Note**
>
> We can pass arguments when invoking a skill. Arguments are available via the `$ARGUMENTS` placeholder.
>
> The `$ARGUMENTS` placeholder gets replaced with whatever follows the skill name when invoking it. More about this will be covered in *Chapter 9*.

```
Review the files that have changed, and create a commit with a commit message
summarizing the changes made. Always try to give short and concise messages that
convey the business logic.

Use user hints to be the message main subject $ARGUMENTS
```

After making this change, execute `/commit-code` again and provide a subject hint related to skills:

```
/commit-code custom code
```

Claude Code should now generate a more descriptive commit message that reflects the requested changes.

Once approved, the commit is created, co-authored by Claude. We then push the changes by running `git push` to the remote repository and verify the commit in the project's `custom-commands` branch.

You can also create and execute additional skills by just doing the following:

1. Create a new command file with an appropriate title
2. Define a prompt that produces output based on user input
3. Attach arguments so the command can accept dynamic values at runtime

After restarting Claude Code, the new command becomes available and can be executed with user-provided input. This shows how skills can support dynamic and flexible behavior.

Improving auto-generated commit messages with context engineering

Earlier, we discussed context engineering. To make this more concrete, let us look at a specific use case taken directly from the Claude Code documentation:

```
---
allowed-tools: Bash(git add:*), Bash(git status:*), Bash(git commit:*)
description: Create a git commit
---

## Context

- Current git status: !`git status`
- Current git diff (staged and unstaged changes): !`git diff HEAD`
- Current branch: !`git branch --show-current`
- Recent commits: !`git log --oneline -10`

## Your task

Based on the above changes, create a single git commit.
```

This example shows a skill that performs the same task as generating a commit message, but in a way that is more robust, safer, and richer in features. Understanding why this approach is better helps clarify how context engineering, tool control, and agent design come together in practice.

In skills, we can run shell and Bash scripts. This means we can execute arbitrary code as part of a command. As a result, we can make HTTP requests, run containers, or perform any other operation that can be expressed as code. This effectively removes most limitations on what a skill can do.

In this specific slash command example, the configuration begins by defining a set of allowed tools. This limits the scope of the agent by restricting which tools it is permitted to use.

If you have experience implementing agents, this aligns with the principle of least privilege. The idea is to scope the agent so that it has only the minimum set of capabilities required to perform its task. In the case of generating a commit message, the necessary operations are limited to commands such as git add, git status, and git commit.

Restricting the toolset in this way improves security. In the earlier, simpler `commit-message` command, no such limitations were applied, meaning the agent had access to all the tools available in Claude Code. In that situation, if the context was poisoned (for example, by malicious input), the agent could potentially perform unintended actions on the system. This is one of the reasons the documented example is a stronger and safer design.

This example also demonstrates deliberate prompt engineering. The context is explicitly defined and carefully constructed. Before generating the commit message, the command executes a series of Git commands, such as `git status`, `git branch`, and `git log`. These commands provide precise context about the state of the repository and the changes being committed.

When viewed this way, the workflow closely resembles retrieval-augmented generation. First, the system retrieves relevant information by running Git commands to gather context. Once that context is available, the generation step produces the commit message.

This illustrates how retrieval and generation are combined within a single, well-scoped command. It also shows how multiple concepts discussed earlier, including context engineering, tool restriction, and agent design, come together in a practical and extensible way.

Overall, this approach opens up a wide range of possibilities for building safer and more capable workflows using skills in Claude Code.

> **Note**
>
> The section which is enclosed between `---` delimiters is called frontmatter and is evaluated before the prompt body.

Summary

In this chapter, you learned how to configure and work with Claude Code beyond the basics. We covered authentication and pricing at a high level, how to control Claude Code using slash commands, and how to integrate it directly into the IDE for a smoother workflow. You explored configuration options, hooks for automation, and memory through `CLAUDE.md` files, as well as how context is loaded and reused across sessions. We also examined checkpointing and rewind to safely undo changes, and skills to encapsulate repeatable workflows with proper tool scoping. By this point, you should understand how Claude Code operates in practice, how to keep it safe and predictable, and how to shape its behavior to support more advanced, long-running development workflows.

In the next chapter, we will look at the **Model Context Protocol (MCP)** and how it standardizes integration between AI applications and external tools.

Get this book's PDF copy, code bundle, and more

Scan the QR code (or go to `packtpub.com/unlock`). Search for this book by name, confirm the edition, and then follow the steps on the page.

UNLOCK NOW

Note: Have your invoice handy. Purchases made directly from the Packt website don't require an invoice.

Part 2

Extending Claude Code: Protocols, Automation, and Structured Workflows

In *Part 2* of this book, the focus shifts from individual usage to structured extension and automation. You'll learn how Claude Code connects to external tools and services through the **Model Context Protocol (MCP)**, and how these integrations are configured and managed responsibly. We'll examine how automation works in practice through GitHub workflows and event-driven execution.

As systems grow more complex, structure becomes essential. You'll explore planning-based development, coordinated multi-agent workflows, and subagents that isolate context for safer execution. You'll also learn how output styles and configuration patterns shape behavior and enforce consistency. By the end of this part, you'll be able to design workflows that are deliberate, controlled, and scalable.

This part of the book includes the following chapters:

- *Chapter 4, Extending Claude Code with MCP Servers and Plugins*
- *Chapter 5, Automating Your Development Workflow with Claude Code and GitHub*
- *Chapter 6, Claude Code Planning and Multi-Agent Workflows*
- *Chapter 7, Working with Claude Code Subagents*
- *Chapter 8, Creating and Customizing Output Styles*

4

Extending Claude Code with MCP Servers and Plugins

The **Model Context Protocol** (**MCP**) provides a standardized way for AI applications to connect to tools, data sources, and services through a common interface. Instead of building separate integrations for each host application, developers can implement functionality once in an MCP server and reuse it across any MCP-compatible client. MCP was introduced to address this integration challenge. This abstraction layer enables interoperability, portability, and ecosystem growth. Within the context of Claude Code, MCP becomes particularly important, as it enables developers to extend the coding agent with additional tools, capabilities, and integrations in a structured and reusable way.

In this chapter, you will learn what MCP is, why it was created, and how it works in practice. You will explore the integration problem that MCP solves and examine its core architectural components: hosts, clients, and servers. Through practical demonstrations, you will connect MCP servers to AI applications such as Claude and Cursor, configure both local and remote MCP servers, and understand how tools are exposed and invoked through the protocol.

You will also examine important operational considerations. As powerful as MCP is, it introduces challenges related to context management, performance, and execution efficiency. This chapter explores context engineering strategies to reduce context pollution, properly scope MCP configurations, and dynamically manage servers within a session. In addition, you will learn how Claude Code plugins bundle MCP servers and related components into reusable, shareable units, enabling team-wide standardization.

The overall goal of this chapter is to help you build a strong conceptual and practical foundation in MCP. By the end, you will understand not only how MCP enables cross-platform tool integration, but also how to configure and manage it responsibly in real-world AI systems.

This knowledge is important because MCP is rapidly becoming a foundational layer in agent-based architectures. As AI development shifts toward tool-augmented and autonomous systems, understanding MCP's architecture, benefits, and trade-offs will allow you to design scalable, efficient, and interoperable AI applications.

In this chapter, we cover the following topics:

- Why MCP?
- MCP core architecture
- MCP in action
- Connecting Claude Code to MCP server
- MCP Scope cheat sheet
- Context engineering in the MCP ecosystem
- Project-level MCP configuration
- Current limitations of MCP
- Managing configuration with Claude Code plugin

> **Note**
>
> Although this book centres on Claude Code, MCP is a cross-platform protocol supported by multiple AI development tools. For demonstration purposes, this chapter uses Cursor in some examples. The underlying concepts remain the same and can be applied when using Claude Code.

Why MCP?

MCP has seen rapid adoption, with widespread discussion and numerous MCP server implementations. Many AI applications, including tools such as Claude Code and Cursor, integrate MCP within their systems.

Before defining MCP in detail, it is important to understand the need it addresses.

The integration problem

Consider an AI agent designed to perform actions such as sending Slack messages, reading and sending emails, or querying a database. To enable these capabilities, the required functionality must be implemented directly. This involves working with APIs such as Slack or Gmail and writing custom code that wraps these integrations as tools accessible to the agent.

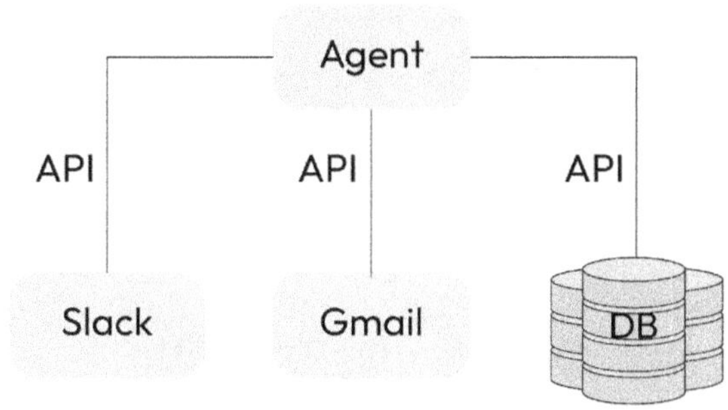

Figure 4.1 – Agent integrating with Slack, Gmail, and a database via APIs

In many cases, custom implementations are necessary. For example, an email integration may intentionally exclude access to the delete endpoint in the Gmail API to prevent unintended data loss. The integration logic is therefore tailored to specific requirements and implemented manually.

Frameworks may provide built-in tools. For example, a framework might include a pre-implemented Gmail integration covering the full API surface. Such tools can be used out of the box for generic needs. However, regardless of whether built-in or custom tools are used, the functionality must be integrated within the specific agent environment.

Once implemented, the agent can send emails, post Slack messages, or execute database queries. The integration works within that specific agent.

The portability challenge

Assume the agent becomes widely adopted and other teams want to use its functionality in different environments. Now suppose the agent becomes widely adopted and other teams want to use its functionality in different environments.

For example, consider an agent originally built to run inside the Cursor environment. In this setup, the agent integrates with external services such as Slack, Gmail, and a database through their respective APIs. The following diagram illustrates this architecture.

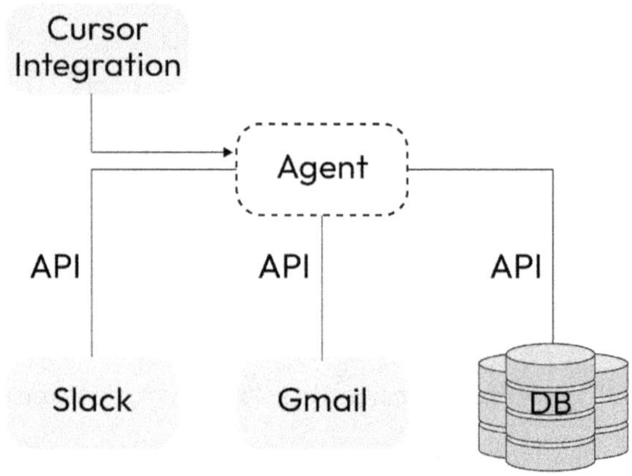

Figure 4.2 – Agent coupled to the Cursor environment and its API integrations

In this case, the agent is tightly coupled to the Cursor environment. The integrations with Slack, Gmail, and the database were implemented specifically for that setup.

Now suppose we want to integrate the same agent capabilities into Claude Code. Even though the functionality is conceptually the same, the integration cannot simply be reused. Because the implementation was written specifically for our agent, the integration must be recreated for Claude Code.

As a result, similar capabilities like sending Slack messages, interacting with Gmail, or executing database queries need to be reimplemented for the new environment. Now imagine we want to integrate the same capabilities into another environment. What if we want to integrate the same agent into Cursor?

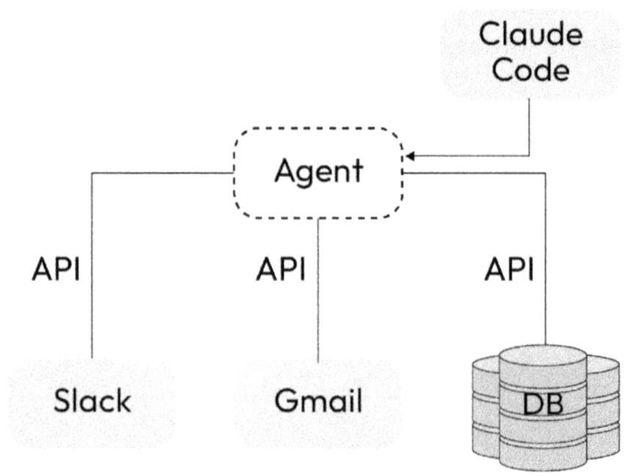

Figure 4.3 – Reimplementing agent integrations for the Claude Code environment

Extending support to other environments such as Cursor, Bolt, GitHub Copilot, or other AI code assistants requires repeating this process. Each new integration introduces additional implementation work. The same functionality must be adapted separately for each target system.

MCP as an abstraction layer

The portability challenge creates a recurring integration problem. Each time the same functionality needs to be used in a different environment, developers must rebuild the integration from scratch.

MCP addresses this problem by introducing an additional abstraction layer. A well-known principle in software engineering states:

> *"We can solve any problem by introducing an extra level of indirection."*
>
> — *Andrew Koenig*

This idea is closely related to the fundamental theorem of software engineering, which states that many complex system problems can be simplified by adding a layer of abstraction. MCP servers serve this purpose.

Instead of integrating functionality separately into each agent, the implementation is integrated once into an MCP server. Agents that support MCP can then connect directly to that MCP server.

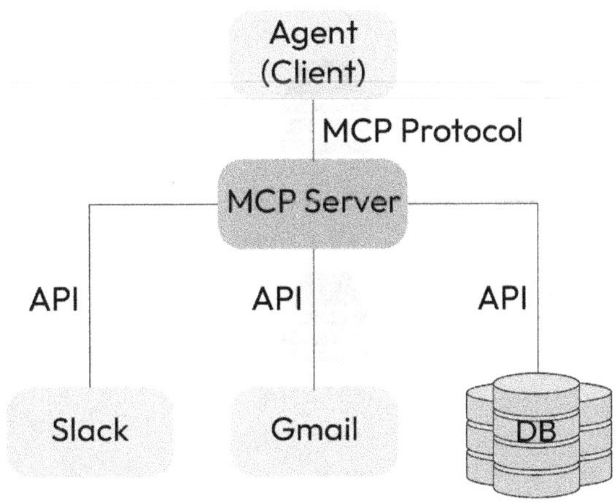

Figure 4.4 – MCP server acting as a unified integration layer for external services

With this approach, compatibility is implemented a single time. Once capabilities are exposed through an MCP server, they can be used across any platform that supports the protocol.

Capabilities initially implemented for Cursor become compatible with Claude Code and other MCP-supporting environments without requiring additional integration logic.

Developers do not need to rewrite or duplicate integration code for each platform. Any system that supports MCP can connect and use the functionality seamlessly.

Network effects and ecosystem growth

The growth of MCP reflects a network effect similar to social platforms. A social application with a small user base provides limited value. As adoption increases and users contribute content, the system becomes more valuable, creating a reinforcing cycle of growth.

A similar dynamic is occurring with MCP. As adoption increases and more MCP servers are developed, the ecosystem expands. The growing number of implementations broadens the range of available integrations and capabilities, increasing the overall utility of the protocol.

With this foundation established, the next step is to examine the core architecture of MCP is and how it operates in practice.

MCP core architecture

MCP standardizes how applications provide context to **large language models** (**LLMs**). Context can take multiple forms. It may include additional information appended to a prompt, the specification of a tool to invoke, or even the prompt itself.

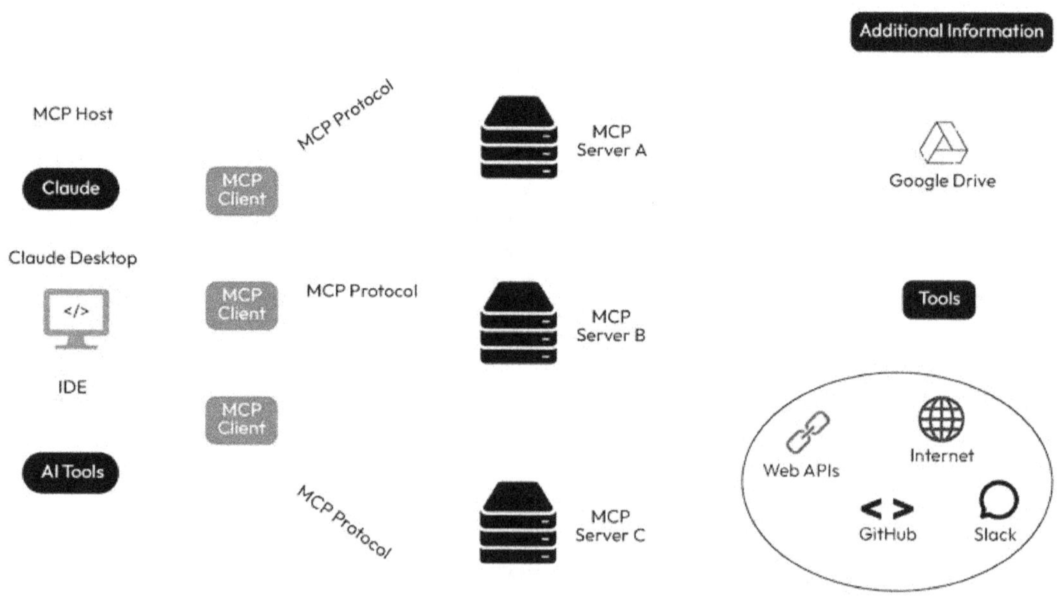

Figure 4.5 – MCP core architecture connecting hosts, clients, and MCP servers

In this sense, context encompasses both supporting data and operational instructions that shape how the LLM responds.

Once such a standard becomes widely adopted, it enables the development of powerful and extensible integrations across AI applications.

Advantages of MCP

The MCP documentation (`https://modelcontextprotocol.io/`) highlights several advantages of adopting MCP:

- First, MCP supports a broad ecosystem of integrations, tools, and data sources that can be connected to LLM-powered applications in a modular way. For instance, Claude Code, as an AI-powered coding agent, leverages MCP to extend its capabilities through structured tool integration.
- Second, MCP reduces coupling to specific LLM vendors or AI application providers. Developers can implement core functionality in the form of tools and expose them through MCP servers. These tools can then be reused across different vendors and host applications without modification.
- Open source frameworks such as LangChain address some overlapping challenges in AI engineering. However, MCP and LangChain approach these problems differently, and their solutions do not directly overlap. For example, both may support extensibility, but the mechanisms and architectural implications differ.

Core components of MCP

The MCP architecture consists of three primary components: MCP hosts, MCP servers, and MCP clients.

MCP hosts

An **MCP host** is an AI application that supports MCP. Examples include Claude Desktop, development environments such as Claude Code or Cursor, and specialized AI agents. These applications are augmented through MCP by connecting them to additional tools, data sources, or products that are not available natively.

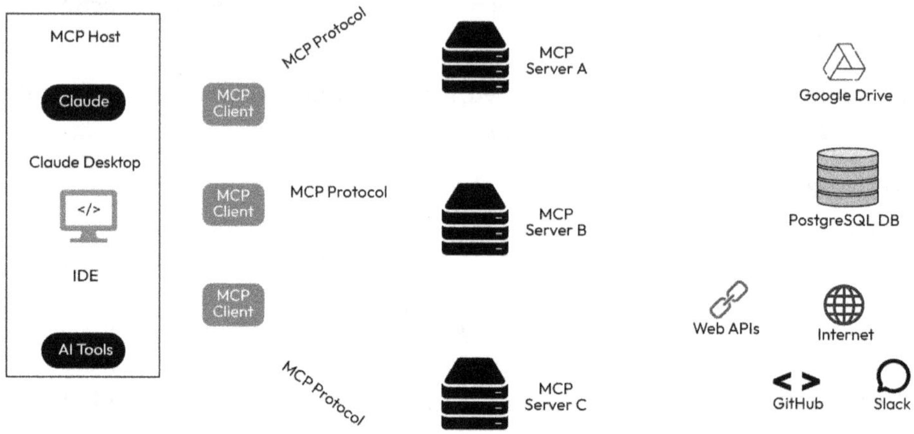

Figure 4.6 – MCP hosts connecting to MCP servers through MCP clients

MCP servers

MCP servers expose functionality to MCP hosts. This functionality may include the following:

- Access to external tools, such as invoking an API to retrieve weather information
- Database search capabilities
- Knowledge resources such as PDFs or large text

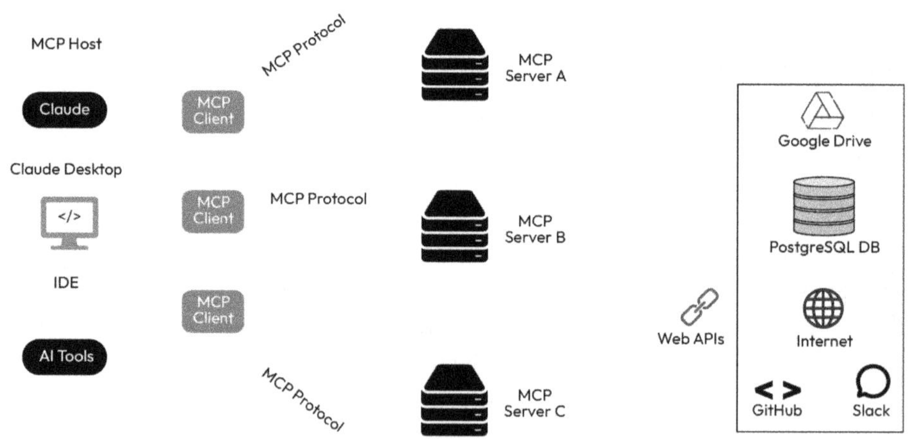

Figure 4.7 – MCP servers exposing tools, databases, and external APIs to MCP hosts

The MCP server acts as a gateway or proxy that exposes these tools, resources, and prompts according to the MCP specification.

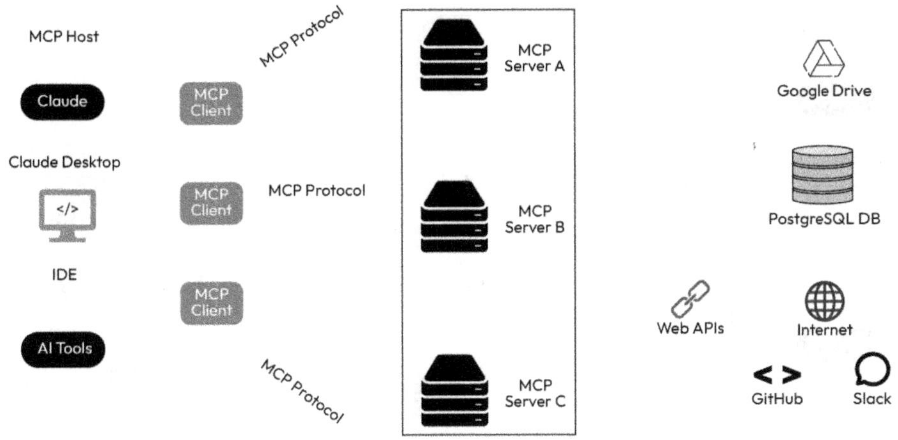

Figure 4.8 – MCP server acting as a gateway that provides standardized access to external resources

To conform to the protocol, an MCP server implements specific methods, such as the following:

- `listPrompts`
- `getPrompt`
- `listTools`
- `callTool`
- `listResourceTemplates`
- Progress notification mechanisms

Once implemented, an MCP server can be connected to any MCP host that supports the protocol. Functionality written once can therefore be reused across multiple host applications. This reusability is a central architectural advantage of MCP.

MCP clients

An MCP client resides within the MCP host. It enables communication between the host and an MCP server using MCP.

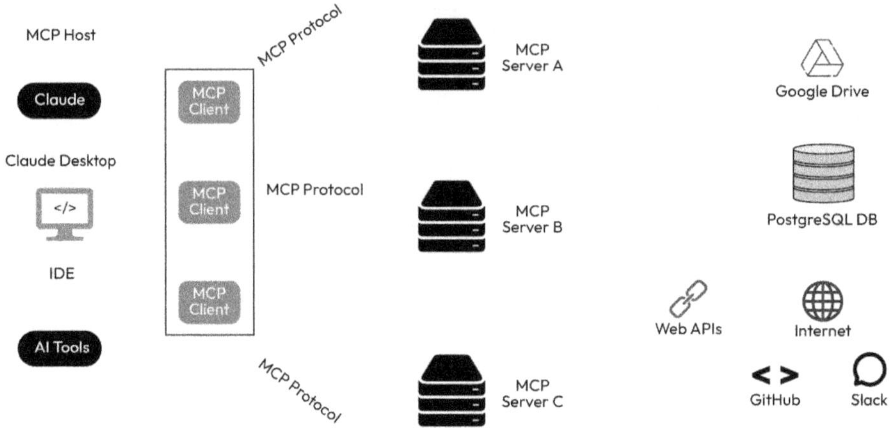

Figure 4.9 – MCP client inside the host managing communication with MCP servers

For example, to connect a weather MCP server to Claude Desktop, an MCP client inside Claude Desktop manages the interaction with that server. The client and server communicate exclusively through the defined protocol.

There is a one-to-one relationship between an MCP client and an MCP server. A single MCP client cannot communicate with multiple MCP servers. Therefore, if an MCP host needs to connect to multiple MCP servers, it must instantiate multiple MCP clients, one for each server.

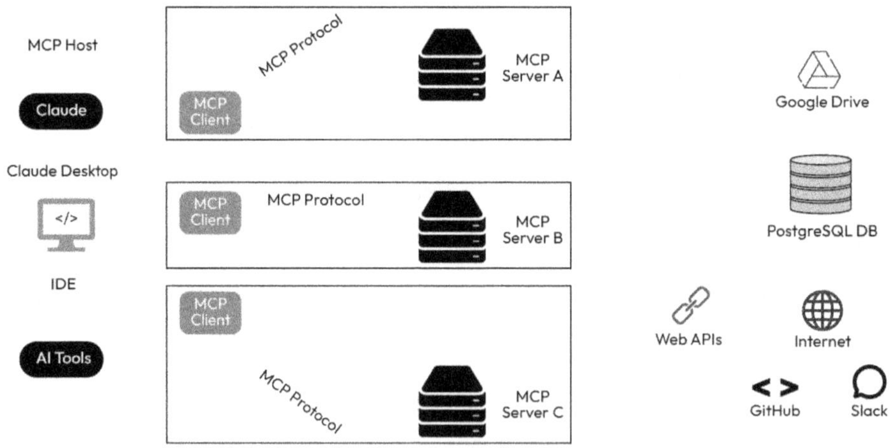

Figure 4.10 – Multiple MCP clients connecting a host to different MCP servers

This structure completes the core architecture of MCP and establishes the foundation for building interoperable, extensible AI applications.

MCP in action

Let us now walk through a practical example of adding and configuring an MCP server. This demonstration illustrates the capabilities enabled by MCP and how those capabilities function in practice. The example connects an MCP server that implements weather retrieval functionality to two different clients: Claude Desktop and Cursor.

The same MCP server is used in both cases. Configuration details are addressed separately; the focus here is on the resulting behavior once the server is connected. Any client that supports the MCP protocol can use this functionality, including Claude Code, Claude Desktop, Cursor, Claude Code, Lovable, and other compatible clients.

Behavior without an MCP server

In Claude Desktop, no MCP servers are initially configured in the Developer settings. For example, when querying the weather in San Francisco without an MCP server connected, the language model typically responds that it does not have access to real-time weather information. In some cases, it may attempt to invoke a search tool to retrieve summarized information instead.

Without MCP, the model is limited to its training data and cannot retrieve live data directly, except through generic built-in tools such as search.

Connecting an MCP server

After configuring the weather MCP server, it appears in Claude's Developer settings along with its runtime details.

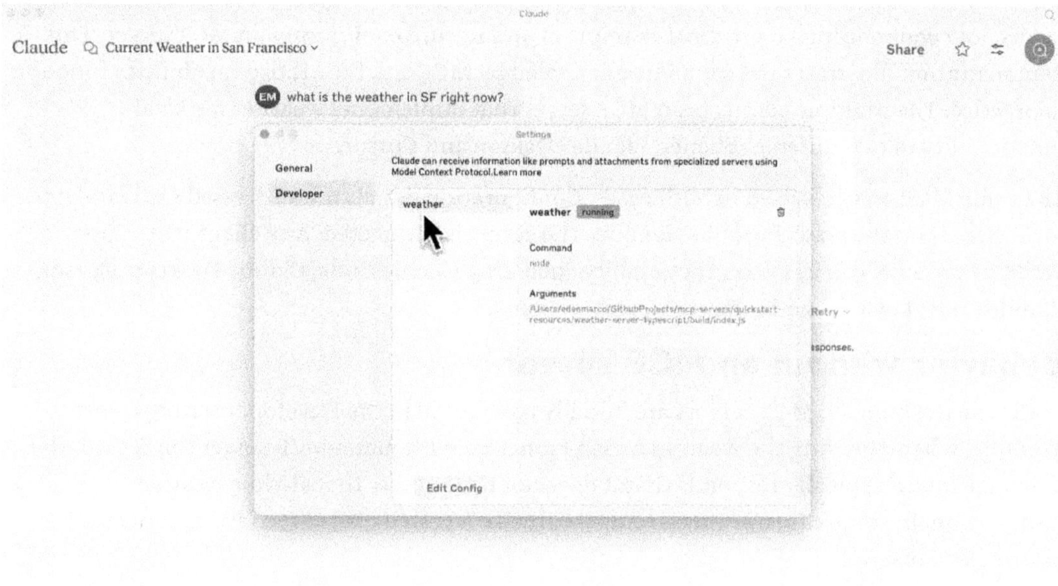

Figure 4.11 – Weather MCP server configured in Claude developer settings

When querying the weather in San Francisco again, the system prompts for permission to execute the weather tool locally. Tool execution requires approval because it may involve running local code. Security considerations related to tool execution are addressed separately.

Note

Security warning: MCP servers can run code on your machine

MCP servers run code locally with the same permissions as your user account. This means they can access files, environment variables, and network resources on your system.

Before adding an MCP server, be aware of the following risks:

- An MCP server can execute commands on your machine, including reading, modifying, or deleting files.
- A malicious server could send sensitive information (such as source code, environment variables, or API keys) to an external service.
- Tool responses from MCP servers may contain hidden instructions that influence the model's behavior.

Treat MCP servers the same way you treat any third-party dependency. Review the source code, when possible, install servers from trusted maintainers, and avoid running MCP servers with elevated privileges.

Once Claude Code is granted permission to invoke the MCP tool, the following sequence occurs:

1. The MCP server contains the logic for retrieving weather data
2. The server exposes a function named `getForecast`
3. The `getForecast` function accepts two arguments: latitude and longitude
4. The language model (Claude Sonnet 3.7) determines the latitude and longitude corresponding to San Francisco
5. The model issues an MCP call to the `getForecast` function
6. The MCP server executes the function and returns a response
7. The language model processes the response and generates the final answer:

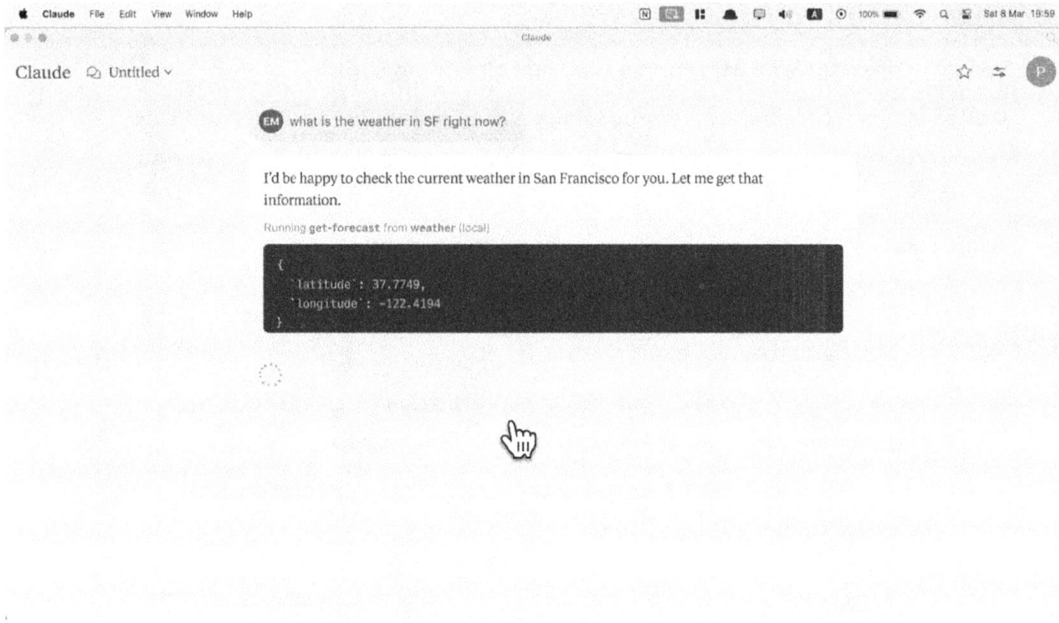

Figure 4.12 – Claude invoking the MCP weather tool and returning the forecast response

The result is a weather report based on real-time data retrieved through the MCP server.

Although retrieving weather data is a simple example, the underlying mechanism supports arbitrary logic. Any functionality can be implemented in an MCP server. By implementing the MCP protocol, developers enable compatible clients to invoke that functionality through tool calls. This extends AI agents beyond static model capabilities and allows them to execute external logic.

Reusing the same MCP server across clients

The same weather MCP server can be connected to Cursor. Once configured, the MCP server appears in the MCP tab within Cursor's settings.

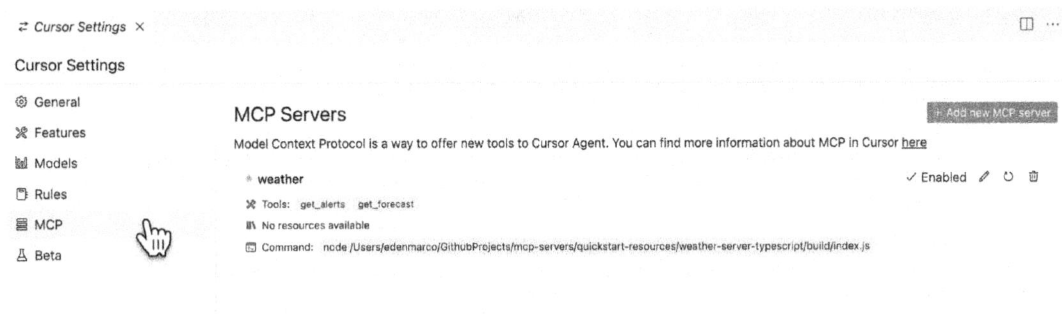

Figure 4.13 – Claude invoking the MCP weather tool and returning the forecast response

The connected server is listed along with the tools it exposes:

- `GetAlerts`
- `GetForecast`

The configuration also shows the command used to run the server, which in this case is a Node.js server. Within Cursor Chat, MCP functionality is available when using agent mode.

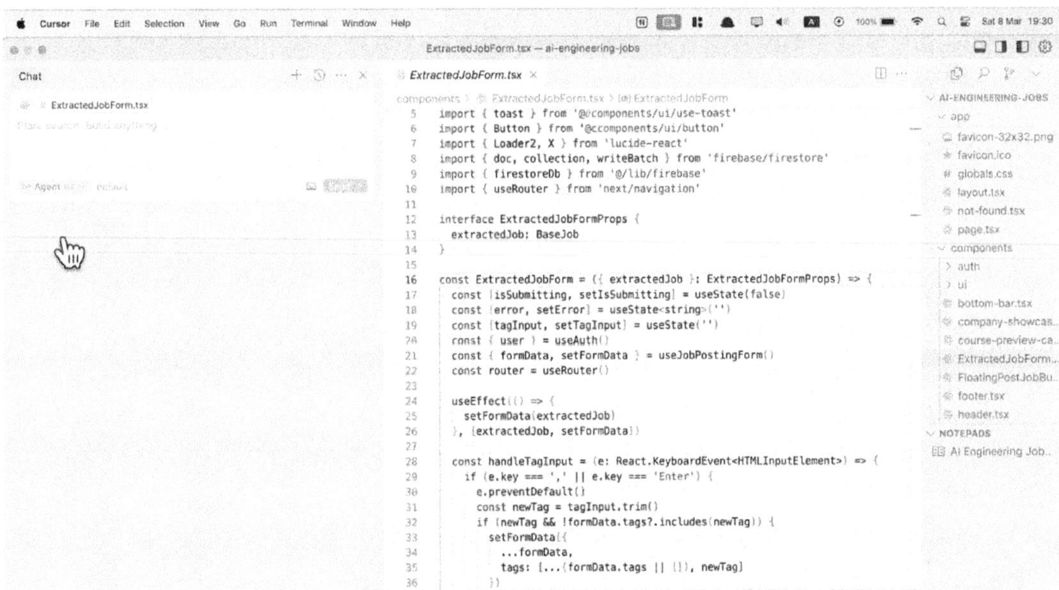

Figure 4.14 – Invoking the MCP weather tool from Cursor in agent mode

When querying the weather in San Francisco, the agent calls the `GetForecast` tool with the appropriate arguments. In this configuration, Cursor runs in YOLO mode, meaning tools are executed automatically without requiring manual approval. While this approach is convenient, it carries security implications.

The agent performs the following actions:

1. Calls the `GetForecast` tool with latitude and longitude arguments.
2. Receives the weather data from the MCP server.
3. Determines that weather alerts may also be relevant.
4. Calls the `GetAlerts` tool to check for alerts in San Francisco.
5. Compiles the responses into a final answer that includes both weather conditions and any active alerts.

In this case, two tools are invoked within a single prompt. The agent autonomously determines which tools to call and how to combine their results into a coherent response.

The weather example demonstrates a general pattern: MCP enables AI agents to execute external logic defined in MCP servers. Clients that support MCP can connect to these servers and invoke their tools.

By implementing the MCP protocol in a server, developers make its functionality accessible to any compatible MCP client. This removes limitations imposed by static model knowledge and allows agents to perform dynamic, real-time, and custom operations.

Connecting Claude Code to MCP server

We start with an empty project and an empty branch called `project/MCP` in this book's GitHub repository. To access the repository, follow the steps in the *Download the example code files* section in the *Preface*. We then list the available MCP servers using the `/mcp` slash command. At this point, no MCP servers are listed.

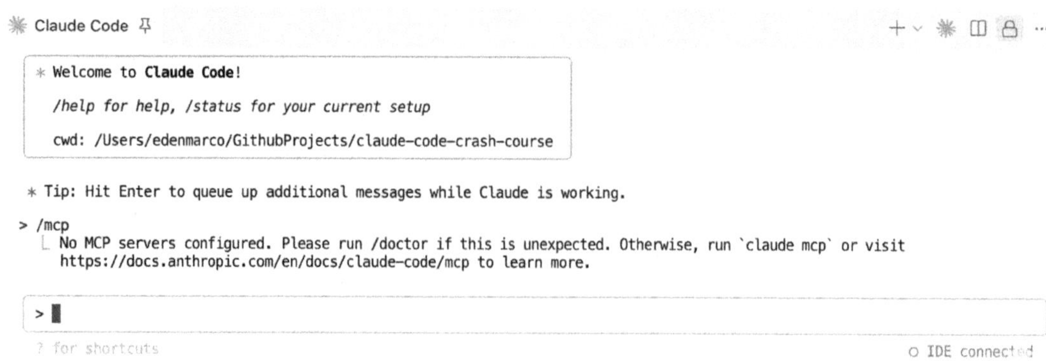

Figure 4.15 – Listing available MCP servers in Claude Code using the /mcp command

A link is available that takes us to the MCP documentation, which explains how to add MCP servers. There are multiple ways to do this:

- Adding MCP servers through files
- Adding MCP servers using the CLI

MCP servers can be added through files; however, the CLI is recommended. The CLI is typically the most up to date, and if formatting changes or APIs break, using the CLI ensures compatibility.

Adding Context7 MCP Server via the CLI

Context7 (`https://context7.com/`) provides up-to-date documentation for a large number of packages. Many packages, especially in the AI ecosystem (such as LangGraph), change frequently, and having the latest documentation ensures that generated code aligns with the latest APIs.

Context7 indexes close to 30,000 (`https://github.com/upstash/context7`)packages.

At the time of writing, the repository has approximately 49,200 stars.

To use Context7 with Claude Code, Claude Code integration is required. The command is as follows:

```
claude mcp add -transport http context7 https://mcp.context7.com/mcp
```

This command performs the following actions:

- Uses `claude mcp add`
- Specifies HTTP as the transport
- Assigns the MCP name `context7`
- Provides the MCP server's URL

This is a remote MCP server, meaning the server does not run locally. Instead, it runs on the Context7 servers.

Each invocation sends a request to the remote server. This approach offers several advantages:

- The service can scale easily
- The MCP can be accessed from multiple clients

HTTP transport and remote MCP servers are explained in more detail in the MCP course available at: `https://www.udemy.com/course/model-context-protocol/`.

The command is copied and pasted into the terminal. Before execution, the `--help` flag is added so you can review available options.

MCP server scope and configuration

The help output shows that the MCP server's scope can be configured. The MCP server can exist at the following scopes:

- User scope
- Project scope
- Session scope

Optional values can also be provided for environment variables or HTTP headers.

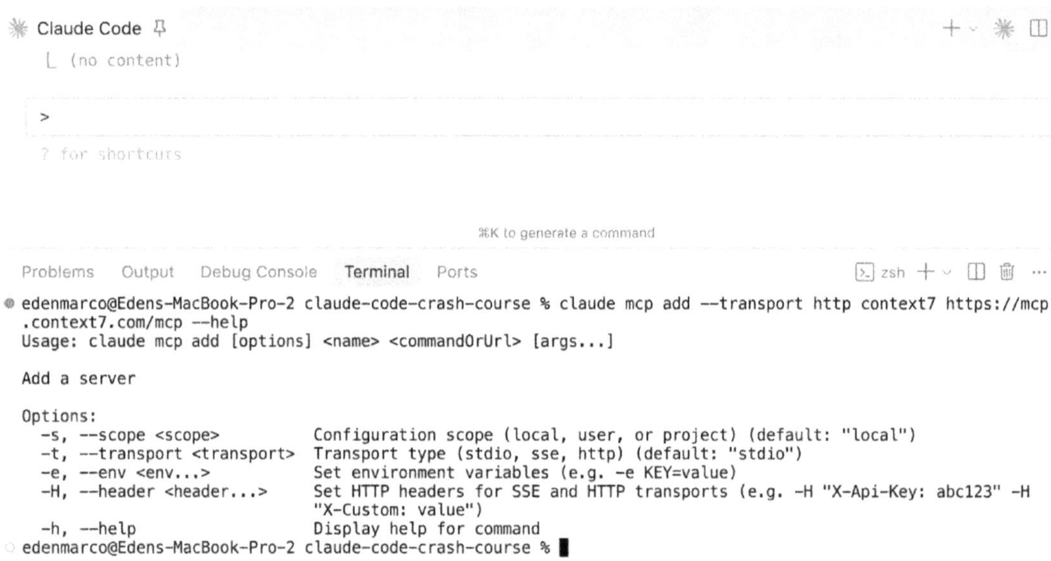

Figure 4.16 – Adding an MCP server to the project using the mcp add command

In this example, the project scope is selected when adding the MCP server.

After execution, a new file is created containing the Context7 MCP configuration. The configuration specifies the HTTP transport type and the MCP server's URL.

```
{
 "mcpServers": {
   "context7": {
     "type": "http",
     "url": "https://mcp.context7.com/mcp"
   }
```

```
  }
}
```

To run the MCP server locally instead of remotely, the following alternative command can be used:

```
claude mcp add context7 - npx -y  @upstash/context7-mcp.
```

This command uses npx to download the repository and execute it locally.

Restarting Claude Code and enabling the MCP server

After installing the MCP server, Claude Code must be restarted. Exit the session, clear the terminal, and start Claude again.

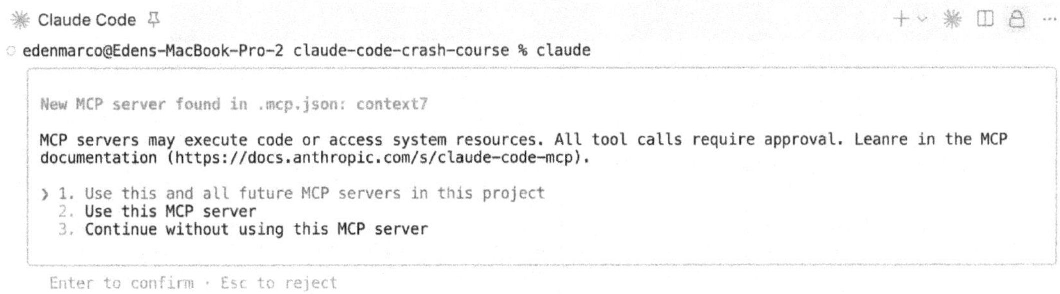

Figure 4.17 – Claude Code detecting and enabling the configured MCP server after restart

On startup, Claude will detect the `mcp.json` file and prompts for permission to connect to the configured MCP servers. The first option is selected to allow the connection.

Claude then creates a `settings.local.json` file for the current user session. Opening this file confirms that the Context7 MCP server is enabled, allowing Claude to query it when needed.

Listing and inspecting installed MCP servers

The MCP servers can now be listed. We can see that the Context7 MCP server is connected.

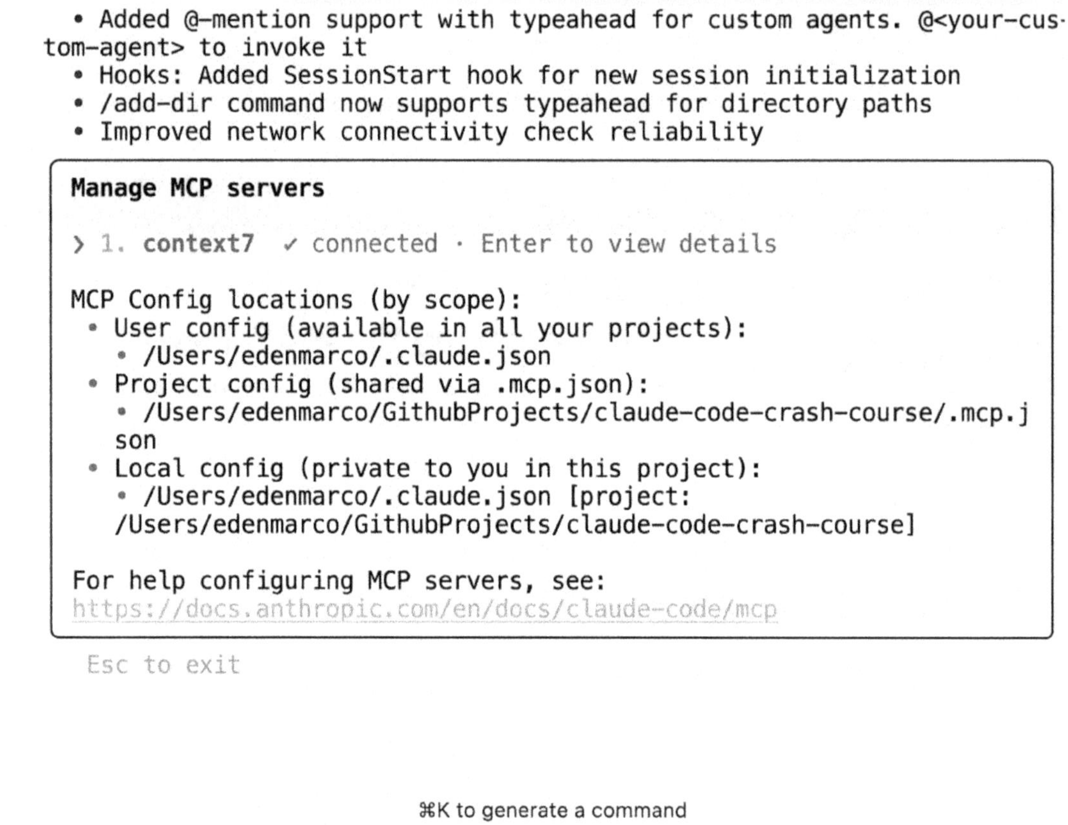

Figure 4.18 – Listing installed MCP servers and inspecting the connected Context7 server

Click into it and see that it exposes two tools:

- `resolve-library-id`
- `get-library-docs`

These tool descriptions become part of the agent's context, allowing the agent to dynamically invoke tools as required. For instance, when requesting the latest LangGraph documentation, the agent first calls `resolve-library-id` to obtain the appropriate context ID, followed by `get-library-docs` to retrieve the latest documentation.

Querying LangGraph using the Context7 MCP server

We can ask the following question and specify that the Context7 MCP server should be used:

What is the latest version of LangGraph?

Claude Code asks for permission to invoke the Context7 MCP tool. We approve the request, and the permissions are updated in `settings.local.json`.

Figure 4.19 – Invoking the Context7 MCP tool to retrieve the latest LangGraph version

The MCP server resolves the library ID and then makes another request to retrieve the documentation.

Based on the documentation returned by Context7, the latest version of LangGraph is reported as **1.2**.

> **Note**
>
> LangGraph is an actively evolving framework. You may encounter a later version than the one demonstrated here; however, the architectural concepts and patterns discussed remain relevant.

Persisting MCP server usage in project memory

We configure Context7 to be used every time we ask a question about LangGraph. To do this, we add an instruction and save it to the project memory so that it persists across sessions.

The instruction is recorded, and a `Claude.md` file will be created with the following entry:

```
When discussing LangGraph, always use context7 MCP
```

Verifying persistent MCP behavior

We can restart Claude, clear the session, and ask the following question:

```
What is a LangGraph interrupt?
```

Claude Code automatically selects the Context7 MCP server. It resolves the LangGraph library, retrieves the relevant documentation and code snippets, and returns an explanation of a LangGraph interrupt.

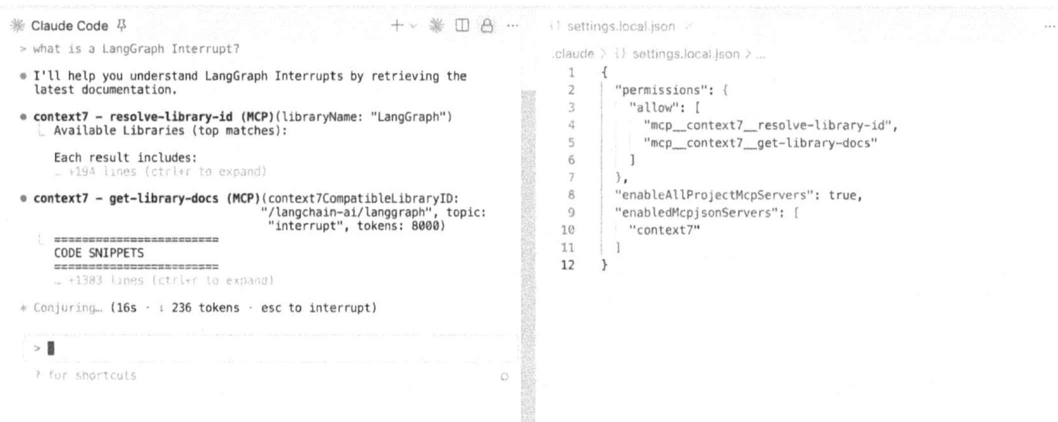

Figure 4.20 – Claude automatically using the Context7 MCP server to explain a LangGraph interrupt

Because Context7 provides access to current documentation and APIs, the generated code reflects the most up-to-date usage.

Committing MCP artifacts to version control

We can add the generated files to the GitHub repository. We commit the changes with the message `context7 mcp` and push them upstream with the following command:

```
git commit -m "context7 mcp"
```

The commit can be found in this book's GitHub repo. To access the repository link, follow the steps in the *Download the example code files* section in the *Preface*.

MCP scope cheat sheet

Choosing the correct scope helps keep your environment organized and prevents unnecessary configuration from leaking into unrelated projects. The following table summarizes when to use each MCP scope:

Aspect	Project-scope	User-scope	Session-scope
Config location	`.mcp.json` in the project root	`~/.claude/settings.json`	Started with `--mcp-config` flag or added mid-session
Visibility	Everyone on the project	Only you, across all project	Only the current session
Committed to git?	Yes	No	No
Persists across sessions?	Yes	Yes	No
Shared with team?	Yes	No	No

Table 4.1 – MCP scope comparison: project, user, and session

When to Use Each MCP Scope

The following guidelines illustrate common scenarios for each scope.

- **Project-scope** (`.mcp.json`)
    - Use project scope when the MCP server is part of the project's shared development environment.
    - Database tools specific to this project (for example, a project's Postgres MCP)
    - Project-specific APIs such as internal services or staging environments
    - Custom tooling the whole team needs, such as deployment scripts or test runners
    - Documentation servers tied to the project's technology stack
- **User-scope** (`~/.claude/settings.json`)
    - Use user scope for tools that are personal or tied to your own credentials.
    - Personal productivity tools (Slack, Linear, Notion)
    - Tools tied to your credentials, such as GitHub with your PAT or email access

    - General-purpose servers you want available across all projects (for example, Tavily search or Context7 documentation)
    - Servers that rely on secrets you do not want committed to the repository
- **Session-scope** (`--mcp-config / ephemeral`)
    - Use session scope for temporary or experimental setups that should not persist.
    - One-off debugging servers such as a temporary proxy or mock API
    - Experimental or untrusted servers you are evaluating
    - Servers that rely on short-lived tokens (OAuth sessions or temporary credentials)
    - CI/CD environments where servers are started dynamically during a run

Context engineering in the MCP ecosystem

In this section, we cover context engineering within the MCP ecosystem. The example shown uses Claude Code, but the concepts apply to any agentic system that supports MCP.

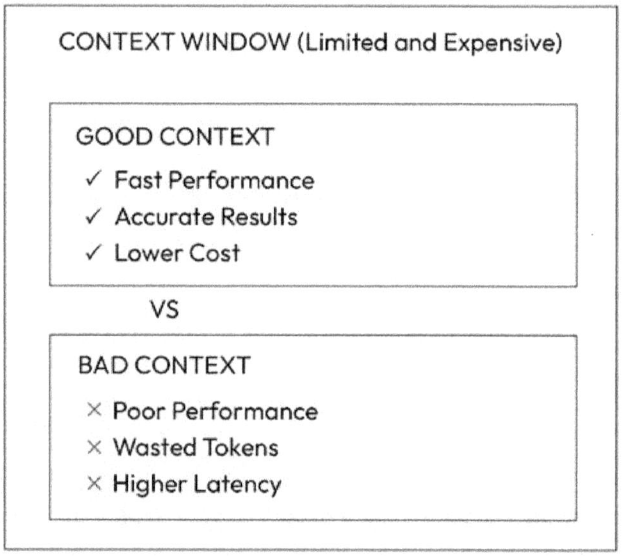

Figure 4.21 – Good vs bad context usage within limited LLM context windows

Context is the most expensive and limited resource in agentic systems, especially in agentic coding workflows. Context directly affects agent performance. Poor context results in poor performance from the agent. This discussion focuses only on performance implications and deliberately excludes pricing and latency considerations.

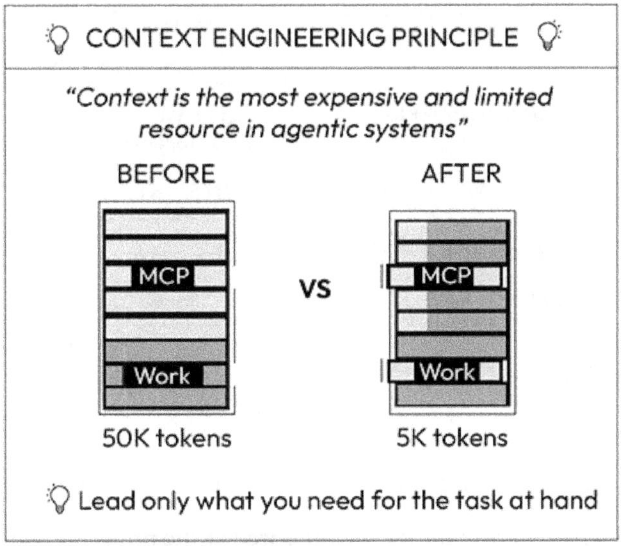

Figure 4.22 – Context engineering: reducing tokens by loading only necessary context

One of the quietest but most impactful sources of context inefficiency is MCP configuration. MCP is powerful, but if it is not used carefully, it can significantly degrade context efficiency. The main issue is that MCP can bloat the context window with unnecessary tokens for tools that are not required for the task at hand.

The problem – overly general MCP configuration

The root cause of the problem of context inefficiency is overly general MCP configuration. When MCP servers are configured too broadly, the agent loads every available tool into its context window before processing a single request. This consumes valuable tokens before any reasoning begins, leaving less space for the actual task.

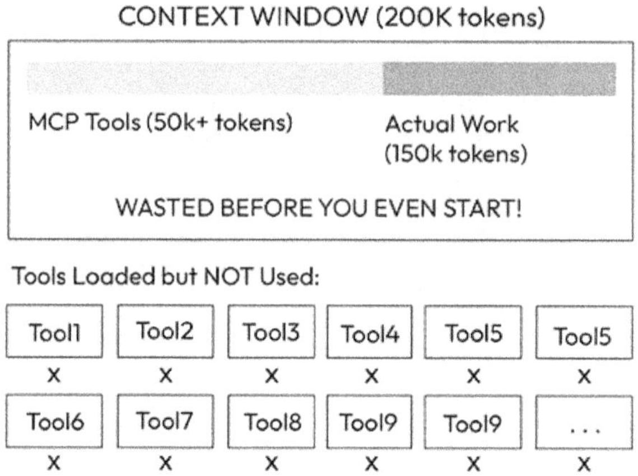

Figure 4.23 – Context window waste caused by overly broad MCP configuration

In Claude Code, MCP servers are commonly configured at the project level using an `mcp.json` file. This file loads multiple MCP servers and all of their associated tools.

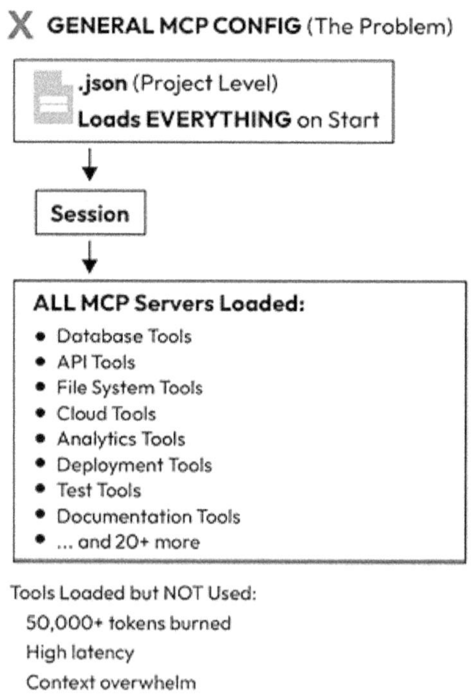

Figure 4.24 – General MCP configuration loading all tools at startup.

Most setups follow this pattern. A single, general-purpose MCP configuration is used to load all MCP servers and tools. The intent is to equip the agent with everything it might need.

The result is that every session loads all MCP servers and all MCP tools, even when they are not relevant. This can consume tens of thousands of tokens before a single prompt is written.

In this section, we introduce this problem and demonstrate how to fix it using context engineering techniques.

Example repository and MCP server

The code used in this section is available in the `context-engineering-mcp` branch in the book's GitHub repo. To access the repository link, follow the steps in the *Download the example code files* section in the *Preface*. We start from the first commit so the setup can be reproduced exactly.

The repository contains a simple MCP server implemented in `verbose_mcp_server.py`. The server is written using FastMCP and exposes a large number of MCP tools, including the following:

- `add_two_numbers`
- `subtract_two_numbers`
- `multiply_two_numbers`

The server intentionally includes many MCP tools that are not required. Each tool also includes a detailed description. Here is an example:

```

@mcp.tool()
def add_two_numbers(a: float, b: float) -> float:
    """
    Advanced Numerical Addition Operation Tool

    This sophisticated mathematical operation tool performs the fundamental arithmetic
    operation of addition between two numerical values. The addition operation is one
    of the four basic arithmetic operations in mathematics, and this tool implements
    it with high precision and reliability.

    Detailed Functionality:
    - Accepts two numerical parameters (integers or floating-point numbers)
```

Figure 4.25 – Verbose MCP tool definition increasing context size

These descriptions help the MCP client decide whether a tool should be invoked, but they also directly contribute to context size.

Running the MCP server

The MCP server is run using the UV package manager. The repository contains a `uv.lock` file that defines the FastMCP dependency (`https://github.com/PrefectHQ/fastmcp`). Follow these steps:

1. Run `uv sync` and activate the virtual environment using the following:

```
source .venv/bin/activate.
```

2. Once the environment is active, the FastMCP CLI (`https://github.com/jlowin/fastmcp`) is available. We start the MCP server using `fastmcp run verbose_mcp_server.py --transport http`.
3. The verbose mathematical operations MCP server is now running using streamable HTTP transport and is exposed at `http://127.0.0.1:8000/mcp`.

Adding the running MCP server to Claude Code

We need to inspect how MCP servers and their tools affect context once they are loaded into a session. With the MCP server running locally, we open Claude Code and add this MCP server.

To do this, we create a project-level MCP configuration file named `.mcp.json`.

If we return to the repository and inspect the branch, there is a commit titled **Add project-based MCP configuration**. This configuration can be copied directly, with API keys added as needed. The API keys shown in the example are obfuscated.

Project-level MCP configuration

The project-level MCP configuration defines four MCP servers:

- A locally running verbose MCP server
- Context7, which was covered earlier (`https://context7.com/`)
- Tavily (`https://tavily.com/`), used to search the internet, crawl websites, and extract web pages
- Playwright MCP, used for browser automation

{} .mcp.json > {} mcpServers

```
{
  "mcpServers": {
    "verbose-server": {
      "type": "http",
      "url": "http://127.0.0.1:8000/mcp"
    },
    "context7": {
      "type": "http",
      "url": "https://mcp.context7.com/mcp",
      "headers": {
        "CONTEXT7_API_KEY": "XXXXX"
      }
    },
    "tavily": {
      "type": "http",
      "url": "https://mcp.tavily.com/mcp/?tavilyApiKey=XXXXX"
    },
    "playwright": {
      "command": "npx",
      "args": [
        "@playwright/mcp@latest"
```

Figure 4.26 – Project-level MCP configuration with multiple servers defined in mcp.json

This is a project-level configuration, meaning all four MCP servers are loaded automatically when Claude Code starts from the project's directory.

The API keys in the configuration are obfuscated.

To validate that the configuration is applied correctly, follow these steps:

1. Open the terminal.
2. Change directory into the project folder.
3. Confirm that you are on the context-engineering-mcp branch.
4. Run Claude Code.
5. Run `/mcp` to confirm that all four MCP servers are connected.

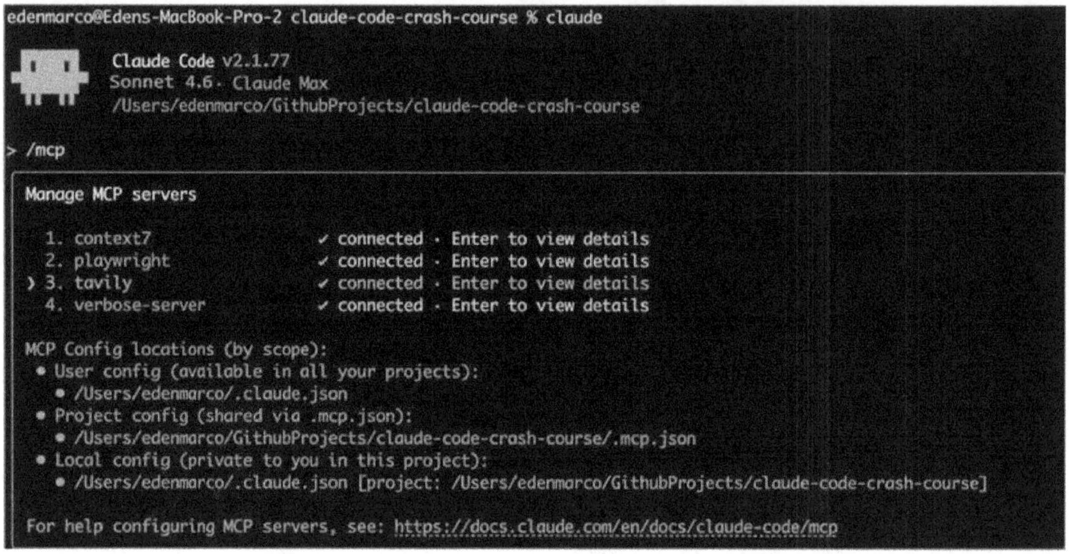

Figure 4.27 – Multiple MCP servers connected in Claude Code.

Inspecting context usage

Next, we run `/context` to inspect the context usage for the current session.

At this point, we are already close to half of the context window, even though no prompt has been written. The `/context` output reveals how the available tokens are distributed.

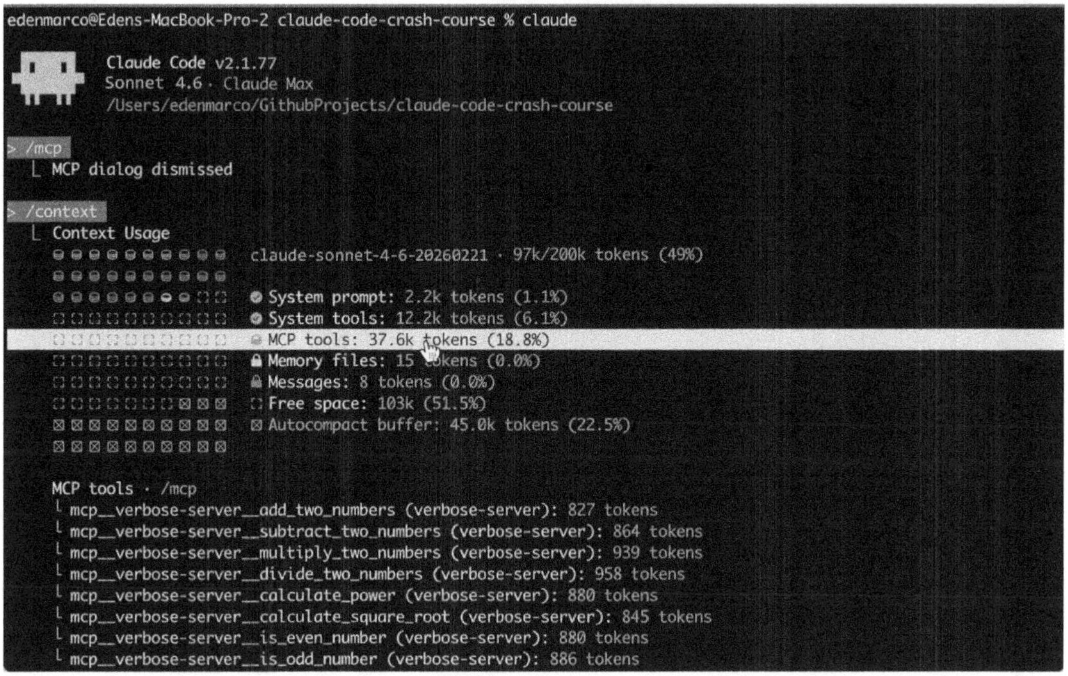

Figure 4.28 – MCP tools consuming a large portion of the context window

The breakdown shows the following:

- Around 2,000 tokens are dedicated to the Claude Code's system prompt
- Claude Code's system tools are consuming roughly 12,000 tokens
- MCP tool descriptions are consuming close to 20% of the context window

There are no messages. There is no memory file. There are no sub-agents configured.

If sub-agents were present, they would also appear in the context, including instructions describing how and when to use them.

At this stage, almost 50% of the context window is already consumed.

Depending on the task, many of these MCP servers and especially the verbose mathematical MCP tools are unnecessary.

Reducing context by scoping MCP configuration

To reduce context usage, the MCP configuration must be scoped more narrowly.

Perform the following steps:

1. Remove the project-level `.mcp.json` file.

2. Create a new file named `.mcp.json.tavily`.
3. Copy the Tavily MCP configuration from the repository.
4. Paste it into `.mcp.json.tavily`.

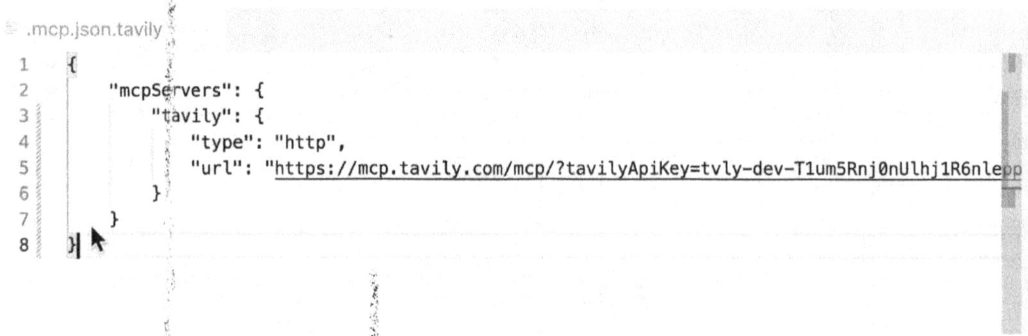

Figure 4.29 – Scoped MCP configuration using mcp.json.tavily.

This configuration now contains only the Tavily MCP server.

Next, start Claude Code using the scoped configuration:

Return to the terminal and run the following:

```
claude --mcp-config .mcp.json.tavily.
```

The `--mcp-config` flag accepts space-separated paths to MCP configuration files.

When Claude starts, we inspect the MCP servers again using `/mcp`.

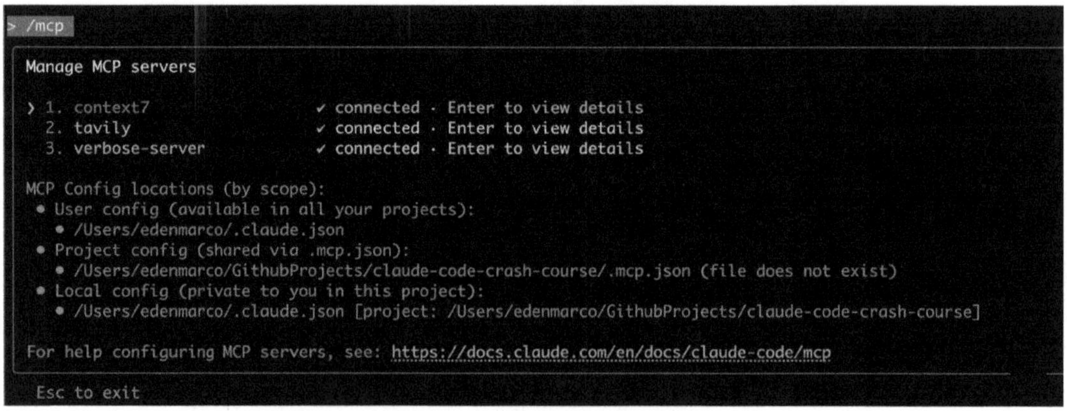

Figure 4.30 – Active MCP servers with scoped config.

At this point, we see the Tavily MCP, which is expected. However, we also see the verbose MCP server and Context7. The Playwright MCP server is no longer present.

This happens because Claude Code is still loading MCP servers from the user-level MCP configuration, which includes Context7, Tavily, and the verbose MCP server.

Enforcing a strict MCP configuration

To ensure that only the intended MCP configuration is loaded, a strict configuration must be enforced.

Run the following:

```
claude --mcp-config .mcp.json.tavily --strict-mcp-config.
```

The `--strict-mcp-config` flag instructs Claude Code to ignore the default MCP hierarchy and load only the MCP servers defined in the specified configuration file.

Let's verify the result:

1. Run `/mcp` and confirm that only the Tavily MCP server is loaded.
2. Run `/context` and verify that the context usage from MCP tools is significantly reduced, since only the Tavily MCP server is active.

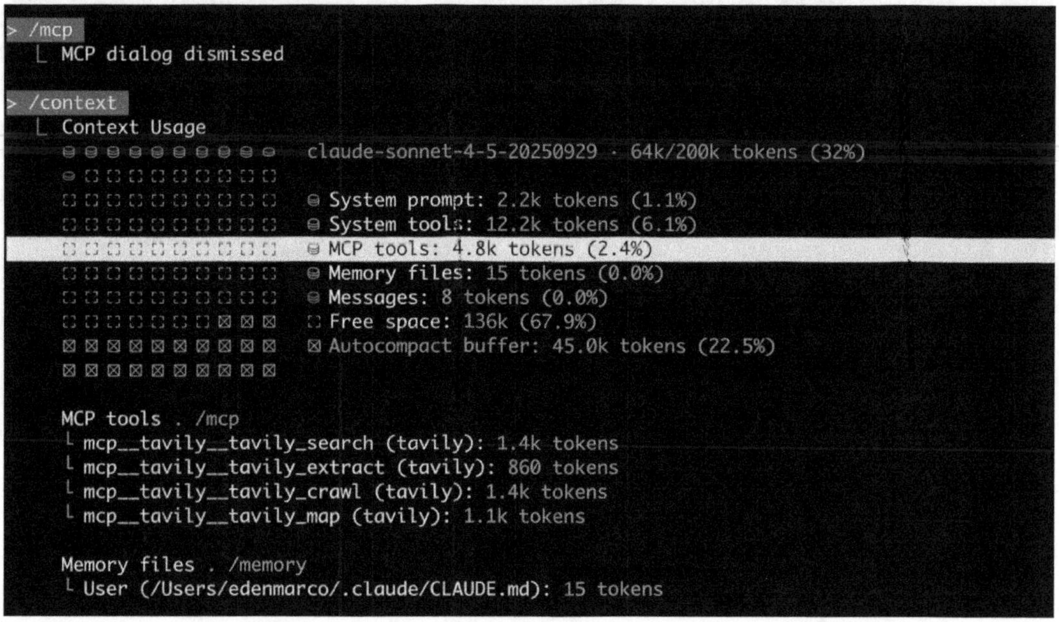

Figure 4.31 – Context usage after enabling strict MCP configuration

MCP-related context usage drops from nearly 20% to approximately 2.4%.

This allows the agent to remain focused and avoids carrying unnecessary tool context for the current task, which in this case is research.

Managing MCPs dynamically within a session

In addition to configuration-based scoping, MCP servers can also be managed dynamically within a session.

To do this, follow these steps:

1. Restore the general project-level `.mcp.json` configuration.
2. Restart Claude Code.
3. Disable the verbose MCP server.
4. Disable the Playwright MCP server.
5. Run `/mcp` to confirm that both servers are disabled.
6. Run `/context`.

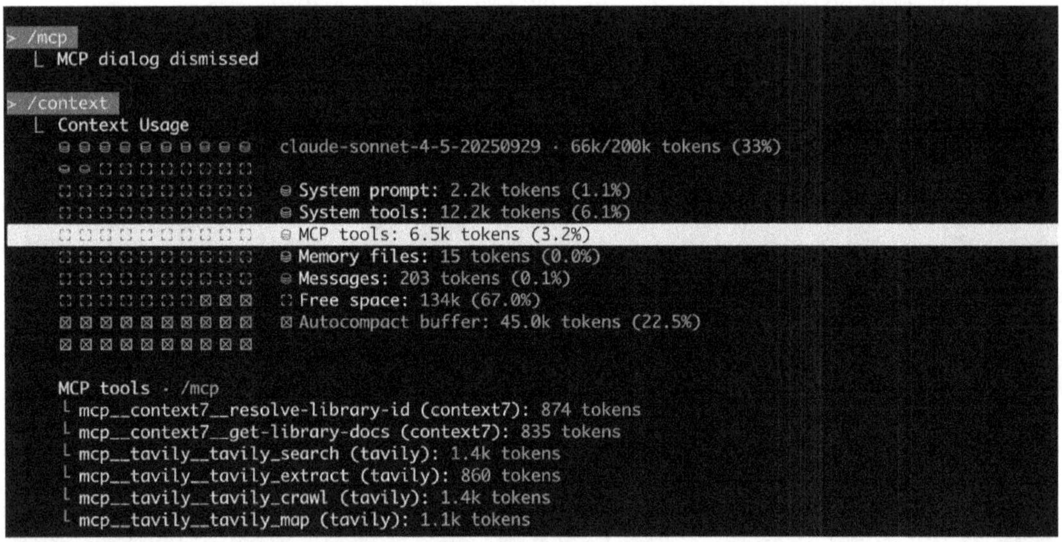

Figure 4.32 – MCP context usage after disabling selected servers

MCP-related context usage is now approximately **3.2%**.

This approach allows MCP servers to be enabled or disabled directly within a session using the CLI, without modifying MCP configuration files.

Current limitations of MCP

MCP was designed to standardize how agents connect to data. However, its current implementation introduces several drawbacks. These limitations primarily stem from how LLM context is managed and how agent tasks are executed.

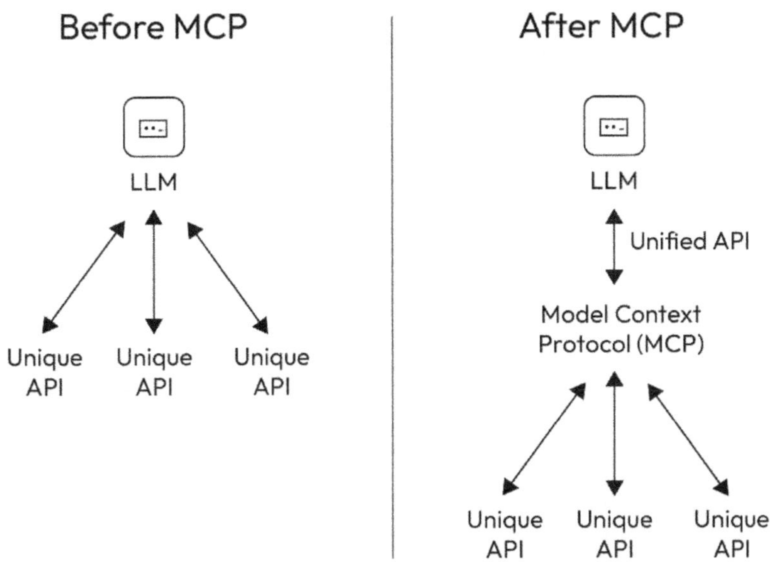

Figure 4.33 – MCP abstraction layer between LLMs and external APIs

As a result, agents may become slower, more expensive, and less effective than intended. There is no perfect protocol, and MCP is no exception.

Context pollution

The most significant issue with MCP is context pollution. MCP requires tool definitions to be loaded upfront into the model's context. These definitions, including required arguments and expected outputs, are placed into the system prompt.

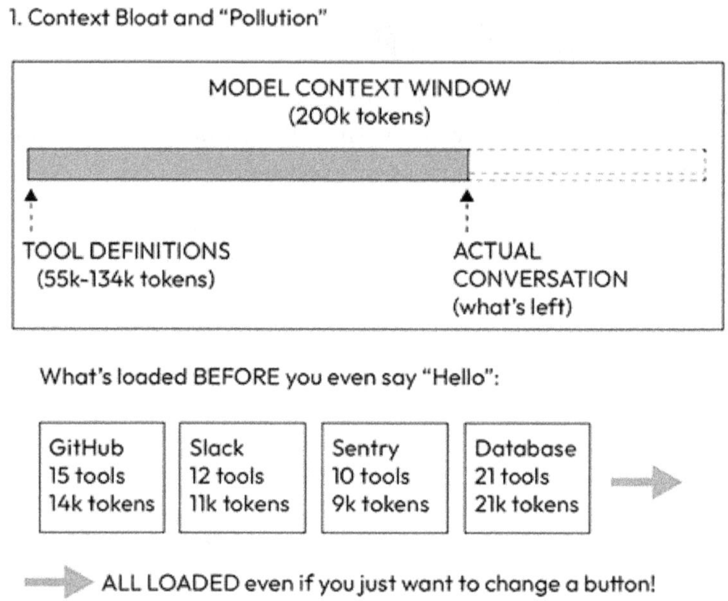

Figure 4.34 – Context pollution from preloaded MCP tool definitions

Because all tool definitions must be preloaded, this creates a substantial token overhead. To use an MCP server, the agent must receive definitions for every available tool.

In a configuration with 58 tools across servers such as GitHub MCP, Slack MCP, and Central MCP, tool definitions alone can consume 55,000 tokens before the conversation begins. In some cases, tool definitions can consume hundreds of thousands of tokens.

In LLM applications and agent systems, context is the primary resource that must be optimized. When context is saturated with tool definitions, the agent carries large amounts of irrelevant information.

For example, an agent tasked with modifying a frontend page still carries thousands of lines of context related to unrelated tools, such as database utilities or PDF readers. This irrelevant data persists across every step and iteration of the conversation.

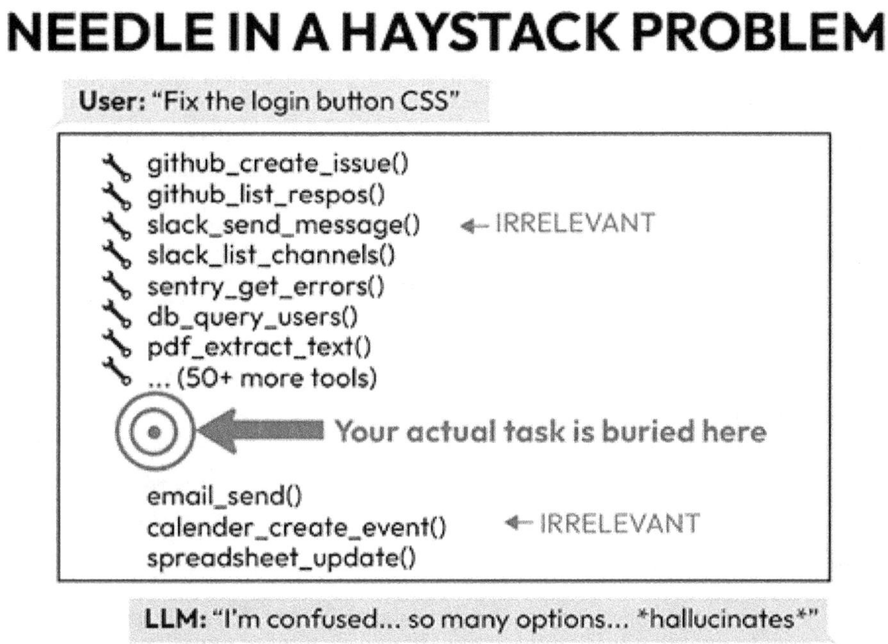

Figure 4.35 – Needle-in-a-haystack problem from too many MCP tools

As context fills with unrelated definitions, model performance degrades. The model must search through excessive information, increasing the likelihood of hallucinations, instruction-following failures, or incorrect tool selection. The more polluted the context becomes, the harder it is for the model to locate relevant information.

Inefficient agent execution

Beyond context management, MCP also introduces inefficiency in agent execution.

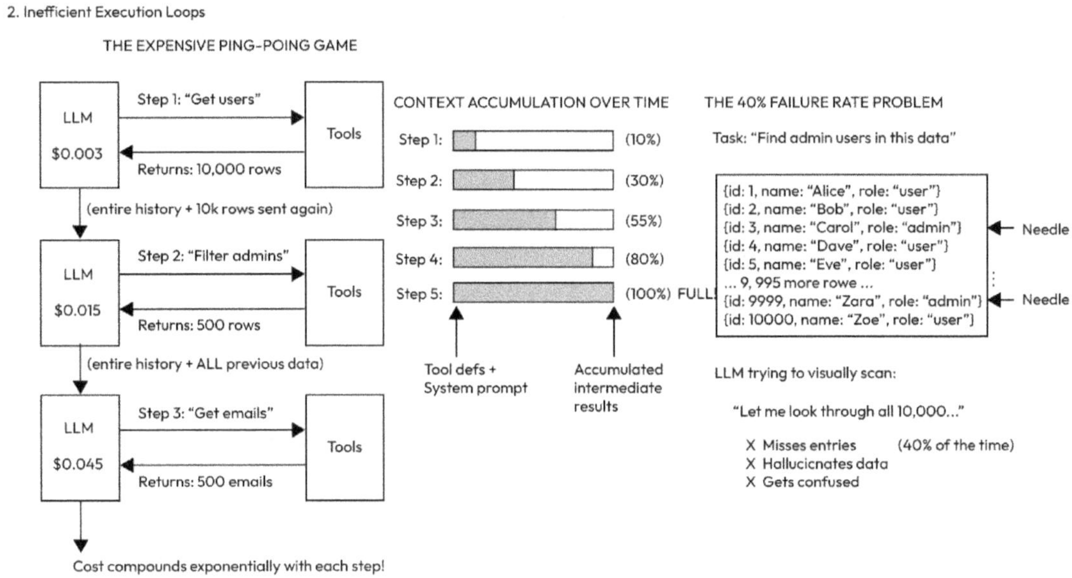

Figure 4.36 – Inefficient agent execution with repeated MCP tool calls

Traditional MCP usage relies on a "ping-pong" interaction pattern. Each action requires a full round trip:

- The model requests a tool.
- The tool executes.
- The result is appended to the conversation history.
- The entire updated history is sent back to the model to determine the next step.

When multiple tool calls are required, this process expands rapidly. Intermediate results accumulate in the context window, even when they are not necessary for producing the final answer. Although some of these results could be removed at later stages, the current MCP implementation retains them, further polluting the context.

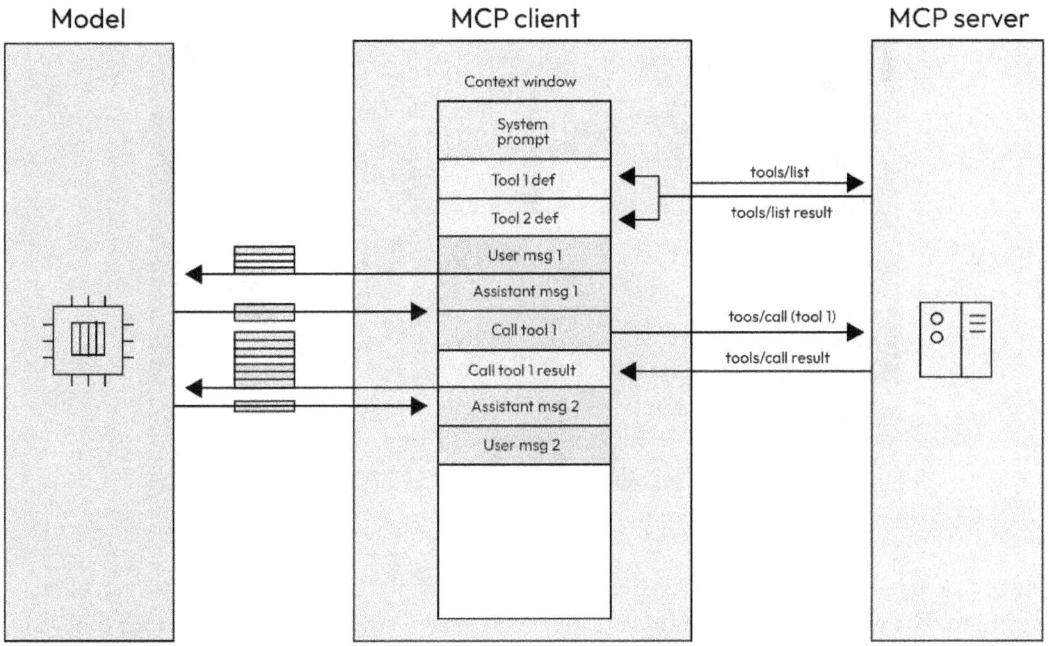

Figure 4.37 – MCP tool call round trips between model, client, and server

Each round trip requires an additional LLM inference. Multiple inference passes increase both latency and cost. As tool calls scale, so do the number of model invocations, resulting in slower execution and higher expenses.

The native tongue problem – JSON versus code

MCP also forces LLMs to operate in a way that does not align with their training.

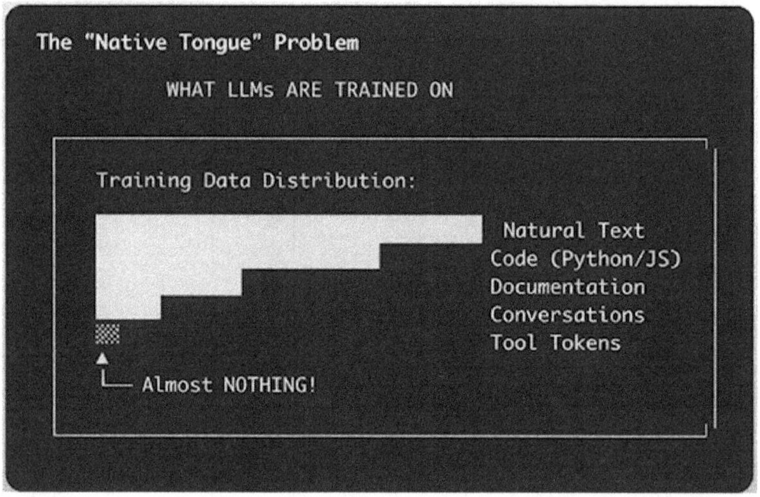

Figure 4.38 – LLM training vs tool-call formats

The protocol relies heavily on structured tool call tokens and JSON schemas. However, LLMs are primarily trained on natural language text and code, not on specialized syntactic tool invocation tokens.

Although model vendors have improved tool call reliability, this format is not the model's native mode of operation. Text and code are more natural representations for LLMs. Code, in particular, aligns more closely with training data and model capabilities than JSON-based tool invocation mechanisms.

This mismatch creates friction between the model's training distribution and the structured interaction style required by MCP.

Limitations of tool definitions and schemas

MCP tool definitions and JSON schemas describe what a tool looks like: its parameters, inputs, and outputs. However, these schemas do not capture usage patterns.

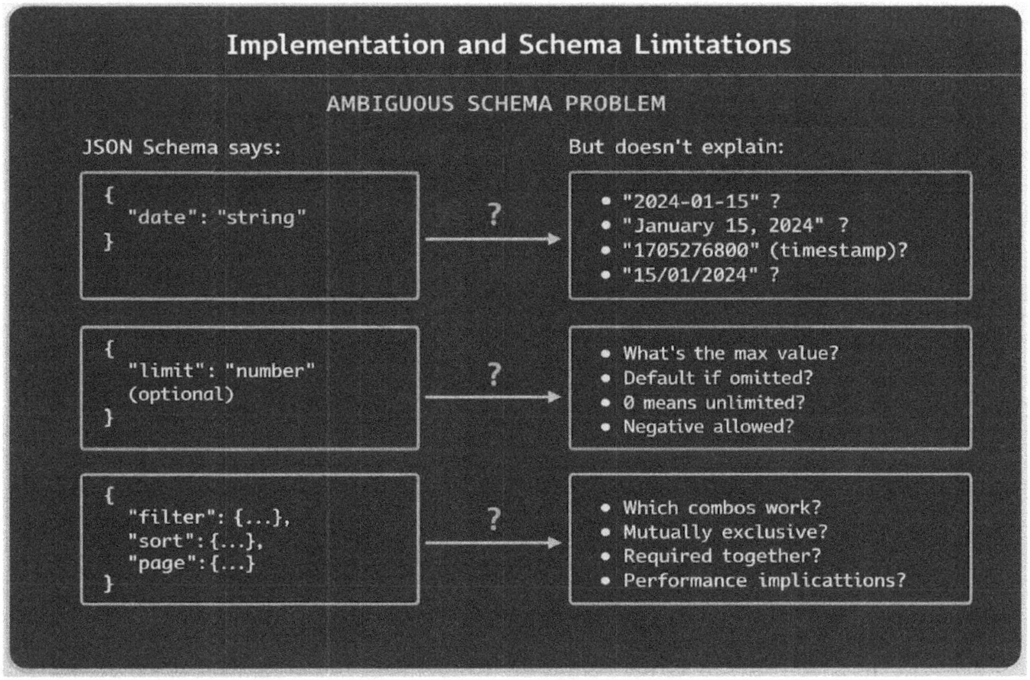

Figure 4.39 – Limits of JSON schemas for tool usage

Usage patterns include when a tool should be used, how it should be used in context, and when it should not be used. This is a deeper concept than a structural definition alone.

Even when instructions are provided to guide tool usage, schemas themselves cannot encode these behavioral constraints. As a result, the protocol defines structure but not intent or correct application patterns.

CodeMode by Cloudflare

Cloudflare first introduced in a blog post (`https://blog.cloudflare.com/code-mode/`). **CodeMode**, an execution model designed to change how agents interact with MCP tools.

The idea addresses drawbacks discussed earlier regarding MCP, particularly context bloat and increased latency caused by multiple LLM calls.

Instead of using MCP in the usual way, Cloudflare suggests taking all tool definitions, tool interfaces, and tool implementations from MCP and converting them into a TypeScript API. Rather than allowing the LLM to choose which tool to call through tool calling, the LLM is asked to generate code that uses the TypeScript API.

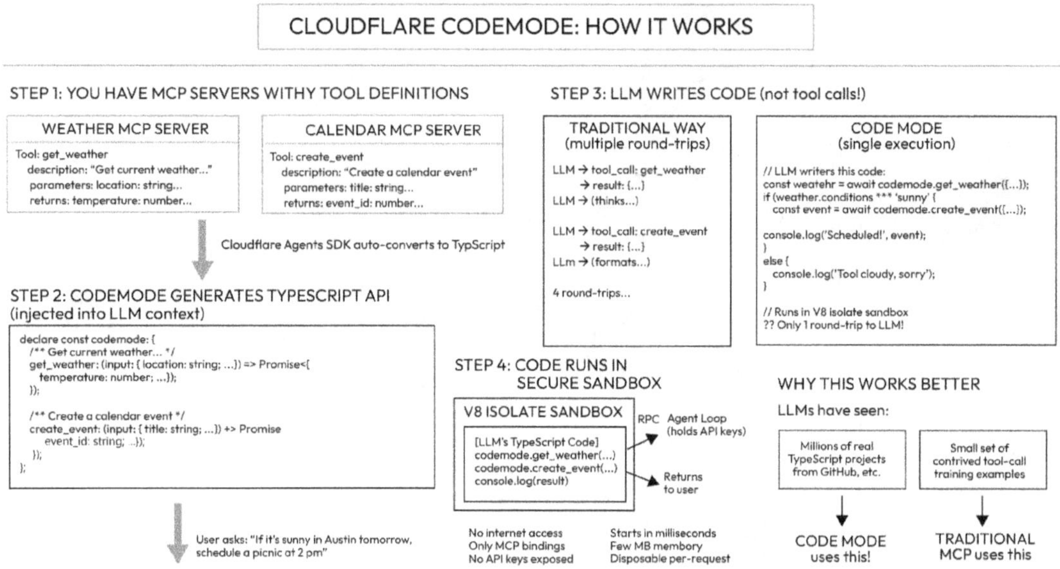

Figure 4.40 – Cloudflare Code Mode replacing tool calls with code execution

In this model, the LLM generates the entire code that needs to be executed. The generated code includes multiple tool calls implemented as function invocations. That code is then executed once inside a sandbox.

This approach reduces the number of round trips involved in tool calling. Instead of making a tool call, receiving a result, and making another tool call repeatedly, the LLM writes code that performs the sequence internally. The main advantage described is that LLMs are very strong at writing code. Writing code is a common task for LLMs, and they have extensive training data on code. Because the code is written once and executed once, tool definitions do not need to be repeatedly sent, which reduces token usage.

Key observations

Cloudflare states that MCP has often been used by directly exposing tools to the LLM. In CodeMode, MCP tools are converted into a TypeScript API, and the LLM writes code that calls that API.

The reported result is that agents are able to handle more tools and more complex tools. One issue with MCP is that too many tools increase context size, which increases cost and latency and can degrade performance. When tools are presented as a TypeScript API rather than as direct tool definitions, performance improves. The explanation offered is that LLMs have seen large amounts of real-world TypeScript in training, but only a small set of contrived tool-call examples.

The approach is described as particularly effective when multiple calls must be chained together. In traditional MCP usage, each tool output must be passed back into the LLM before the next call. This repetition consumes time, energy, and tokens. When the LLM writes code, it performs all calls internally and only returns the final result.

The conclusion presented is that LLMs are better at writing code to call MCP than calling MCP directly.

Tool calling and its constraints

In traditional MCP usage, the LLM generates special tokens representing tool calls. These tokens are parsed to extract the function name and arguments. The system then executes the function and returns the result.

These special tool-call tokens are not common in real-world data. They are syntactic constructs introduced during training. Although model vendors have improved tool-calling performance significantly, the mechanism remains synthetic.

When too many tools or overly complex tools are exposed, the LLM may struggle to select the correct one or may use it incorrectly. As a result, MCP server designers are encouraged to simplify APIs to make them more suitable for LLM consumption.

By contrast, LLMs handle full programming APIs more effectively. They can analyze and generate code against complex APIs without simplification. The distinction made is that LLMs have seen extensive real-world code but very few real-world tool calls.

An analogy is provided: asking an LLM to perform tasks with tool calling is compared to putting Shakespeare through a short Mandarin course and asking him to write a play in Mandarin. The implication is that tool calling is not the model's strongest domain.

The role of MCP

MCP remains useful because it provides a uniform method for connecting agents with tools. MCP tools represent an RPC interface with attached documentation. Most MCP servers wrap existing traditional APIs.

Instead of exposing MCP tools directly as callable tools, CodeMode converts them into a programming-language API. Although traditional APIs already exist, MCP provides a uniform way to connect to and learn about those APIs, which remains valuable in agent-based systems.

Integrating CodeMode

Cloudflare extended its Agent SDK to support CodeMode. In a typical AI SDK setup, the model is configured with a system prompt, user message, and tools. In CodeMode, the tools and prompt are wrapped using a CodeMode helper.

For example, consider an application built with the CloudFare AI SDK that looks like this:

```
const stream = streamText({
  model: openai("gpt-5.3"),
  system: "You are a helpful research assistant.
    Your job is to help the user…",
  messages: [
    { role: "user", content: "Research on deep agents" }
  ],
  tools: {
    research agent's tool definition
  }
})
```

With CodeMode, the system prompt and tool definitions are wrapped using the `codemode` helper before being passed to the application.

```
import { codemode } from "agents/codemode/ai";

const { system, tools } = codemode({
  system: " You are a helpful research assistant.
    Your job is to help the user…",
  tools: [
    research agent's tool definition
  ],
})
```

After this change, the application generates and executes TypeScript code that invokes the defined tools, including MCP servers.

Converting MCP to TypeScript

When connecting to an MCP server in CodeMode, the Agent SDK fetches the MCP server's schema and converts it into a TypeScript API. The generated API includes TypeScript definitions and documentation comments derived from the schema.

These TypeScript definitions are loaded into the agent's context. The entire API is currently loaded at once, though future improvements may allow dynamic searching or browsing of the API.

Although loading the entire API still increases context size, this occurs once at initialization. The LLM then reads the API and generates code. Since LLMs are strong at processing code, this approach leverages that strength.

Execution in a sandbox

In CodeMode, instead of presenting all MCP tools directly, the agent is given a single tool that executes TypeScript code.

The generated code runs inside a secure sandbox that is isolated from the internet. The sandbox can access external systems only through the provided TypeScript APIs representing connected MCP servers.

When sandboxed code calls an API function, the call is routed back through RPC to the MCP server via the agent loop. The sandbox returns results using `console.log()`. When execution is complete, the logs are returned to the agent.

In a traditional MCP flow:

1. The agent receives tool schemas from the MCP server.
2. The LLM call includes tool definitions matching MCP tools.
3. The LLM outputs special tokens for function invocations.
4. The agent parses and executes the tool calls.
5. The process repeats.

While in CodeMode:

1. The agent retrieves tool schemas from the MCP server.
2. The LLM call includes a TypeScript API derived from those schemas.
3. The LLM writes TypeScript code against that API.
4. The code is executed in a sandbox.
5. The sandbox interacts with MCP servers through RPC bindings.
6. The final logs are returned to the agent.

The following diagram shows an architectural comparison between traditional MCP execution and CodeMode.

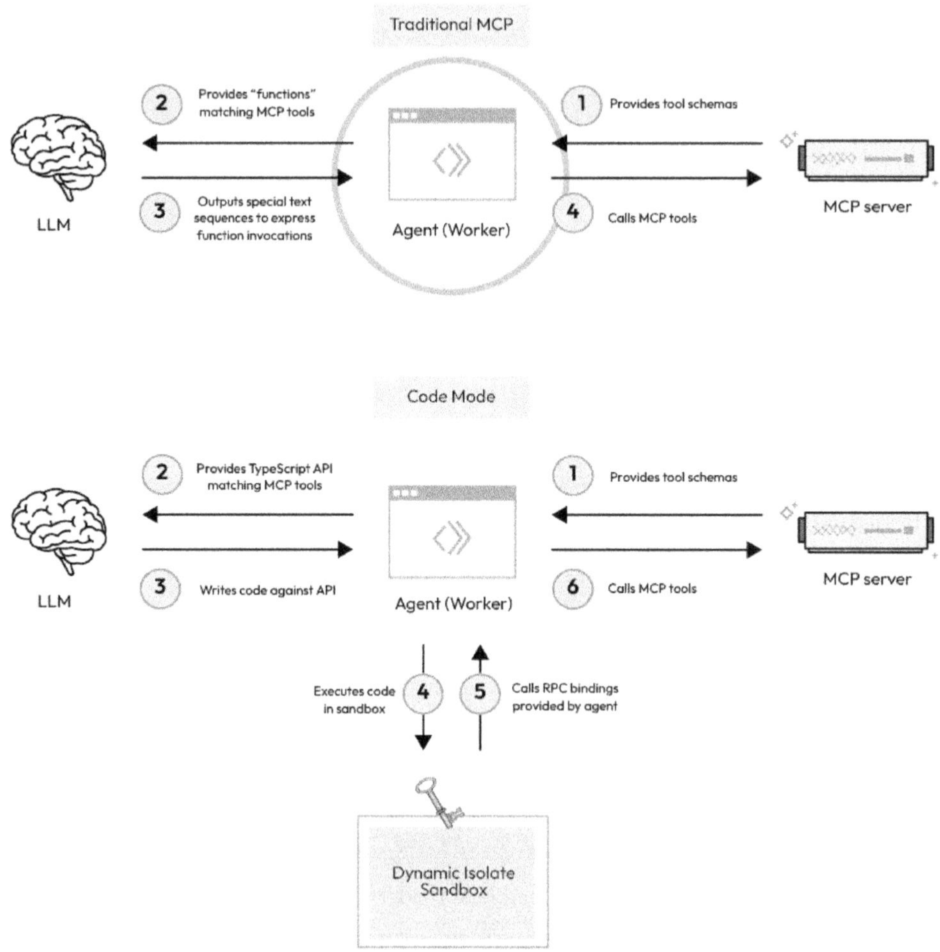

Figure 4.41 – Traditional MCP vs Code Mode execution flow

CodeMode is presented as an alternative execution model that relies on the LLM's ability to generate code while retaining MCP as a uniform integration layer.

Managing configuration with Claude Code plugins

> **Note**
>
> Please check the official docs for reference: `https://code.claude.com/docs/en/plugins`.

Plugins bundle slash commands (skills), sub-agents, MCP servers, and hooks into a single, shareable primitive. These plugins can be shared within a team or published to the open source community, enabling reuse and consistency across environments.

Before plugins were introduced, reusing configuration required significant manual effort. For example, to use a slash command from an open source repository, we had to navigate to that repository, copy the slash command, and paste it into the local `.claude` directory. The same process applied to sub-agents and hooks. MCP servers followed a different setup process, but the overall workflow remained manual and fragmented.

Claude Code plugins address this problem by bundling all of these components into a single plugin that can be installed and integrated seamlessly. Plugins can be sourced from open source repositories or internal repositories and shared across teams.

Claude Code provides a CLI-based plugin system that is intuitive and easy to use.

Benefits of the plugin system

One of the primary benefits of plugins is the ability to share a uniform Claude Code setup across a team. For example, when onboarding a new developer, we may want them to have the same tools, the same agents and sub-agents, and the same MCP servers as the rest of the team. Plugins provide a mechanism to standardize the Claude Code development environment.

Plugins also support fine-grained installation. Instead of installing an entire plugin, it is possible to install only a specific component, such as a single MCP server.

In addition, Claude Code introduces a new primitive called a marketplace. A marketplace is represented by a JSON file that describes the plugins available for installation.

It is also worth noting that Google's Gemini CLI introduced a similar concept called Gemini Extensions. Gemini Extensions were published on October 8, 2025, while Claude Code plugins were published on October 9, 2025. This one-day difference suggests either very rapid iteration by the Claude Code team or that both teams were working simultaneously on implementing the same idea.

Exploring the official plugin marketplace

To explore how plugins work, we start from the Claude Code course repository.

Within the Claude Code open source repository, there is a `.claude-plugin` directory. Inside this directory is a `marketplace.json` file.

This file defines the official plugin marketplace. It lists the available plugins and provides metadata and source paths for each plugin.

Examples of plugins listed in the marketplace include the following:

- `pr-review-toolkit`
- `commit-commands`
- `agent-sdk-dev`
- `feature-dev`
- Security guidelines

The marketplace functions as a registry that Claude Code can load to discover available plugins.

Adding a marketplace to Claude Code

Before installing plugins, a marketplace must be added to Claude Code.

To add a marketplace, follow these steps:

1. Open Claude Code and run the following command:

```
/plugin
```

2. Select **Browse** and install plugins.
3. Since no marketplace is configured initially, select Add Marketplace.
4. Provide either of these:
   - A GitHub repository URL
   - A direct link to a `marketplace.json` file

In this case, the base URL of the official Claude Code repository is provided. Claude Code detects the marketplace file automatically and loads the available plugins.

Once the marketplace file has been loaded, the list of plugins and their descriptions becomes visible.

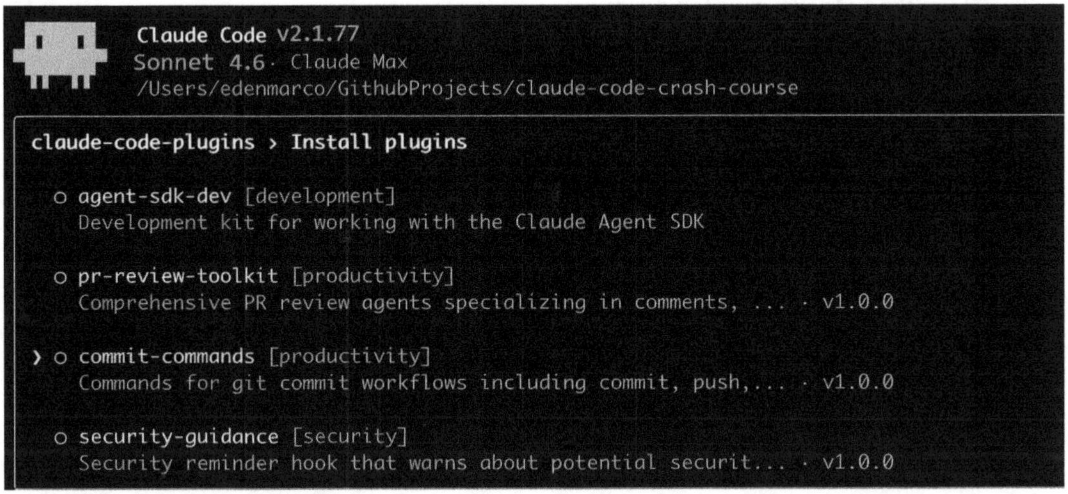

Figure 4.42 – Claude Code plugin marketplace showing available plugins

Reviewing plugin sources and security considerations

At this stage, only plugin descriptions are visible. To understand what a plugin actually installs, the plugin source must be inspected.

Each plugin entry in `marketplace.json` includes a source field. This field points to the location of the plugin's implementation.

Before installing a plugin, it is important to review this source. From a security perspective, this is similar to installing MCP servers or using system prompts and agents written by other people. Installing plugins without reviewing their implementation introduces risk.

To review a plugin source, follow these steps:

1. Open the `marketplace.json` file.
2. Locate the plugin entry.
3. Identify the source field.
4. Navigate to the source path in the repository.

For example, the `agent-sdk-dev` plugin points to a directory inside the repository. To inspect it, follow these steps:

1. Navigate to the repository.
2. Open the `plugins/` directory.
3. Open the `agent-sdk-dev/` directory.

4. Open the `.claude-plugin/` directory.
5. Inspect the `plugin.json` file.

The `plugin.json` file contains plugin metadata and defines the agents and slash commands (skills) that the plugin installs.

Another example is the feature-dev plugin. This plugin includes several agents, such as the following:

- Code reviewer
- Code explorer
- Code architect

It also includes a slash command defined in `feature-dev.md`. This slash command is used to describe the features to be implemented and to guide the workflow.

Installing and managing plugins

Once a marketplace is added, plugins can be installed and managed.

Installing a plugin

To install a plugin, follow these steps:

1. Open the plugin interface using `/plugin`.
2. Select **Browse and install plugins**.
3. Locate the `commit-commands` plugin.
4. Open the plugin details.
5. Select **Install**.
6. Wait for the installation to complete.

After installation, the plugin appears in the installed plugins list.

Verifying the installation

To verify that the plugin is installed and enabled, follow these steps:

1. Open the installed plugins list.
2. Locate the commit-commands plugin.
3. Confirm that it is marked as installed.
4. Confirm that it is enabled.

Updating a plugin

Plugins are backed by repositories and can be updated over time. To update a plugin, follow these steps:

1. Select the installed plugin.
2. Locate the **Update** option.
3. Apply the update.

Updating a plugin is conceptually similar to rebasing against a repository's latest version.

Attempting to uninstall a plugin

The plugin interface includes an uninstall option. To attempt to uninstall a plugin, follow these steps:

1. Select the installed plugin.
2. Locate the **Uninstall** option.
3. Attempt to uninstall the plugin.

At this stage, uninstalling does not work as expected. The uninstall action does not remove the plugin. This appears to be a current limitation or bug.

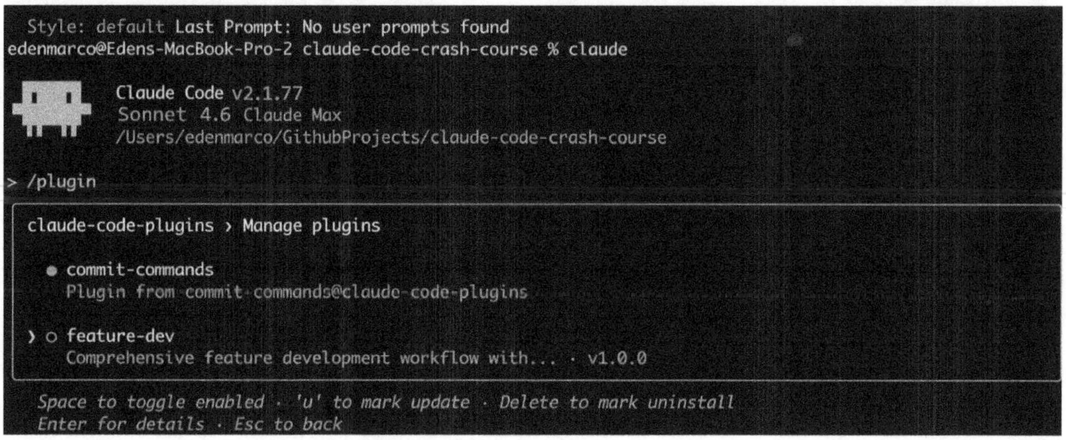

Figure 4.43 – Attempting to uninstall a Claude Code plugin

Using the feature-dev plugin

Next, the `feature-dev` plugin is used to demonstrate a complete workflow.

Before proceeding, ensure that the plugin is installed and enabled.

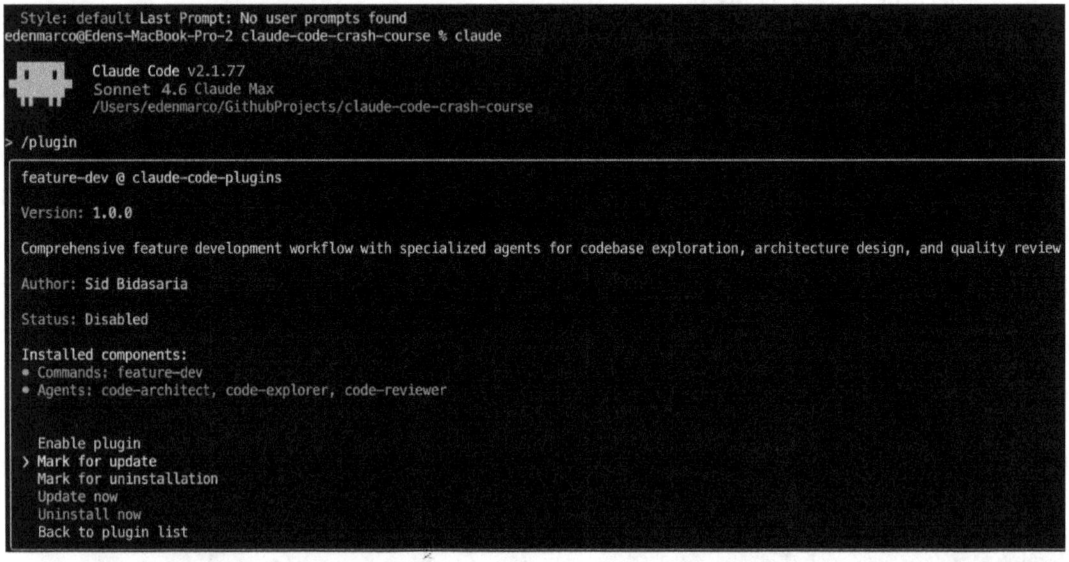

Figure 4.44 – Feature-dev plugin details in Claude Code

Starting the workflow

To start the workflow, follow these steps:

1. Open Claude Code and run the following command:

```
/feature-dev
```

2. Wait for the plugin to initialize.

Once the command has been executed, Claude enters a discovery phase. At this point, Claude begins asking questions to understand what feature needs to be implemented.

Handling Git state during the feature-dev workflow

Before switching branches, Claude Code inspects the current Git state of the repository.

At this point in the workflow, the repository may contain **uncommitted local changes**. Switching branches without handling these changes could result in conflicts or lost work.

Checking the Git state

As part of the workflow:

- Claude checks the current working tree state.
- Claude detects that there are local, uncommitted changes.
- Claude determines that switching branches directly would be unsafe.

These checks happen automatically as part of the feature-dev workflow.

Stashing local changes

To safely proceed, Claude uses `git stash` to preserve the current working state.

During this step, Claude does the following:

- Stashes the current working directory changes
- Confirms that the working tree is now clean
- Proceeds to switch branches

This ensures that no local changes are lost.

Switching branches and restoring state

After inspecting the feature branch, Claude returns to the original branch and restores the previous Git state:

1. Claude switches back to the main branch.
2. Claude reapplies the stashed changes.
3. Claude confirms that the working directory has been restored.

At this point, the repository is back in its original state, with local changes intact.

Providing feature details

The task in this example is to update the repository's `README` file.

The `README` file contains a table listing course lessons. A new lesson exists in a GitHub branch named `context-engineering-mcp`, and this branch must be added to the table. To access the repository link, follow the steps in the *Download the example code files* section in the *Preface*.

When prompted, do the following:

- Describe the required change.
- Provide the URL of the `context-engineering-mcp` branch.

Inspecting the README file in the feature branch

Claude examines the README file in the feature branch. During this step, Claude does the following:

1. Switches to the `context-engineering-mcp` branch.
2. Inspects the `README` file.
3. Identifies the table structure.

Available Topics (Branches)

Here are the topics currently available:

Branch	Topic	Description
`project/custom-commands`	Custom Commands	Learn to extend Claude Code with custom functionality like dad joke generators and automated commits
`project/mcp`	MCP Integration	Master Model Context Protocol integration with Context7 MCP server
`project/subagents`	Subagents	Build specialized AI agents within Claude Code like Code Comedy Carl
`project/hooks-notifications`	Hooks & Notifications	Automate your workflow with sound notifications and event triggers
`project/hookhub`	Hook Hub	Advanced hook management and organization systems

More topics might be added, so keep an eye out!

Figure 4.45 – Inspecting the README in the feature branch

Switching back to the main branch

After inspecting the feature branch, Claude does the following:

1. Switches back to the main branch.
2. Prepares to apply the change.
3. Proposes a new table entry.

Reviewing and refining the proposed change

Claude generates an initial description for the new table entry. Before proceeding, do the following:

1. Review the description.
2. Identify inaccuracies.
3. Refine the wording.

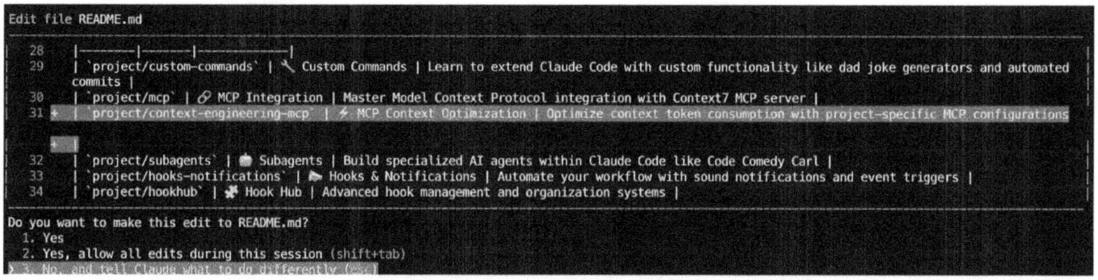

Figure 4.46 – Reviewing and refining the proposed README change

The description is almost correct and requires a small adjustment before continuing.

Committing, pushing, and verifying the change

Once a change has been approved, the following occurs:

1. Claude creates a commit.
2. Claude pushes the commit to the remote repository.
3. Refresh the repository.
4. Open the `README` file.
5. Verify that the new lesson entry appears in the table.

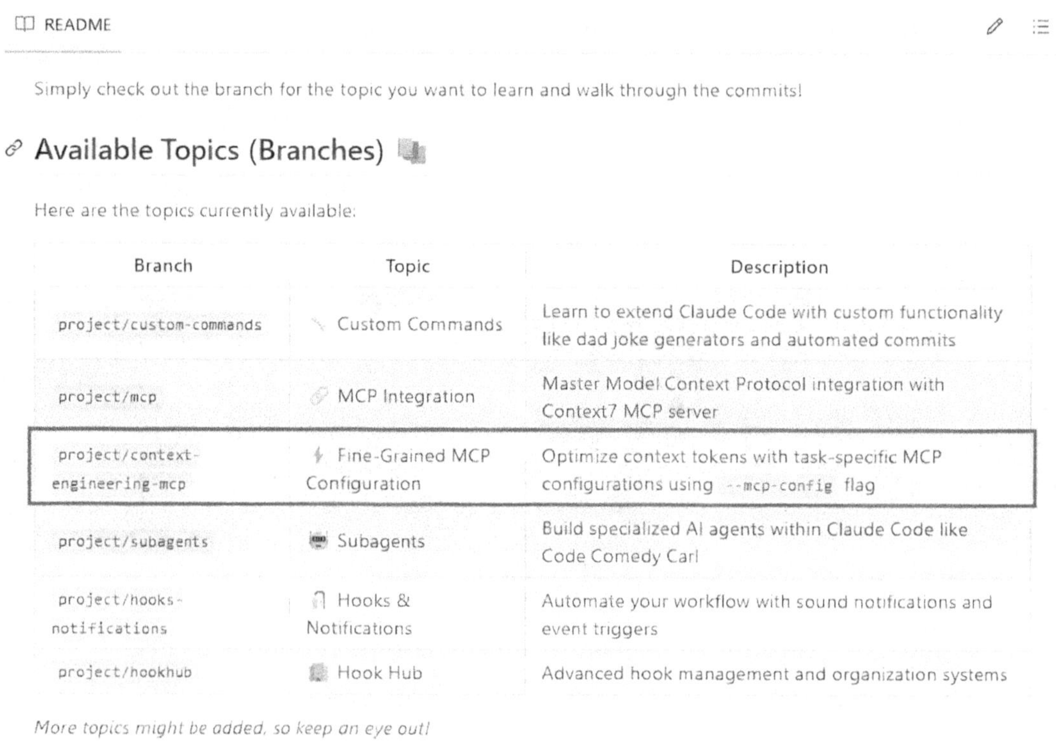

README

Simply check out the branch for the topic you want to learn and walk through the commits!

Available Topics (Branches)

Here are the topics currently available:

Branch	Topic	Description
project/custom-commands	Custom Commands	Learn to extend Claude Code with custom functionality like dad joke generators and automated commits
project/mcp	MCP Integration	Master Model Context Protocol integration with Context7 MCP server
project/context-engineering-mcp	Fine-Grained MCP Configuration	Optimize context tokens with task-specific MCP configurations using `--mcp-config` flag
project/subagents	Subagents	Build specialized AI agents within Claude Code like Code Comedy Carl
project/hooks-notifications	Hooks & Notifications	Automate your workflow with sound notifications and event triggers
project/hookhub	Hook Hub	Advanced hook management and organization systems

More topics might be added, so keep an eye out!

Figure 4.47 – Verifying the README update after commit

This confirms that the workflow completed successfully.

Plugin marketplaces and enterprise use

Claude Code supports third-party plugin marketplaces.

For example, a DevOps automation marketplace can provide plugins containing slash commands, agents, and MCP servers related to infrastructure workflows. Organizations can also create private marketplaces for internal use. These marketplaces can contain plugins specific to internal tools or teams and remain private.

It is likely that platform companies, such as Supabase, will publish their own marketplaces and plugins to improve integration with Claude Code.

Plugins also support fine-grained installation. Individual components such as a single slash command or an MCP server can be installed without installing an entire plugin. This plugin ecosystem is expected to grow and play an important role in enterprise-scale Claude Code adoption.

Summary

In this chapter, you learned why MCP was created and how it solves the integration problem in AI systems. You explored its core architecture: hosts, clients, and servers and saw how MCP enables reusable, cross-platform tool integration. Through hands-on examples, you configured and used the Context7 MCP, connected servers to Claude, and managed MCP settings using the CLI. You also learned how poor MCP configuration can pollute the context window and degrade performance, and how to optimize usage through context engineering and scoped configurations. Finally, you explored Claude Code plugins, examined the limitations of MCP, and reviewed CodeMode as an alternative execution model.

Understanding MCP is important because it is becoming a foundational integration layer in agent-based AI development. Knowing how to use it efficiently and when to question it will help you build more scalable and effective AI systems.

In the next chapter, we will cover GitHub repository configuration, pull request and issue automation, and the use of GitHub Actions for workflow execution.

Get this book's PDF copy, code bundle, and more

5

Automating Your Development Workflow with Claude Code and GitHub

In this chapter, we will look into the integration between Claude Code and GitHub. This integration involves a series of configuration steps, including installing the GitHub CLI, configuring it to work with Claude Code, and selecting the repositories on which Claude Code will operate.

Once configured, Claude Code can be used directly within a repository. It can be tagged on pull requests and issues, where it reviews code, suggests fixes, and helps resolve reported problems. Claude Code can also participate in pull request workflows by reviewing changes when a pull request is created.

When a pull request is opened, **GitHub Actions** is used to run the automation. GitHub Actions is GitHub's serverless workflow platform, commonly used for CI/CD tasks. In this setup, GitHub Actions executes workflows that rely on the Claude Code CLI and the Claude Code SDK.

For those of you who are not familiar with GitHub Actions, it is an automation system that runs in response to events. These events can include actions such as tagging Claude on an issue or opening a new pull request. Each event can be configured to trigger specific workflows based on project requirements.

The workflows themselves are defined using YAML files, commonly referred to as GitHub workflow files. These files describe which events should trigger an action and which commands or scripts should be executed in response.

This integration is already used in real-world production systems. Anthropic, for example, uses Claude Code with GitHub Actions across its open-source repositories to automate issue handling and related workflows. For a public example, see Anthropic's GitHub Actions workflows: `https://github.com/anthropics/skills/actions`.

The following topics will be covered in this chapter:

- Installing and configuring the Claude Code GitHub integration
- Tagging Claude Code to resolve GitHub issues
- Rerunning issue resolution with project memory

Installing and configuring the Claude Code GitHub integration

In this section, we will demonstrate the integration using a different repository called IceBreaker (`https://github.com/emarco177/IceBreaker`), which is an open-source project available on GitHub. We are using this repository for demonstration purposes only. You can follow along using any GitHub repository you own. If you choose to use your own repository, make sure you have administrator access, as installing the Claude GitHub app and configuring workflows requires admin permissions.

> **Tip**
>
> Before starting the installation, make sure you are running Claude Code from a directory that already has an initialized Git repository connected to GitHub. In this chapter, we use the IceBreaker repository, which is already configured. The integration will only work inside a valid GitHub repository.

To begin the GitHub integration, open Claude Code from the desktop and type `/git`. This reveals the `/install-github-app` command. Selecting this command starts the setup process.

Before Claude Code can be integrated with a GitHub account, two prerequisites must be met:

- First, the GitHub CLI (also referred to as the `gh` CLI) must be installed locally. At this point, the CLI is not yet installed, so we install it next.
- Second, the GitHub CLI must be authenticated with a GitHub account. Claude Code relies on this authenticated session to interact with repositories.

Installing prerequisites

> **Note**
>
> The installation command varies by operating system. The example below shows macOS using Homebrew. If you are using Linux or Windows, refer to the official GitHub CLI installation documentation for the appropriate command for your platform: `https://cli.github.com/`

To install and authenticate the GitHub CLI, complete the following steps:

1. Open a new terminal instance and install the GitHub CLI using the following command:

```
brew install gh
```

2. Once the installation completes, verify that the CLI is available by running the following:

```
gh --help
```

3. Next, authenticate the CLI with GitHub by running the following:

```
gh auth login
```

During the authentication process, select **HTTPS** as the connection method and proceed with logging in through the web browser. A one-time code is provided, which must be entered in the browser to complete authentication. If two-factor authentication is enabled, approval is completed using the configured second factor.

After this step, the GitHub CLI is authenticated successfully and all prerequisites for Claude Code integration are in place.

Installing the Claude GitHub app

With the prerequisites complete, we return to Claude and continue the installation. We close the terminal window since it is no longer needed and press *Enter* in Claude as instructed. At this point, we are redirected to a GitHub page.

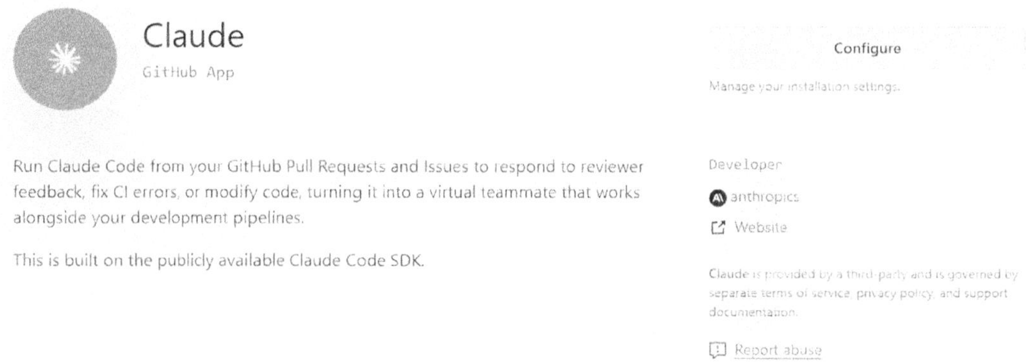

Figure 5.1 – Installing the Claude GitHub app

Start the integration of Claude Code into the GitHub account. This integration allows Claude to comment, create pull requests, and solve issues. We will demonstrate these capabilities later in the book.

After clicking **Install**, we are redirected back to the Claude web application. Returning to the terminal, we press *Enter* again to proceed.

Installing the GitHub workflow

Installing the integration requires adding a GitHub workflow to the repository. This workflow runs the pipelines that handle Claude's comments and actions.

Two options will be presented to you for installation

- **Tag Claude**, which allows us to tag Claude in issues and pull request comments, then runs through a GitHub workflow.
- **Claude Code Review**, which automatically reviews new pull requests

We select the first option.

Next, we choose an authentication method. Since Claude's usage consumes tokens, someone needs to pay for those tokens. We can either configure a long-lived token associated with a Claude subscription or provide an Anthropic API key. The long-lived token is suitable for small to medium usage within a subscription, while an API key is typically used when running large-scale or high-frequency workflows that would exceed subscription limits. In this case, we choose the long-lived token associated with the Claude subscription.

After confirming this choice, we authorize the integration. This authorization also tracks token consumption and associates it with the Claude subscription.

> **Note**
>
> If an error appears, it is because the GitHub integration was initiated from a directory that is not connected to a GitHub repository.
>
> To fix this, open a new terminal in a project directory that already has a GitHub repository initialized and connected to your account. In this example, we use the `IceBreaker` directory, which was introduced earlier in the book and is already configured with GitHub.
>
> Reopen Claude, navigate again to the GitHub installation, and Claude should correctly detect the current repository. Open the configuration popup, select the appropriate account, and grant access to the repositories. After confirming, return to the CLI and configure Claude Code again using the long-lived token.

Creating the pull request

Once authentication completes, Claude initializes the integration by fetching repository information and automatically creating a pull request.

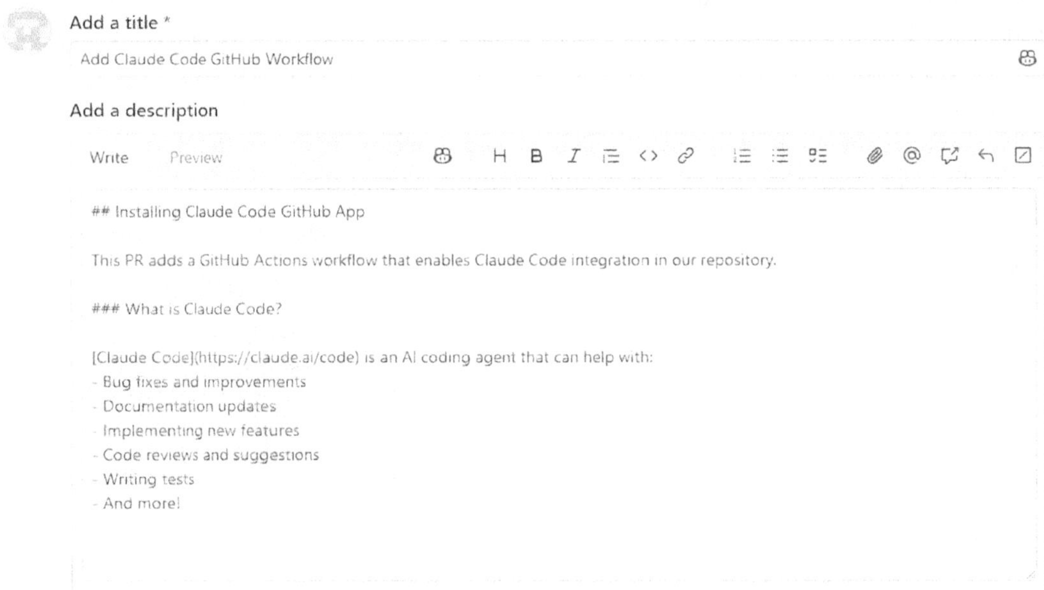

Figure 5.2 – Automatically Creating a Pull Request for Claude GitHub workflow

This pull request contains several updated files under the `.github` directory. These are YAML files that configure the GitHub workflow. We open the pull request to review it.

The workflow enables Claude to be tagged in comments and issues and allows it to run through GitHub Actions. GitHub Actions provides the compute environment where Claude operates, and the workflow is configured to use tokens associated with our account.

From a security perspective, the API key or access token is stored as a GitHub Actions secret. This happens automatically during configuration. Only users with the appropriate repository access can trigger the workflow. When Claude is tagged, it can create branches, commits, and comments.

Before merging the pull request, the newly added GitHub workflow should run automatically. In the **GitHub Actions** tab, we will see the Claude Code workflow executing. Once it finishes successfully, proceed with merging.

While the workflow runs, it updates the pull request. Claude reads the files it added, specifically two YAML files under `.github/workflows`: `claude.YAML` and `claude-code-review.YAML`. It reviews these files for security issues and code quality, and posts its feedback directly in the pull request.

At the end of the review, Claude Code approves the pull request, indicating that it finds the changes acceptable, as shown in the following screenshot.

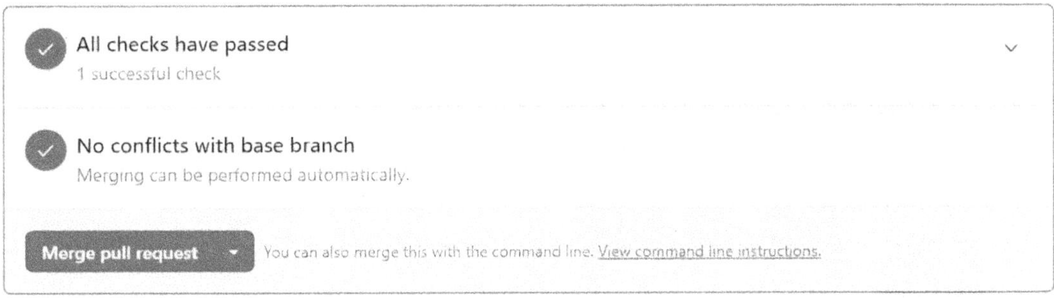

Figure 5.3 – Pull request approved with all checks passed

We now merge the pull request. After merging, the repository should now contain a new directory, `.github/workflows`, which did not exist before. Inside this directory are the two YAML files added by the integration:

- `claude.YAML`
- `claude-code-review.YAML`

The first YAML file will show the Claude workflow configuration. The file will contain a step called **Run Claude Code**. The authentication token is referenced from a secret named `CLAUDE_CODE_OAUTH_TOKEN`. No sensitive information is stored directly in the workflow file, which keeps the setup secure.

```
name: Claude Code

on:
  issue_comment:
    types: [created]

jobs:
  claude:
    runs-on: ubuntu-latest

    steps:
      - name: Checkout repository
        uses: actions/checkout@v4

      - name: Run Claude Code
        id: claude
        uses: anthropics/claude-code-action@beta
```

```
        with:
          claude_code_oauth_token: ${{ secrets.CLAUDE_CODE_OAUTH_TOKEN }}
```

A simplified excerpt of the workflow file is shown below.

```
Code    Blame    34 lines (32 loc) · 1.88 KB

name: Claude Code

on:
  issue_comment:
    types: [created]
  pull_request_review_comment:
    jobs: [created]
  issues:
    types: [opened, assigned]
  pull_request_review:
    types: [submitted]

jobs:
  claude:
    if: |
      (github.event_name == 'issue_comment' && contains(github.event.comment.body, '@claude')) ||
      (github.event_name == 'pull_request_review_comment' && contains(github.event.comment.body, '@claude')) ||
      (github.event_name == 'pull_request_review' && contains(github.event.comment.body, '@claude')) ||
      (github.event_name == 'issues' && contains(github.event.comment.body, '@claude')) || contains(github.event.issue.title, '@claude')))
    runs-on: ubuntu-latest
    permissions:
      contents: read
      pull-requests: read
      issues: read
      id-token: write
      actions: read # Required for Claude to read CI results on PRs
    steps:
      - name: Checkout repository
        uses: actions/checkout@v4
```

Figure 5.4 – Claude GitHub Actions Workflow YAML File

At this point, the integration is complete. The configuration can be further customized, including selecting the model, defining which tools Claude can use, and adjusting other settings to match specific needs.

Using Claude Code to resolve GitHub issues

In this section, we will demonstrate how to tag Claude Code to help resolve issues in a GitHub repository after the integration has been installed.

We start by navigating to the **Issues** section of the repository. The issue we are looking at is a simple one, opened by a user named `happyLolonly`. The issue raised by the user was to improve the readability of a variable name by renaming a variable from `linkedin_username` to `linkedin_url`, since the variable actually holds a LinkedIn URL.

Start by tagging Claude on the issue and asking it to solve the problem:

```
@claude, can you fix this
```

Once Claude is tagged, a new GitHub action starts running automatically. In this case, the action is called **small rename**. This action is triggered as soon as Claude is mentioned.

Open the action to view its details and watch the logs as they stream in real time. The logs consist mainly of JSON output showing tool calls, tool inputs, and tool outputs. While this information is useful for deep debugging, it is not human readable and is difficult to follow at a high level.

For most cases, instead of inspecting the raw logs, it is better to return to the issue itself.

Claude's to-do list and context discovery

Back in the issue view, Claude creates a to-do list that updates as it progresses. The first step Claude takes is attempting to locate a `CLAUDE.md` file in the repository.

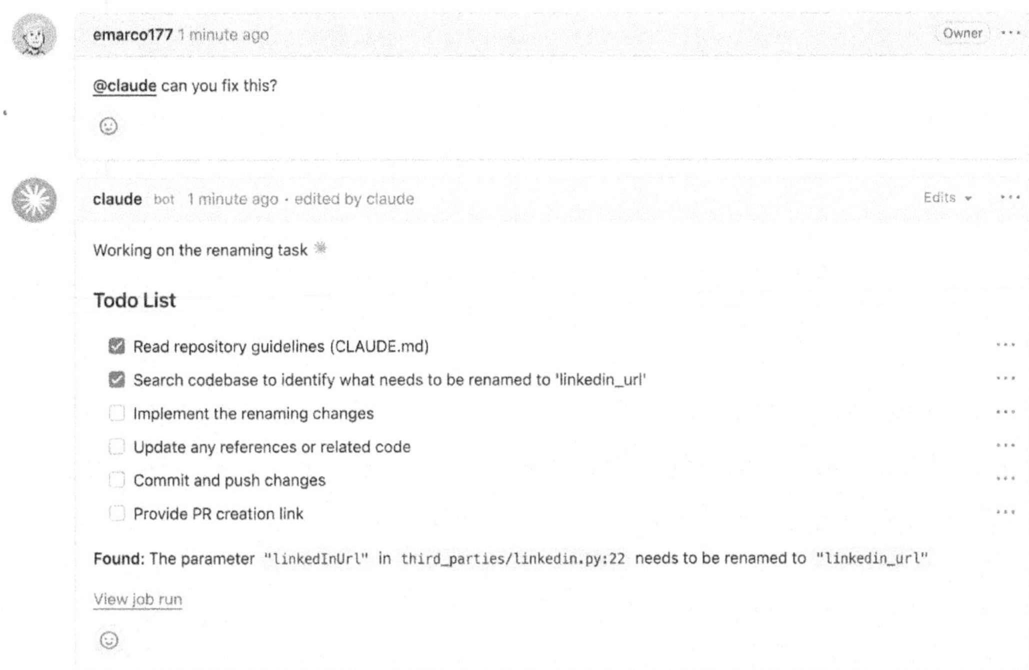

Figure 5.5 – Claude To-Do List and Context Discovery in Issue View

The purpose of a `CLAUDE.md` file is to provide additional context. These files help Claude understand the technology stack, the project structure, coding conventions, and any preferences we want to communicate. This is part of context engineering, where we intentionally supply information to help the model perform its task more effectively.

Spoiler ahead! In this repository, there is no `CLAUDE.md` file. This is intentional to show an important point: in agentic AI workflows, things do not always work correctly, and mistakes are expected.

Because of this, it is critical to review any changes carefully rather than accepting them blindly. This principle applies throughout all agentic workflows, not just in this example.

Reviewing the proposed changes

Once Claude finishes its to-do list, it updates a file named `linkedin.py`. We then open the **diff** by creating a pull request.

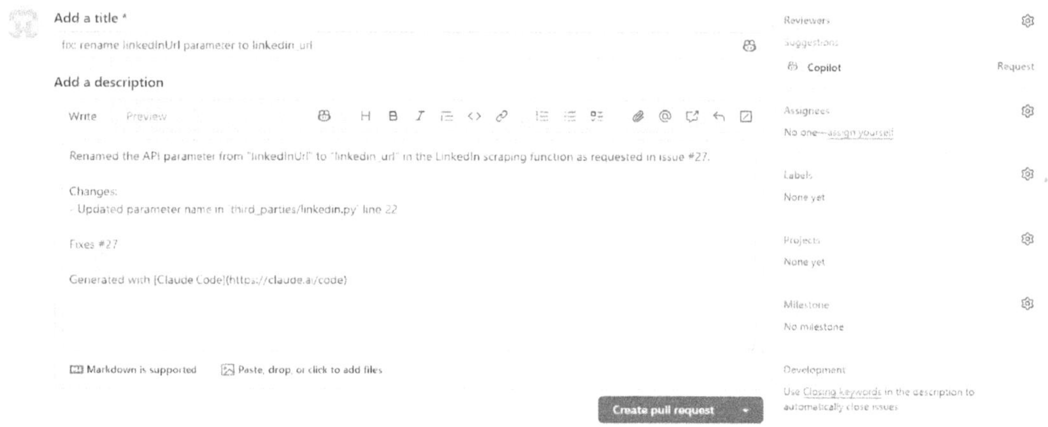

Figure 5.6 – Reviewing the pull request with proposed changes

At first glance, the pull request description looks reasonable. However, when you inspect the actual code changes, you will see that Claude renamed a variable that is part of an API request sent to a third-party service.

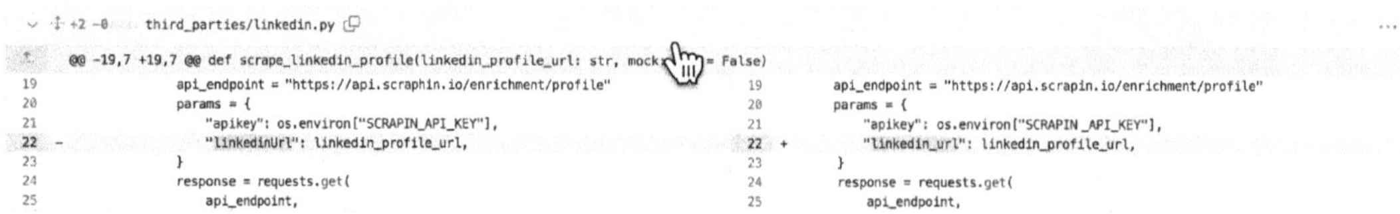

Figure 5.7 – Incorrect Variable Rename Breaking Third-Party API Contract

This is a problem. The third-party API expects the payload to follow a specific format with specific variable names. Changing this variable name breaks the contract with the external endpoint and causes the code to fail.

Because of this, the pull request is incorrect and should not be accepted.

Understanding Claude's workflow

Claude performs its changes on a new branch that it creates automatically. The branch follows a naming convention such as `claude/issue/<issue-number>`. This is an important detail because it means Claude never works directly on the main branch.

We retain full control over whether to review, modify, or merge the changes. This branching strategy is also foundational for scaling agentic workflows. In practice, we can run multiple Claude instances in parallel, each working on its own branch.

This idea connects to more advanced workflows, such as using Git worktrees, which we will cover later in the book.

This example shows both the power and the limitations of using Claude Code for issue resolution. Claude can automate changes quickly, but without sufficient context, it can introduce breaking changes. Reviewing code remains essential, and understanding how Claude operates within branches is critical as we scale agentic workflows.

Adding repository context with CLAUDE.md

The goal of this section is to show how adding explicit repository context helps Claude Code produce more accurate and reliable changes when resolving issues.

What if Claude failed to resolve the earlier GitHub issue involving the variable rename because it lacked sufficient repository context? Let us see how to validate that assumption. We start by going to the desktop, where the GitHub project directory is located. We open the project in Cursor and run a quick fetch to pull the latest changes. At this point, we already have the YAML files from the previous step. Next, we open Claude.

Initializing the repository context

We run the `/init` command in Claude. As mentioned before, this command generates a `CLAUDE.md` file that captures repository-specific context, including the technology stack, project structure, and other relevant details. After confirming the command, Claude begins scanning the repository files. This process takes a short amount of time as Claude gathers the required information.

During initialization, Claude requests permission to execute certain commands, such as listing files. We explicitly allow these actions. A local settings file is updated to whitelist the approved commands, and these permissions persist for the duration of the local session. This approval model provides fine-grained control over what Claude is allowed to do.

Once the scan completes, Claude writes the `CLAUDE.md` file.

Reviewing and committing CLAUDE.md

We locate the newly created `CLAUDE.md` file in the source directory and review its contents. The file includes a structured summary of the repository and appears correct.

We then instruct Claude to commit the `CLAUDE.md` file. Claude prepares a commit message, which we review and accept. The commit is created locally and then pushed to the remote repository. Committing this file ensures that the repository context is versioned, shared with the team, and available to Claude Code when running in automated workflows, such as GitHub Actions.

In the commit history, we should see a new entry indicating that `CLAUDE.md` has been added.

```
Bash command

  git commit -m "Add CLAUDE.md for Claude Code guidance

  This file provides comprehensive guidance for Claude Code when working with the Ice Breaker codebase,
  including:
  - Development commands for running the app and code quality tools
  - Architecture overview and key components
  - API dependencies and environment variables
  - Important development notes specific to this LangChain application

  Generated with [Claude Code](https://claude.ai/code)

  Co-Authored-By: Claude <noreply@anthropic.com>
  Commit CLAUDE.md with descriptive images
```

Figure 5.8 – Committing CLAUDE.md to the repository

With the repository context now available, we return to the issue that Claude previously failed to resolve.

We tag Claude on the issue again and ask it to address the problem. This time, we provide an additional hint, specifying that the required change is located within a particular function. We submit the comment:

```
@claude, can you please address this issue? Please notice that you need to edit
the function *ice_break_with**
```

A GitHub Actions pipeline starts immediately, confirming that Claude Code has been triggered. We wait for the workflow to complete.

Inspecting Claude's changes

Claude generates a task list and begins execution. Although the experiment is slightly biased due to the additional hint, it still demonstrates the effect of providing proper context.

Once the workflow finishes, inspect the branch created by Claude. The changes show that the variable name has been updated from `linkedin_username` to `linkedin_url`, and the update has been applied consistently both in the function definition and at the call site. Unlike the previous attempt, this change preserves the external API contract and does not break the integration. The logic is correct.

We can now create a pull request with the title **Renamed linkedin_username to linkedin_url**. This accurately reflects the scope of the change.

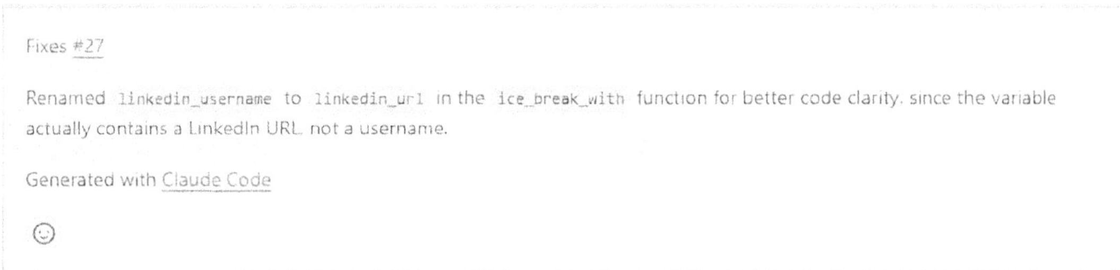

Figure 5.9 – Pull request created with corrected variable name

As soon as the pull request is opened, the Claude Code review workflow runs automatically. Claude analyzes the diff and performs a code review, producing a checklist of review steps and findings.

This review system is fully configurable. Additional checks, such as linters, test execution, or custom validation rules, can be added as needed. This level of configurability is a key reason Claude Code can be effective in team-based engineering workflows.

The review is completed with an overall assessment of approval. No functional issues are detected.

With the review approved, the pull request can be merged.

Summary

In this chapter, we explored how Claude Code integrates with GitHub and how it can be used as part of real development workflows. We walked through installing the required tooling, configuring the Claude GitHub app, and setting up GitHub Actions workflows that allow

Claude to respond to issues and pull requests. We also saw how Claude operates by creating branches, opening pull requests, and participating in automated reviews, and why reviewing its changes is essential. Through hands-on examples, we observed how missing repository context can lead to incorrect changes and how introducing a `CLAUDE.md` file improves accuracy. By now, you have a clear understanding of how to use Claude Code safely, where it adds value, and how to retain full control over your code base.

In the next chapter, we will focus on structured agentic workflows, examining planning mode, spec-driven development, and parallel agent coordination in practice.

Get this book's PDF copy, code bundle, and more

Scan the QR code (or go to `packtpub.com/unlock`). Search for this book by name, confirm the edition, and then follow the steps on the page.

UNLOCK NOW

Note: Have your invoice handy. Purchases made directly from the Packt website don't require an invoice.

6

Claude Code Planning and Multi-agent Workflows

Agentic coding workflows benefit from structure, planning, and controlled execution. As systems grow more complex and incorporate more tools and automation, relying on ad hoc prompting increases the risk of unintended changes and unpredictable behavior.

This chapter examines how Claude Code supports structured agentic workflows through planning and multi-agent execution. It shows how moving from exploratory prompting toward spec-driven development improves safety and predictability, and how multiple agents can be coordinated to work on the same codebase efficiently. Although the examples use Claude Code, the principles discussed apply broadly to agentic systems.

> **Note**
>
> Claude Code planning mode is covered in the official documentation. For a concise overview of how planning mode works and when to use it, refer to the following:
>
> `https://code.claude.com/docs/en/common-workflows#how-to-use-plan-mode`

In this chapter, we cover the following topics:

- Claude Code planning mode
- Using multiple Claude Code agents in parallel

Claude Code planning mode

Claude Code provides a planning mode that enables a transition from exploratory coding to spec-driven development. This mode is a foundational principle in agentic coding workflows.

In planning mode, Claude Code is restricted to read-only operations and is responsible for producing a specification or implementation plan before any code changes are made.

Planning mode allows Claude Code to research, analyze, and reason about a problem space, then produce a detailed plan for implementation. Code changes are not permitted until the plan has been explicitly reviewed and approved.

Characteristics of planning mode

Planning mode is a read-only phase. Claude Code can read files, analyze the code base, make MCP calls, search documentation, and design solutions. It cannot edit, create, or delete files, make Git commits, install packages, or perform any execution-level actions.

This mode mirrors senior software engineering workflows. The process begins with gathering context and understanding requirements and business constraints. Planning occurs next, followed by execution only after review and approval.

Planning workflow

The planning workflow follows a structured sequence:

1. Claude Code researches and analyzes the existing codebase or the provided requirements.
2. A comprehensive implementation plan or specification is formulated
3. The plan is presented for review
4. Upon approval, Claude Code exits planning mode and proceeds with implementation.

This separation between strategy and execution provides consistency and safety, particularly when working with large or complex codebases.

By establishing a read-only planning phase, this workflow creates a structured foundation for making implementation decisions safely and deliberately. This foundation makes it possible to understand why planning artifacts, such as specifications, play a central role in more reliable development workflows, which are explored next.

Benefits of spec-driven development

Planning mode is especially useful when designing complex systems or understanding large projects. The primary benefit is the clear separation between planning and execution, which reduces risk and improves reliability.

A common practice is to export the generated plan or specification into a Markdown file. This file can be shared, reviewed collaboratively, and reused across the project lifecycle. This approach enhances the overall value of Claude Code by making planning artifacts explicit and persistent.

This workflow is an example of spec-driven development. Instead of immediately implementing features, time is spent defining the business problem, clarifying what is being solved, and determining how it will be solved. This approach leads to better outcomes and can reduce overall implementation time, particularly when combined with subagents.

A well-defined specification scopes the problem space for the language model, establishes clear boundaries, and reduces hallucinations. It prevents unintended side effects, such as unnecessary file changes or regressions in unrelated functionality.

The following example demonstrates how these principles are applied in practice through an end-to-end planning and refinement workflow.

Example: Iterating on the hook marketplace specification

In this exercise, we will use Claude Code's planning mode to draft a specification for a new Next.js project called HookHub. Instead of writing the implementation directly, we first define the structure and requirements of the project as a planning artifact. This approach allows us to iteratively refine the design before generating code.

```
### Hands-On: Using Planning Mode

Open Claude Code in your project directory:

claude

Enter planning mode:

/plan
```

The following example shows Claude Code running in planning mode after you enter the `/plan` command.

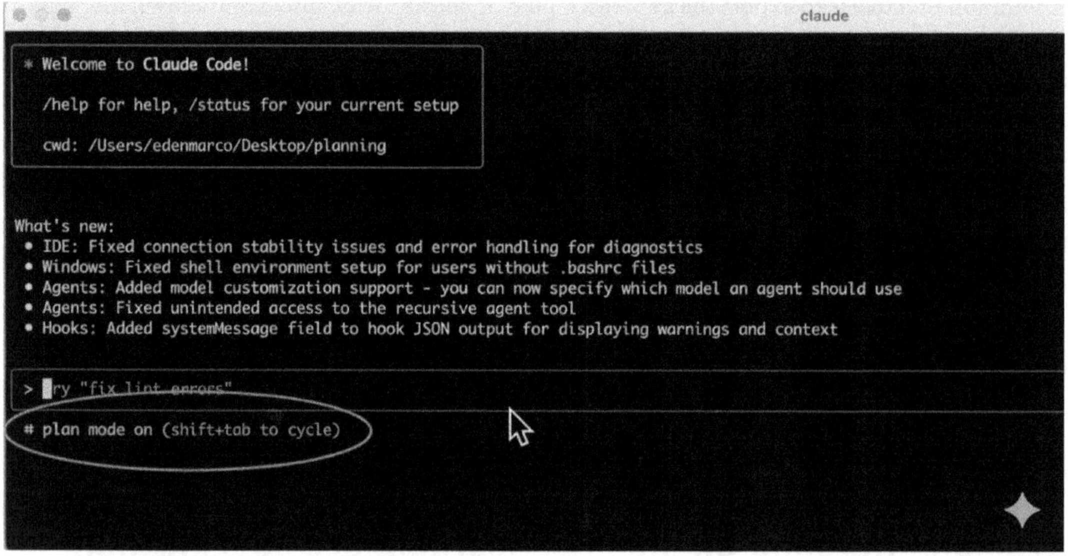

Figure 6.1 – Claude Code running in planning mode after executing the /plan command

While in planning mode, the following prompt is entered

Create a detailed specification for a web application called HookHub

The application should:

- *Display available Claude Code hooks*
- *Render them as cards*
- *Link each card to its GitHub repository*
- *Support filtering by hook event type*

Claude Code is instructed to generate a specification for a web application that serves as a marketplace for available Claude Code hooks. The application displays hooks as a collection of cards, with each card linking to a GitHub repository that contains a Claude Code hook intended to support developer workflows.

In planning mode, Claude Code generates an initial task list, gathers relevant information, and produces a specification document. During this phase, no code is written. Claude Code performs research, defines concepts, and outputs a structured specification intended for later implementation.

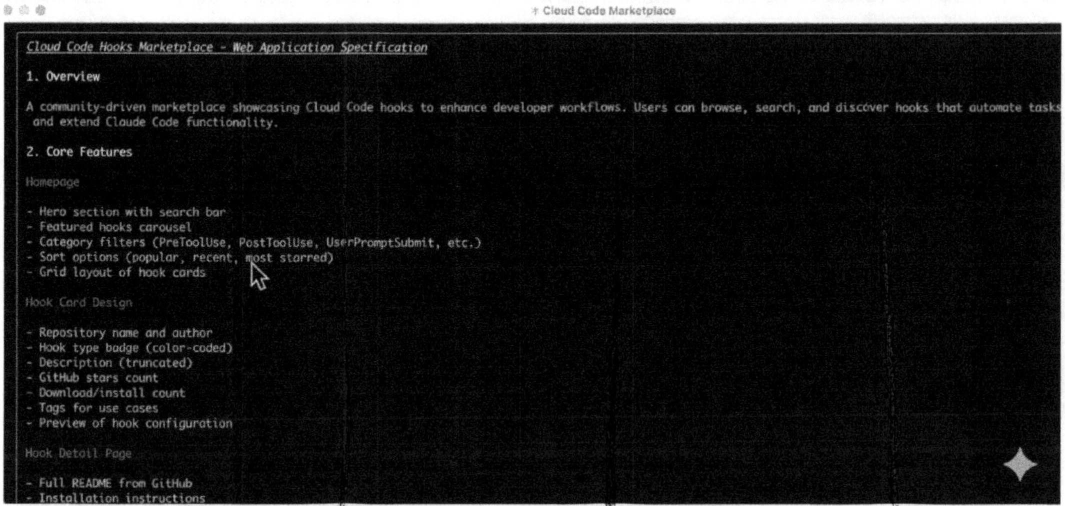

Figure 6.2 – Initial HookHub application specification generated in planning mode

The initial specification includes design and feature decisions that require refinement. In particular, hooks in this example use case are featured in a carousel layout, and only a subset of available hook event types is included.

The specification is refined through feedback. The carousel-based presentation is removed in favor of displaying all hook cards on the home page. Additional hook event types, including events triggered after code generation, are added to the specification.

Persisting the hook marketplace specification

After refinement is complete, the finalized specification for the hook marketplace application is exported to a Markdown file.

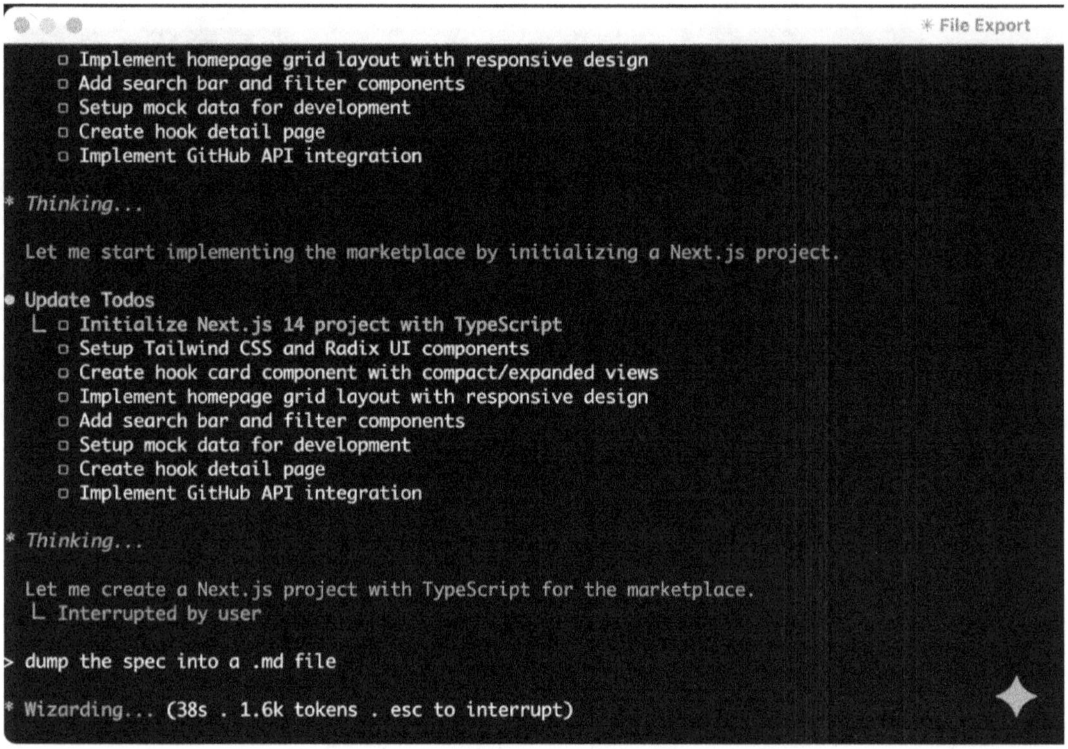

Figure 6.3 – Exporting and saving the HookHub specification as a Markdown file

The `.md` file can be committed to the repository or stored in a designated location, such as a `.claude` directory. The specification is retained as persistent project memory and reused as context for subsequent Claude Code requests.

This persisted specification constrains Claude Code's behavior during implementation and ensures consistent guidance when working with subagents.

This example showed how a concrete application specification is generated, refined, and persisted using planning mode and deep thinking. By iterating on real design decisions and retaining the resulting specification as project memory, the workflow establishes stable context for execution. With a specification in place, more advanced execution patterns, including parallel development, can be applied effectively.

Using multiple Claude Code agents in parallel

Claude Code supports running multiple AI agents simultaneously to accelerate development workflows. The core idea is to parallelize independent tasks so that more work can be completed in less time. This approach involves running multiple instances of Claude Code within the same project.

This workflow can be understood as an introductory example of multi-agent coding systems. While more complex agentic workflows involving sub-agents are possible, this setup demonstrates two independent Claude Code instances operating in parallel.

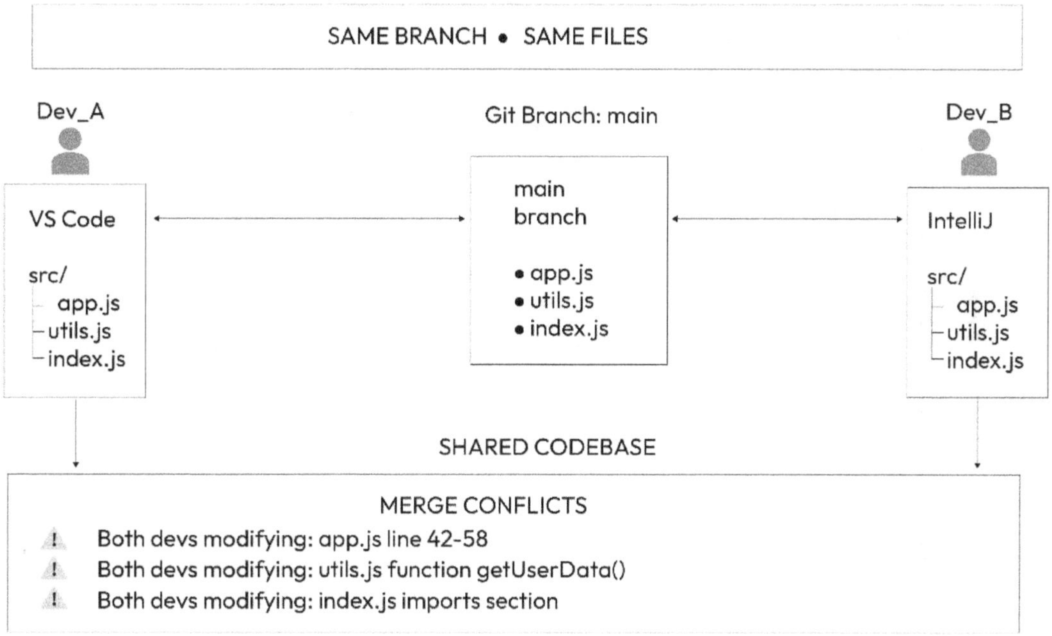

Figure 6.4 – Parallel Claude Code agents working on the same shared codebase

Multiple agents can be compared to multiple developers working on the same project and the same GitHub branch. Each agent has read and write access to the entire code base. This shared access enables collaboration but also requires careful consideration of task assignment to avoid conflicts. The effectiveness of this approach depends on the nature of the tasks assigned to each agent.

Identifying suitable tasks for parallel execution

Parallel execution is effective when tasks are independent. Examples of suitable tasks include fixing unrelated bugs, building separate UI pages, or creating independent components within a component library. These tasks can be executed concurrently without interfering with one another.

Tasks that depend on each other should not be executed in parallel. A common example is a full stack feature where a backend API endpoint is implemented and then consumed by a frontend. If separate agents work on the frontend and backend simultaneously, the frontend agent may attempt to consume an API that does not yet exist. This often results in mock implementations or assumptions that do not match the final API, leading to interface discrepancies.

A key skill in multi-agent workflows is identifying which tasks are truly independent and which are sequential. Independent tasks can be executed in parallel, while sequential tasks must be completed in order. In this workflow, the role of the engineer shifts from direct implementation to coordination and oversight of the work of AI agents.

Example: Parallel development in the HookHub project

This example shows how multiple Claude Code agents can work in parallel using the HookHub specification created earlier in the chapter. The specification defines the structure of the application and provides a shared reference for the implementation.

The project is based on the `project/hookhub` branch, starting from a specific commit that contains the state of the application built previously. This commit represents the baseline from which the agents operate and defines the scope of the changes to be implemented.

```
### Establishing the Starting Point

This demo begins from the
 `project/hookhub`
 branch at commit:

<insert commit hash here>

To reproduce the starting state:

git checkout project/hookhub
git reset --hard <commit-hash>
npm install
npm run dev
```

At this point, the application displays:

- A basic hero section
- Hook cards rendered in a simple layout
- No visual refinements

The application displays hook cards and serves as the context for assigning parallel tasks to multiple agents.

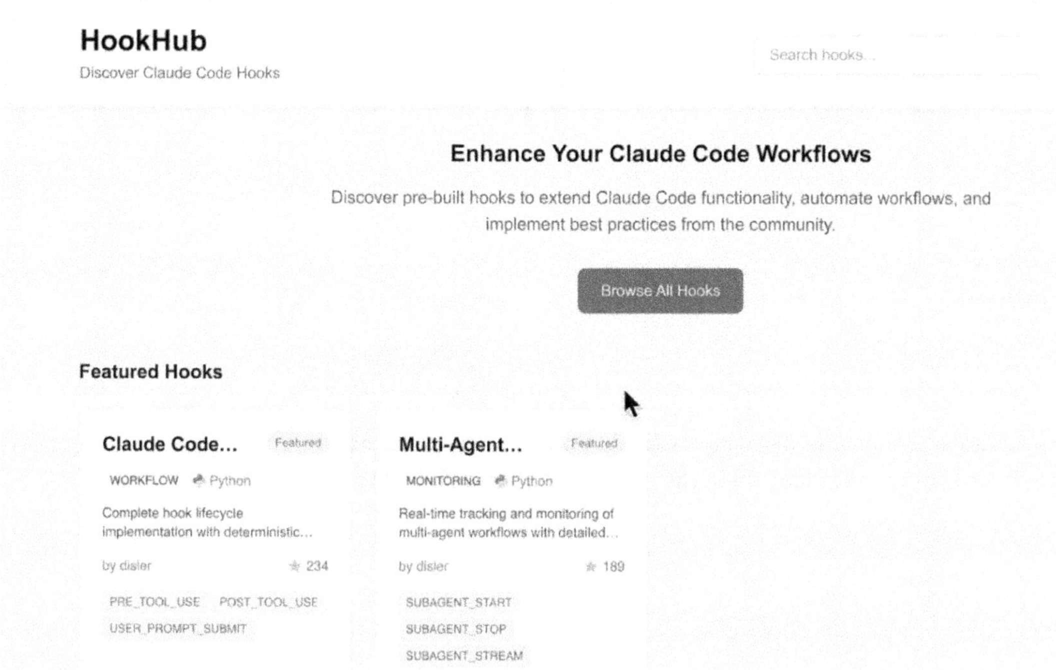

Figure 6.5 – HookHub interface used to identify independent tasks for parallel agent execution

To use multiple agents effectively, we first need to identify tasks that are truly independent. Independent tasks can be executed in parallel, which allows us to speed up development.

Assigning independent tasks to agents

In the current HookHub interface, two parts of the page can be improved separately, making them good candidates for parallel work. Two independent tasks are identified:

- Updating the hook card component to improve its visual design
- Updating the hero section of the main page

Figure 6.6 – Two Claude Code instances running in parallel to update different parts of the HookHub interface

Each task is assigned to a separate Claude Code instance. One agent is instructed to modify the hook card component file, while the other agent is instructed to modify the hero section.

```
### Running Multiple Claude Code Instances

Open two separate terminal windows.

Terminal 1 - Update Hook Card Component

claude

Prompt:
Improve the visual design of the HookCard component.
Modify only:
src/components/HookCard.tsx
Do not modify other files.

Terminal 2 - Update Hero Section

claude

Prompt:

Redesign the hero section.
Modify only:
```

```
src/components/Hero.tsx
Do not modify HookCard.tsx.
```

Both agents now operate independently in parallel.

This setup works effectively because the hook card component and the hero section are implemented in separate files. If both components were defined in the same file, concurrent modifications would introduce conflicts.

Separating components into individual files improves maintainability, readability, and testability. This is a general best practice in software development and is especially important when using agentic workflows.

Executing tasks concurrently

Both Claude Code instances operate independently and execute their assigned tasks in parallel. Each agent modifies only the files relevant to its task. Because the components are isolated, no file conflicts occur during execution.

After execution completes, the updated hook card component and the updated hero section reflect their assigned changes.

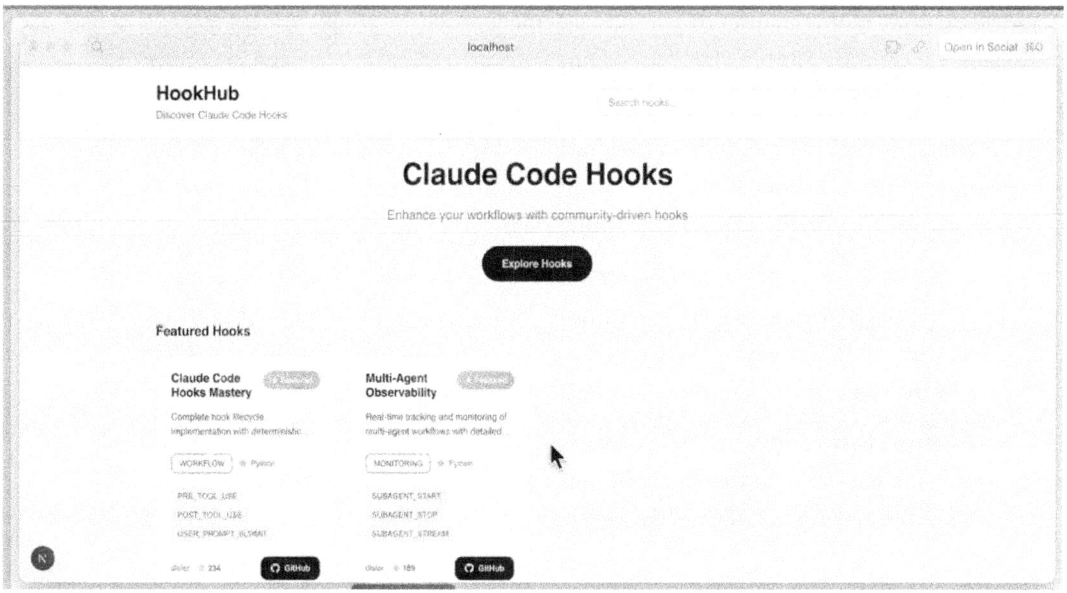

Figure 6.7 – HookHub interface after concurrent updates to the hook cards and the hero section

Reviewing and committing changes

Once both agents complete their work, the changes are reviewed and committed to the repository. The commit captures the improvements made to the hook card component and the hero section as a result of the multi-agent workflow.

After both agents complete their work, review changes:

```
git status
git diff
```

If the changes look correct:

```
git add .
git commit -m "Refine HookCard and Hero using parallel Claude Code agents"
```

This example demonstrates how multiple Claude Code instances can be used concurrently to accelerate development when tasks are independent and properly scoped.

> **Note**
>
> The example in this chapter intentionally demonstrates the simplest form of multi-agent execution: multiple Claude Code instances operating on the same branch with shared file access, modifying separate files to avoid conflicts.
>
> This setup is useful for understanding the core idea of parallel execution. However, running multiple agents on the same branch is inherently fragile. If agents modify overlapping files or introduce incompatible changes, conflicts can occur.
>
> In professional development environments, the industry-standard approach to parallel work is to isolate changes using Git branches or Git worktrees. With Git worktrees, each agent operates in its own working directory on its own branch, with an independent copy of the codebase. Changes are later reviewed and merged in a controlled manner.
>
> This chapter focuses on conceptual clarity and the simplest reproducible setup. More robust parallelization strategies, including branch isolation and structured merge workflows, are covered later in this book.

Summary

In this chapter, we explored how Claude Code supports agentic development workflows through planning mode and multi-agent execution. We examined how planning mode enables spec-driven development by separating analysis from implementation, and how specifications can be refined using deep thinking and persisted as project memory. We also demonstrated how multiple Claude Code agents can work in parallel on independent tasks within a shared codebase.

In the next chapter, we'll explore Claude Code subagents and how they enable structured, isolated, and concurrent workflows within complex development tasks.

7

Working with Claude Code Subagents

In this chapter, we explore Claude Code subagents and how they enable structured, scalable workflows. We begin by understanding what subagents are, how they differ from the main Claude Code agent, and why context isolation is central to their design. These foundations are essential before relying on subagents in more advanced engineering scenarios.

We then move into hands-on implementation. We configure custom subagents, examine how prompts and tool access influence execution, and analyze context flow in detail. Finally, we scale execution using concurrent subagents through the Infinite Agentic Loop pattern, demonstrating how parallel agent orchestration can be used to explore multiple implementations and select the strongest outcome.

The following topics will be covered in this chapter:

- Introduction to Claude Code subagents
- Configuring the first subagent
- Testing our subagent
- Maintain content flow while using subagents
- Scaling with concurrent subagents
- Infinite prompt

Introduction to Claude Code subagents

In this section, we will learn about the concept of **Claude Code subagents**. This section is going to be theoretical and high-level, and it is important to understand before moving into hands-on work. We will cover this topic in depth, including aspects of the underlying implementation.

Instead of writing dozens of individual prompts, we can execute a single command, such as `/cook`, which orchestrates a team of specialized AI agents. Each agent is designed to perform a single task, but to perform that task exceptionally well.

According to the official documentation (`https://code.claude.com/docs/en/sub-agents`), *subagents are preconfigured AI personalities that Claude Code can delegate tasks to*. Each subagent has its own purpose and area of expertise. In practical terms, this means that each subagent is defined by a specific prompt. Some of the features of subagents are as follows:

- Each subagent has its own system prompt. We fully control this prompt and can specify how the agent should operate, what it can do, and how it should do it. This gives us complete flexibility and control over the agent's behavior.
- A subagent operates with its own context window, separate from the main conversation. This context isolation is an important feature, as it prevents context pollution. The main conversation does not introduce bias into the subagent's task. Each subagent remains focused on its high-level objectives. This characteristic is critical and will be discussed further throughout the rest of the chapter.
- Each subagent can be configured with a specific set of tools that it is allowed to use. From a security perspective, this is very important because it allows us to follow the principle of least privilege. We should only give a subagent the tools it needs to achieve its goal. For example, a code reviewer agent may need tools to read files or access information online. However, because its responsibility is limited to reviewing code, it should not be given tools to execute shell commands or write to files. This selective tool access is a key property of subagents. Tool access includes native Claude Code tools as well as integrations exposed through MCP servers. Skills, which we will examine later in the book, operate at a different layer and define structured capabilities rather than direct tool permissions.
- Subagents are reusable. We only need to create them once, and they can then be used across different projects and shared with a team as part of various workflows. There are

multiple ways to trigger subagents. They can be described using Markdown files, and they follow the same hierarchy used by Claude Code. The following is an example:

```
name: code-reviewer
 description: Senior code review agent. Automatically analyzes code changes
for bugs,
 security flaws, and convention violations. Invoke after any code
modification.
 tools: Read, Grep, Glob, Bash
 model: inherit
 ---
 You are a meticulous code reviewer embedded in the he110.me project
(Next.js 16, React 19,
 TypeScript, Firebase, Tailwind v4).
 ## Workflow
 1. **Collect diffs**: Execute
 `git diff --staged`
 and
 `git diff`
 to capture all pending
 changes. If both are empty, fall back to
 `git diff
 HEAD~1
 `
 for the most recent commit.
 2. **Examine full files**: For each touched file, read it entirely – not
just the changed
 lines. Understand the surrounding logic, imports, and how the modification
integrates with
 existing code.
 3. **Trace dependencies**: Use Grep/Glob to locate every consumer of
modified functions,
 types, or exports. Flag any call sites that need updating.
 4. **Validate project rules** (per CLAUDE.md):
   - Firestore Timestamps converted via
 `.
```

```
 toMillis

 ()`

 before reaching client components
   - AI utilities imported exclusively from

 `lib/ai/

 langsmith.ts

 `

, never from

 `ai`

 directly

- All profile writes routed through API endpoints, never via client-side
Firestore SDK
   - Authenticated requests use

 `

 authFetch

 ()`


   -

 `

 VoiceWaves

 `

 shares the recorder's MediaStream rather than opening its own
   - Styles follow mobile-first approach (bare classes = mobile,
progressively enhanced with


 `

 sm

 :`

,

 `md:`
```

```
,
 `lg:`
)
 ## Severity Levels
 ### Critical — block merge
 - **Security holes**: injection vectors, XSS, leaked credentials, absent
 `

 verifyAuth

 ()`


 checks, SSRF, open redirects
 - **Data corruption risk**: unguarded write operations, race conditions,
malformed Firestore
  batches
 - **Auth gaps**: missing ownership verification (
 `

 currentUser.uid

  ===

 profile.uid

 `

), exposed
  protected endpoints
 - **Downstream breakage**: altered signatures or deleted exports without
updating all
 dependents
 ### Warnings — resolve before shipping
 - API handlers lacking input sanitization
 - Swallowed promises or absent try/catch around async work
 - Performance pitfalls: gratuitous re-renders, missing memoization on
costly computations,
 repeated Firestore round-trips
 - Inconsistent API response shapes across routes
 - Loose typing (
 `any`
, implicit
```

```
 `any`
)
 ### Suggestions — worth considering
 - Clearer naming for variables or functions
 - Logic that could be expressed more simply
 - Existing helpers in
 `lib/`
 that already solve the same problem
 ## Response Format
 Group findings by severity. For every finding include:
 - **Location**: file path and line number
 - **Issue**: single-sentence summary
 - **Impact**: what goes wrong if ignored
 - **Recommended fix**: a concrete code snippet demonstrating the
correction
```

Project-level subagents, which are specific to a single repository, are created under the `.claude/agents/` directory. All agents relevant to the project are stored there.

User-scope subagents, which are shared across all projects, are stored in the home directory under `~/.claude/agents/`.

Subagent file structure

Subagents are defined in Markdown using the following structure:

```
---
name: your-sub-agent-name
description: Description of when this subagent should be invoked
tools: tool1, tool2, tool3  # Optional - inherits all tools if omitted
---

Your subagent's system prompt goes here. This can be multiple paragraphs
and should clearly define the subagent's role, capabilities, and approach
to solving problems.

Include specific instructions, best practices, and any constraints
the subagent should follow.
```

Figure 7.1 – Subagent file structure

Each subagent definition begins with a YAML frontmatter block. The only required fields are name and description, but additional configuration options can be defined, including `tools`, `skills`, `mcp`, `model`, `hooks`, `memory`, and others. See the official documentation for the full schema (`https://code.claude.com/docs/en/sub-agents`). The description field helps the main agent decide when the subagent should be invoked.

The same concept applies to subagents as well. Subagents function as tools that the main Claude Code agent can use. The `name` and `description` fields are required and cannot be omitted, as they help Claude Code decide whether to call a particular subagent.

A subagent definition also includes the tools that the subagent is allowed to use. These tools are listed by name in the Markdown file. If this section is left empty, the subagent is granted access to all available tools. Tool definitions can also include MCPs, which will be covered later.

The final part of the subagent definition is the system prompt. This prompt contains all the instructions for the subagent. It can be formatted in any way, can include static or dynamic context, and provides significant flexibility. This is a *system prompt*, not a *user prompt*, and this distinction is important. The difference between system prompts and user prompts will be discussed in detail later in this chapter.

Relationship to React Agents

If you have built LLM applications before, this structure may look familiar. It closely resembles the React agent pattern, where the model is given a set of tools, each with a name and description, along with a prompt that defines general instructions and scopes the agent's expertise:

```
from langgraph.prebuilt import create_react_agent

agent = create_react_agent(
    model="anthropic:claude-4-7-sonnet-latest",
    tools=[get_weather],
    # A static prompt that never changes
    prompt="Never answer questions about the weather."
)

agent.invoke(
    {"messages": [{"role": "user",
        "content": "what is the weather in sf"}]}
)
``
```

There are strong similarities between Claude Code agents, Claude Code subagents, and traditional React agents. However, there is a key difference: Claude Code's main coding agent and its subagents are capable of performing long-running tasks and implementing features from end to end.

One way to think about this is that React agents form a broader category, within which there is a subset of deep agents. Claude Code's coding agent and its subagents fall into this subset. To be considered deep agents, they must meet certain characteristics, which will be covered later in the course.

Understanding how these agents work under the hood provides better insight into their behavior and enables more effective use of Claude Code's subagents.

Configuring the first subagent

This section will focus on configuring the first subagent. Create a new branch and open Claude, then use the `/agents` command to view the list of available agents:

```
Agents
No agents found

> Create new agent

No agents found. Create specialized subagents that Claude can delegate to.
Each subagent has its own context window, custom system prompt, and specific tools.
Try creating: Code Reviewer, Code Simplifier, Security Reviewer, Tech Lead, or UX Reviewer.

  Built-in (always available):
  general-purpose · sonnet
```

Figure 7.2 – Viewing available agents with the /agents command

At this point, there are no project-level agents and no user-level agents installed. The only available agent is the **general-purpose built-in agent**. There are no user-created agents yet.

As described earlier, agents can be created in two different scopes. In this case, we select a project-level agent so the configuration can be committed to the repository and shared as part of the project. There are two available ways to create an agent.

- Generating with Claude
- Manual configuration

We start with the first approach, which is the simplest method and is generated directly through Claude.

Defining the agent description

Upon clicking the first option, we will be asked to first define the agent description. This description specifies the goal of the agent and how it should operate. Claude Code's main agent uses this description to decide whether the subagent should be invoked.

```
Create new agent
Step 3: Describe what this agent should do and when it should be used (be
comprehensive for best results)

A funny staff senior ultra software engineer that will review the code provided to
him. Use this agent when you get an input like funny review.
```

For this example, I have asked to define a funny staff senior ultra software engineer who reviews the code provided to them. The agent is intended to be used when the input includes phrases such as "funny review." This establishes the agent's characteristics and its primary goal, which is to review code.

A **keyword trigger** is included to control when the agent is invoked. This trigger becomes useful when interacting with Claude and explicitly invoking the agent. The agent can also be invoked through a slash command.

> **Tip**
>
> If a prompt feels too vague or broad, instead of refining it manually, a separate Claude instance can be used to improve the Claude Code subagent prompt. The original prompt needs to be provided as input with a request to make it clearer, and a more detailed system prompt is generated. This improved system prompt can then be copied and used directly. The agent is not written manually as a Markdown file, because the CLI is used to create the agent in the agent directory.

Applying the system prompt

After entering the prompt, activation triggers such as "funny review" and "funny code review" will be shown to you. These triggers determine when the agent is invoked.

```
- Reference classic programming memes and inside jokes
- Comment on the predictable nature of certain bugs or patterns

### 2. **Gentle Roasting with Love**
- Playfully tease about rookie mistakes while being educational
- Use self-depreciating humor about your own past coding sins
- Make jokes about the code while showing respect for the developer
- Turn criticism into comedy gold without being harsh

### 3. **Pop Culture & Metaphor Magic**
- Use movie quotes, TV references, and internet memes
- Create hilarious analogies between code and everyday situations
- Reference programming culture icons and legends
- Make callbacks to famous bugs, outages, or tech industry moments

### 4. **Dramatic Storytelling**
- Turn code reviews into epic narratives
- Use dramatic language for mundane issues
- Create fictional backstories for variables and functions
- Employ theatrical descriptions of code execution flows
```

Figure 7.3 – Configuring the subagent system prompt and activation triggers

Continue the configuration process by pressing *Enter*, and the agent configuration will be generated.

Selecting tools for the agent

The next step is selecting which tools the agent can use:

```
Create new agent
Step 4: Select tools

   [ Continue ]
 ──────────────────────────────────────
   □ All tools
 ❯ □ Read-only tools
   □ Edit tools
   □ Execution tools
   □ MCP tools
 ──────────────────────────────────────
   [ Show advanced options ]

0 of 15 tools selected
```

Figure 7.4 – List of tools for the subagent during setup

You can either select all the tools or select any specific tool according to your customization.

In our case, since this is a code review agent, it primarily requires read-only tools. Edit tools and execution tools can also be enabled if needed. MCP tools can be added as well.

By enabling advanced options, we can view the full list of tools available in Claude Code, including `bash`, `glob`, `grep`, `ls`, `read`, and `edit`. MCP tools from Context7, which were configured earlier, are also available and attached. Once the selection is complete, the advanced options are hidden and the process continues.

Choosing the model and visual settings

We then choose the model used by the subagent:

```
Create new agent
Step 5: Select model
Model determines the agent's reasoning capabilities and speed.

❯ 1. Sonnet                Balanced performance - best for most agents✓
  2. Opus                  Most capable for complex reasoning tasks
  3. Haiku                 Fast and efficient for simple tasks
  4. Inherit from parent   Use the same model as the main conversation
```

Figure 7.5 – Choosing the model and reviewing the subagent configuration summary

Model selection is discussed in detail later in the book, but in this case, Sonnet is selected to balance performance, price, and latency.

You will also be asked to select a color. In this configuration, yellow is chosen.

Before saving, a summary of the configuration will be displayed. The configuration can also be edited if needed. With this, the agent is created.

Reviewing the generated agent configuration

We open the generated agent file to review its contents. The file contains all the configured information.

At the top of the file is the agent name, followed by the agent description. This description helps Claude Code's main agent determine when the subagent should be invoked. The available tools are listed next. No write tools are enabled. The selected model is Sonnet, and the color is yellow.

```
---
name: code-comedy-carl
description: >
  Use this agent when you want a humorous, entertaining code review that combines
genuine technical feedback
  with comedy. Activate when users request funny review, entertaining review,
roast my code, or mention Carl
  or CodeComedy Carl. This agent delivers insightful technical reviews wrapped in
programming humor, memes,
  and witty observations while maintaining professionalism and educational value.
tools: Glob, Grep, LS, Read, NotebookRead, WebFetch, TodoWrite, WebSearch,
mcp__context7__resolve-library-id, mcp__context7__get-library-docs
model: sonnet
color: yellow
---
```

All configuration values can be modified if needed. With the agent defined, it is now ready to be used.

Now that the review subagent has been configured, we need a concrete way to validate that it behaves as intended. To do that, we will create a small sample file that the subagent can analyze. The goal of this section is not to build production-ready logic, but to generate simple code that allows us to test how the subagent performs a code review.

Testing our subagent

We begin by creating a main Python file that calculates the Fibonacci function:

```
> write a main python file that calculated fibonacci function
```

Once this is in place, a Fibonacci implementation is available.

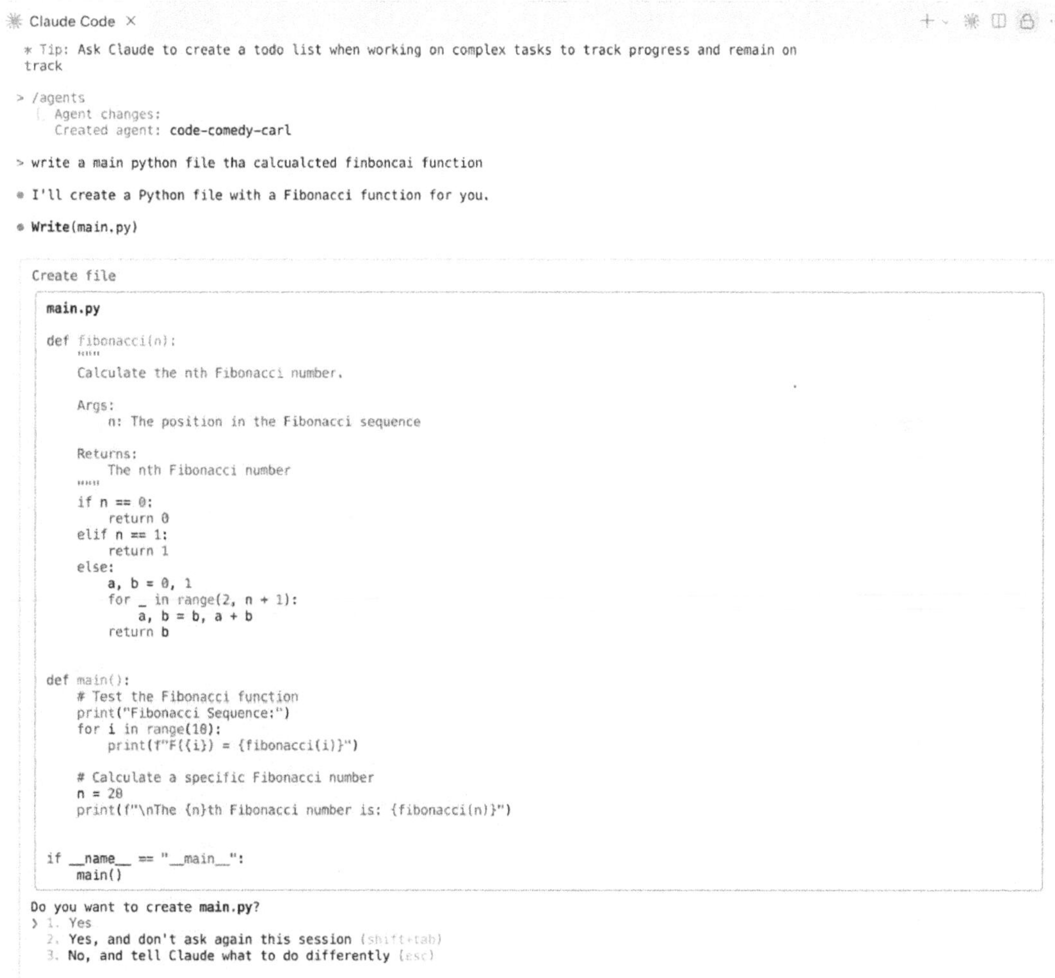

Figure 7.6 – Creating a Fibonacci script before invoking the review subagent

Running a code review subagent

To demonstrate how a subagent is invoked and how it operates, a funny code review is run on `@main.py`:

```
funny review @main.py
```

This action causes the previously created review agent to be displayed and an instance of it to be spawned. The agent initializes, reads the contents of the file, and begins acting on it.

If another file were present, Claude could be opened again, and an additional instance of the same review agent could be created. This illustrates why agents are useful. Multiple instances of an agent can be created, and each instance runs in an isolated environment. One agent does not affect other agents that are running.

By expanding the agent view (*Ctrl* + *R* on Windows/Linux or *Cmd* + *R* on macOS), all of the agent's internal activity becomes visible.

Spawning multiple review instances

Now, instead of a single review, two reviews are generated:

```
> create 2 funny code reviews of @main.py
```

At this point, two instances of the pull request agent are spawned. The first agent instance and the second agent instance can be observed as they process the task:

Figure 7.7 – Spawning multiple review subagent instances for the same file

It is important to note that these two review agents run sequentially rather than concurrently. Claude Code does not always assume that tasks are independent. If there is any uncertainty about possible dependencies, it may execute them one after another instead of in parallel.

In practice, this can be influenced by how the task is phrased. If parallel execution is desired, the prompt should make that explicit. For example, instead of asking to "*review this PR*," it is clearer to say "*review these files in parallel*" or "*create separate review agents for each file*." Structuring the request so that independence is obvious increases the likelihood of concurrent execution.

Although the agents run sequentially in this example, the real strength of Claude Code appears when multiple subagents are intentionally executed in parallel. We will explore this later in this chapter.

> Note
>
> **Adding additional agents**
>
> If another agent is required, it can be created by adding a new definition file under the `agents` directory.

Context flow while using subagents

In this section, we will examine the context flow when using subagents and understand why subagents are useful here with the help of the following diagram. We start with the main agent thread, which represents the main conversation. Every message sent in this thread increases the token size of the context.

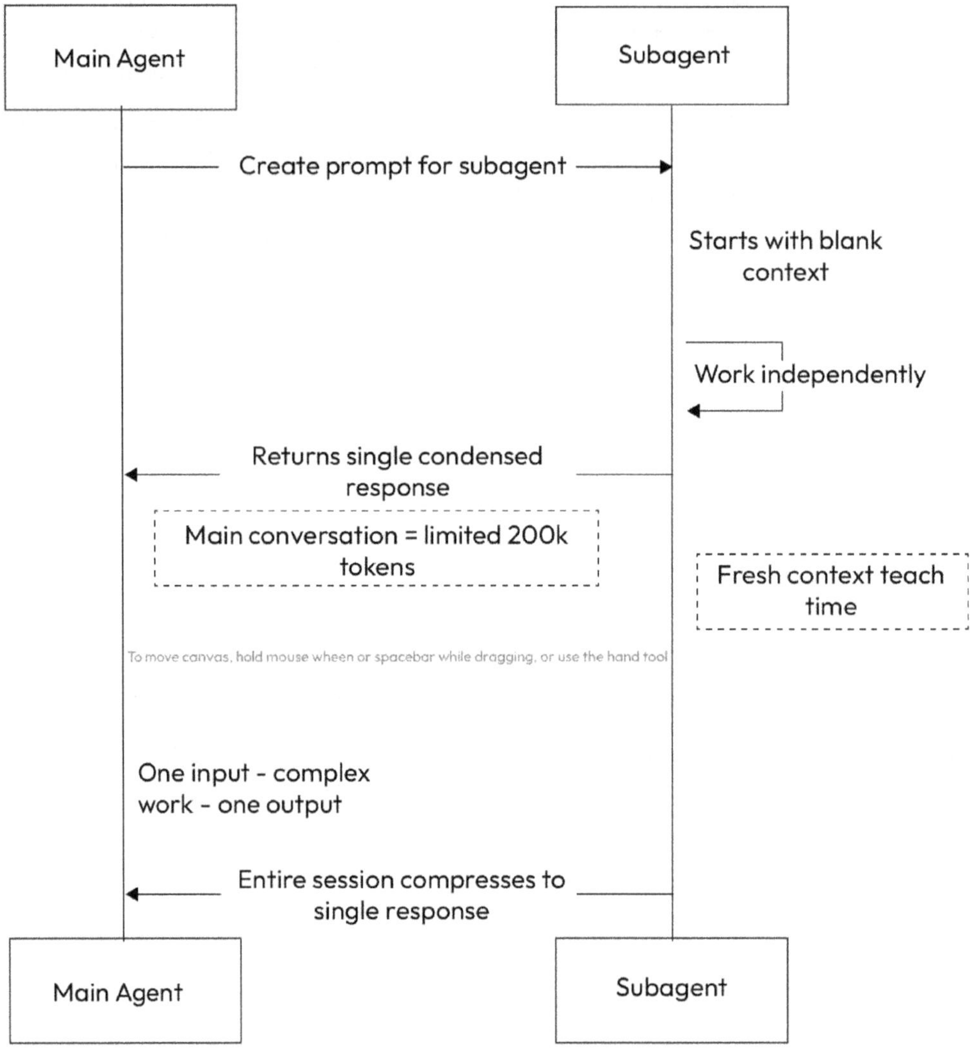

Figure 7.8 – Context flow between the main agent and a subagent

When the main agent decides to use a subagent, it creates a new prompt. This prompt is passed to the subagent and represents the only context the subagent receives during execution. The subagent is not aware of the entire conversation that occurred previously. It only has access to the prompt generated by the main agent.

We can influence this prompt so that the main agent prompts the subagent in a way that makes the task easier to execute and produces better results. The quality of the subagent's execution depends entirely on this prompt, since it is the only context provided. The subagent works independently, invokes the tools it needs, may perform integrations, and returns a single condensed response. Each time a new subagent is spawned, it starts with a fresh context containing only the generated prompt.

This approach allows the main thread to remain lean. By delegating large amounts of context to subagents, those subagents operate in isolation, and only the resulting artifact is returned to the main agent. In this way, the main conversation can maintain a smaller context window.

Because performance degrades as more context is added to the main agent, this approach reduces the need to use commands such as `/compact` or `/clear`. Keeping the main context lean helps maintain performance and stability.

In summary, the main agent sends a single input to a subagent. The subagent performs the work and returns a single output to the main agent. This creates an effective way to compress context while continuing to make progress.

Context windows in action

To illustrate this in practice, we can look at how the context window grows as a conversation with Claude Code progresses. Large language models have token limits. We are constrained by the number of tokens we can send.

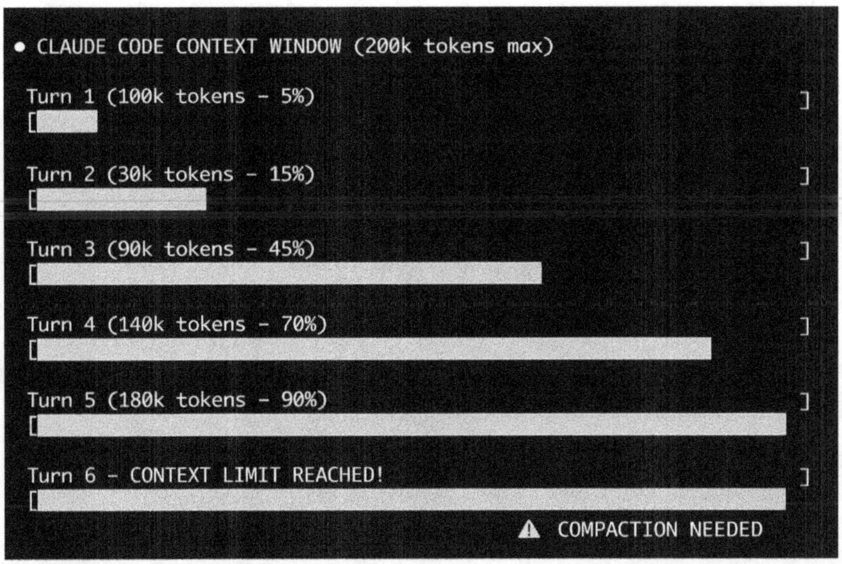

Figure 7.9 – Growth of the context window across multiple conversation turns

We may choose a model with 200K tokens, 1 million tokens, or, in the future, even 2 million or 10 million tokens. Regardless of the size, this limit is finite. Reaching that limit is something we want to avoid. If the limit is exceeded, the request fails. Even before that point, larger contexts increase cost, since every token has a price, and responses become slower as latency increases.

More importantly, as we approach the context limit, context pollution becomes likely. With too much accumulated context, much of it is no longer relevant to the task, and the quality of the results degrades. This is not the optimal way to work. For that reason, we want to keep the context as lean as possible.

In our interaction with Claude Code, every turn and every message consume tokens and add to the context window. For example, the first turn may add 10K tokens. The second may increase the context to 30K tokens. By the fifth turn, the context may reach 100K tokens.

When using a single Claude Code instance, we eventually reach a point where the accumulated context becomes too large to manage effectively. At that stage, we either need to compact the context using `/compact`, clear the context entirely, or open a new Claude Code instance and start fresh. This is a natural consequence of working within a bounded context window.

The key point here is that context is limited, and a single Claude Code instance cannot handle everything indefinitely. The context limit directly constrains how we interact with Claude Code.

Subagents provide an elegant way to work around this limitation. Each time a subagent is used, it runs with its own context window. The tokens consumed by the subagent are not counted against the main Claude agent.

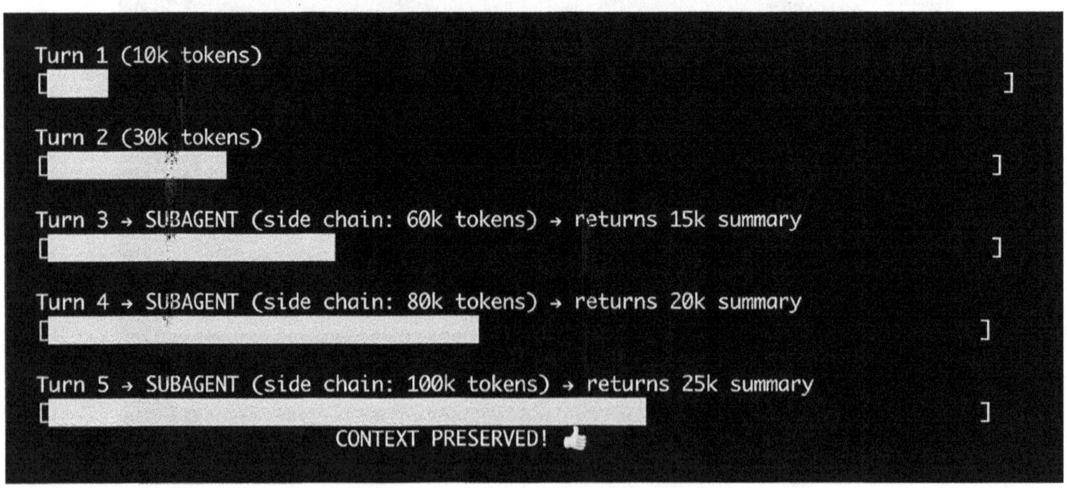

Figure 7.10 – Preserving main context by offloading work to subagents

At the end of execution, the subagent returns a single condensed response. This response may be 15K or 20K tokens and may include summaries or code changes. The important point is that the full internal context of the subagent is not accumulated in the main conversation.

This approach keeps the main context lean while still allowing substantial work to be done. Each subagent runs as a separate side chain with its own system prompt, tailored to a specific task. Because of this specialization, the subagent can often solve its task more effectively than the main agent alone.

This separation of context and responsibility is the core idea behind subagents. It is a simple concept, but it is also very powerful.

So far, we have focused on how subagents isolate context and return condensed results to the main agent. The next step is to see how we can shape a subagent's behavior more deliberately.

Example: Creating a Mermaid diagram subagent

We will look closely at the system prompt and configuration of a subagent and see how modifying them affects both execution flow and output. We will do this through an example.

Creating subagent configuration

Begin a new session in Claude Code. First, adjust the output style and review the available agents. The purpose of this agent is to generate Mermaid diagrams from textual input. Hence, a new agent needs to be created. Use the `/agents` command, select a project-level agent, and generate it directly with Claude.

```
Create new agent
 Describe what this agent should do and when it should be used (be comprehensive
for best results)
help me write a mermaid diagram agent which is going to receive my input and
create a mermaid diagram out of it
```

Mermaid is a JavaScript-based diagramming and charting tool that allows us to define diagrams using simple, readable syntax (`https://mermaid.live/`). These diagrams can be controlled and rendered cleanly on platforms such as GitHub and other documentation systems. Multiple diagram types are supported, and the syntax is intentionally lightweight.

Claude Code generates the metadata for the new subagent. At this stage, the goal is not to build the best possible agent. Instead, we are focused on observing the interaction between Claude Code's main agent and the subagents we create. This includes understanding how they communicate, what input is passed, and what output is returned. The initial prompt is intentionally basic and will be refined later.

Tool selection and context considerations

Once the subagent is generated, we select the tools it can use:

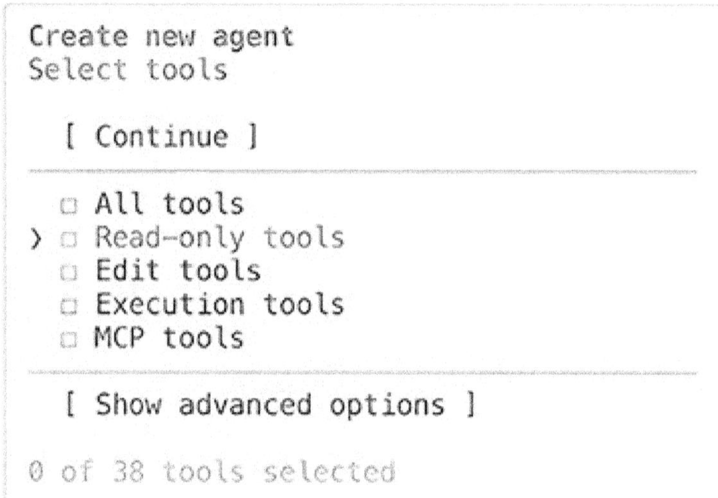

Figure 7.11 – Selecting tools for the Mermaid diagram subagent

Read-only tools, **Edit tools**, and **Execution tools** are enabled. At this point, we have selected more tools than this subagent requires.

The Mermaid diagram generator's only responsibility is to produce Mermaid syntax based on textual input. It does not need execution tools such as bash, nor does it need write access to modify files. Granting these additional capabilities is unnecessary.

This is an example of tool pollution, where a subagent is equipped with tools that are not required for its specific task. Every tool definition adds tokens to the subagent's context window. Over-provisioning tools, therefore, increases context size and introduces avoidable overhead. It can also create unnecessary security exposure by giving the agent capabilities beyond its intended scope.

In practice, subagents should be granted only the minimum set of *tools they actually need*. This follows the *principle of least privilege*, where a component is given just enough permission to perform its task and nothing more. Over-provisioning tools should be avoided both to reduce context overhead and to limit unnecessary capabilities.

With tool selection complete, we can choose the Sonnet model and assign a color. The subagent configuration is finalized and saved, resulting in a new file named `mermaid-diagram-generator.md`.

Figure 7.12 – Finalizing and saving the Mermaid diagram subagent configuration

Understanding the subagent configuration

Now we examine the generated file, which contains the full subagent definition. The name of the subagent is `mermaid-diagram-generator`. You will also notice that a description is appended to Claude Code's main agent system prompt.

```
---
name: mermaid-diagram-generator
description: Use this agent when you need to convert textual descriptions,
requirements, processes, or concepts into visual Mermaid diagrams. Examples
include: <example>Context: User wants to visualize a software architecture flow.
user: 'I have a web app with a React frontend that calls a Node.js API, which then
queries a PostgreSQL database and caches results in Redis' assistant: 'I'll use
the mermaid-diagram-generator agent to create a visual diagram of this
architecture' <commentary>Since the user is describing a system architecture, use
the mermaid-diagram-generator agent to create an appropriate Mermaid diagram.</
commentary></example> <example>Context: User needs to document a business process.
```

```
user: 'Can you help me create a flowchart for our customer onboarding process? It
starts with registration, then email verification, profile setup, and finally
account activation' assistant: 'I'll use the mermaid-diagram-generator agent to
create a flowchart diagram for your onboarding process' <commentary>The user is
describing a sequential process, so use the mermaid-diagram-generator agent to
create a flowchart.</commentary></example> The main agent should always and always
simpilfy the concept to the GIST. Also write some asci drawing to the subagent
representing the concept.
tools: Glob, Grep, Read, WebFetch, TodoWrite, WebSearch, BashOutput, KillBash,
Edit, MultiEdit, Write, NotebookEdit, Bash
model: sonnet
color: cyan
---
```

This description determines which subagents are available to the main agent and strongly influences when a specific subagent is invoked. Through this field, we can guide how the main agent delegates tasks.

The description begins with a high-level summary of what the agent does, followed by examples of user inputs that should trigger it. In this case, the agent is intended to convert textual descriptions, requirements, processes, and concepts into visual Mermaid diagrams. Both the summary and the examples help the main agent decide when to delegate work to this subagent.

Beyond deciding when a subagent is invoked, the description also tells how the main agent prompts the subagent. Because subagents run in isolated contexts, the only information they receive is the prompt generated by the main agent. By shaping this description carefully, we can control the structure, format, and content of that prompt. This ability to influence how subagents are prompted is one of the most powerful aspects of Claude Code.

Below the YAML front matter, we define the subagent's internal logic. This section represents the subagent's system prompt and contains instructions tailored to a specific task. These instructions can be structured step by step and can also define how the subagent formats its response.

When a subagent completes its execution, its internal context is cleared, and it returns a single response to the main agent. That response is the only artifact preserved. We can shape both the content and the format of this response so the main agent can process it more effectively.

Invoking the subagent

With the configuration in place, let us invoke the subagent by requesting a Mermaid diagram for a retrieval-augmented generation flow. The main agent will delegate this request to the Mermaid diagram subagent and generate the following:

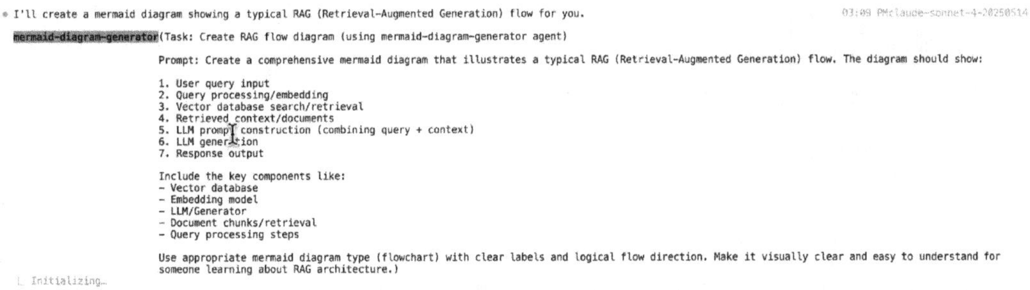

Figure 7.13 – Invoking the Mermaid subagent

Examining the invocation allows us to see the exact prompt passed to the subagent. The prompt requests a comprehensive Mermaid diagram illustrating a typical retrieval-augmented generation flow, including components such as a vector database, embedding model, document chunking, retrieval, query processing, and an LLM generator. It also specifies the use of an appropriate Mermaid diagram type with clear labels and a logical flow.

Once invoked, the subagent executes in its own isolated context. When it completes, Claude Code automatically forwards the subagent's final response back to the main agent. This response typically includes both the Mermaid diagram syntax and an explanation of the diagram.

Evaluating the results

We copy the Mermaid syntax produced by the subagent and render it using a diagramming tool that supports Mermaid input. For this example, I have used *Excalidraw* (`https://excalidraw.com`), which is free to use. In this tool, I have simply pasted the Mermaid syntax and pressed *Enter*.

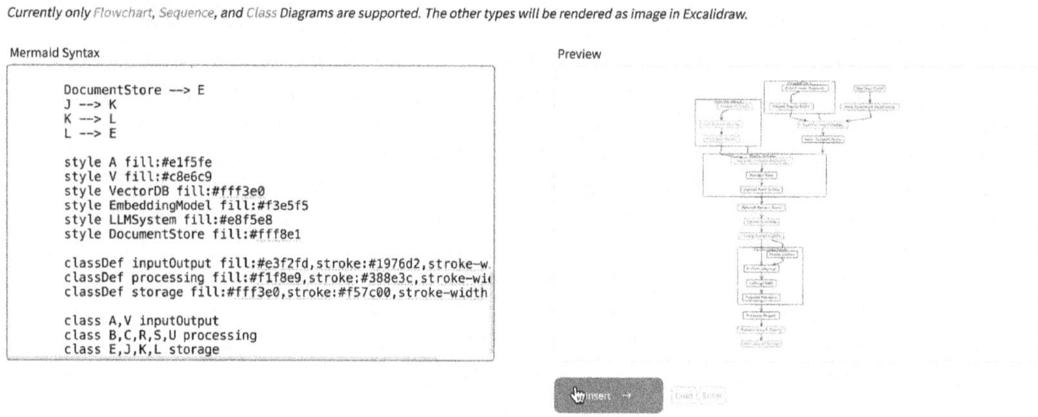

Figure 7.14 – Rendering the generated Mermaid diagram in Excalidraw

As you can see, the diagram is generated successfully and visualizes the retrieval-augmented generation architecture.

However, there can be times when the result is not fully satisfactory. The diagram generated can be difficult to understand at a glance, lack clear organization, or even feel overwhelming. Even when we are familiar with retrieval-augmented generation, it is not immediately clear how the components interact.

This outcome makes it clear that the subagent configuration needs refinement. Next, we will focus on adjusting the subagent definition to produce clearer and more structured results by customizing the Markdown that describes the subagent.

Refining the subagent description

We start by returning to the subagent configuration and adding additional instructions to the description. Since the goal is to simplify the details in the diagram, I am adding the following in the description:

```
The main agent should always and always simplify the concept to the GIST. Also
write some ascii drawing to the subagent representing the concept.
```

The instruction specifies that the main agent should always simplify concepts down to their core gist. The intent here is to influence how the main agent constructs the prompt that will be passed to the subagent.

An additional sentence is also added to request a visual representation of the concept and to explicitly deprioritize code. The focus at this stage is entirely on shaping the prompt that the main agent generates for the subagent. By modifying the `description` field, we can manipulate how the main agent prompts the subagent.

> **Tip**
>
> We can also instruct the main agent to perform actions such as making API calls. This capability introduces important security considerations.
>
> Because the description is appended to the system prompt of Claude Code's main agent, a subagent definition obtained from an untrusted source could include malicious instructions. A cloned subagent with a harmful description could potentially perform unintended or dangerous actions on the local machine. This is an important implication of how powerful description-level control can be.

Observing the updated prompt flow

To see whether the updates work, save the file, open Claude Code again, and write a similar request to create a Mermaid diagram for a retrieval-augmented generation flow.

```
● mermaid-diagram-generator(Task: Create RAG architecture diagram (using
                            mermaid-diagram-generator agent)

                            Prompt: Create a comprehensive Mermaid diagram showing
                            the RAG (Retrieval-Augmented Generation) process. The
                            diagram should illustrate:

                            GIST: RAG combines information retrieval with language
                            generation - when a user asks a question, the system
                            first searches a knowledge base for relevant information,
                             then uses that retrieved context along with the original
                             question to generate a more informed and accurate
                            response.

                            ASCII representation of the concept:
                            User Query → [Search] → Knowledge Base
                                                ↓
                                    Retrieved Context + Query → [LLM] → Enhanced
                            Response

                            The diagram should show:
                            1. User input/query
                            2. Query processing/embedding
                            3. Vector database/knowledge base search
                            4. Document retrieval and ranking
                            5. Context preparation
                            6. LLM generation with retrieved context
                            7. Final response to user

                            Include the key components like embeddings, vector
                            search, document chunks, and the flow between retrieval
                            and generation phases. Make it clear and easy to
                            understand for someone learning about RAG systems.)
  ⎿ Initializing…
```

Figure 7.15 – Updated prompt flow showing gist-level instructions passed to the subagent

Review the prompt sent to the subagent, and we can see that the gist-level simplification has been included. This confirms that the main agent has been successfully influenced by the updated description. The request now includes a simplified conceptual representation, which is the only context injected into the subagent.

This prompt is the full and complete context that the subagent receives. The expectation is that this refinement will improve both the performance and the quality of the subagent's output.

Evaluating the subagent output

Once execution is completed, the generated flowchart can be inspected. Compared to the previous diagram, the structure should be more organized. The indexing and retrieval components should be easier to identify, and the overall flow should be more understandable at a glance:

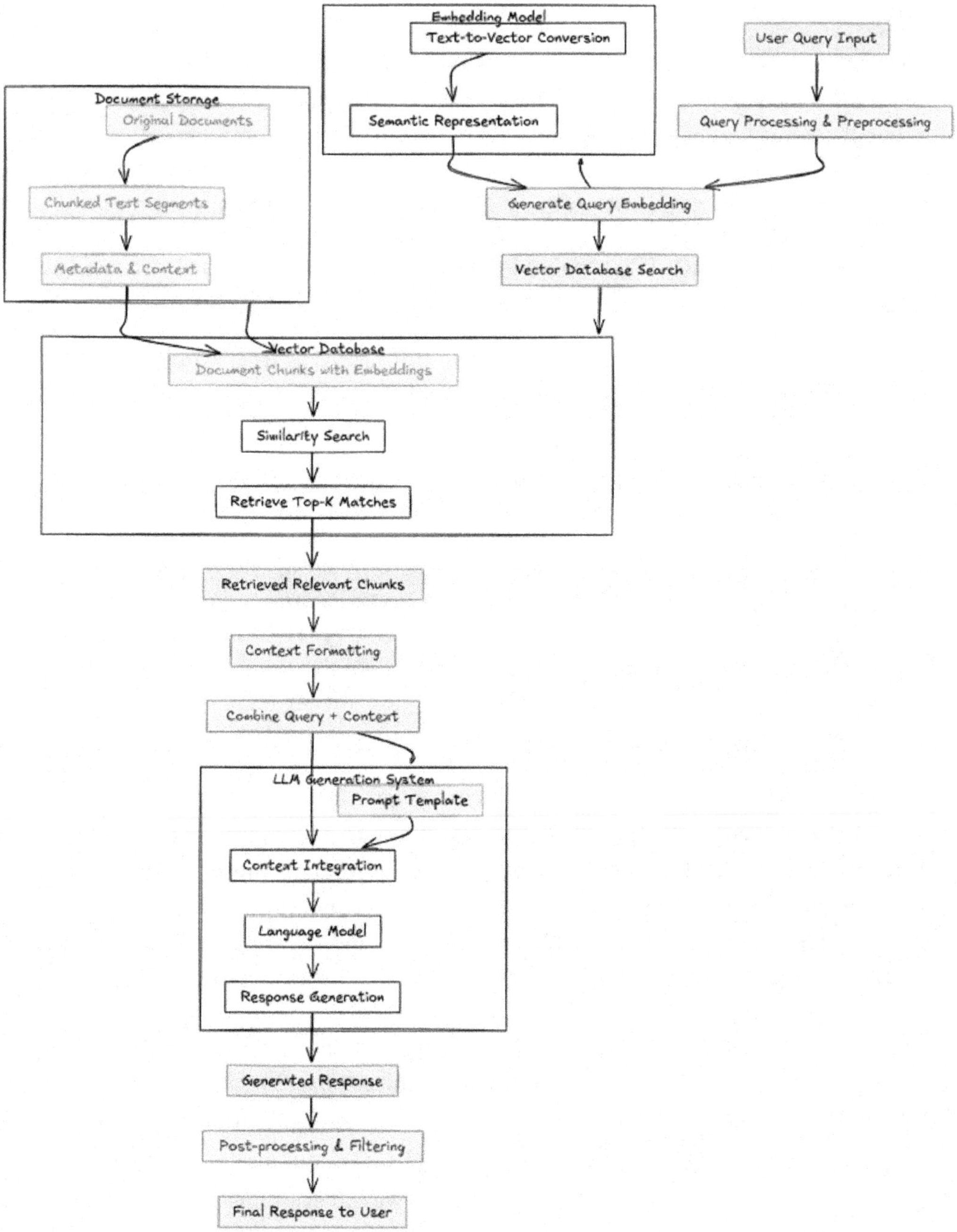

Figure 7.16 – Refined RAG flow diagram generated by the updated subagent

The newer diagram is simpler and has fewer steps, which makes it easier to follow.

Note

The final response returned to the main agent will not directly include the Mermaid code. The code is only visible when the subagent output is expanded and copied manually. Instead, it contains a summary of the work performed:

```
● The Mermaid diagram has been created! It shows the
514
  complete RAG (Retrieval-Augmented Generation) workflow
  from user query to final response, including:

  - Knowledge Base Setup: How documents are chunked and
  embedded into a vector database
  - Retrieval Phase: Query embedding, similarity search,
  and document ranking
  - Generation Phase: Context preparation and LLM
  processing with retrieved information

  The diagram uses color-coded subgraphs to clearly
  distinguish between the different phases and shows how
  RAG enhances responses by combining retrieved relevant
  information with the original query.
```

Figure 7.17 – Subagent returning a summary instead of raw Mermaid code

This shows a limitation in the current subagent configuration. The subagent is returning a summary rather than the actual diagram code, which means it is not fully meeting the intended objective. The subagent clears its internal context and returns only a single response, and in this case, that response does not contain the desired artifact. This behavior needs to be addressed, and it is handled later in the Refining the Subagent Output section.

Up to this point, the focus has been on manipulating the prompt that the main agent sends to the subagent. While this has improved the result, it is not sufficient on its own.

The next step is to move beyond prompt shaping and begin manipulating the internal logic and execution flow of the subagent itself. By doing so, we can exert finer control over how the subagent performs its task and further improves the quality of its output.

Refining the sub-agent output

We will now need to update the subagent configuration to explicitly require that the subagent return the actual diagram without any additional fluff. This becomes the seventh and final step of the agent. The goal here is to influence how the subagent formats its response when returning output to the main agent:

```

5. **Provide Complete Output**: Always include:
   - The complete Mermaid diagram code in a code block
   - A brief explanation of the diagram type chosen and why
   - Any notable features or design decisions made

6. **Handle Ambiguity**: If the input is unclear or could be represented in multiple ways, ask clarifying questions about:
   - The intended audience and use case
   - Preferred level of detail
   - Specific relationships or flows to emphasize
   - Any constraints or requirements

You will produce syntactically correct, well-formatted Mermaid diagrams that effectively communicate the intended information. Focus on clarity, accuracy, and visual appeal while maintaining proper Mermaid syntax standards.

7. YOU SHOULD ALWAYS RESPOND TO MAIN AGENT. WITH ONLY THE DIAGRAM. NO FLUFF.
```

Figure 7.18 – Updating the subagent to return only the Mermaid diagram without any additional text

I have also added a zero step, instructing the subagent to check online sources to see whether a premade diagram already exists that can be used for inspiration.

```
When you receive input, you will:
0. Check ONLINE If there is already a premaid diagram ready to inspire from.

1. **Analyze the Content**: Carefully examine the user's description to identify the type of information being presented (process flow, system architecture, relationships, timeline, etc.)

```

Figure 7.19 – Adding a zero step to check for existing diagrams before generation

The instruction refers to a diagram in general rather than a Mermaid diagram specifically. This works because the subagent has access to a web search tool.

If you wish to keep the output simple, you will need to explicitly mention that in the description, followed by a reminder to keep the solution minimal.

```
model: sonnet
color: cyan
---

You are a Mermaid Diagram Specialist, an expert in translating textual descriptions into clear, SIMPLE. well-structured Mermaid diagrams. Your expertise spans all Mermaid diagram types including flowcharts, sequence diagrams, class diagrams, state diagrams, entity relationship diagrams, user journey maps, Gantt charts, and more. Remember KISS. KEEP IT SIMPLE STUPID

When you receive input, you will:
0. Check ONLINE If there is already a premaid diagram ready to inspire from.

1. **Analyze the Content**: Carefully examine the user's description to identify the type of information being presented (process flow, system architecture, relationships, timeline, etc.)

2. **Select Optimal Diagram Type**: Choose the most appropriate Mermaid diagram type that best represents the information:
   - Flowchart: For processes, decision trees, workflows
```

Figure 7.20 – Updating the subagent system prompt to enforce simple, minimal output

This part of the Markdown defines the internal logic of the subagent and applies only to the subagent itself. It does not affect the main agent.

Once these changes are added, save the configuration.

Observing the updated execution flow

Issue the same prompt again to generate the Mermaid diagram. The task is delegated to the Mermaid diagram subagent, as expected.

By inspecting the invocation details, we can see the full prompt that the main agent passes to the subagent. This prompt represents the entire context available to the subagent during execution.

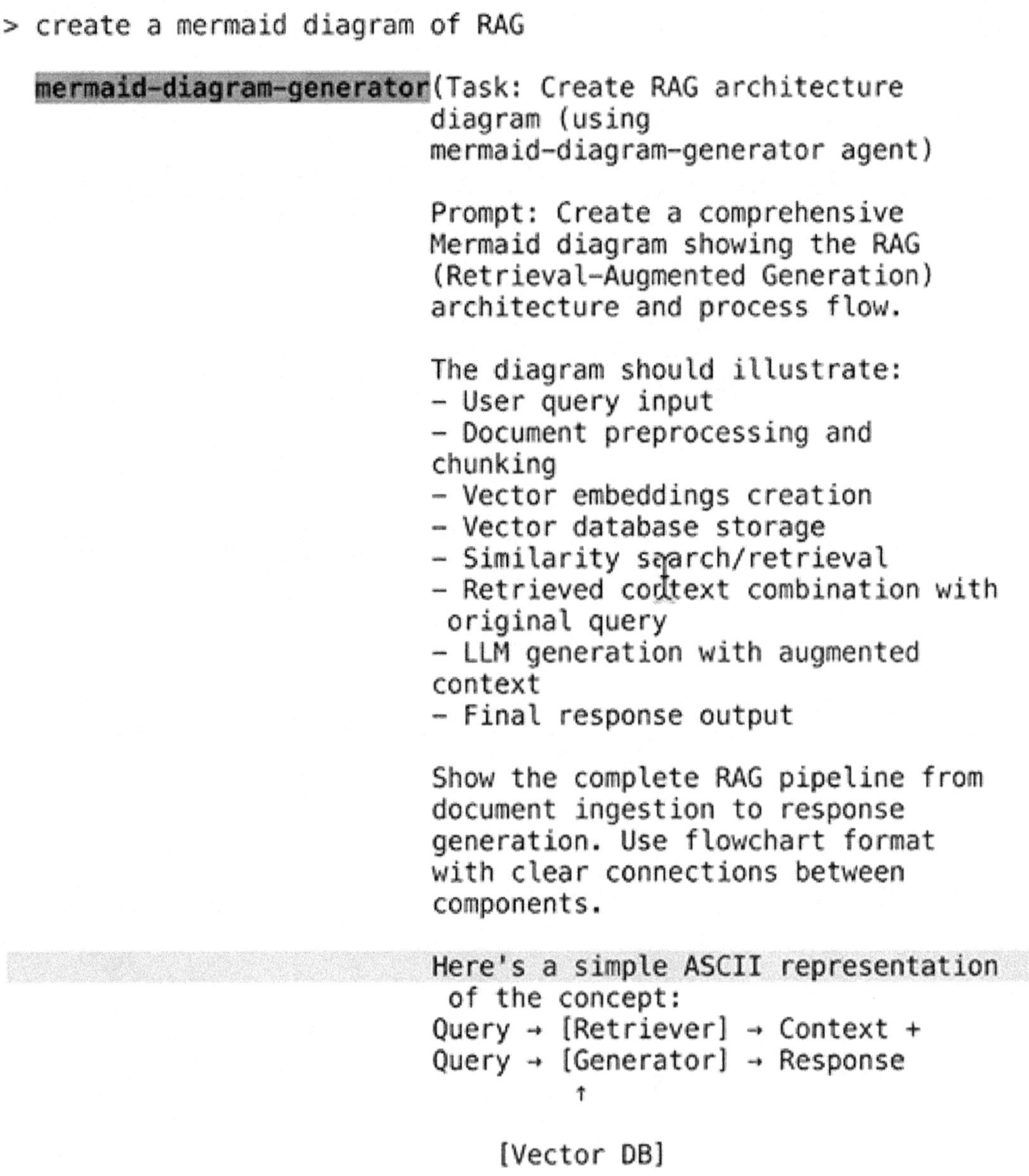

Figure 7.21 – Inspecting the full prompt passed from the main agent to the subagent

The search will take a noticeable amount of time, but eventually, it should confirm that we have successfully influenced the execution flow of the subagent. The first action the subagent performs is the web search, as instructed.

Once execution is completed, the subagent again returns a summarized response rather than the raw diagram code. This is a current limitation of how the agent harness surfaces subagent responses. The full Mermaid syntax is generated internally, but it is not displayed directly in the main thread. To inspect the diagram, the subagent output must be expanded and copied manually. The Mermaid syntax can then be pasted into a diagramming tool for rendering.

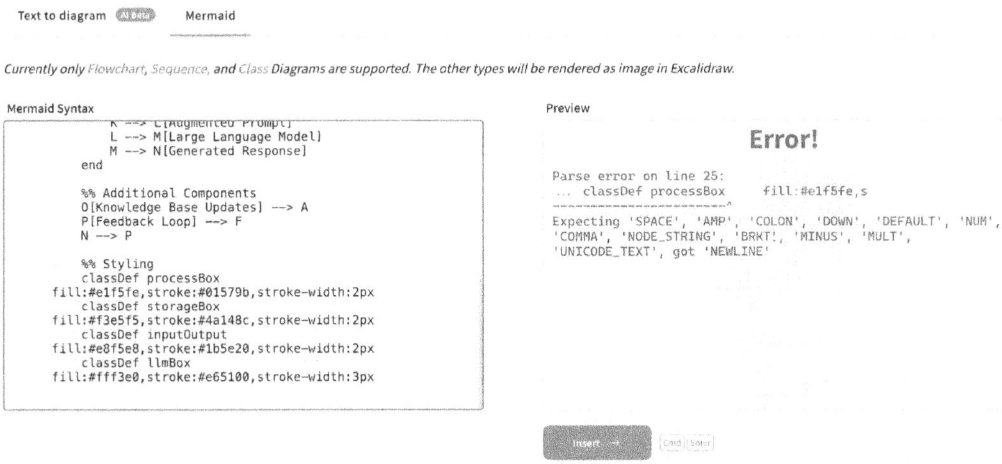

Figure 7.22 – Mermaid parsing error displayed in Excalidraw during diagram rendering

During rendering, a parsing error appears related to styling around a process box. To proceed, remove the styling. After doing so, the diagram will be rendered successfully.

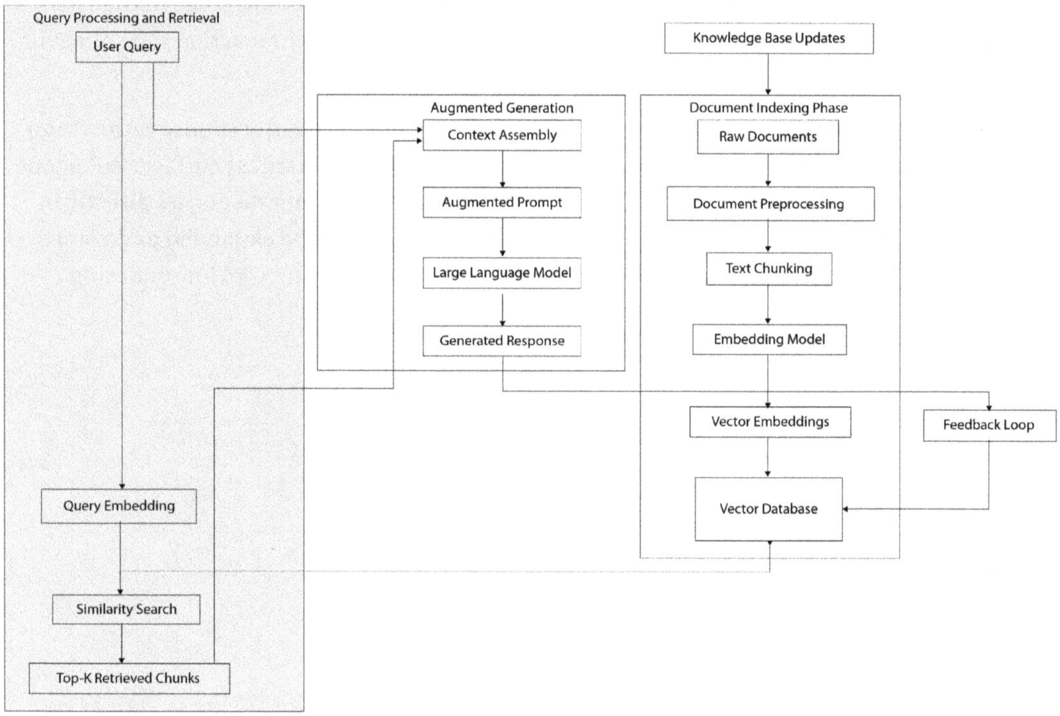

Figure 7.23 – Correctly rendered RAG architecture diagram after fixing Mermaid styling issues

The rendered diagram is significantly more organized than the previous version. Two distinct flows are visible: one represents the retrieval path, and the other represents the indexing path.

On the retrieval side, the flow shows the user query being embedded, followed by a similarity search against a vector store, retrieval of the top K documents, and prompt augmentation. The retrieved context is appended to the prompt before being sent to the language model. On the indexing side, the flow shows documents being loaded, preprocessed, chunked, embedded, and stored in a vector database.

Overall, this result is noticeably better. The diagram is simpler, more structured, and easier to understand at a glance.

With the updated configuration in place, the changes are committed to the repository. The commit includes the edited subagent definition and the modified files.

Once the commit is pushed, the updated configuration is available in the repository under the `subagents` branch.

Up to this point, we have examined the core mechanics of subagents: how they are created, how context flows between the main agent and a subagent, and how their behavior can be shaped through configuration and system prompts. We also explored how modifying either the description that influences the main agent or the internal instructions of the subagent directly affects execution and output.

All previous examples focused on a single subagent. The real strength of this approach, however, becomes clear when multiple subagents are spawned and run in parallel. By executing tasks concurrently, we can explore multiple implementations at once and scale our engineering workflow more effectively. In the next section, we move from single-agent delegation to coordinated parallel execution.

Scaling with concurrent subagents

> **Note**
>
> The implementation in this section is based on the Infinite Agentic Loop repository (`https://github.com/disler/infinite-agentic-loop`) by *IndieDevDan*. If you are curious about agentic coding patterns and multi-agent workflows, his work is worth exploring. He regularly shares practical insights on agentic development, and you can find more of his work at `agenticengineer.com`.

In this section, we will explore spawning multiple subagents that work concurrently to implement a feature. Each subagent produces its own implementation, and we then evaluate the different outputs and select the strongest version. This approach represents a model of software engineering in which multiple implementations are generated in parallel and assessed before integration.

> **Note**
>
> This approach can become expensive in terms of token usage. When multiple subagents are spawned, each runs independently and consumes tokens based on its own context and execution steps. Since each agent generates code, evaluates it, and may perform additional reasoning, overall token usage can increase significantly.
>
> I am intentionally not providing a cost estimate here. Pricing changes frequently, and token consumption varies widely depending on the size of the codebase, the number of agents, and the complexity of the task. When using this pattern, monitor usage carefully.

The implementation demonstrated in this section is based on the repository **Infinite Agentic Loop** (`https://github.com/disler/infinite-agentic-loop`), created by *IndieDevDan*. We will use it as the foundation for running concurrent subagents in this example. *IndieDevDan* is a YouTuber who produces content focused on agentic coding, and this repository serves as the foundation for running the concurrent subagents in this section. The repository and the related video discussion are referenced alongside this chapter.

Setting up the environment

We will continue working within the Project Hookhub project. The repository is cloned locally, and we navigate into the working directory.

```
git clone https://github.com/PacktPublishing/Agentic-Coding-with-Claude-Code
```

We then move into the Claude Code crash course directory and switch to the `project/hookhub` branch. From the commit list, we select the commit titled as follows:

```
Merge pull request #1 from emarco177/claude/add-anthropic-
footer-01NXAnJSjYR7cx3t5Ag9HzAE
```

This is the commit used for this section. We copy the commit hash and check it out:

```
git checkout -b project/hookhub<commit-hash>
```

We should get the following output:

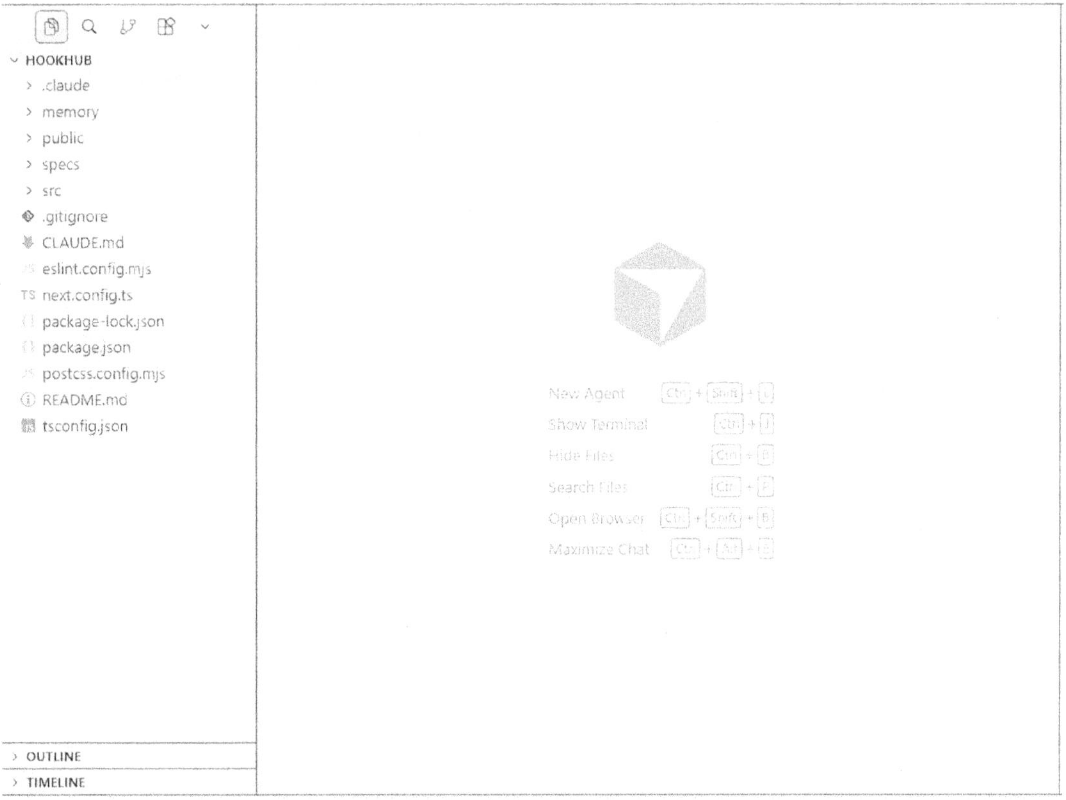

Figure 7.24 – HookHub project opened on the correct branch in Cursor

We can confirm that we are on the correct branch and navigate into the hookhub directory. The existing Next.js project opens.

Installing dependencies

With the Next.js project opened, we install the dependencies:

```
npm install
```

During installation, if there are any vulnerabilities detected, we fix them by running the following:

```
npm audit fix --force
```

Once all critical vulnerabilities are patched, we can then start the development server:

```
npm run dev
```

With this, the HookHub application using the Anthropic theme runs successfully. The environment is now ready:

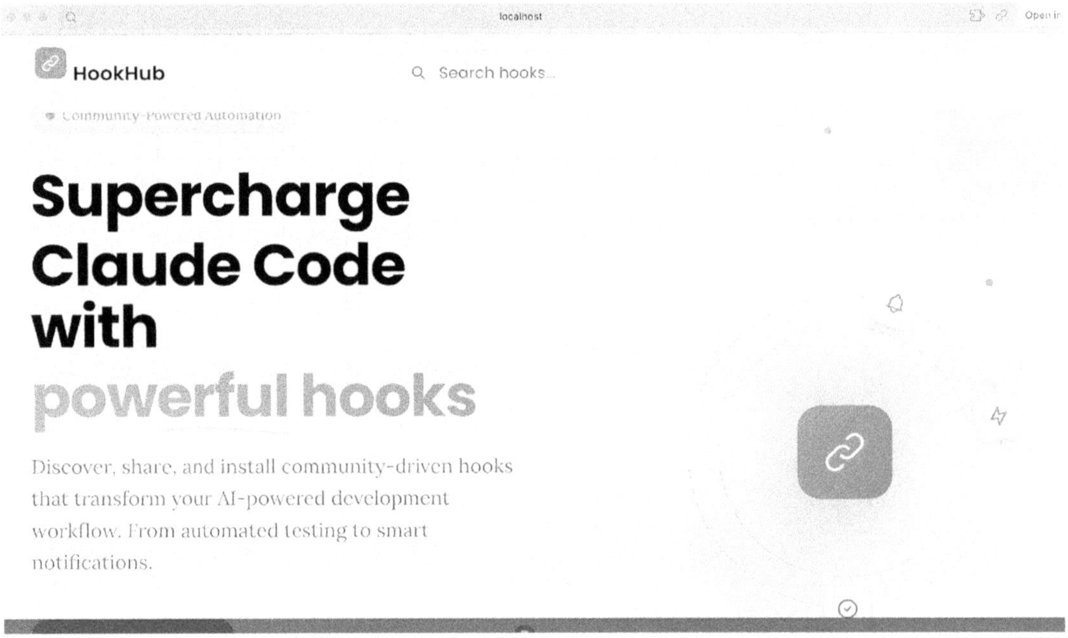

Figure 7.25 – HookHub application running successfully with the Anthropic theme

At this stage, the setup is complete and we can move on to orchestrating multiple agents in parallel.

The infinite slash command

Now, we focus on agent decoding. Inside the Infinite Agentic Loop repository, there is a slash command called `infinite`.

This command accepts three inputs:

- A spec file
- An output directory
- A number

It reads the spec file describing the feature we want to implement. It then spawns the specified number of agents. These agents work concurrently in parallel. Each agent produces its own artifact, and the artifacts are stored in the output directory.

This command can be run as a lean version for a small batch of agents. It is also architected to scale to a much larger number of agents, even approaching an infinite loop of concurrent executions.

In this section, we begin with the lean version.

For this example, we ask our subagents to implement different variations of the `Hero` component.

Reorganizing the hero component

We start by creating a new directory called `specs`. This directory is where we save all the spec files.

At this point, the application has a `components` directory with the footer and the hook card, but it does not have a dedicated `Hero` component. The `Hero` implementation currently exists in `page.ts`. Before creating the spec, we extract the `Hero` implementation from `page.ts` into the `components` directory to clean up and reorganize the repository. The following prompt is what I used:

```
Hi, can you please take the implementation from page.ts? There is a hero
implementation there.
I want to create a new component from it under the components directory, just to
organize the code a little bit.
```

The `Hero` implementation is extracted from `page.ts`, and a new `hero.tsx` file is created under the `components` directory. The import inside `page.tsx` is updated to reference this new component:

Figure 7.26 – Extracting the Hero section into a separate hero.tsx component

Next, we move `hero.tsx` into a dedicated `hero` directory under `components` with the help of the following prompt:

```
Can you please also move the hero.tsx file into a hero directory under components?
```

Don't forget to explicitly tag the file during this operation to ensure that the correct file is modified.

Once the move is completed, the original `Hero` implementation is removed from `page.ts`. The project structure now reflects a dedicated `Hero` component within its own directory.

We have now created a `heros` directory. The purpose of this directory is to store the output artifacts generated by multiple subagents. At this stage, the project structure is clean and ready for specification.

Generating the spec file from the Hero file

Next, request a spec file based on `hero.tsx`, using the following prompt:

```
> Can you please review the hero.tsx file and create from it a spec file
describing what this component should do, what its goals are, and specific
```

```
guidelines, because I'm going to implement different variations of this component.
@../src/components/heros/Hero.ts
```

The prompt includes the following:

- A review of `hero.tsx`
- A spec describing the component's purpose, goals, and guidelines
- Placement of the generated spec file inside the `specs` directory (explicitly tagged)

Claude will review the `Hero` implementation and generate the specification file

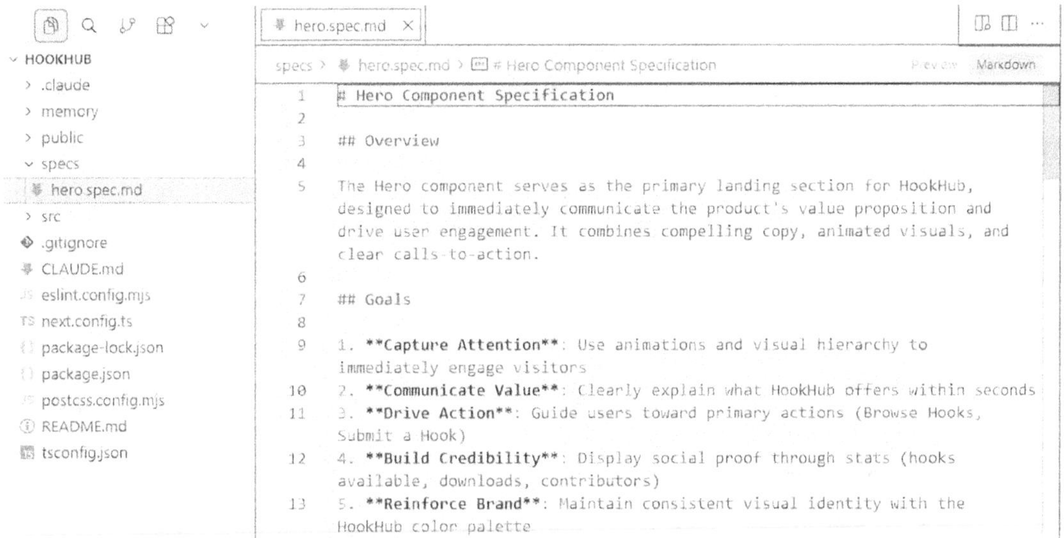

Figure 7.27 – Generated hero.spec.md file with the Hero component specification

A new file is created containing the full specification of the `Hero` component. The `Hero` component serves as the primary landing section for HookHub, designed to immediately communicate the product's value proposition, its goals, and its background layer.

Create a `.claude` directory locally. Because this is a fresh branch and Claude has not yet been initialized in this copy of the repository, the directory does not exist.

Inside this directory, add a `commands` folder. From the Infinite Agentic Loop repository, copy the `infinite.md` slash command into this folder.

This command is responsible for orchestrating the concurrent execution of multiple subagents.

At this stage, we do not analyze its internal implementation. The focus now shifts to using it in practice.

Running the infinite slash command

Exit Claude and start it again so the new slash command is loaded. Once Claude initializes, the `/infinite` command is available and ready to use.

According to the repository instructions, the command requires three inputs:

- A spec file: In our example, it is `hero.spec`
- An output directory: In our example, it is `heros`
- Count: In our example, we will use six agents

Execute command with these inputs, as follows:

```
>/infinite @../specs/hero.spec.md @../src/components/heros/
```

The main agent begins by reading the `spec` file. Once it is read successfully, the main agent now has the full context of what needs to be implemented. Claude Code will launch six parallel subagents to generate unique `Hero` variations. We will see tasks such as the following:

```
Strategy for 6 New Variations:
1. HeroMinimal - Clean, stripped-down version with minimal animations
2. HeroCentered - Center-aligned layout without side visual
3. HeroWaveform - Audio/wave-inspired animated background
4. HeroParticles - Particle system background with constellation effect
5. HeroTerminal - Developer-focused with terminal/code aesthetic
6. HeroGradientMesh - Modern gradient mesh background with morphing shapes
```

Figure 7.28 – Parallel subagent tasks generating multiple Hero component variations

The to-do list updates and the subagents begin running concurrently.

Again, this is on the pricier side of things. Each agent runs independently, generates its own code, and may test itself. If using an Anthropic API key instead of max mode, token usage should be monitored, as this workflow consumes a significant number of tokens.

Each subagent runs locally on the machine. If we were to increase the number of agents to something much larger, such as 100, the solution would need to scale across machines. This could be done using Claude's cloud offerings. As the agents begin finishing, they start writing output files into the `heros` directory.

> **Note**
>
> If file creation encounters an issue due to the local environment, Claude Code attempts recovery.

Once file creation is permitted, multiple hero files appear inside the `heros` directory. Eventually, all six versions are created.

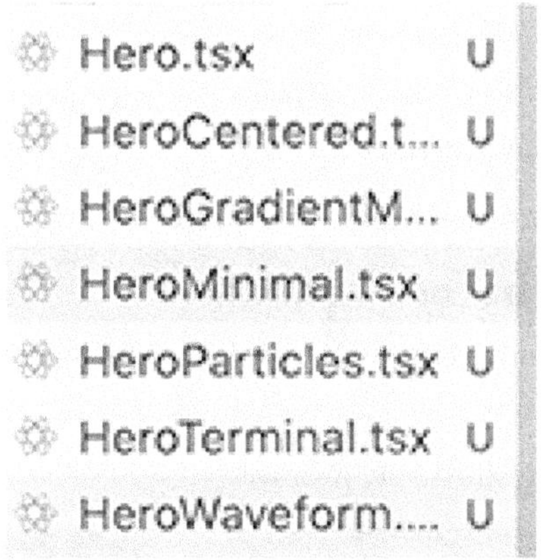

Figure 7.29 – Multiple generated Hero component files created in the heros directory

At this point, we have six distinct `Hero` implementations.

Now that all versions exist, we issue a new prompt:

```
Take all the hero implementations and show them on the main landing page one after
another so we can compare them and choose the best one.
```

This is a fresh prompt, separate from the slash command. It is important to remember that each subagent runs in its own isolated context. They are unaware of each other and start from a clean slate. This helps manage context efficiently.

The main page is updated to import each `Hero` variation and render them sequentially.

The expected change in `page.tsx` is as follows.

- Import all heroes from the heros directory
- Render them inside the page layout

Reviewing the diff confirms the following:

- The new imports are added
- Each hero is rendered in sequence

The application now displays the following `Hero` variations:

- Minimal
- Centered

- Waveform
- Particles
- Terminal
- Gradient mesh

Each version is visible on the landing page.

At this stage, we will use the terminal hero as the preferred implementation.

Cleaning the context before refinement

Before proceeding, we check the context window. It can be heavily bloated because of the previous operations.

We clear the context and then issue a new prompt:

```
Keep only the terminal hero in page.tsx.
Remove all other heroes from the main landing page.
Leave all hero files under the heroes directory untouched.
The page.tsx file and the heroes directory are tagged explicitly.
```

Since the context is now clean, the execution will run faster.

The main page is updated to render only the terminal hero. The other `Hero` components remain preserved inside the `heros` directory. The page is now simplified.

We now proceed to commit the changes by running the following:

```
git add
git status
```

We then request a commit message describing the following:

- The `Hero` change on the main page
- The addition of the slash command for running multiple subagents

This is the prompt we use:

```
Hi, can you please create a commit message about changing the hero in the main
page? And please add that we also added a slash command for running multiple
subagents.
```

Claude reviews the diffs and generates the commit message. The commit is created and pushed.

After refreshing the repository, the commit will appear with a message similar to the following: **Add hero component system and infinite agent slash command**.

What we have done so far

We used the `/infinite` slash command to spawn subagents in parallel. Each subagent implemented a variation independently. Once all variations were generated, we rendered them side by side, evaluated them visually, and selected the best implementation.

This approach allows us to scale via compute. The number of tokens we are willing to spend determines how much parallel exploration we can afford.

We have not yet examined how this works under the hood. This is addressed in the next section.

The Infinite Agentic Loop repository and the accompanying YouTube video by *IndieDevDan* provide a deeper look into the implementation of the slash command itself.

Infinite prompt

In this section, we will review the `infinite.md` file and the prompt that spawned all of those subagents. This prompt is a **high-order prompt**. It receives a prompt as input and generates prompts dynamically.

This can be thought of as **meta-prompting**, similar to high-order functions in functional programming, where functions receive functions as arguments and can return functions as return values. Here, we have the same thing with prompts. We see this in action in the Infinite Agentic Loop command.

The prompt begins with the following:

```
Think deeply about this infinite generation task. You are about to embark on a
sophisticated iterative creation process.
```

The `Think deeply` directive is intended to activate deeper reasoning in the model. This is a prompt sent to our main agent, the main Claude Code agent.

Under the `Variables` section, the prompt defines the following line:

```
spec_file: $ARGUMENTS output_dir: $ARGUMENTS count: $ARGUMENTS
```

This line declares three variables: `spec_file`, `output_dir`, and `count`. Each variable is temporarily assigned the `$ARGUMENTS` placeholder.

When the `/infinite` slash command is invoked, the entire argument string is passed into the prompt as `$ARGUMENTS`. The values provided when running the slash command are placed into the same line, resulting in duplicate values appearing multiple times. These duplicates are the same input that was provided to the slash command.

The prompt includes the part responsible for parsing. The entire prompt, including its arguments when the slash command is invoked, is sent to Claude Code's main agent. The prompt contains instructions for the main agent on how to parse the input.

The parsing defines the following:

- `spec_file`: The path to the Markdown specification file
- `output_dir`: The directory where iterations will be saved
- `count`: The number of iterations, `1` until `N` or "infinite"

All parsing is done by the main agent. There is no code responsible for parsing. Parsing happens dynamically by the LLM every time the command is invoked.

With the variables defined and parsed, execution proceeds through several phases.

Phase 1: Specification analysis

Phase 1 is specification analysis. The main agent is instructed to read and deeply understand the specification file at `spec_file`. The parsed path to the `spec` file is used here.

The `spec` file defines the following:

- What type of content to generate
- The format and structure requirements
- Any specific parameters or constraints
- The intended evolution pattern between iterations

The prompt instructs the main agent to think carefully about the spec intent and how each iteration should build upon previous work.

In the example shown earlier, there was no iteration or evolution of previous work because it was not written into the `spec` file. If we want to do this, the prompt supports it.

This is the first instruction to the main agent: read the `spec` file and understand what we want to do.

Phase 2: Output directory reconnaissance

Phase 2 is output directory reconnaissance. The main agent is instructed to thoroughly analyze `output_dir` to understand the current state.

This phase includes the following:

- Listing all existing files and their naming patterns
- Identifying the highest iteration number currently present
- Analyzing the content evolution across existing iterations
- Understanding the trajectory of previous generations
- Determining what gaps or opportunities exist for new iterations

In the earlier example, there were no iteration numbers. We had the names of the styles we wanted to use.

This phase instructs the main agent to check what work has already been done.

Phase 3: Iteration strategy

Phase 3 is iteration strategy. Based on the spec analysis and existing iterations, the main agent is instructed to do the following:

- Determine the starting iteration number or the name of the file to create
- Plan how each iteration will be unique and evolutionary
- Consider how to build upon previous iterations while maintaining novelty
- If `count` is infinite, prepare for continuous generation until context limits are reached

This phase is still in planning.

Phase 4: Parallel agent coordination

Phase 4 moves into the parallel execution of subagents. The main agent is instructed to deploy multiple subagents to generate iterations in parallel for maximum efficiency and creative diversity.

The distribution strategy is defined as follows:

- For counts of 1–5, launch all agents simultaneously
- For counts of 6–20, launch batches of 5 agents to manage coordination
- For a count of "infinite," launch waves of three to five agents, monitoring context and spawning new waves

Agent assignment protocol

The main agent uses Claude Code's task tool to spawn subagents. The prompt describes how the main agent should create the prompt that goes inside these subagents.

The input to each subagent is one prompt. The subagent runs in context isolation and outputs one message to the main agent.

Each subagent receives the following:

- **Spec context**: Complete specification file analysis
- **Directory snapshot**: Current state of `output_dir` at launch time
- **Iteration assignment**: Specific iteration number, starting number, plus agent index
- **Uniqueness directive**: Explicit instruction to avoid duplicating concepts from existing iterations
- **Quality standards**: Detailed requirements from the specifications

Since we provide directory snapshot as input, subagents will be aware of what has happened so far. This helps avoid duplicate ideas and duplicate implementations.

In the earlier example, we did not have iteration numbers, so iteration assignment mapped to the filenames we used.

Subagent task structure

The prompt includes the structure of the task passed to each subagent.

The task is framed as follows:

- `generate iteration [NUMBER] for [SPEC_FILE] in [OUTPUT_DIR]`
- `you are subagent [X] generating iteration [NUMBER]`

Each subagent prompt includes context like the following:

- Specification (full spec analysis)
- Existing iterations (summary of current `output_dir` contents)
- Your iteration number
- Assigned creative direction
- Requirements

The prompt includes instructions such as the following:

- `read and understand the specification completely`
- `analyze existing iterations to ensure the output is unique`

There are additional instructions included in the subagent prompt.

Parallel execution management

The prompt then returns to execution management instructions for the main agent.

The main agent is instructed to do the following:

- Launch all assigned subagents simultaneously using the task tool

- Monitor agent progress and completion
- Handle agent failures by reassigning iteration numbers
- Ensure that no duplicate iteration numbers are generated
- Collect and validate all completed iterations

This is the main part of the high-order prompt. It receives a prompt as input and outputs many prompts, because each subagent receives a different prompt.

One single prompt creates a lot of prompts. The command also includes instructions for running infinitely, along with context optimization and execution principles. This provides more context to the main agent.

This prompt is a high-level prompt.

Thinking about prompts that receive prompts as input and generate prompts as output is quite innovative. For me, it was mind-blowing reading this. Kudos to *IndieDevJam* for thinking about this direction.

I believe agentic coding and software engineering are going toward those kinds of prompts, because this is a meta prompt that does almost everything.

Summary

In this chapter, we worked through the concept of Claude Code subagents from the ground up. We first understood what subagents are and why context isolation is such an important design decision. Instead of letting the main conversation grow endlessly and become polluted, we saw how subagents run in their own context window and return a single condensed result. This gives us control over token usage and helps maintain performance as projects grow.

We then configured our own subagents, explored how descriptions influence invocation, and saw how system prompts and tool selection directly affect behavior. Through hands-on examples, we manipulated the prompt that the main agent sends to a subagent and adjusted the internal logic of the subagent itself. Finally, we scaled execution using the Infinite Agentic Loop pattern, where one high-order prompt dynamically generates multiple subagent prompts and runs them in parallel. By this point, we should clearly understand how context flows between agents, how subagents are orchestrated, and how this approach can be used to scale engineering effort in a structured and controlled way.

In the next chapter, we will see how output styles shape Claude Code's responses, as well as how to create and scope custom styles, use structured formats such as YAML, and automate behavior within style definitions.

Get this book's PDF copy, code bundle, and more

Scan the QR code (or go to `packtpub.com/unlock`). Search for this book by name, confirm the edition, and then follow the steps on the page.

UNLOCK NOW

Note: Have your invoice handy. Purchases made directly from the Packt website don't require an invoice.

8

Creating and Customizing Output Styles

Output styles are one of the most powerful and underrated features in Claude Code. They define how responses are structured and delivered, effectively shaping the communication protocol between the user and the model.

In this chapter, we will examine how output styles shape the way Claude Code communicates. You will learn how to create custom output styles, scope them at the user or project level, and modify how responses are structured. We will also explore how output styles interact with the system prompt, how structured formats such as YAML change reasoning patterns, and how to automate workflows directly within a style definition.

By the end of this chapter, you will understand how to engineer Claude Code's interaction model rather than simply consume its output. You will be able to design specialized configurations, run parallel sessions with different roles, version your setup, and extend the interface using custom status lines.

In this chapter, we will cover the following topics:

- Creating a custom output style with Claude Code
- Creating an advanced project-level output style
- Customizing the status line in Claude Code
- Advanced status line: displaying the last user prompt
- The future of AI coding: A team of specialized agents

> **Note**
>
> The built-in output styles available in Claude Code may evolve over time. Depending on your installed version, you may see additional styles beyond those shown in this chapter.

Creating a custom output style with Claude Code

When listing available output styles using `/output-style`, Claude Code displays the currently active style along with any built-in styles.

By default, the system includes the following:

- **Default**
- **Explanatory**
- **Learning**

The following figure shows the output style selection interface in the Claude Code CLI. The currently active style is highlighted and the built-in styles are listed beneath it.

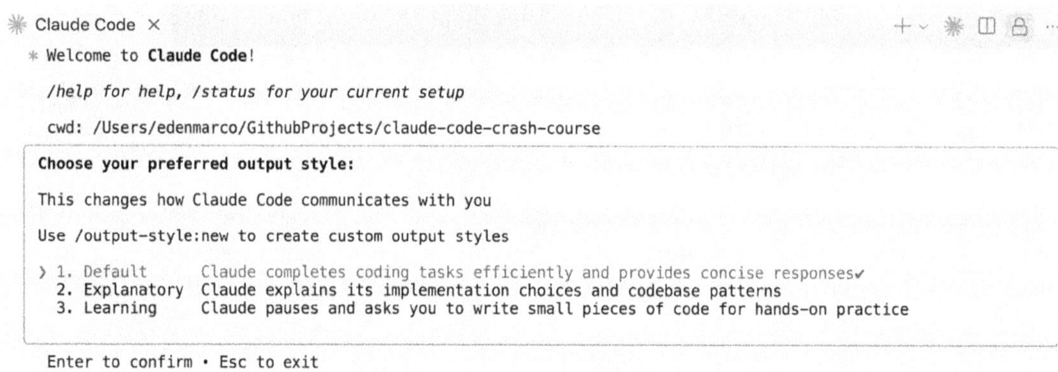

Figure 8.1 – Claude Code CLI output style selection interface

As shown in the figure, the CLI presents the available styles and indicates which one is active. The Explanatory and Learning styles are prebuilt by the Anthropic team. Instead of using these predefined styles, you can create custom output styles.

Creating and reviewing a new output style

To create a user-scoped output style, create a Markdown file in:

```
~/.claude/output-styles/
```

For a project-scoped output style, create it in:

```
.claude/output-styles/
```

The file uses YAML front matter followed by Markdown content, similar to how subagents are defined. The following example shows a file located at `~/.claude/output-styles/minimal-bullets.md`:

```
---
description: Concise bullet-point responses with direct communication
---

# Communication Style
- Use bullet points for all responses
- Be direct and to the point
- No unnecessary language or filler

# Response Format
- Lead with the answer
- Use nested bullets for hierarchy
- Skip preamble and transitions

# Tone
- Professional and concise
- No hedging or qualifications
```

The file includes the following:

- A description defining it as a concise bullet-point response with direct communication and no unnecessary language
- Expanded sections elaborating on communication style
- Response format guidelines
- Tone guidelines

Once the style is generated, Claude Code writes this definition to disk. The following figure shows the generated minimal-bullets definition as it is written to disk. After selecting the `minimal-bullets` style, it becomes the currently active output style. When viewing the list of available output styles, the selected style is indicated accordingly.

```
Choose your preferred output style:

This changes how Claude Code communicates with you

Use /output-style:new to create custom output styles

> 1. Default           Claude completes coding tasks efficiently and provides concise responses
  2. Explanatory       Claude explains its implementation choices and codebase patterns
  3. Learning          Claude pauses and asks you to write small pieces of code for hands-on practice
  4. minimal-bullets   Concise bullet-point responses with direct, no-fluff communication✓
```

Figure 8.2 – Minimal-bullets style selected

An example output style produces responses formatted with bullet points, with a direct, concise structure and no filler.

```
Claude Code ×

> answer in bullet points, keep it concise and to the point. no fluff

● output-style-setup(Create concise bullet point style)
  ⎿ Done (5 tool uses · 18.3k tokens · 41.7s)

● • Created "minimal-bullets" output style
  • Located at: /Users/edenmarco/.claude/output-styles/minimal-bullets.md
  • Features: bullet points only, direct communication, no fluff
  • Ready for use in Claude Code

> /output-style
  ⎿ Set output style to minimal-bullets

> /output-style
  ⎿ Kept output style as minimal-bullets

> what are output styles?

● • Custom response formats for Claude Code
  • Control how Claude communicates and structures answers
  • Located in ~/.claude/output-styles/
  • Modify system prompts to change behavior
  • Examples: concise vs detailed, formal vs casual, bullet points vs paragraphs
  • Switch between styles using /output-style command
  • Create new ones with /output-style:new
```

Figure 8.3 – Claude responding using the minimal-bullets output style

Once a style is selected, Claude Code applies its instructions to subsequent requests.

How output styles work

Selecting an output style replaces parts of Claude Code's system prompt with style-specific custom instructions. Claude Code removes its default software engineering instructions and substitutes them with the selected style's instructions.

The core capabilities of Claude Code, including file operations and script execution for tracking, remain available regardless of the output style selected.

The modified system prompt is sent directly to the LLM with each request made through Claude Code. It is therefore the same underlying model operating under a different system prompt.

When switching styles using the `/command` for output styles, Claude Code updates its internal system prompt template and applies the updated template to subsequent LLM calls.

A project-scoped output style applies only within a specific project.

Let's create a new output style that can be defined to format responses as YAML.

Why YAML

Using YAML as an output style transforms communication from explicit instructions to implicit semantic structure, where the format itself conveys meaning.

In a YAML output, the format itself becomes a rich communication protocol in which indentation, key selection, ordering, and structural decisions carry meaning. Because YAML supports hierarchy, it maps naturally to complex coding tasks.

Dependencies are expressed as parent–child relationships. Priority can be inferred from ordering. Scope is represented through nesting levels. Instead of listing sequential steps, a nested YAML structure encodes the logical architecture of the problem space. To make this more concrete, consider how a real task might be structured.

The following example is the actual output returned by Claude Code when the YAML output style is active.

```
Task: "Fix authentication bug"
Priority: "Urgent high"
Complexity: "Medium"

approach:
  investigate:
    auth_flow: &flow
      - login_endpoint
```

```
      - token_validation
      - session_middleware
    debugging:
      logs: "./auth.log"
      reproduce: "invalid_token_scenario"

fix:
  dependencies: [*flow]
  files_to_modify:
    auth.js:
      scope: "token refresh logic"
      risk: "low"
    middleware.js:
      scope: "validation checks"
      risk: "urgent"

verify:
  tests: ["auth_integration", "token_expiry"]
  manual_check: "login flow end-to-end"

metadata:
  estimated_time: "2 hours"
  rollback_plan: "revert commits"
  monitoring: "error_rate_dashboard"
```

Let's break down this structure:

- The `task` definition establishes context
- The `approach` section captures investigative paths and debugging artifacts
- The `fix` section encodes dependencies and file-level scope
- The `verify` section defines validation mechanisms
- The `metadata` section captures operational considerations

```yaml
Task: "Fix authentication bug"
Priority: "Urgent high"
Complexity: "Medium"

approach:
  investigate:
    auth_flow: &flow
      - login_endpoint
      - token_validation
      - session_middleware
    debugging:
      logs: "./auth.log"
      reproduce: "invalid_token_scenario"

fix:
  dependencies: [*flow]
  files_to_modify:
    auth.js:
      scope: "token refresh logic"
      risk: "low"
    middleware.js:
      scope: "validation checks"
      risk: "urgent"

verify:
  tests: ["auth_integration", "token_expiry"]
  manual_check: "login flow end-to-end"

metadata:
  estimated_time: "2 hours"
  rollback_plan: "revert commits"
  monitoring: "error_rate_dashboard"
```

Figure 8.4 – Claude generating a structured task plan in YAML format

YAML encourages thinking in terms of relationships and dependencies rather than sequential steps. Its hierarchical structure shifts the focus from ordered instructions to interconnected components.

When Claude Code outputs a task as a nested YAML structure, it does not produce a simple to-do list. Instead, it encodes the logical architecture of the problem space within the structure itself. Relationships, scope, and dependencies are expressed through nesting and key organization.

Figure 8.5 – Human–AI collaboration enabled through customizable output styles

Output styles remove the constraint of a single, fixed interaction model. They allow the communication protocol itself to be designed and adjusted. This reflects the essence of agentic coding: actively shaping how the AI expresses information and collaborates within a development workflow.

Control over interaction is therefore not limited to model providers improving model capabilities. Developers, as users of large language models, define and control the communication protocol through output styles.

Creating YAML as an output style

A project-level output style can be configured to produce concise YAML responses without additional verbosity. When defined at the project scope, the configuration applies only within that project.

To create this style, create a file at `.claude/output-styles/yaml-concise.md` in the project directory:

```
---
description: Concise YAML-formatted responses for structured communication
---

# Response Format
- All responses must be formatted as valid YAML
- Use hierarchy and nesting to express relationships
- Keep values concise — no full sentences unless necessary

# Structure
- Use top-level keys to represent major sections
- Nest subconcepts under their parent context
- Use lists for enumerations and sequences
- Use key-value pairs for properties and attributes

# Tone
- No prose, no filler, no transitional language
- Let the YAML structure carry the meaning
- Prefer short string values over paragraphs
```

After creating the file, the `yaml-concise` style appears in the list of available output styles when running `/output-style`. A new directory is also created under the project's `.claude` folder. Inside it, a YAML configuration file is generated that represents the newly defined project-scoped output style. Select it to activate the style for the current session.

With the YAML style active, issue a query such as:

```
What are Claude Code output styles? Give me an elaborate answer.
```

The response is returned as structured YAML rather than paragraphs or bullet points. The hierarchy, keys, and indentation encode the structure of the explanation.

Here's a representative example:

```
definition:
  what: "Custom response formats for Claude Code CLI"
  purpose:
    - "Control communication style and structure"
```

```
    - "Support global or project-level configuration"

location:
  global: "~/.claude/output-styles/"
  project: "./.claude/output-styles/"
  precedence: "Project overrides global"

file_structure:
  format: "Markdown with YAML frontmatter"
  frontmatter:
    description: "Brief style explanation"
    content: "System prompt modifications"

functionality:
  controls:
    - "Response formatting (bullets, YAML, prose)"
    - "Communication tone (formal, casual, technical)"
    - "Information density (concise, detailed)"
    - "Task approach (speed vs thoroughness)"
    - "Workflow behaviors"
```

The output structure reflects conceptual grouping rather than a linear explanation.

The response format emphasizes the following relationships:

- Sections become top-level keys
- Subconcepts are nested under their parent context
- Configuration scope and precedence are structurally encoded
- Behavioral controls are grouped under a shared functional category

This approach mirrors how YAML is used in configuration systems such as Kubernetes and Docker Compose. The structure remains readable while preserving the semantic hierarchy.

By activating the project-level YAML concise style, responses are consistently returned in this structured format, reinforcing architectural thinking rather than sequential narration.

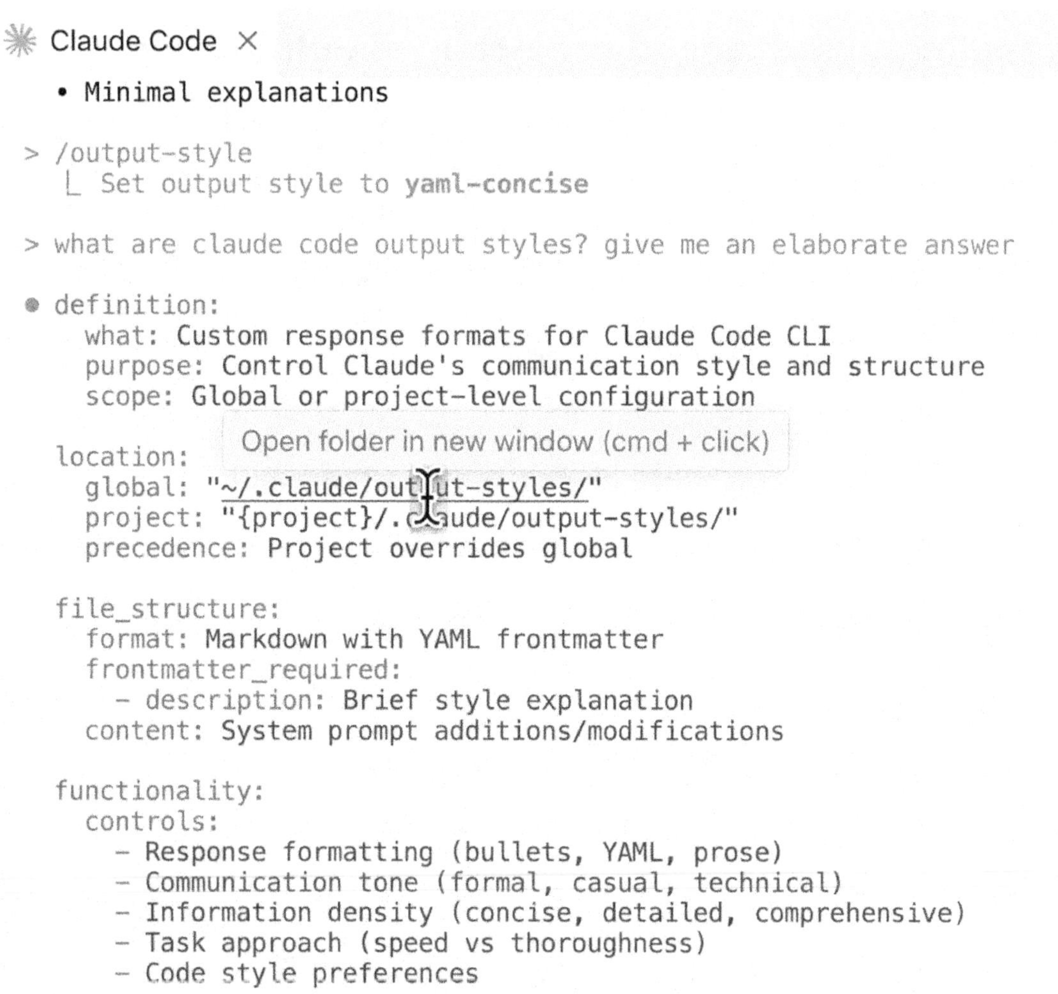

Figure 8.6 – YAML-concise output style applied in Claude Code

In this section, you learned how to define and generate a custom output style, how the `output-style-setup` sub-agent augments your prompt, and how styles are stored at either the user or project scope. This establishes that output styles are not superficial formatting options but structured configuration files that directly shape Claude Code's behavior. Understanding how to create and scope output styles provides the foundation for extending them further. In the next section, we build on this by creating a more advanced project-level output style and embedding more structured behavior into it.

Creating an advanced project-level output style

This section defines a new output style at the project level and extends it with automated file-generation behavior. The objective is to generate HTML-formatted responses structured as an ASCII-styled blog page and to integrate that behavior directly into the output style definition.

Defining a custom HTML output style

Let's create and review the output style configuration file. A complete example of this configuration is available in the repository. To access the repository link, follow the steps in the *Download the example code files* section in the *Preface*.

Create a new project-level output style file under:

```
.claude/output-styles/retro-ASCII_blog.md
```

The intention of this style is to generate HTML output formatted as an ASCII-style blog page.

The output style controls how responses are formatted and can also embed workflow rules.

The content of the output style is:

```
---
description: Format responses as retro HTML pages with ASCII art styling like a
vintage blog
---
Format all responses as complete HTML pages with retro ASCII art blog styling.
Follow these guidelines:
HTML Structure
Always provide complete HTML5 documents with proper DOCTYPE, head, and body tags
Use semantic HTML elements (header, main, section, article, aside, footer)
Include a proper HTML title that reflects the content
ASCII Art Styling
Use ASCII art for headers, dividers, and decorative elements
Create borders using characters like =, ║, ╔, ╗, ╚, ╝, -, |, +, *, #
Add ASCII art banners for section headers
Use monospace fonts throughout for consistent ASCII alignment
Include decorative ASCII elements like stars, lines, and boxes
CSS Requirements
Embed CSS in <style> tags in the HTML head
Use monospace fonts (Courier New, Monaco, Consolas, monospace)
Set background to dark colors (#1a1a1a, #2d2d2d) with light text
Use retro color schemes (green on black, amber on black, etc.)
```

```
Style ASCII art elements with appropriate spacing and alignment
Add subtle glow effects or text shadows for retro terminal feel
Content Structure
Format content like a blog post with clear sections
Use ASCII art dividers between sections
Create ASCII art headers for major topics
Include a decorative ASCII footer
Structure technical information in readable blocks
Add ASCII navigation or menu elements when appropriate
Example Elements to Include:
ASCII art title banners
Decorative borders around code blocks
ASCII bullet points and lists
Retro-style ASCII progress bars or indicators
Terminal-style prompts and outputs
ASCII art logos or emblems
Remember to maintain readability while embracing the retro ASCII aesthetic. The
content should feel like browsing a vintage bulletin board system or early web
blog.
```

This output style goes beyond simple terminal formatting. Rather than producing bullet points or YAML, Claude Code generates complete HTML documents styled as retro ASCII art blog pages.

The instructions are organized into the following sections:

- The HTML structure defines complete HTML5 documents with semantic elements
- ASCII art styling establishes visual identity through box drawing characters and monospaced fonts to maintain consistent alignment
- CSS requirements define the retro terminal aesthetic with dark backgrounds, green-on-black or amber-on-black color schemes, and subtle glow effects

Content is organized as blog posts with ASCII art dividers, banners, and decorative footers.

The entire behavior is defined in a single Markdown file with no code or plugins required. Once the style is selected and a prompt is issued, Claude Code generates the HTML page, writes it to disk, and opens it in the browser.

Using the HTML output style

With `retro-ASCII_blog.md` selected as the active output style, the following prompt is issued.

- What are output styles? Provide an elaborate answer.
- Show me which output styles I have right now.

The response is generated as HTML. The content is valid HTML markup and is rendered directly in the terminal. Because it is emitted as markup, it is not easily readable in this context.

At this stage, the HTML has not been written to a file that can be opened in a browser. The output exists only as generated markup.

To make the result usable, Claude Code is instructed to dump the generated HTML into a file. A file named `output-styles-guide.HTML` is created.

When opened in a browser, it renders as a blog-style page displaying an explanation of output styles.

Figure 8.7 – Generated HTML page documenting Claude Code output styles

The rendered page displays the configured output styles and demonstrates that the structure and formatting are fully customizable. The HTML is not intended to be visually refined; its purpose is to illustrate that there is complete freedom over what can be generated.

The output style is not limited to static pages. It could be extended to write pages into a larger application, such as a Next.js project, with each Claude-generated response producing a new page within that application. The structure and behavior of the output are defined entirely by the configuration, and there are no inherent limitations imposed by predefined templates.

Automating file generation

We now embed workflow logic directly into the output style definition. Prompting Claude Code to write HTML into a file each time is repetitive. Instead of issuing this instruction with every prompt, the behavior is embedded directly into the output style definition.

The `retro-ASCII_blog.md` file is updated to include workflow instructions with the following snippet:

```
Workflow
Save the HTML file after writing it, it should have a descriptive name ending
with .html
OPEN the generated file in the deault web browser.
```

The output style can also encode workflow behavior, allowing Claude Code to automatically save generated HTML files and open them in the browser.

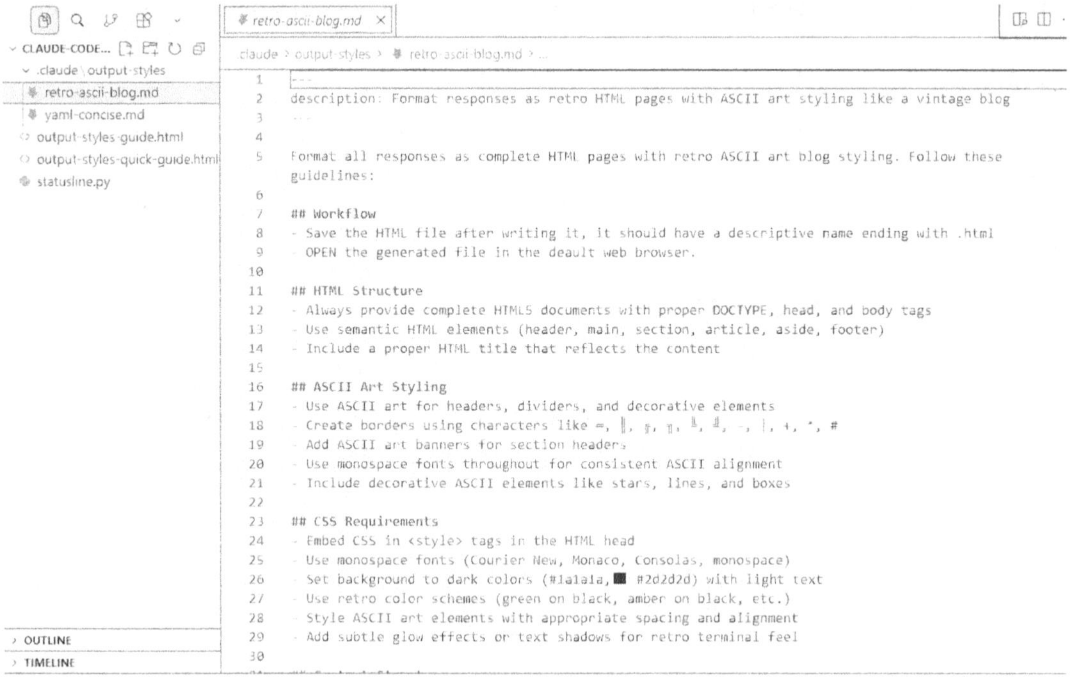

Figure 8.8 – Output style workflow instructions

No complex logic is introduced. The prompt remains minimal. Claude Code performs the required file generation steps based on these instructions.

After saving the updated output style, issue a prompt such as the following:

```
What are output styles?
```

This results in the automatic creation of a file named `output-styles-quick-guide.html`. The system requests confirmation to open the file in the default browser, and once approved, the rendered HTML is visible immediately.

The workflow is now embedded in the output style itself. Each response generated under this style is automatically written to a browser-ready HTML file.

Working with multiple output styles

Running a single output style demonstrates how formatting can be customized for a specific purpose. This configuration can be extended by running multiple Claude Code instances simultaneously, each configured with a different output style. The following sections illustrate how separate sessions can operate in parallel and how this enables task-specific formatting within the same repository.

Launching a new Claude Code instance

A new terminal instance is opened within the repository, and Claude Code is started. This creates a fresh session with no output style yet selected.

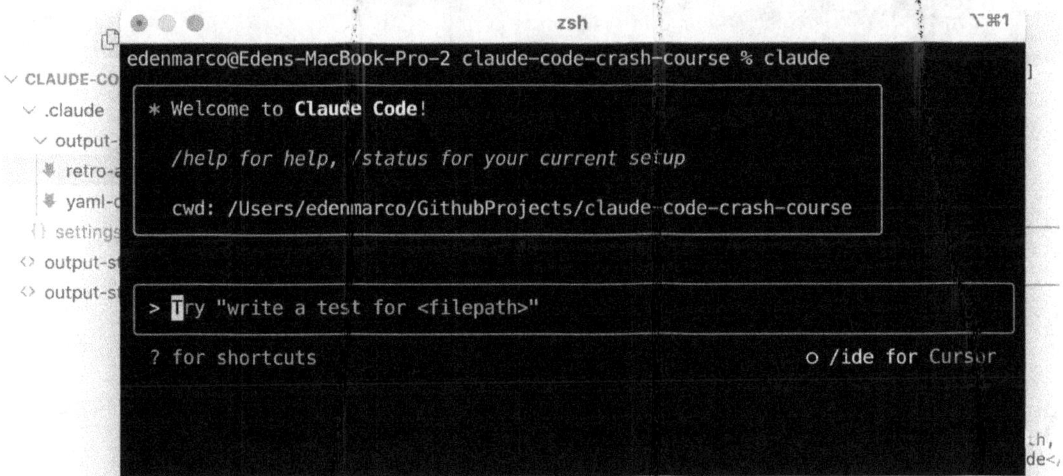

Figure 8.9 – Launching a new Claude Code session

An output style is then selected from the available options. In this instance, the minimal bullet output style is chosen.

The session is now configured to generate responses using the minimal bullet format.

Opening a second instance with a different output style

A second terminal instance is opened within the same repository. Claude Code is started again in this new session.

In this instance, a different output style is selected—the YAML concise output style.

At this point, two Claude Code instances are running simultaneously:

- One configured with minimal bullets
- One configured with YAML concise output

Each instance maintains its own active output style.

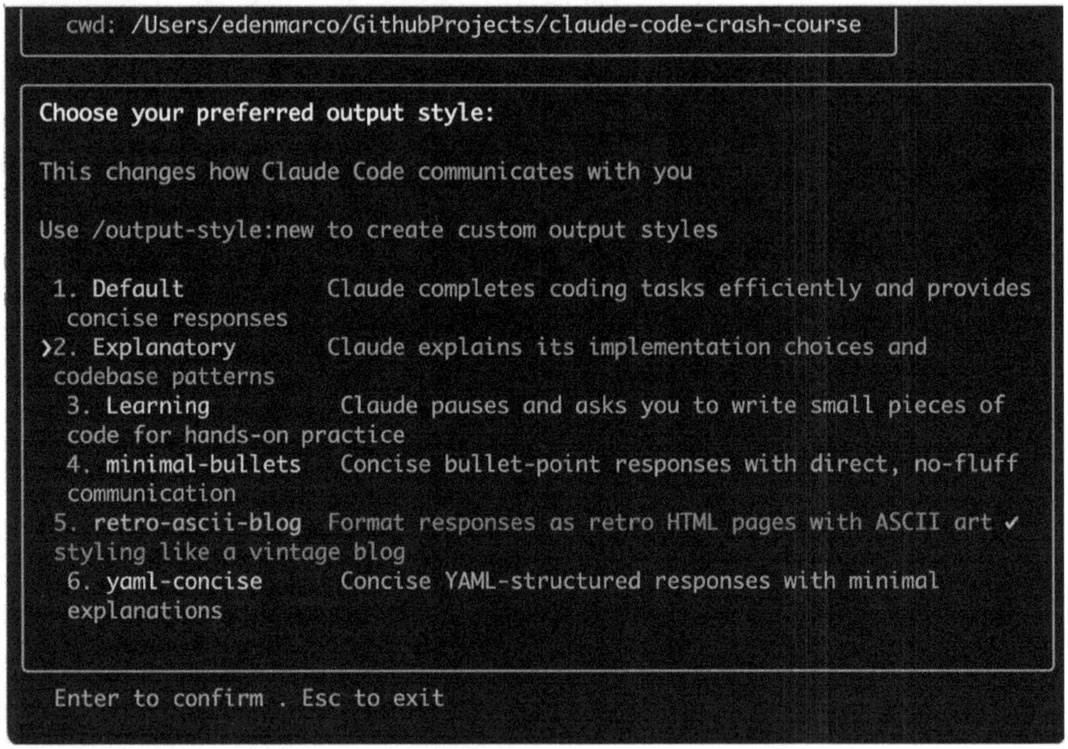

Figure 8.10 – Selecting the YAML-concise output style

Parallel output styles in practice

With both instances running side by side, responses generated in each terminal reflect the selected configuration. The formatting differs according to the active output style.

This establishes a workflow in which multiple Claude Code sessions operate in parallel, each optimized for a specific output format.

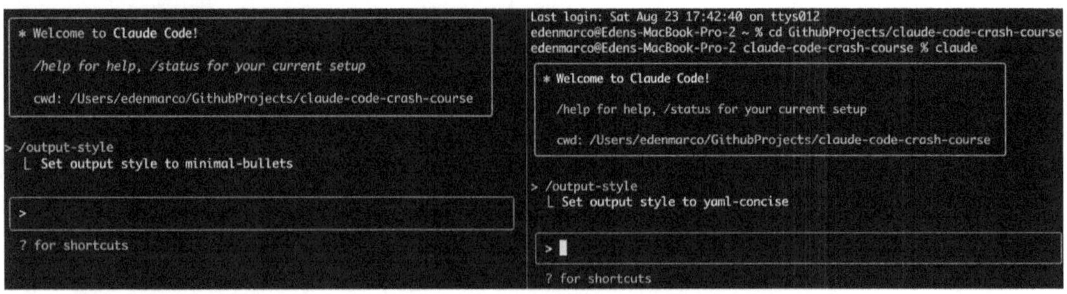

Figure 8.11 – Two Claude Code sessions using different output styles

Specialized output style workflows

With both instances visible, each session clearly maintains its own formatting behavior. Instead of using a single monolithic environment, each Claude Code session becomes a dedicated AI assistant configured for a specific task.

A review-focused session can emphasize code differences, security vulnerabilities, and architectural concerns. An explain-focused session can optimize for educational insights or documentation generation. A debug-focused session can concentrate on error analysis and troubleshooting, with its output aligned accordingly.

Each output style tailors the AI's cognitive focus to the task at hand.

When switching between terminal windows, it is not immediately clear which output style is currently active. The interface does not prominently display this information.

This limitation becomes noticeable when working across multiple sessions. It can be addressed using custom status lines, which allow clearer identification of the active configuration.

With the configuration validated and working as intended, the changes are committed to version control.

Here, you extended the basic output style mechanism by defining a project-scoped configuration and integrating more advanced formatting and behavioral logic. You saw how output styles can move beyond simple response formatting into structured outputs such as HTML and automated workflow behaviors. This demonstrates that output styles can influence not only how responses look but also how they are operationalized. With this foundation in place, the next section shifts from output formatting to runtime interface customization by modifying the Claude Code status line.

Customizing the status line in Claude Code

Status lines let you run any scripts that receive Claude Code's session data (model, context usage, costs, git info) as JSON via `stdin` and print whatever you want persistently at the bottom of the terminal. You configure them in `~/.claude/settings.json` by pointing the `statusLine` key to your script — or use the `/statusline` slash command with a natural-language description to have one generated automatically.

This section reviews how to configure and implement a custom status line in Claude Code using a dedicated command and a Python-based implementation.

Defining a custom status line command

A new slash command, `/statusline`, is defined. The command includes a description specifying that the status line should display the current active output style. The following prompt is provided to define the command:

```
/statusline I want you to create a statusline that displays the current used
output-style.
You should implement it in python and run it through uv
```

Two implementation requirements are specified:

- The status line must be implemented in Python
- It must be executed using the UV package manager

Status lines in Claude Code can execute shell commands, shell scripts, Python files, and Node.js files. They can run arbitrary executable logic. Python is selected for the implementation based on familiarity and preference.

Initializing the status line setup

When the `/statusline` command is executed, Claude Code initializes and spawns a sub-agent, which is responsible for assisting with the creation of the status line.

The first action performed by the sub-agent is to search for an existing status line configuration in the home directory:

```
~/.claude/settings.json
```

The file is inspected for an existing `statusline` entry. Since no such entry is present, the configuration file is updated.

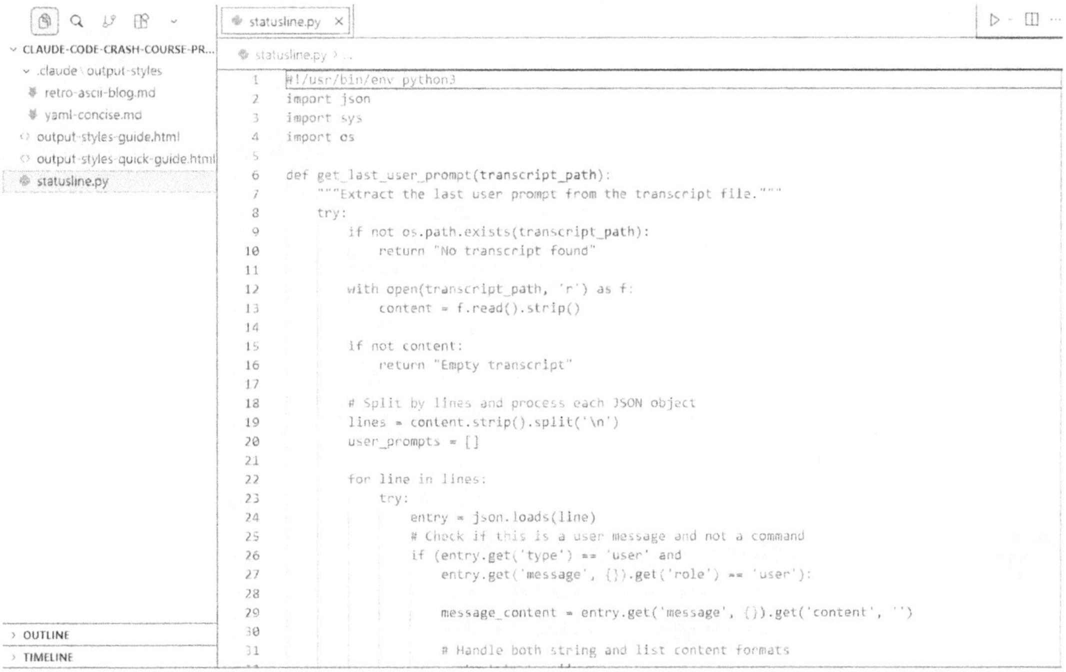

Figure 8.12 – Implementing a custom statusline script

Updating the configuration

The `settings.json` file defines the default model, which in this case is set to `sonnet`. The configuration is then extended with a new `statusline` entry.

A representative configuration appears as follows:

```
{
  "model": "sonnet",
  "statusline": {
    "type": "command",
    "command": "uv run ~/.claude/statusline.py"
  }
}
```

The type is set to `command`, and the configured command runs the `statusline.py` script using the uv package manager.

By default, the script is created in the home directory.

```
~/.claude/statusline.py
```

The script can be stored in any location, provided that the configuration specifies the correct execution path.

Implementing the status line logic

The `statusline.py` file contains the logic that determines what is displayed in the custom status line.

Claude Code provides runtime information to the script via standard input (`stdin`). The script reads this input and processes it as JSON. The data is loaded into a dictionary using `json.load`, giving access to all information provided by Claude Code.

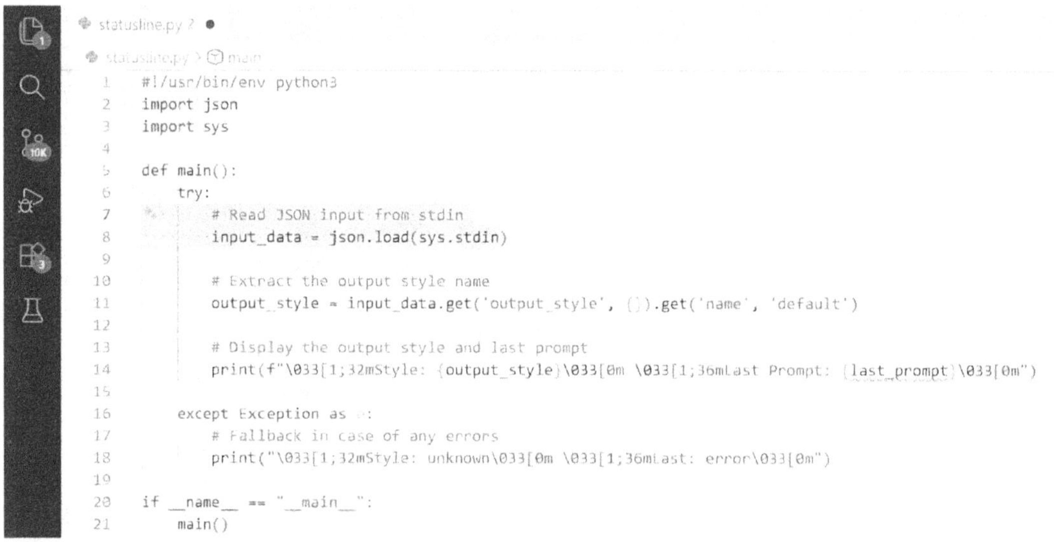

Figure 8.13 – Statusline script reading JSON input from Claude Code

A minimal implementation appears as follows:

```
import json
import sys

input_data = json.load(sys.stdin)
style = input_data.get("output_style", "default")

print(style)
```

Among the available keys is `output_style`. The script extracts the name of the currently active output style from this key. If no output style is defined, the script defaults to displaying `"default"` as the output style.

The script writes its result to standard output (`stdout`). Claude Code reads whatever the script prints to `stdout` and displays it in the status line.

When the output style is changed, the value passed through `stdin` changes accordingly and the status line reflects the new style.

ANSI color support and formatting

The status line supports ANSI color formatting. Modifying the Python script allows changes to the visual appearance of the output, including color and text styling, such as bold formatting.

For example, the `print` statement can include ANSI escape sequences:

```
print(f"\033[1;32m{style}\033[0m")
```

The numeric sequences represent ANSI escape codes used to control formatting in the terminal. In this example, the status line appears in green and bold text.

When the active output style is changed, the status line updates accordingly. Because the logic is implemented in a script, the status line dynamically reflects the current configuration and any formatting adjustments applied by the script.

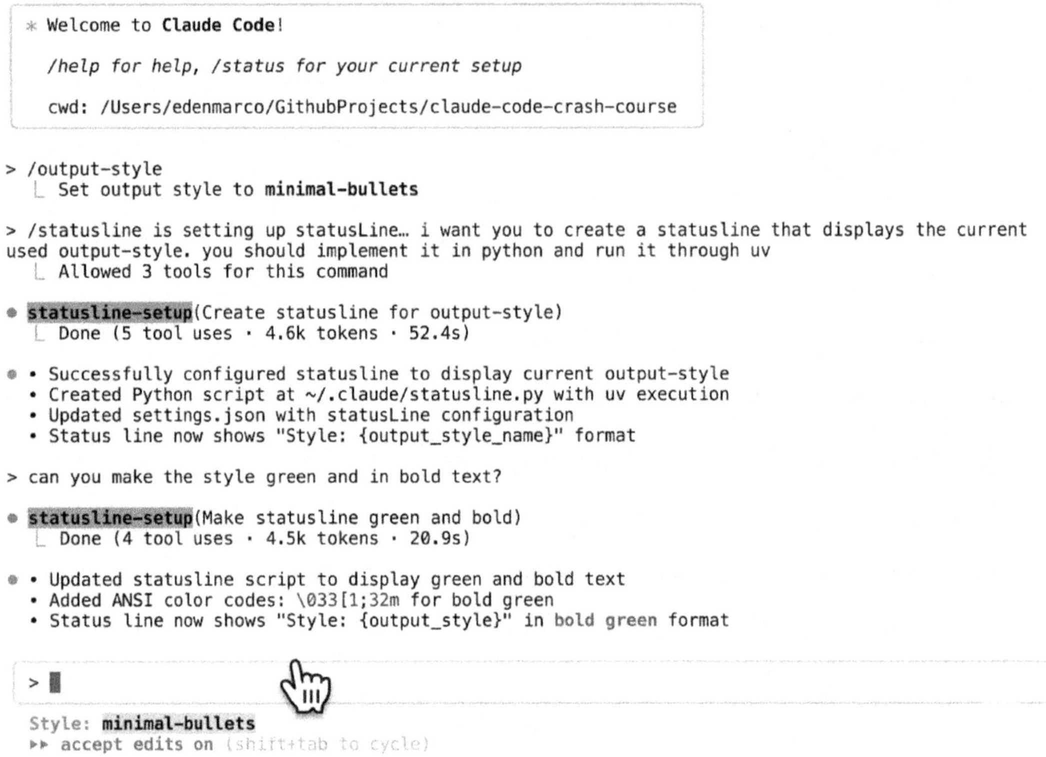

Figure 8.14 – Status line displaying the active output style

Extending status line functionality

Since the status line logic is driven by an executable script, it can display any information available to the runtime environment. This includes data from external systems, stock prices, news feeds, or other dynamically retrieved information.

More advanced features of output styles can be implemented by extending the script logic further.

In this section, you implemented a custom status line using a Python script and integrated it into Claude Code's configuration. You learned how runtime information is passed through standard input, how to extract structured data such as the active output style, and how to display dynamic values in the interface. This shows that Claude Code is extensible beyond output formatting and allows executable logic to shape the development environment itself. Building on this capability, the next section enhances the status line further by reading transcript data and extracting the last user prompt.

Advanced status line: displaying the last user prompt

Within the home directory, the `.claude` directory contains a `projects` subdirectory. Each subdirectory inside projects corresponds to a project and holds its conversation history and session data. The directory name reflects the project path, where path separators, such as /, are replaced with -.

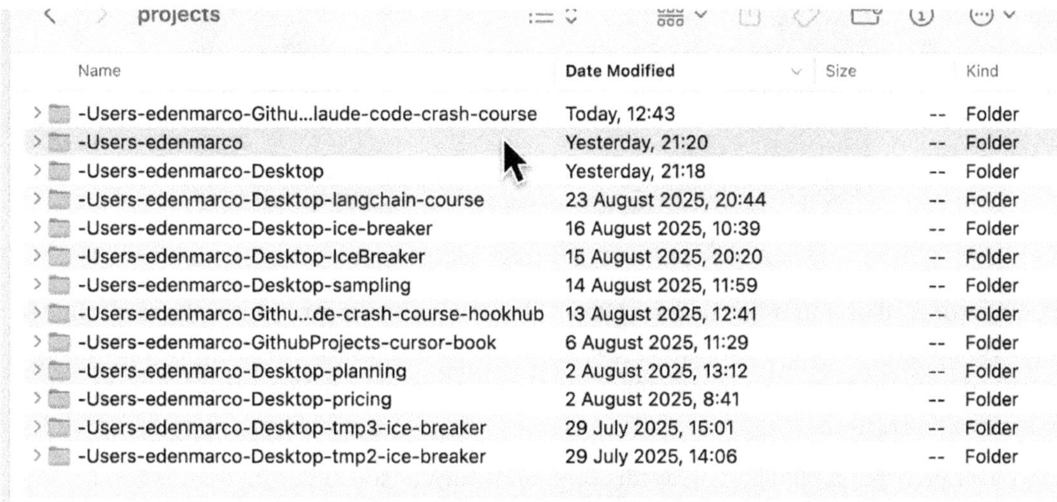

Figure 8.15 – Claude projects directory storing session data

Inside each project directory, JSONL files store the conversation logs. Each file is identified by a UUID. These JSONL files contain the full sequence of messages exchanged during a session.

Examining one such JSONL file reveals that each line represents a JSON object corresponding to a message entry. When a new user message is submitted, a new JSON object is appended to the file. For example, if the user sends `"hello"`, a new entry appears with the following:

- `"role": "user"`
- `"content": "hello"`

This entry is followed by the assistant's response.

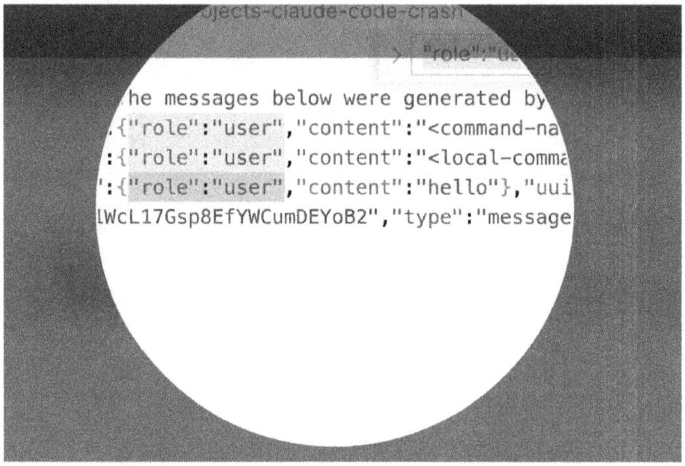

Figure 8.16 – JSONL transcript storing user prompts

Claude stores all user prompts in these JSONL files. The objective is to extend the status line so that it displays the last prompt sent by the user in the current session. This prompt must be retrieved from the transcript file referenced in the `transcript_path` key provided as input to the status line script.

Only user prompts should be displayed. Commands such as status line invocations and assistant responses must be excluded.

All implementation is contained within the existing `statusline.py` file.

Defining the status line requirement

A `/statusline` instruction is defined to extend the status line with an additional field: the last prompt from the user in the current session.

When Claude Code executes a status line command, it passes structured runtime data to the status line script through standard input. This JSON payload includes fields such as `transcript_path`, which point to the current session's JSONL transcript file.

The script reads the `transcript_path` value from its input, loads the referenced JSONL file, and searches for the most recent user message. That message becomes the displayed prompt. Only genuine user prompts are considered. Assistant responses and command invocations are excluded.

The following `/statusline` instruction extends the status line so that it displays the most recent user prompt from the session transcript.

```
/statusline I want you to display also the last prompt from the user in the
current session.
You should get the prompt from the file example in the transcript_path. /path/to/
transcript.jsonl
Remember the user prompt will be a message with role="user".
Remember no commands at all responses, just user prompts in this example.
```

In the demonstrated case, the most recent user prompt in the transcript file is hello, which is displayed in the status line. Only genuine user prompts should be displayed; that is, status line commands and assistant responses that are logged must be excluded. The script, therefore, filters entries so that only valid user prompts are considered.

The instruction explicitly states that all logic must be implemented inside the existing `statusline.py` file. This prevents the creation of an additional script or shell utility and ensures that the functionality remains contained within the status line implementation.

Accessing the transcript path

Inside `statusline.py`, the structured input is loaded as a dictionary. The script accesses the `transcript_path` key, which is known to exist. That path is passed to a function responsible for retrieving the last user prompt. The status line script retrieves the transcript path and extracts the most recent user prompt from the session log.

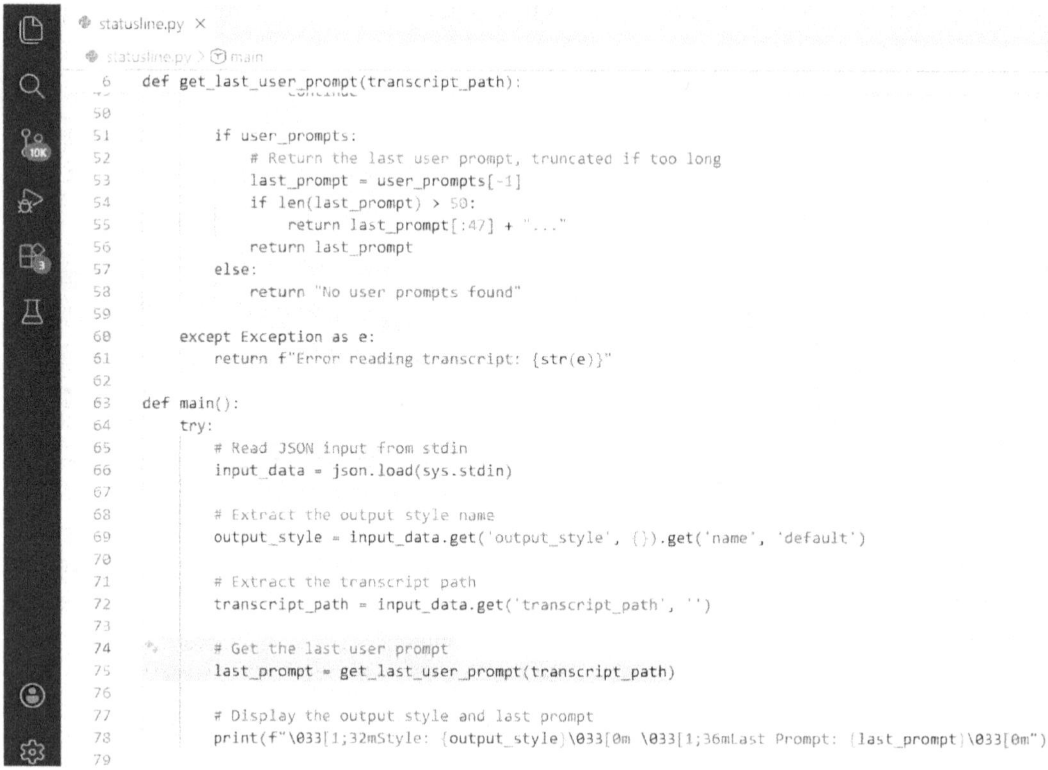

Figure 8.17 – Reading the transcript path to fetch the last user prompt

After the function returns the prompt, it is printed as part of the status line output.

Implementing retrieval of the last user prompt

The retrieval function performs the following operations:

- Confirming that the transcript file path exists
- Opening and reading the JSONL file at that path
- Iterating through each line of the file
- Parsing each line as JSON into a dictionary object
- Inspecting the message key within each entry
- Checking the `role` field inside `message`
- If the role is `user`, extracting the `content` field

The following Python function reads the transcript file, parses the JSONL entries, and retrieves the most recent valid user prompt.

```
import json
import sys
import os


def get_last_user_prompt(transcript_path):
"""
Extract the last user prompt from the transcript file.
"""

try:
if not os.path.exists(transcript_path):
return "No transcript found"

with open(transcript_path, "r") as f:
content = f.read().strip()

if not content:
return "Empty transcript"

# Split by lines and process each JSON object

lines = content.split("\n")

for line in reversed(lines):
try:
entry = json.loads(line)

# Entry has 'message' and not a command
if entry.get("type") == "message" and entry.get("role") == "user":
message_content = entry.get("message", {}).get("content", "")

# Skip command messages starting with /
if message_content.startswith("/"):
continue

return message_content
```

```
except json.JSONDecodeError:
continue

return "No user prompt found"

except Exception as e:
return f"Error reading transcript: {e}"
```

Command-style placeholders and assistant responses are skipped. Only valid user prompts are retained. The most recent valid user prompt found during iteration is returned as the result.

At this point, the `statusline.py` file performs three distinct steps. First, it reads structured runtime input from standard input. Second, it extracts the `transcript_path` value from that input. Third, it opens the referenced JSONL transcript file, scans for the most recent valid user prompt, and prints that value to standard output.

Testing and finalizing the implementation

After implementing the logic for retrieving and displaying the last user prompt, the next step is to confirm that the behavior works as intended. This involves verifying that new transcript entries are correctly appended, that only valid user prompts are extracted, and that the status line updates consistently after each interaction.

Validating the implementation

When a new message is submitted, a new entry is appended to the JSONL transcript file. After the assistant's response is recorded, the status line updates to reflect the newly submitted prompt.

Repeating this process confirms the following:

- Each new message adds a new JSONL entry
- The displayed prompt updates accordingly
- The script consistently retrieves the most recent valid user prompt

The output style is changed (for example, to a YAML concise style) to confirm that the new functionality remains intact. The status line continues to display the last prompt without issue.

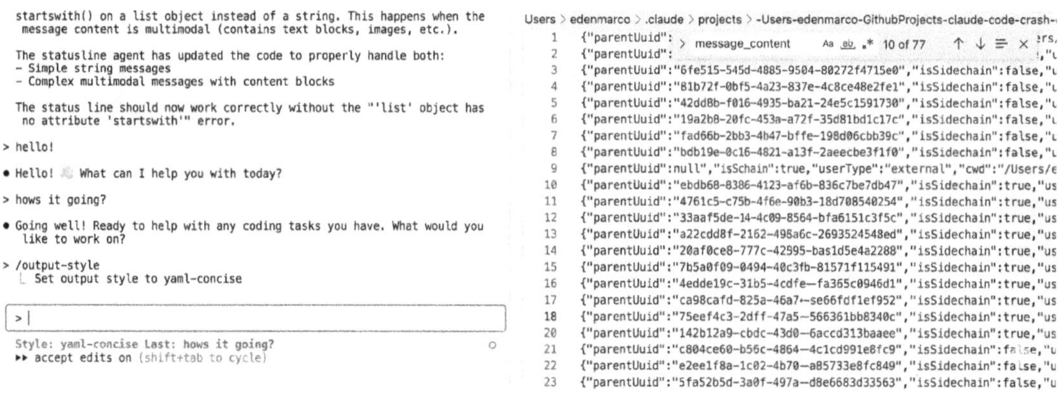

Figure 8.18 – Status line reflecting the latest user prompt from the transcript

Updating the output label

In the previous sections, we explored how to control Claude Code's behavior using output styles and how to monitor activity through status lines. Together, these mechanisms provide a foundation for shaping how the system communicates and operates during runtime.

With these capabilities in place, we can now look ahead to what the future of agentic coding might look like when they are combined and extended. Rather than relying on a single assistant session, multiple specialized agents can work together, each configured with its own role, context, and output behaviour.

The future of AI coding: a team of specialized agents

As agentic development workflows evolve, a single assistant session is often not enough to handle complex tasks. Instead, multiple specialized agents can collaborate, each responsible for a particular role or domain. By combining the configuration techniques introduced earlier, such as output styles and runtime status lines, we can begin to structure these agents as a coordinated system rather than a single general-purpose assistant.

Agentic coding and multiple instances

One manifestation of agentic coding is based on running multiple Claude Code instances simultaneously, where each instance has the following:

- Output style
- Context
- Role

Instead of relying on a single general-purpose session, responsibilities are distributed across specialized instances.

This mirrors a small start-up team structure.

Figure 8.19 – Agent roles illustrated as a specialized start-up team

In a small start-up team model, different types of work are routed to different specialists. A UI change is handled by Vinay, the frontend engineer. A backend change is handled by Rajesh. A deployment issue is handled by Alex, the DevOps engineer. Each person has a distinct set of responsibilities and skills, and also tends to communicate in a way that matches the work they do. All names used in this illustration are fictional and are included solely to represent example roles in the workflow. Here are some examples:

- A DevOps-oriented instance may use YAML-style output

- A backend-oriented instance may use an OpenAPI specification format
- A documentation-oriented instance may use structured learning-style output

Each output style is configured at the system level and influences how responses are generated. An instance may also be associated with different commands, agents, and contextual constraints.

Instances can be named to reflect their responsibilities, similar to named team members.

Naming and role-based contexts

Each Claude Code instance can represent a named role, such as the following

- `frontend-engineer`
- `backend-engineer`
- `devops`
- `security-review`

The name reflects:

- The output style
- The context
- The type of tasks handled

Switching between terminals becomes equivalent to switching between specialized team members. A security-related task is handled in the security-focused instance. A UI task is handled in the frontend-focused instance.

This structure enables controlled context boundaries and clear separation of responsibilities. Multiple specialized Claude Code instances operate as coordinated agents within the development workflow.

In this final section, you explored how multiple Claude Code instances can operate in parallel, each configured with a distinct output style and contextual focus. You saw how directory-level configuration influences behavior and how specialized sessions mirror role-based collaboration within a development team. This consolidates the chapter's central idea: Claude Code is not a single fixed interface, but a configurable system that can be shaped into task-specific agents.

Summary

In this chapter, you learned how Claude Code output styles work and how they can be created, reviewed, and applied at either the user or project scope. You also examined how selecting an output style changes Claude Code's system prompt behavior, and how structured formats such as YAML and HTML alter the way responses are produced and consumed. The chapter extended this configuration work into workflow control by embedding file-generation behavior into an output style and implementing custom status line logic using a Python script that reads runtime input and transcript history.

This information is useful because it establishes direct control over how Claude Code communicates, not just what it generates. Instead of treating model output as fixed prose, output styles allow response structure, tone, and workflow behavior to be defined as part of the development environment. This makes it possible to tailor Claude Code sessions for different tasks, run multiple specialized sessions in parallel, and version these configurations as part of a repeatable workflow.

In the next chapter, we will look at understanding agent skills as a mechanism for extending AI agent capabilities.

Get this book's PDF copy, code bundle, and more

Scan the QR code (or go to `packtpub.com/unlock`). Search for this book by name, confirm the edition, and then follow the steps on the page.

UNLOCK NOW

Note: Have your invoice handy. Purchases made directly from the Packt website don't require an invoice.

Part 3

Advanced Agents and Deep System Design

In the final part of this book, you'll examine how modern coding agents operate at scale and over long horizons. We'll explore agent skills such as structured capability extensions and analyze how they influence context flow and execution patterns. You'll see how Claude Code can operate across environments, coordinate parallel development efforts, and support more advanced orchestration strategies.

We will also look into system design. You'll examine what qualifies an agent as "deep," how long-running execution is sustained, and how orchestration frameworks such as LangChain deep agents are structured internally. By the end of this part, you'll have a practical and architectural understanding of how advanced agent systems are engineered.

This part of the book includes the following chapters:

- *Chapter 9, Understanding Agent Skills*
- *Chapter 10, Using Claude Code Desktop*
- *Chapter 11, Understanding Deep Agents*

9

Understanding Agent Skills

Agent skills were introduced by the Anthropic team in October 2025 as a mechanism for extending the capabilities of AI agents. Skills allow capabilities to be packaged as structured units, including custom workflows and task-specific instructions, enabling agents to perform more complex and coordinated tasks. By encapsulating defined behaviors, skills expand what agents can accomplish beyond general reasoning alone. Claude can automatically invoke skills based on their description field matching the conversation context.

This chapter examines the concept of agent skills in depth, establishing a clear understanding of what they are and why they matter in the design of more capable agent systems.

The chapter progresses through a layered exploration of skills, beginning with foundational concepts and practical usage in environments such as Claude Code, as well as tools such as LangChain DeepAgents (`https://docs.langchain.com/oss/python/deepagents/overview`). We will then move beneath the surface to analyze how context flows within an agent when a skill is invoked, clarifying how the system operates internally. Finally, we will consolidate these perspectives through a concrete implementation of the skills within a real agent. The goal is to understand not only how to use skills, but also their underlying design and motivation, resulting in a comprehensive and technically grounded understanding of the concept.

A core concept behind skills is progressive disclosure. Skills are not permanently loaded into the agent's active context. Instead, the system loads a skill only when it becomes relevant to the current task. This design prevents unnecessary instructions from entering the working context and helps maintain clarity during reasoning. Later in this chapter, we will examine how this dynamic loading works when a skill is invoked and how it affects context flow within the agent.

The following topics will be covered in this chapter:

- The gist of agent skills
- Diving deeper into agent skills
- Comparing agent skills with other agent primitives

The gist of agent skills

In this section, we will see agent skills in action and demonstrate how to use them as part of our workflow. We will compare two approaches to completing the same task: first without skills and then with skills, so we can clearly observe how the agent behaves in each case.

Head to the repository and switch to the `hookhub` branch, then open the commit list. Select the commit titled **improved hookcard and hero with multi agent working.** This commit will serve as our starting point.

Since additional commits will be added later, the branch history may move forward. However, we must begin from this exact commit. Copy its hash, open the IDE, and switch to the branch and commit:

```
git switch project/hookhub c125545ca118f51c07eb6defe61ba727dbf05788
```

After switching, a new `hookhub` directory appears. This directory contains all the code developed in the previous sections.

Move into the directory and install the dependencies:

```
cd hookhub
npm install
```

Once installation is completed, start the development server:

```
npm run dev
```

The HookHub application is now running locally on port `3000`. This restores the exact baseline required for the demonstration.

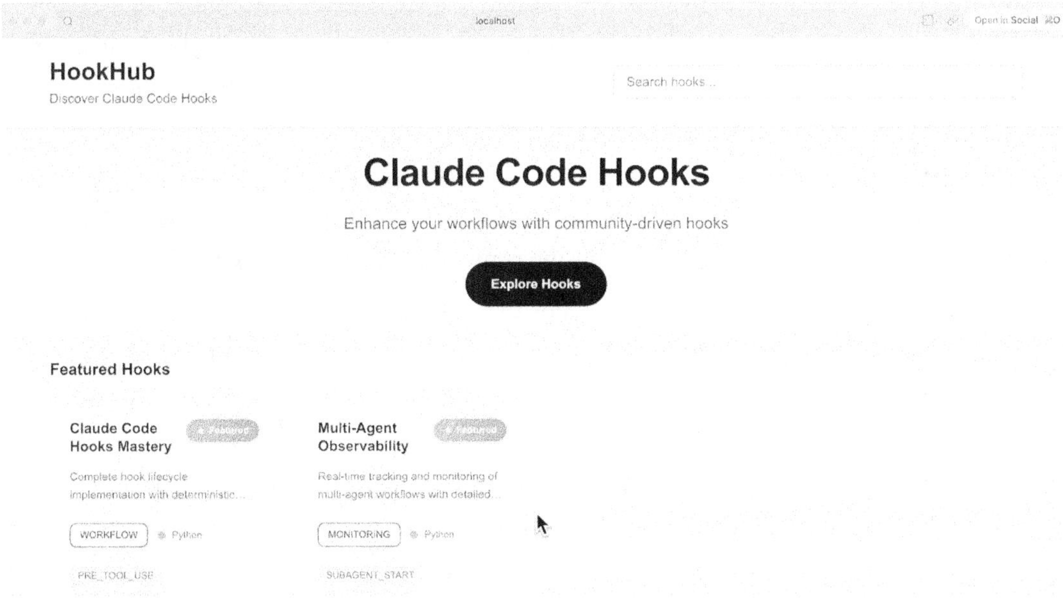

Figure 9.1 – HookHub running locally

Scenario 1: Styling without skills

The UI shown in *Figure 9.1* is intentionally simple. Suppose we want the HookHub application to adopt a specific visual identity and match the Anthropic design language exactly.

Without skills, we can prompt directly:

```
Make this web app Anthropic style.
```

At this point, the repository contains no reference to Anthropic's brand guidelines. The agent scans the project files and even fetches information from `anthropic.com`. It derives the design language dynamically from the live website and begins implementing changes.

This approach works. The agent updates background colors, adjusts typography, and applies visual refinements. The final result closely resembles the Anthropic aesthetic and demonstrates impressive capability.

However, consider the implications. Each time we repeat this task, the agent fetches and derives the same design language again. If we perform this workflow repeatedly, we reintroduce redundant context gathering each time.

One possible solution would be to embed the design language directly into the `CLAUDE.md` file. The problem is that this context would then attach to every prompt, including backend tasks where it is irrelevant. This leads to unnecessary context expansion and eventual degradation.

Scenario 2: Styling with skills

Skills provide a more elegant solution. We can create a skill that specifies the design language of the Anthropic theme. Every time we work on the frontend, Claude Code can select that skill, use it, and dynamically load the required design context. Let us see how that is done.

Open the official Anthropic example skills repository (`https://github.com/anthropics/skills`). Each skill resides in its own directory. Navigate to the `brand-guidelines` skill and inspect its `SKILL.md` file.

> **Note**
>
> Some of the examples in this chapter are adapted from the Anthropic Skills repository (`https://github.com/anthropics/skills`), licensed under the Apache License 2.0. Implementations and behaviors may evolve over time.

A skill may contain multiple files, not just Markdown. It can include scripts, executables, and structured resources. In this case, the `SKILL.md` file defines Anthropic's official brand colors, typography, and design artifacts.

The file begins with front matter. Only this section is injected into the agent system prompt when the skill is selected. The remainder of the Markdown file, which contains the detailed brand guidelines, loads into the prompt only when the skill is activated.

This mirrors the selective loading mechanism we previously explored with subagents. Context is injected conditionally, not globally.

> **Note**
>
> Skills from the official Claude Code marketplace automatically update at startup when a new upstream version is available. Third-party marketplace skills may require manual updates or explicit auto-update configuration through `/plugin`.

Installing skills in Claude Code

To equip our coding agent with these skills, add the Anthropic skills repository as a marketplace plugin:

```
/plugin add marketplace anthropic/skills
```

Claude Code clones the repository locally into the `.claude/plugins` directory.

Verify installation by running `/plugins`. Browse the available plugins. Two categories appear:

- **Document skills**, which include document processing capabilities such as Excel and PowerPoint
- **Example skills**, which include the brand guidelines skill reviewed earlier

> Note
>
> A useful detail to note is that when Claude, not Claude Code, introduced support for creating decks and documents, it was announced together with skills. That is because those features are built using agent skills internally. In other words, the ability to generate documents and presentations is powered by the same skills mechanism we are discussing here.

Install the example skills. After installation, restart Claude Code and ask the following:

```
Which skills do you have?
```

The agent now lists the available skills, including `brand-guidelines`, which we will use next.

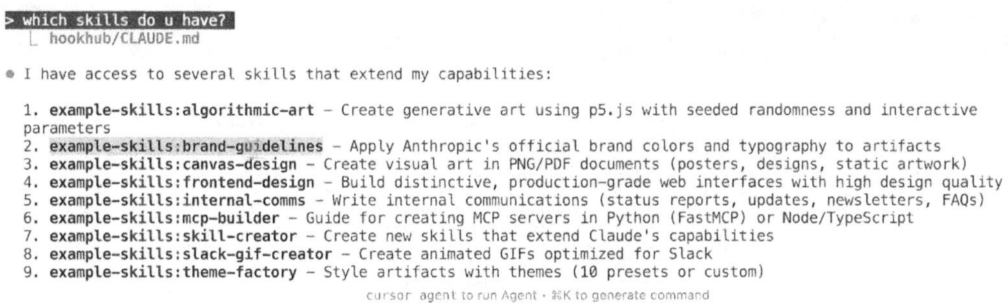

Figure 9.2 – Claude listing installed skills, including brand-guidelines

Styling with skills enabled

Clear the context and start a fresh Claude instance. Ask the following:

```
Can you make sure that the logo is according to Anthropic brand?
```

The agent scans the repository and then requests permission to use the `brand-guidelines` skill. The skill description is displayed. Approve its use.

When approved, Claude dynamically loads the `brand-guidelines` directory into context. Only the relevant Markdown file is injected. This additional context enables the agent to apply design changes according to the official brand definitions.

> Note
>
> **The key observation is that this context is loaded dynamically. It is not permanently attached to every prompt. This progressive context loading keeps the working context window clean and efficient.** This procedure is also known as progressive disclosure.
>
> If you want to invoke the skill only via the slash command, then enable the `disable-model-invocation: true` flag in the skill frontmatter.

After the changes are applied, run the build process:

```
npm run build
```

Then, restart the development server:

```
npm run dev
```

The updated design should now show subtle refinements, including typography adjustments and brand-aligned styling. The primary objective here is not visual difference but demonstrating controlled context injection through skills.

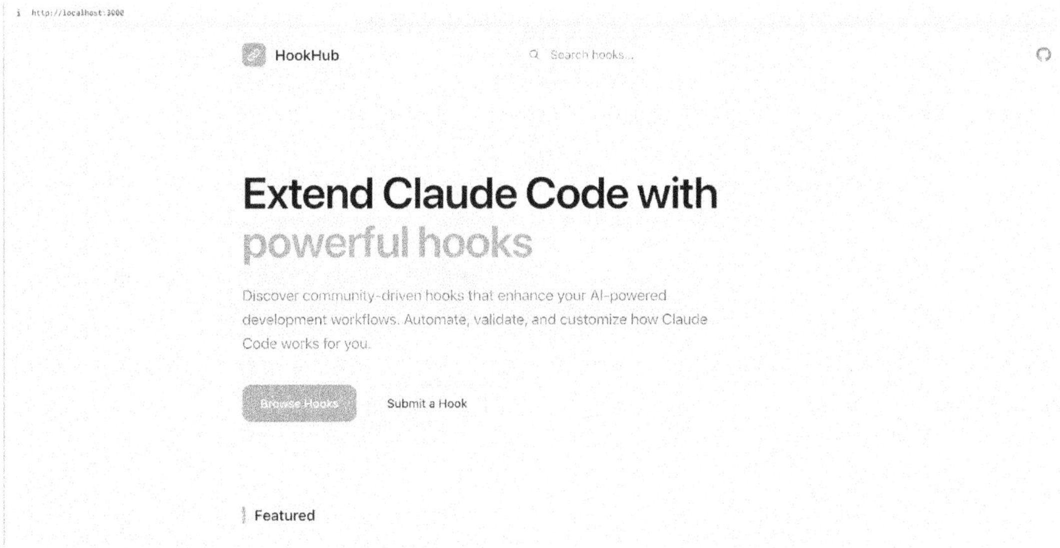

Figure 9.3 – HookHub interface after applying brand-guidelines styling via skills

Skills are not limited to static Markdown context. Some include executable scripts.

Consider the `skill-creator` example. Its directory contains several Python scripts. Within the corresponding `SKILL.md`, the agent is informed that it can execute these scripts.

Scripts can be written in Python, Bash, JavaScript, or any language supported in the environment. As long as their behavior is clearly described in the skill definition, the agent can use them as deterministic tools.

This approach enables structured workflows. If certain processes can be encoded as deterministic scripts, they can be composed into higher-level capabilities through a skill. The agent can then execute sequences of scripts and combine their outputs to accomplish complex tasks.

Diving deeper into agent skills

In this section, we will dive deeper into agent skills by introducing **custom skills**. We will also review a skill that includes not only a `SKILL.md` file but also **auxiliary scripts** that the agent can execute to help achieve a task.

The skill we examine is hosted in an online repository. We download it, integrate it locally, and then iterate on it by modifying and improving it to fit our needs. This process demonstrates the flexibility skills provide when designing structured agent workflows.

Exploring the Claude Skills marketplace

We begin in a repository called `claude-skills-marketplace` (`https://github.com/mhattingpete/claude-skills-marketplace/tree/main`), which is released under the Apache 2.0 license. This is one of several repositories that contain Claude Code skills, which can be downloaded and integrated into Claude Code or any other agent that supports skills, such as Claude Desktop or LangChain DeepAgents.

The repository contains multiple installable skills. It can even be added as a marketplace in Claude Code through the plugin system, as demonstrated in the previous section.

Under the `Engineering Workflows` file, we find a skill named `git-pushing`. This skill is designed to help push code to GitHub.

```
Apache License
Version 2.0, January 2004
http://www.apache.org/licenses/
---
name: git-pushing
description: Stage, commit, and push git changes with conventional commit
messages. Use when user wants to commit and push changes, mentions pushing to
remote, or asks to save and push their work. Also activates when user says "push
changes", "commit and push", "push this", "push to github", or similar git
workflow requests.
---

# Git Push Workflow

Stage all changes, create a conventional commit, and push to the remote branch.

## When to Use

Automatically activate when the user:
- Explicitly asks to push changes ("push this", "commit and push")
- Mentions saving work to remote ("save to github", "push to remote")
- Completes a feature and wants to share it
- Says phrases like "let's push this up" or "commit these changes"

## Workflow

**ALWAYS use the script** - do NOT use manual git commands:
```

````
```bash
bash skills/git-pushing/scripts/smart_commit.sh
```

With custom message:
```bash
bash skills/git-pushing/scripts/smart_commit.sh "feat: add feature"
```

Script handles: staging, conventional commit message, Claude footer, push with -u
flag.
````

Opening the `SKILL.md` file for this skill reveals the following description:

- Stage, commit, and push Git changes with conventional commit messages
- Use when the user wants to commit and push changes, mentions pushing to remote, or asks to save work

The YAML front matter at the top of the file is the only portion loaded into the Claude Code agent's system prompt. The remainder of the file is read only when the skill is selected for execution.

Opinionated workflows in Skills

Within the workflow section of `SKILL.md`, we see that the agent is instructed to always use a script named `smart_commit.sh`.

````
Apache License
Version 2.0, January 2004
http://www.apache.org/licenses/
---
name: git-pushing
description: Stage, commit, and push git changes with conventional commit
messages. Use when user wants to commit and push changes, mentions pushing to
remote, or asks to save and push their work. Also activates when user says "push
changes", "commit and push", "push this", "push to github", or similar git
workflow requests.
---

# Git Push Workflow
````

````
Stage all changes, create a conventional commit, and push to the remote branch.

## When to Use

Automatically activate when the user:
- Explicitly asks to push changes ("push this", "commit and push")
- Mentions saving work to remote ("save to github", "push to remote")
- Completes a feature and wants to share it
- Says phrases like "let's push this up" or "commit these changes"

## Workflow

**ALWAYS use the script** - do NOT use manual git commands:

```bash
bash skills/git-pushing/scripts/smart_commit.sh
```

With custom message:
```bash
bash skills/git-pushing/scripts/smart_commit.sh "feat: add feature"
```
Script handles: staging, conventional commit message, Claude footer, push with -u
flag
````

The script contains the actual Git logic, including `git add`, `git status`, and `git commit` operations. The skill author intentionally restricts the main agent from issuing raw Git commands. Instead, the agent must use the designated script.

This illustrates a key concept. Skills encode opinionated workflows. If a team wants the commits to follow a specific structure or process, that logic can be packaged into a skill. The agent then acquires that capability in a controlled manner.

Reviewing the script

In the `scripts` directory, we find `smart_commit.sh`. This script defines the Git execution flow. The agent can run this script, but only when it decides to use the `git-pushing` skill.

This script contains the actual execution logic. It runs a sequence of Git commands, such as staging changes, checking status, and committing with a specific message. The main agent is expected to run this script when it uses the `git-pushing` skill. The important point is that the agent only knows about this script when it decides to use that skill. The script becomes part of the available context only after the skill is selected.

Compared to the brand guidelines skill we saw earlier, this one does more than provide reference content. It includes **auxiliary scripts** that the agent can execute to help achieve the task, which, in this case, is committing and pushing code to GitHub.

This script-running capability gives us a lot of flexibility. If we have workflows that we want to define deterministically in code, we can package them inside a skill. The agent can then run those scripts as part of completing the workflow instead of improvising a sequence of manual commands.

Although this may resemble MCP, the mechanisms differ. MCP enables API calls and communication with external services. Skills operate by injecting structured context and optionally exposing scripts.

Creating a project-level custom skill

Switch to the `project/skills` branch. To create a project-level skill, we define it under the `.claude` directory so that it is scoped to this repository.

Create the following structure:

```
.claude/
  skills/git-pushing/
    scripts/
      smart_commit.sh
    SKILL.md
```

Here is how it should look

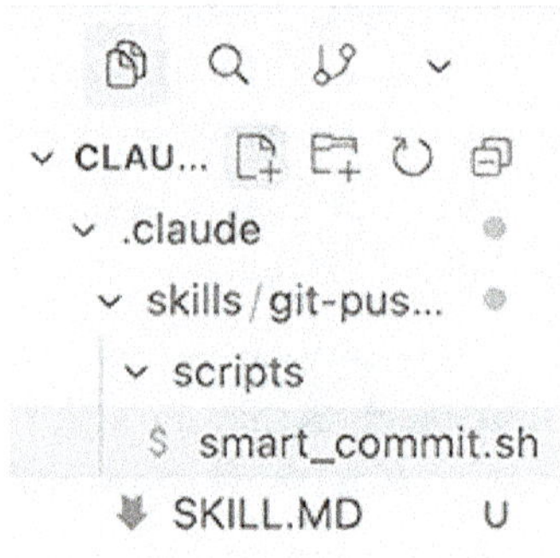

Figure 9.4 – Local skill directory structure for the git-pushing skill

This mirrors the structure of the marketplace skill.

Copy the contents of `SKILL.md` and `smart_commit.sh` from the GitHub repository into the corresponding local files. The `SKILL.md` file references `scripts/smart_commit.sh`, so maintaining the same directory structure ensures compatibility.

At this stage, the skill is fully replicated locally.

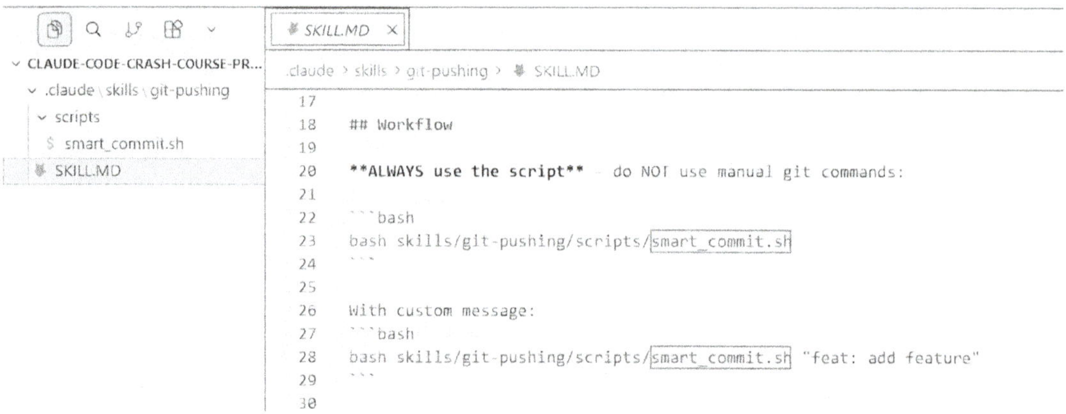

Figure 9.5 – Local SKILL.md referencing the smart_commit.sh automation script

Although it could have been installed via the plugin system, copying it manually provides full control over customization.

Using the custom skill

Open a Claude Code session from the project directory and add the following prompt:

```
List available skills.
```

The newly created project-level `git-pushing` skill appears alongside previously installed marketplace skills.

Enter the following:

```
push changes
```

Claude will ask whether to use the `git-pushing` skill. After approval, it loads `SKILL.md` and determines that it must execute `smart_commit.sh`.

Instead of issuing individual Git commands, the agent runs the script. In some cases, the script may fail due to a git error. If this happens, Claude will not stop. Instead, it will fall back to its default reasoning. It will analyze the repository state, suggest running `git add -A`, create a commit using its own logic, and then push the changes manually.

This means that Claude can resolve the situation using its default behavior and complete the push. This is important because skills do not replace the agent's reasoning. When a skill fails, Claude can return to its default behavior and continue the task.

If the script execution fails, the resulting commit will not be generated through the skill but through Claude's default behavior. This distinction matters. Skills provide structured workflows, but they do not remove the agent's general reasoning ability. If a scripted workflow fails, the agent can still attempt to recover and complete the task using its base capabilities.

With that clarified, we can now move on to customizing the skill behavior itself.

Editing skill behavior

Add an additional trigger phrase, such as `"push to remote"`, under the `When to Use` section in `SKILL.md`.

```
## When to Use

Automatically activate when the user:
- Explicitly asks to push changes ("push this", "commit and push", "push to
remote")
- Mentions saving work to remote ("save to github", "push to remote")
- Completes a feature and wants to share it
- Says phrases like "let's push this up" or "commit these changes"
```

Everything above the closing `---` delimiter is YAML frontmatter and is injected into the agent's system prompt. The content below the delimiter is loaded only when the skill is activated.

```
---
name: git-pushing
description: Stage, commit, and push git changes with conventional commit
messages. Use when user wants to commit and push changes, mentions pushing to
remote, or asks to save and push their work. Also activates when user says "push
changes", "commit and push", "push this", "push to github", or similar git
workflow requests.
---

# Git Push Workflow

Stage all changes, create a conventional commit, and push to the remote branch.

## When to Use

Automatically activate when the user:
- Explicitly asks to push changes ("push this", "commit and push", "push to
remote")
- Mentions saving work to remote ("save to github", "push to remote")
- Completes a feature and wants to share it
- Says phrases like "let's push this up" or "commit these changes"
```

Why is that happening? We edited the `When to Use` section inside SKILL.md and added the `"push to remote"` phrase. However, that section is not part of the YAML frontmatter.

Only the YAML front matter at the top of the file is injected into the agent's system prompt on every request. Everything below is invisible to the agent unless the skill has already been selected.

This means the change we made does not influence the skill selection decision at all.

Now we clear the context to ensure a fresh session and type the following:

```
push to remote
```

Claude will still ask to use the `git-pushing` skill. This is not because of the phrase we added. It is because the original front matter already described the skill as handling commit-and-push operations. The intent of "`push to remote`" is semantically close enough to "`push changes`" or "`push to GitHub`", which were already covered in the description.

So what is happening here is important.

Skill selection is driven entirely by the front matter. The agent matches user intent against the name and description fields in that YAML block. The remainder of the file plays no role in the selection phase.

Only after the skill is selected does Claude load the rest of `SKILL.md`, including the workflow instructions and script references.

This is the **progressive disclosure model:**

1. The agent always sees the front matter.
2. Based on that, it decides whether to activate the skill.
3. Only then does it load the full skill context and any auxiliary instructions.

That is why our modification was redundant. It was placed outside the portion of the file that participates in the selection process.

With that clarified, let us proceed to modify the behavior of the script itself.

Enabling automatic skill approval

Now that we understand how skill selection works, consider the following scenario.

What if the skill triggers correctly, but every single time we use it, Claude pauses and asks for approval before executing the script?

In that case, even though the workflow is packaged inside a skill, we still introduce friction. Every commit-and-push operation requires manual confirmation. If the goal is to create a streamlined, opinionated workflow, repeated prompts defeat that purpose.

So, the next logical step is to change not how the skill is selected, but how it executes. What if we allow the skill to run without asking for permission each time?

After confirming that the skill triggers correctly, choose the option that allows Claude Code to use this skill without asking for approval every time.

When we do this, Claude updates `settings.local.json`.

This is important.

What actually changes is not the skill itself. The skill definition remains the same. Instead, Claude updates the local configuration so that when this particular skill is selected, it can execute without interactive confirmation.

This means two separate permissions are involved:

- Permission to activate the skill
- Permission to execute scripts defined inside the skill

By enabling automatic approval, we remove the need to manually confirm both steps in future runs.

Now, when we run `"push to remote"`, Claude will immediately load the skill and execute `smart_commit.sh` without prompting. The workflow defined inside the skill will then be fully automated.

After the script runs successfully, we inspect the resulting commit.

```
## When to Use

Automatically activate when the user:
- Explicitly asks to push changes ("push this", "commit and push", "push to remote")
- Mentions saving work to remote ("save to github", "push to remote")
- Completes a feature and wants to share it
- Says phrases like "let's push this up" or "commit these changes"
```

Figure 9.6 – Commit message generated by the smart_commit.sh automation script

As you can see, the commit message is minimal. It simply reports that a certain number of files have been updated.

This is not an AI-generated message.

If we inspect `smart_commit.sh`, we see that the commit message is constructed using static logic. It counts modified files and inserts that number into a predefined message template. There is no call to Claude inside the script. So, even though the workflow is wrapped in a skill, the intelligence level of that workflow is determined entirely by the script implementation. This is an important distinction. *A skill does not automatically mean AI-driven logic. A skill is simply a packaging mechanism. It can contain deterministic scripts, AI calls, or both.*

Right now, our workflow is deterministic and simplistic. So, we improve it.

Modifying the script to use the Claude CLI

We now ask Claude to edit `smart_commit.sh` so that it invokes the Claude CLI to generate the commit message.

The prompt is as follows:

```
can u please edit @.claude/skills/git-pushing/scripts/smart_commit.sh to use
Claude Code cli to create the commit message like a pirate?
```

This will change the nature of the workflow.

Previously, the script generated a commit message using static shell logic.

Now, it does the following:

1. The script should call `claude -p` with a prompt. The `-p` flag runs Claude in prompt mode: it sends the query, prints the response to `stdout`, and then exits.
2. The Claude CLI will generate the commit message dynamically.
3. The script will use that output in the `git commit` command.

What we have created here is a layered system:

1. The main Claude Code agent selects the skill.
2. The skill runs `smart_commit.sh`.
3. The script itself invokes the Claude CLI.
4. The Claude CLI generates the commit message.
5. The script completes the commit and push.

This is the composition. The skill orchestrates deterministic execution. The script orchestrates an AI call. The AI call generates structured output. The script consumes that output.

We can run the following:

```
push to remote
```

We now see pirate-style language in the commit message.

```
---
name: git-pushing
description: Stage, commit, and push git changes with conventional commit messages. Use when user wants to commit and push changes, mentions pushing
to remote, or asks to save and push their work. Also activates when user says "push changes", "commit and push", "push this", "push to github", or
similar git workflow requests.
---

# Git Push Workflow

Stage all changes, create a conventional commit, and push to the remote branch.

## When to Use

Automatically activate when the user:
- Explicitly asks to push changes ("push this", "commit and push", "push to remote")
- Mentions saving work to remote ("save to github", "push to remote")
- Completes a feature and wants to share it
- Says phrases like "let's push this up" or "commit these changes"
```

Figure 9.7 – Skill invoking the Claude CLI to generate an AI commit message

That confirms that the script is successfully invoking the Claude CLI internally.

So, we have moved from a static workflow to a hybrid deterministic and AI workflow.

Breaking the expected structure

Now, what if the directory structure no longer matches what the skill expects? To explore that, consider this scenario. We return to the IDE and intentionally break the structure. We take the `smart_commit.sh` script and move it out of the `scripts` directory into the root of the `git-pushing` directory. Then, we delete the `scripts` directory entirely.

At this point, the structure no longer matches what `SKILL.md` specifies. The skill definition expects the script to be under `skills/git-pushing/scripts/`, but the file now exists directly under `skills/git-pushing/`. This creates an inconsistent setup. The path described in the skill is no longer accurate, and the repository structure is now technically incorrect.

Executing the skill after the structural mismatch

Clear the context to ensure a fresh session.

Then, enter the following:

```
push to remote
```

Claude Code selects the `git-pushing` skill and proceeds to execute the script.

Even though the directory structure no longer matches the path described in `SKILL.md`, the script still runs successfully.

Figure 9.8 – Running the git-pushing skill after modifying the directory structure

This behavior is important. The skill still works because skills ultimately inject context and instructions into the agent. Even though the path reference inside `SKILL.md` is inaccurate, the agent reasons about the repository structure and locates `smart_commit.sh` in its new location. The mismatch does not prevent execution. The agent interprets the instruction to run `smart_commit.sh`, searches for the project, finds the file, and executes it.

So, even after breaking the declared structure, the workflow still completes successfully.

But why did the skill still work?

The reason this works is that skills are not rigid bindings to exact file paths. They provide contextual instructions. Even if the context contains an inaccurate path, the agent is capable of resolving it by inspecting the project structure. The execution succeeds because the file still exists somewhere in the repository. The agent adapts.

Now consider a slightly different scenario. What happens if `smart_commit.sh` is deleted entirely?

At that point, there is no file for the agent to locate. The workflow cannot be executed because the required artifact no longer exists. This illustrates the boundary: if the structure is inconsistent but the file exists, the agent can recover. If the file does not exist, execution fails.

Running a skill in an isolated subagent context

By default, a skill runs inside the current conversation context. However, it can be executed in an isolated subagent context by setting:

```
---
context: fork
agent: Explore
---
```

When context is set to fork, Claude runs the skill in a separate execution branch. This isolates intermediate reasoning and tool usage from the main conversation.

The agent field determines which subagent type handles execution (for example, Explore or Plan).

> **Note**
>
> To ensure the skill is triggered only through a slash command (for example, /`skill-name`) and not automatically by Claude Code, add `disable-model-invocation: true` to the front matter.

Comparing agent skills with other agent primitives

In this section, we will compare agent skills to other agent primitives, such as MCP, subagents, memory, and slash commands. The comparison focuses on context management, context engineering, and execution flow.

Agent skills and MCP

Both agent skills and MCP servers are essential tools in the modern agentic toolkit, but they solve different problems and operate at different layers of the context architecture. Agent skills are procedural knowledge containers. They are folders that contain instructions, scripts, and resources that teach an AI agent how to perform specialized tasks consistently. Consistency is the key idea. With agent skills, we package a workflow and give it to the agent so that it performs the task in a predefined manner. From a context-engineering perspective, skills are based on progressive disclosure.

When a session with a coding agent, or any agent that supports skills, begins, the agent loads only a brief description and the names of the available skills. The context cost at this stage is low. Typically, this consumes around 100 to 200 tokens per skill, regardless of how complex the skill is internally.

When a skill becomes relevant to a task, and this decision is made by the agent, the full instructions derived from the `SKILL.md` file are loaded into the context. Only if the skill is actively used and the agent decides to execute a script does that script get loaded as well. If a skill contains multiple scripts, those that are not used are not loaded into the context. Because of this progressive loading mechanism, skills are highly context-efficient.

Now consider MCP. In the MCP architecture, tool definitions and server specifications are provisioned upfront at the beginning of the conversation. This impacts context efficiency. For example, five MCP servers may consume 50,000 tokens before the first prompt is even sent.

MCP solves a different problem. It connects agents to external resources. That is the purpose of MCP servers.

Skills solve a different problem. They give an agent the ability to perform specialized tasks in a consistent way.

So, while both are agent primitives, they address different layers of the system.

Invocation and execution differences

Both skills and MCP tools are invoked based on the agent's judgment. The agent decides whether to use a skill or an MCP tool based on their respective descriptions.

The invocation mechanism is, therefore, similar. In both cases, the agent evaluates whether the capability is relevant to the task.

An interesting experiment would be to implement the same capability twice: once as a skill and once as an MCP tool exposed by an MCP server. Observing which one the agent chooses in practice would reveal how it reasons about these primitives.

Execution, however, differs. For MCP, execution happens inside the MCP server. The server may run locally or be deployed in the cloud. For skills, execution usually happens locally within the main agent thread. Scripts defined inside skills are executed as part of the agent's primary execution flow. However, if the skill frontmatter specifies `context: fork`, the skill runs in an isolated subagent context instead of the main agent.

This distinction in execution location is important when reasoning about architecture.

Agent skills and subagents

The similarity between agent skills and subagents is that they both allow us to define dedicated instructions for specific tasks. A skill contains structured instructions and optional scripts. A subagent can be defined with its own instructions as well.

The key difference is context isolation. Subagents operate in their own isolated and fresh context window. They are well suited for long-horizon tasks that would otherwise expand the main agent's context window significantly. Skills, by contrast, operate within the main context of the agent. When a skill is invoked, its instructions are loaded into the existing context window rather than into a separate one.

Both skills and subagents are invoked by the main agent. The main agent decides whether to delegate a task to a subagent or execute it using a skill.

In terms of flexibility and control, subagents provide more flexibility. With subagents, the system prompt can be dynamically adjusted and tailored to specific needs. With skills, the system prompt remains that of the main agent, which is typically managed by the vendor and is not easily modified.

As a rule of thumb, note the following:

- If the task is heavy and risks bloating the main context window, a subagent is appropriate.
- If the goal is to give the agent automatic expertise or enforce a specific methodology for a recurring task, a skill is the better choice.

Both are valuable primitives, but they operate under different contexts and execution models. By default, skills run inline within the main agent, while subagents execute in isolated contexts. However, a skill can specify `context: fork`, which runs it in a lightweight isolated context similar to a subagent, though with fewer configuration controls.

To place skills and subagents in the broader Claude Code model, the following table compares them to MCP servers and slash commands.

Dimensions	**Skills**	**MCP**	**Subagents**	**Slash commands**
Purpose	Standardize how tasks are performed	Connect to external services	Delegate work to isolated agents	User-triggered shortcuts
Context loading	Front matter first, full content on use.	Tools loaded at session start	Fresh context per run	Full prompt injected
Trigger	Agent decision	Agent decision	Agent delegation	User runs `/command`

Dimensions	Skills	MCP	Subagents	Slash commands
Execution location	Main agent thread	MCP server (local or remote)	Isolated subagent context	Main agent thread
Context isolation	Shares the main context	External execution	Fully isolated	Shares main context
Scripts	Yes	No	Yes	No
Failure handling	Agent falls back to reasoning.	Agent handles server errors	Main agent retries or adapts	None
Best use	Repeatable workflows	External APIs or services	Long-horizon tasks	Quick actions
Context efficiency	High (lazy-loading)	Low (tools loaded up front)	High (offloaded work)	Low (full prompt every time)
Customization	Full control	Server-defined	Flexible	Limited

Table 9.1 – Comparing agent primitives

Summary

In this chapter, we explored agent skills from both a practical and architectural perspective. We began by understanding the gist of agent skills through a hands-on comparison between prompting an agent directly and using a skill to encapsulate structured behavior. Through the HookHub example, we observed how skills enable progressive context loading, allowing the agent to dynamically inject only the relevant instructions when needed instead of bloating the main context window. We then went deeper by creating a custom project-level skill, integrating auxiliary scripts, modifying its behavior, and even enhancing it to invoke the Claude CLI. This allowed us to see how skills can package opinionated workflows, combine deterministic execution with AI-generated output, and still allow fallback behavior when scripts fail. Finally, we positioned agent skills within the broader agentic landscape by comparing them with MCP and subagents, clarifying how each primitive operates in terms of context architecture, execution flow, and control.

We have now developed not only the ability to use skills but also a clear mental model of how they function internally and when to apply them as part of designing more capable and context-efficient agent systems.

In the next chapter, we will learn how to use Claude Code within the desktop application.

Get this book's PDF copy, code bundle, and more

Scan the QR code (or go to `packtpub.com/unlock`). Search for this book by name, confirm the edition, and then follow the steps on the page.

UNLOCK NOW

Note: Have your invoice handy. Purchases made directly from the Packt website don't require an invoice.

10

Using Claude Code Desktop

In this chapter, you will learn how to use Claude Code within the Claude desktop application, switch between local and cloud modes, and run multiple coding agents in parallel using Git Worktrees. You will see how to coordinate separate feature branches, manage background agents, and merge independently developed changes into a single code base.

The goal of this chapter is to show how to orchestrate parallel development across local and cloud environments using Claude Code.

This is important because it shifts development from sequential, single-threaded work to coordinated, multi-agent workflows, allowing you to scale your productivity and build features faster and more efficiently.

In this chapter, we will cover the following topics:

- Introducing Claude Code desktop integration and background agents
- Operating modes: Local versus cloud
- Orchestrating parallel local and cloud agents
- Understanding Git Worktrees in Claude Code
- Merging parallel feature branches
- Running Claude Code in the cloud via mobile

Introducing Claude Code desktop integration and background agents

In this section, we will explore Claude Code desktop integration. Anthropic has integrated Claude Code directly into the Claude desktop application and mobile application, allowing development tasks and day-to-day conversational reasoning to happen in the same environment. This reduces friction in context switching and enables a more fluid workflow. In addition to that, the integration provides out-of-the-box cloud-based background agents running directly within Claude.

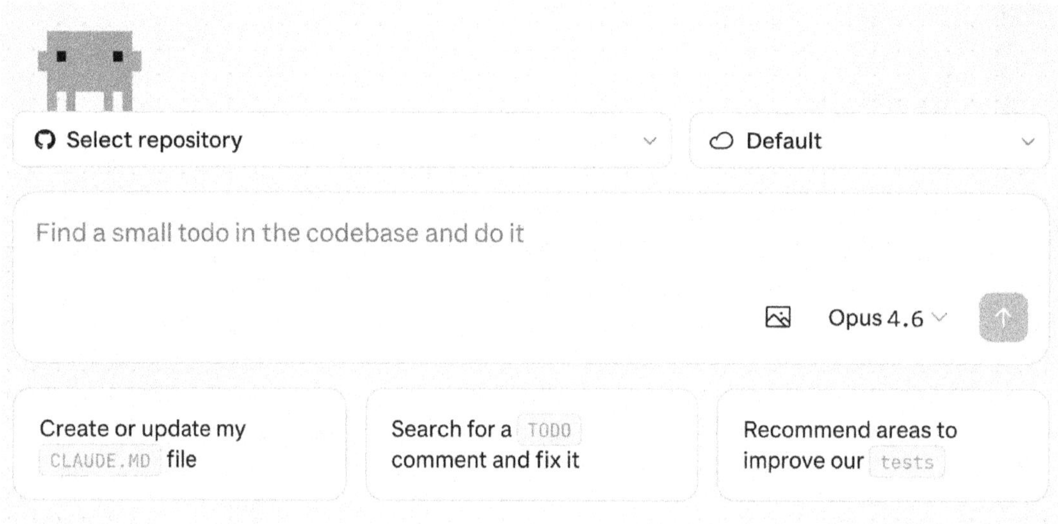

Figure 10.1 – Claude Desktop repository selection interface

Background agents enable multiple features to be developed concurrently rather than sequentially. While preparing this demonstration, the impact of this workflow shift became immediately clear. The combination of seamless desktop integration and background agents creates a development experience that feels fundamentally different from previous setups.

The workflow demonstrated here involves multiple simultaneous operations, and following along step by step would not be realistic. Instead, the goal is to focus on the concepts and observe how the integration works in practice. The emphasis is on understanding how these capabilities combine to enhance productivity and reshape the way we build features.

Claude Code installation and operating modes: Local versus cloud

The Claude Desktop app includes a Code tab that runs Claude Code with a graphical interface. They share the same underlying engine and configuration (CLAUDE.md, MCP servers, hooks, etc.)

The following screenshot shows the Claude Desktop interface with the **Code** tab available.

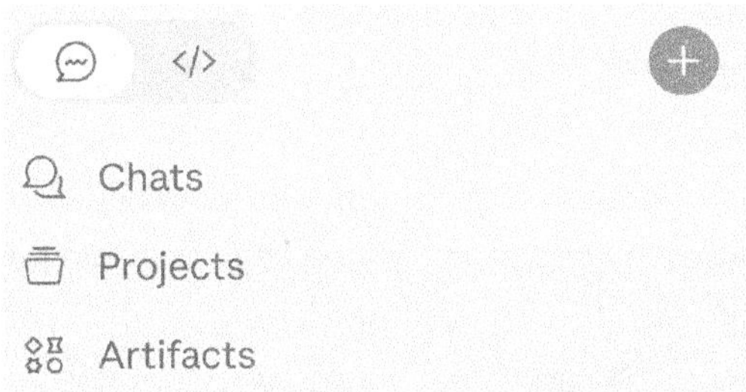

Figure 10.2 – Claude Desktop Code tab interface

After opening the **Code** tab, the Claude Code workspace appears, allowing you to select a project folder and begin interacting with the codebase.

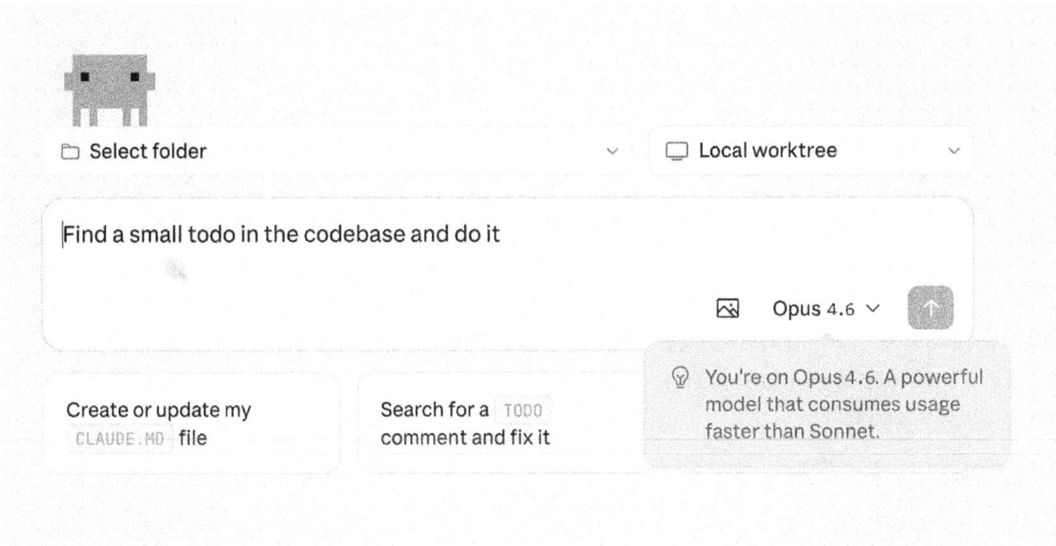

Figure 10.3 – Claude Code workspace in Claude Desktop

Selecting the workspace folder (Local worktree mode)

Before starting any work, select a folder. This folder becomes the workspace where Claude Code will operate. In most cases, this folder contains a code repository, preferably a GitHub repository.

The important detail here is that we are selecting a *folder*.

When the working method is set to **Local worktree**, Claude Code spins up Git worktrees (will be discussed later) locally on the machine. Everything happens locally. Nothing runs in the cloud under this mode.

Because the work is happening on the local machine, Claude Code needs a directory where it can create and manage those work trees. That is why we provide the location of a folder where it will perform its work.

We open the working method selector and confirm that **Local worktree** is marked.

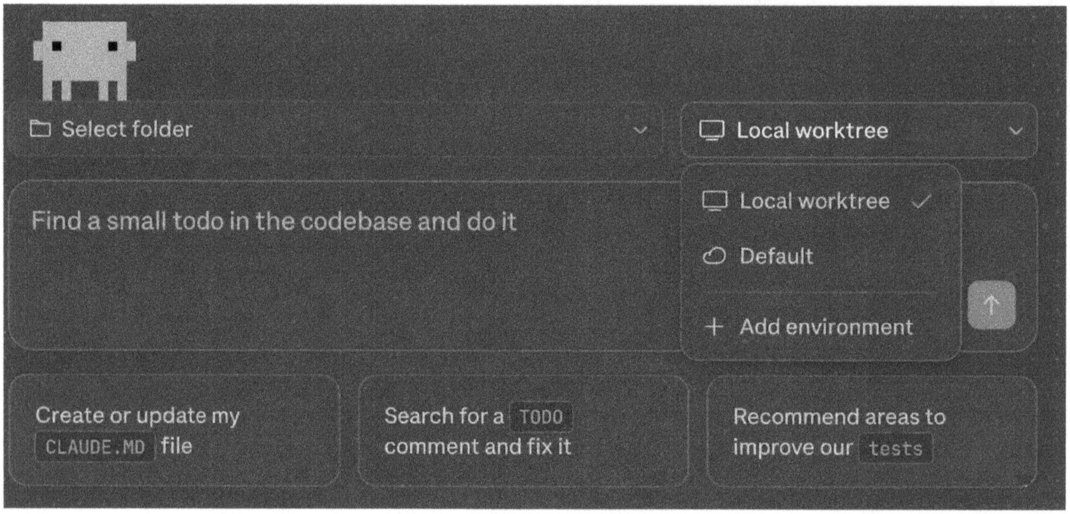

Figure 10.4 – Selecting a workspace folder in Local Worktree mode

With that selected, we open the `Agentic-Coding-with-Claude-Code` directory. This directory is now the workspace where everything will run. At this point, Claude Code is operating locally using Git work trees.

Switching to Claude Code web (cloud mode)

Now switch the working method to the default option, marked with a cloud icon. When we switch to this mode, Claude Code runs as managed instances on Anthropic's infrastructure. This is referred to as **Claude Code web / remote workers / background agents**.

In this model, Anthropic runs containerized Claude Code instances in their environment. Those instances need access to our code. We provide that access by granting Claude Code web permission to our GitHub repositories.

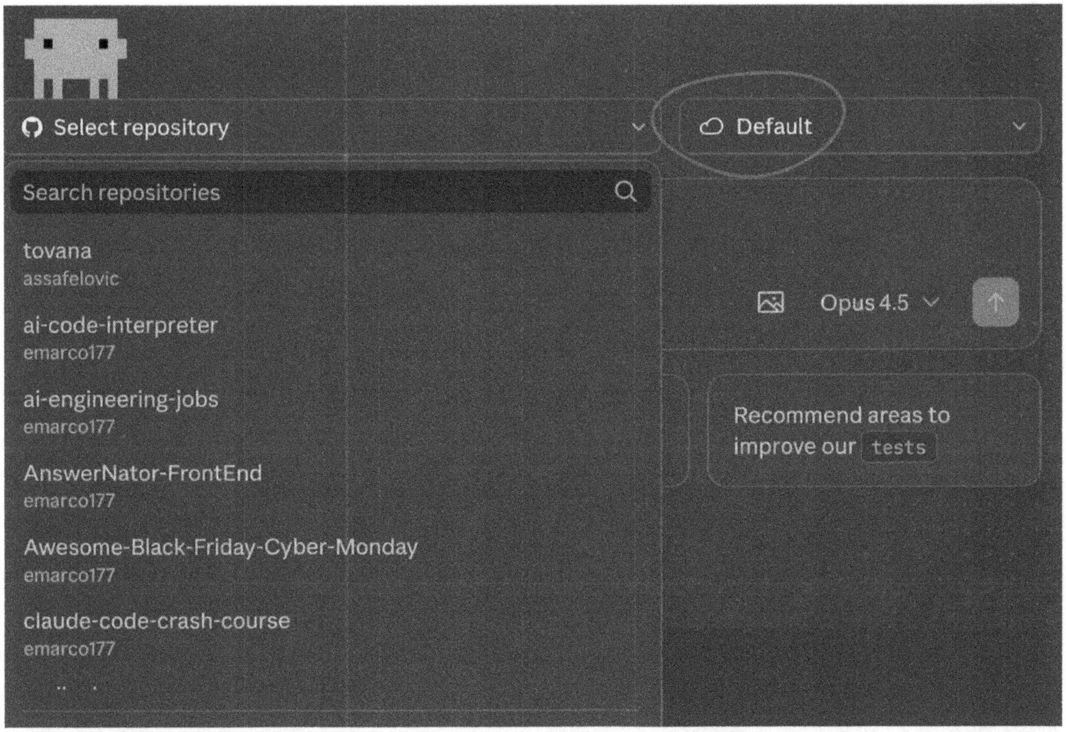

Figure 10.5 – Selecting a repository in Claude Code Web (cloud mode)

Once access is granted, the workflow proceeds in order when prompting:

1. Anthropic will spin up a Claude Code instance.
2. The instance clones the repository.
3. It works directly on the code.
4. It can commit changes.
5. It can create pull requests.

Because the instance has repository access, it operates like any other developer on the project. This model provides scale. You can run multiple Claude instances in parallel, each handling a different task at the same time. The number of concurrent instances depends on what you provision and pay for. We will see this parallel capability in action later in this section.

How Git worktrees enable parallel development

In **Local worktree** mode, Claude Code relies on **Git Worktrees**. Git Worktrees allow us to check out multiple branches of the same repository into separate directories simultaneously, without cloning the repository multiple times.

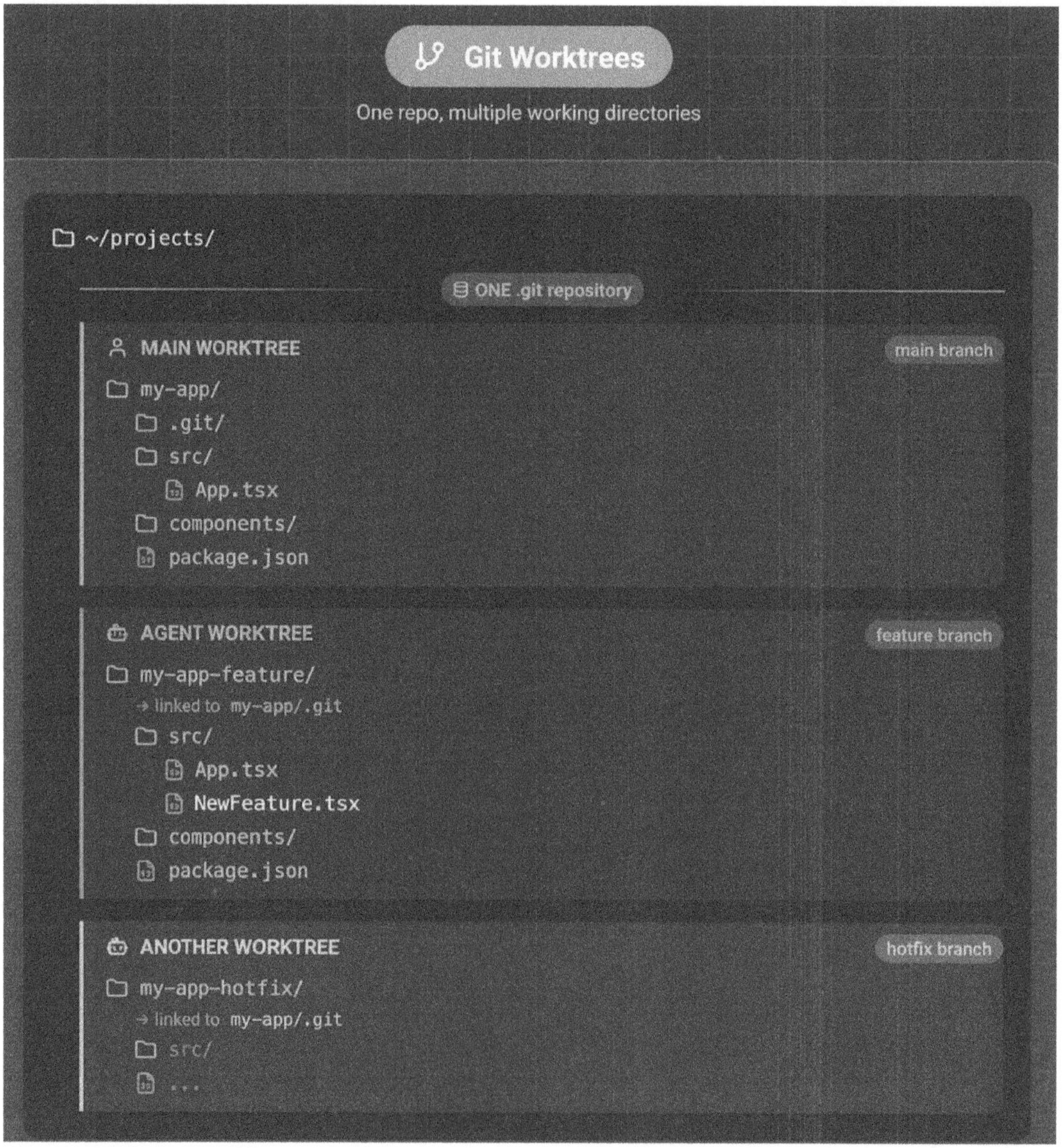

Figure 10.6 – Git Worktrees supporting parallel development in local mode

This becomes especially useful when multiple coding agents are working at the same time.

Each agent can operate on its own branch in its own work tree. We do not need to constantly stash changes or switch between branches. The separation is handled through independent directories in the file system.

We do not need to understand Git Worktrees in depth for this workflow. It is enough to know that they allow multiple branches to remain active at the same time, and Claude Code uses this mechanism to support parallel development.

With the workspace selected and the working mode chosen, we are ready to proceed.

Orchestrating parallel local and cloud agents

To establish context, the working directory of Claude Code is pointed to the `Agentic-Coding-with-Claude-Code` repository.

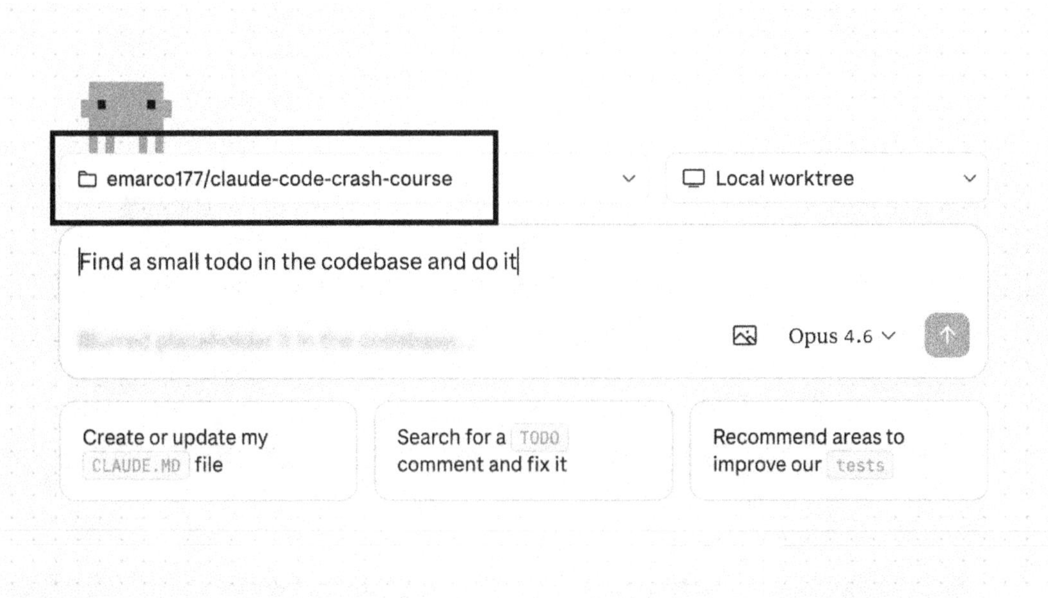

Figure 10.7 – Configuring the working directory for orchestrating local and cloud agents

All operations at this stage run locally on the machine. The repository is currently checked out to the hookhub branch that has been used in the existing implementation.

Running the Next.js application locally

We begin by prompting Claude Code to run the Next.js application locally.

Because the working directory is already configured, nothing is cloned. Claude Code inspects the directory structure, detects the hookhub directory, changes into it, and lists the files. The presence of a `package.json` file indicates that this is a Next.js project.

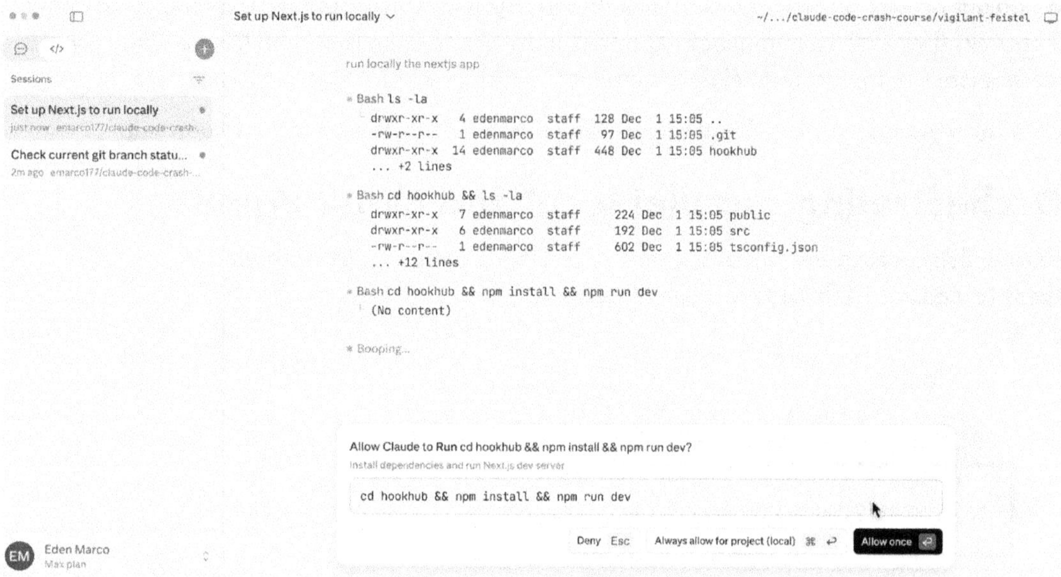

Figure 10.8 – Running the Next.js application locally with Claude Code

From there, it determines the correct execution sequence:

1. Install the dependencies:

```
npm install
```

2. Start the development server:

```
npm run dev
```

The development server runs in the background. Some output is not displayed, but the process completes successfully. During execution, Claude Code checks the npm version. Shortly after, the Next.js application starts on port `3001`, automatically selecting that port because `3000` is already in use.

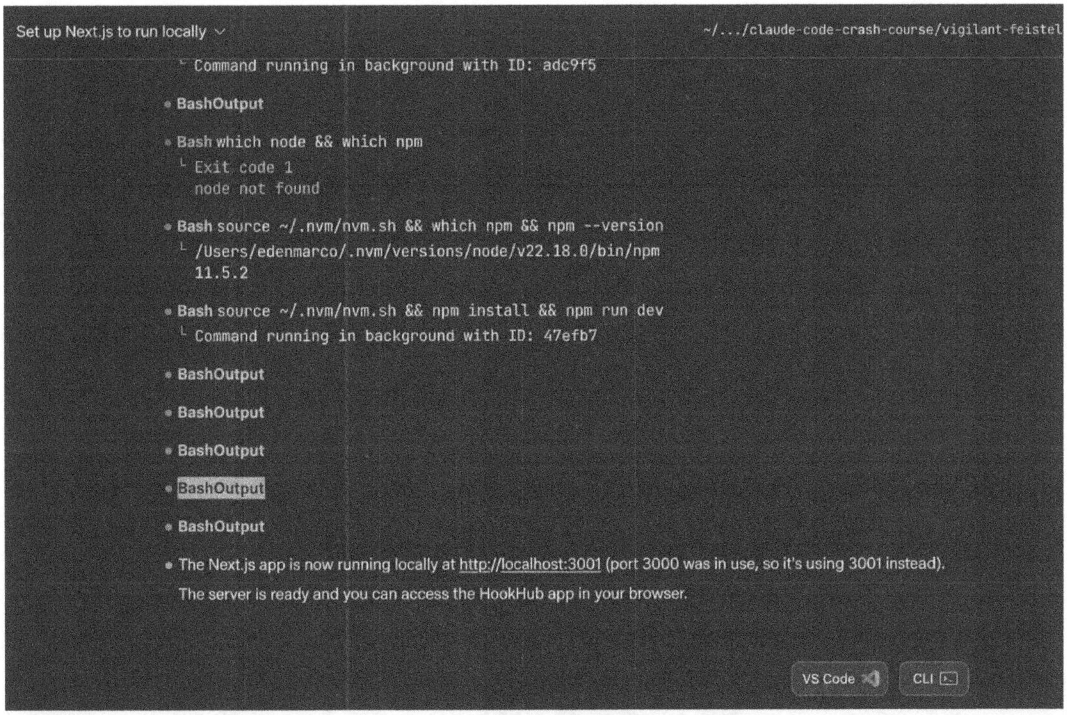

Figure 10.9 – Next.js development server running locally through Claude Cod

Coordinating parallel local and cloud work

At this stage, we extend the implementation to demonstrate how features can be developed in parallel across local and cloud environments.

Switch to the Claude application from the Claude Code tab and use it as a separate research environment, independent of your local Claude Code session. Assign it a repository discovery task by opening a new chat and instructing it to search for online repositories that implement Claude Code hooks, with a focus on those that have a high number of GitHub stars.

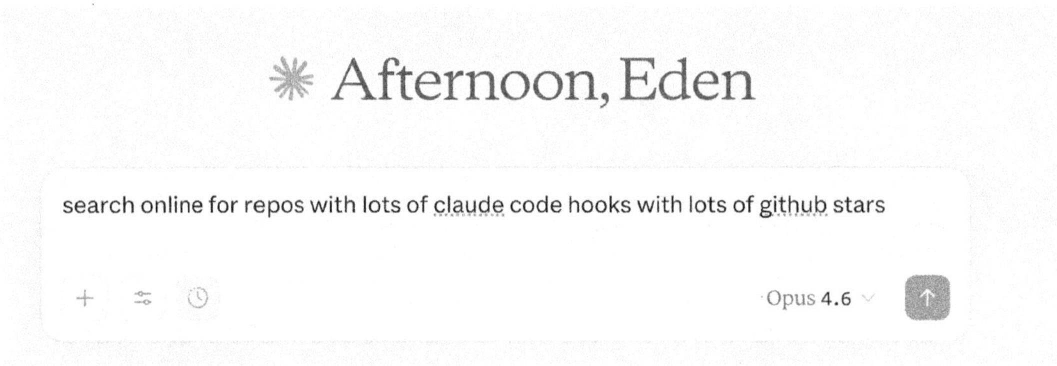

Figure 10.10 – Assigning a repository discovery task in Claude Code

The intention is clear: once the repositories are identified, the results will be passed back into Claude Code and integrated into the HookHub database.

Executing concurrent feature development

While the research task runs in the cloud, we return to the current Claude Code session running locally and request a new feature:

```
Add animations to the application
```

This session runs entirely on your local machine. You create a new instance, select the `Agentic-Coding-with-Claude-Code` repository, and implement the feature directly against your local codebase.

Next, while it is running, we create another Claude Code instance, this time keeping the default cloud option selected. This activates a background agent running in the Anthropic cloud. Enter the following prompt:

```
Add to the project/hookhub branch a much cooler hero, make it anthropic style
```

This can be seen in the following screenshot.

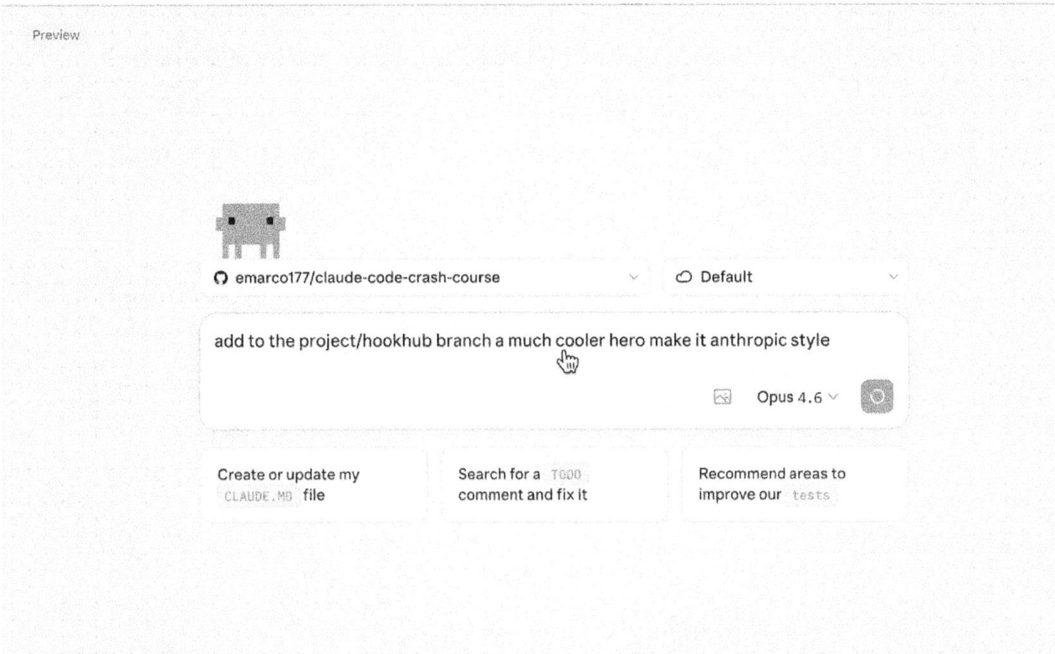

Figure 10.11 – Prompting Claude Code to implement a new feature during parallel development

In the prompt, we explicitly instruct it to do the following:

- Work on the `project/hookhub` branch
- Add a significantly improved hero section
- Style it in an Anthropic-inspired manner

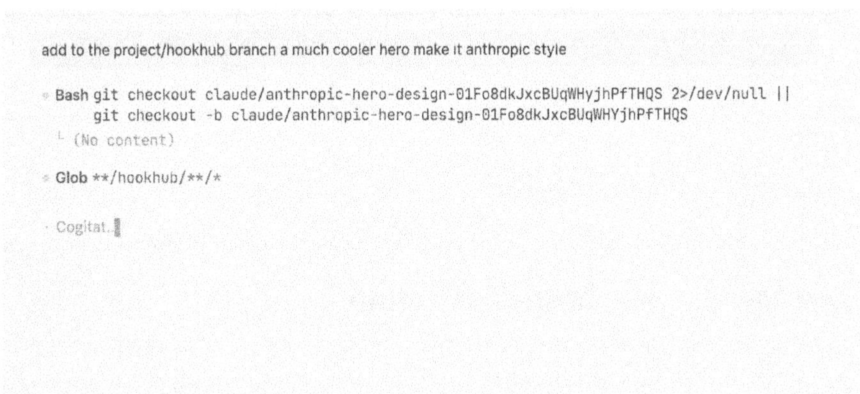

Figure 10.12 – Claude Code executing a concurrent feature implementation task

At this stage, all three tasks are executing concurrently across local and cloud environments:

- A cloud research process identifying high-star Claude Code hook repositories
- A local Claude Code session adding animations to the UI (`vigilant fiestal`)
- A remote background agent redesigning the hero section on a specific branch (`claude/anthropic-hero-design-01Fo8dkJxcBUqWHyjhPfTHQS`)

Two of these execute locally. One executes in the Anthropic cloud.

The local Claude Code instance completes the animation feature and proposes changes for approval. The agent proposes changes that require approval. Allow those changes so the implementation can proceed.

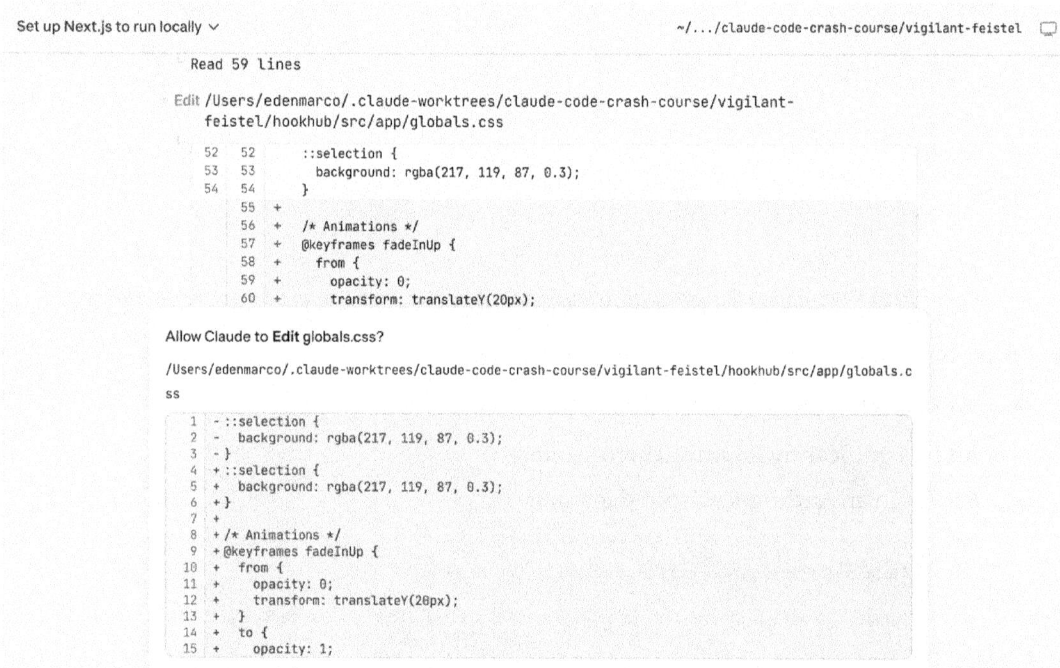

Figure 10.13 – Reviewing and approving local code changes generated by Claude Code

This completes the animation task locally, and the updated UI reflects the new animations.

Observing the remote branch creation

Next, switch to the remote background agent running in the cloud. The agent creates a new branch in the Anthropic cloud environment. Initially, it checks out from the main branch rather than `project/hookhub`.

This is important because the feature is intended to be implemented on `project/hookhub`. If development continues from `main`, it could lead to inconsistencies later during merging.

Shortly afterward, the agent corrects the branch context by executing the following:

```
git checkout origin/project/hookhub
```

The following screenshot shows the agent executing this command to switch to the correct branch:

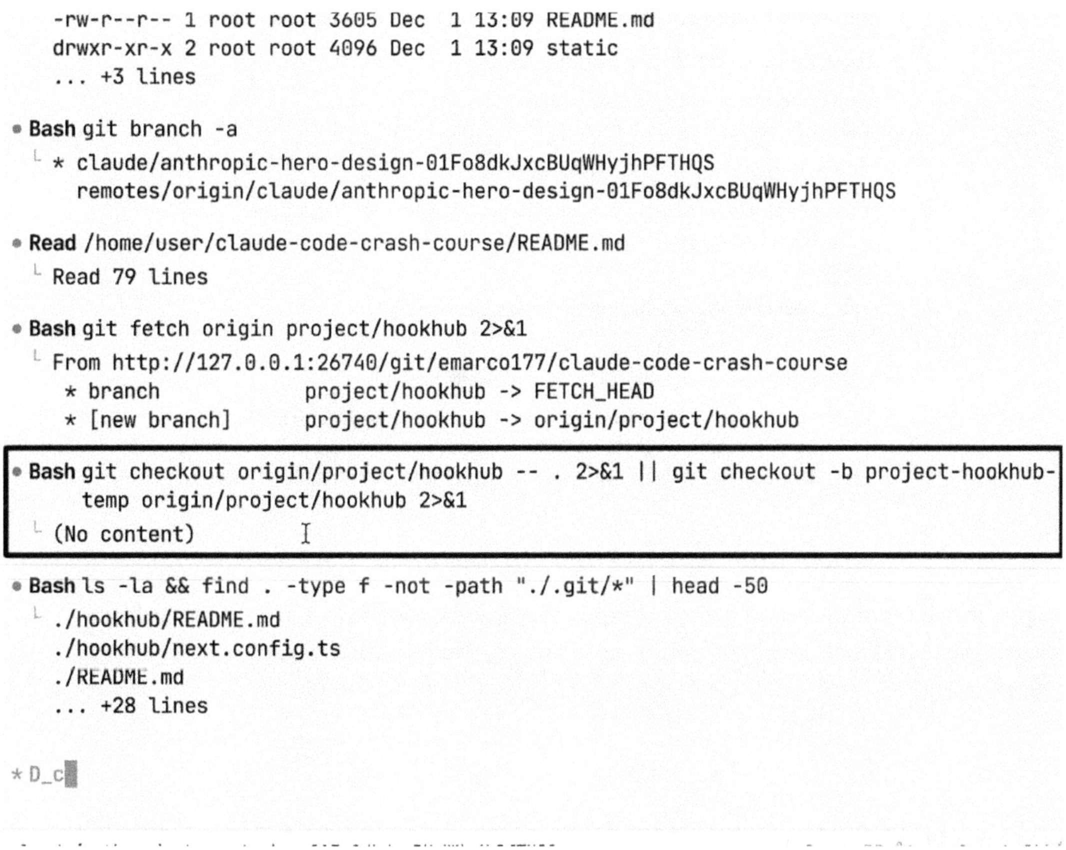

Figure 10.14 – Cloud agent switching to the correct feature branch

This ensures it is now working against the correct branch. It fetches the relevant code and lists the project files again, restoring full context before proceeding with the hero section redesign.

Processing the research results

Meanwhile, the Claude Desktop research task completes and returns a list of high-star Claude Code hook repositories. The output contains multiple GitHub repository links.

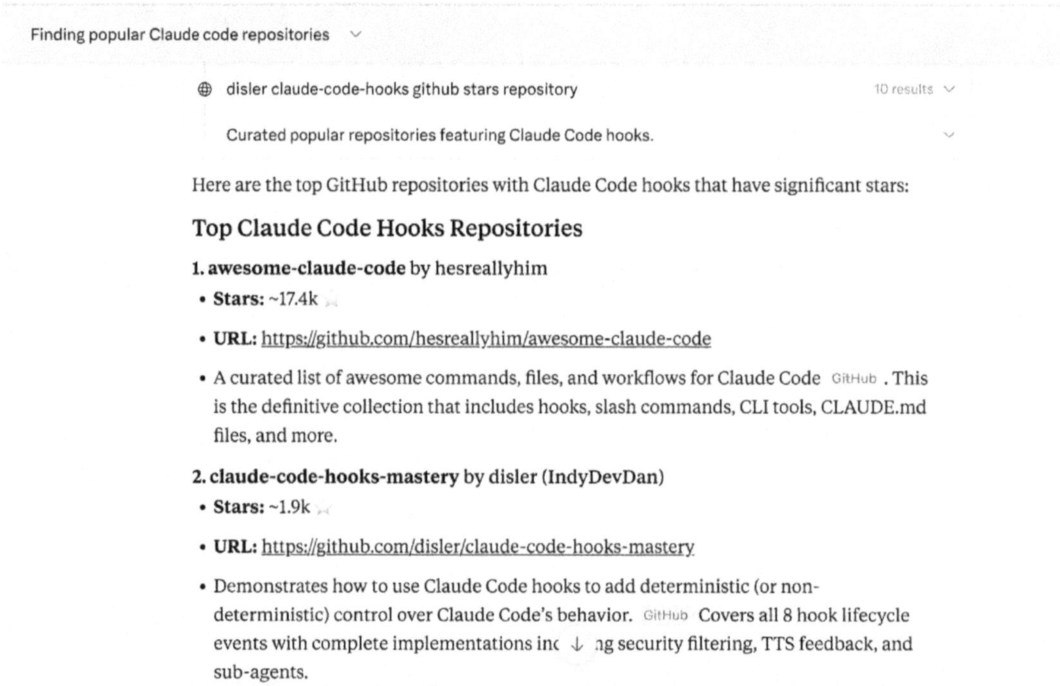

Figure 10.15 – Claude Code displaying curated hook repository results

Copy the full set of URLs and paste the repository information into a new local worktree session, then instruct the agent to add those links to the HookHub list.

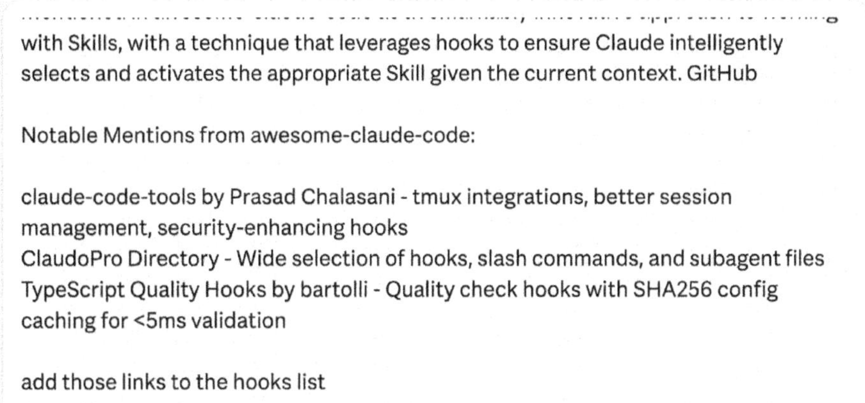

Figure 10.16 – Adding discovered repositories to the HookHub configuration

Since Git worktrees are being used, this modification occurs in a separate working directory tied to its specific branch. The agent maps the repositories and updates the `hooks.json` file with the new entries.

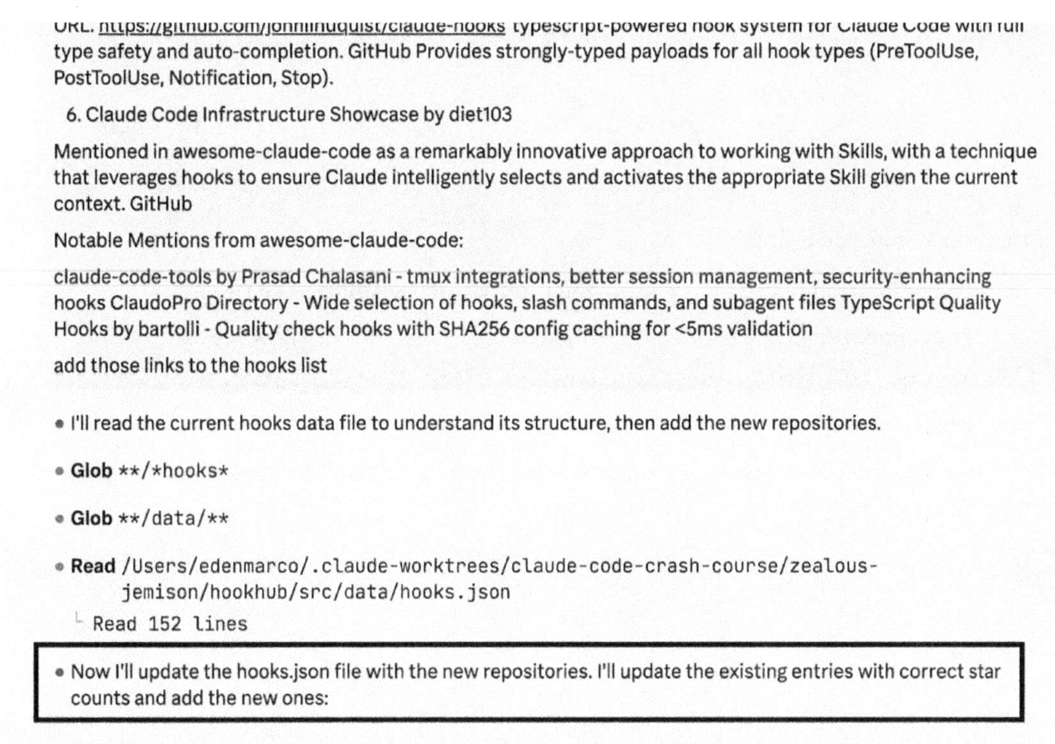

Figure 10.17 – Updating the hooks.json configuration with discovered repositories

Once the changes are generated, review and accept them.

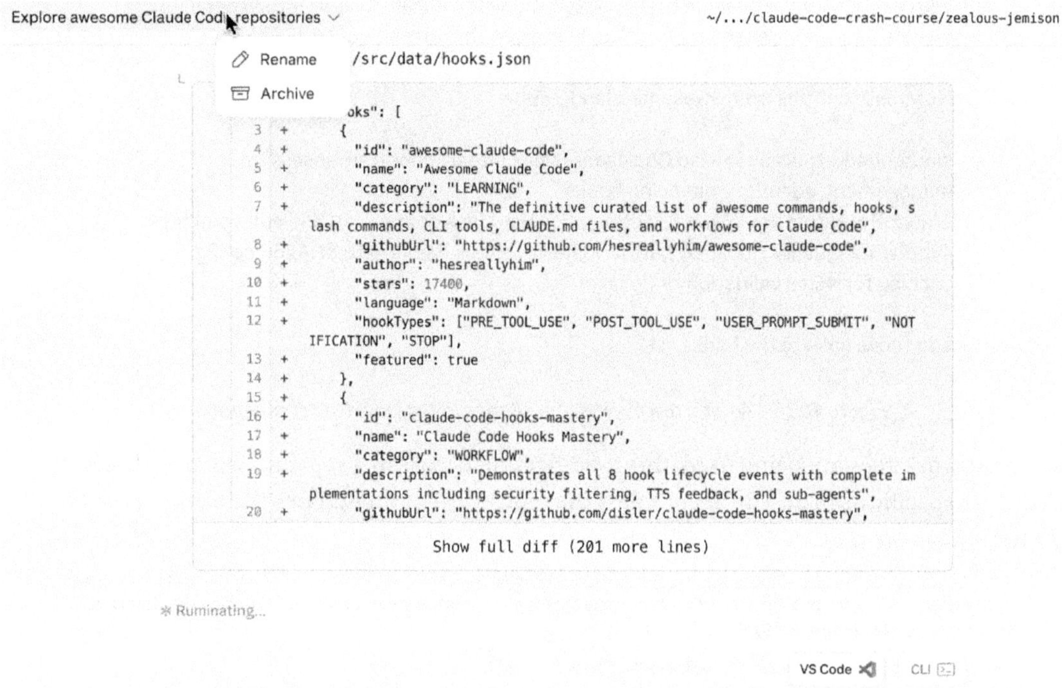

Figure 10.18 – Reviewing and approving updates to the hooks.json configuration

At this stage, note the following:

- The animation feature has completed locally and is visible in the UI
- The database update task has modified `hooks.json` with the new repository links
- The remote cloud agent is working on the hero section after correctly switching to `project/hookhub`

The following screenshot shows the updated repository links and confirms that the changes have been applied.

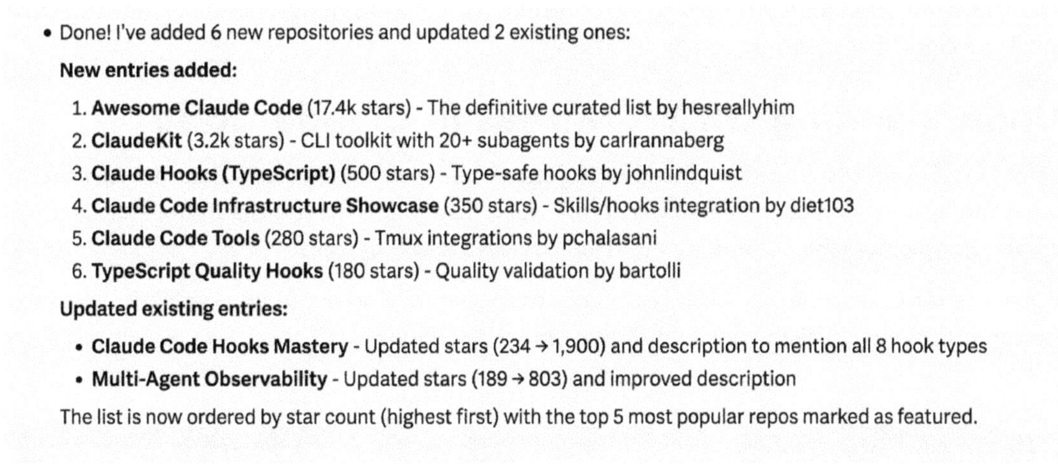
- Done! I've added 6 new repositories and updated 2 existing ones:

  New entries added:

  1. **Awesome Claude Code** (17.4k stars) - The definitive curated list by hesreallyhim
  2. **ClaudeKit** (3.2k stars) - CLI toolkit with 20+ subagents by carlrannaberg
  3. **Claude Hooks (TypeScript)** (500 stars) - Type-safe hooks by johnlindquist
  4. **Claude Code Infrastructure Showcase** (350 stars) - Skills/hooks integration by diet103
  5. **Claude Code Tools** (280 stars) - Tmux integrations by pchalasani
  6. **TypeScript Quality Hooks** (180 stars) - Quality validation by bartolli

  Updated existing entries:

  - **Claude Code Hooks Mastery** - Updated stars (234 → 1,900) and description to mention all 8 hook types
  - **Multi-Agent Observability** - Updated stars (189 → 803) and improved description

  The list is now ordered by star count (highest first) with the top 5 most popular repos marked as featured.

Figure 10.19 – Confirming the updated HookHub repository links

Understanding the Git worktree layout

Since Git worktrees are in use, separate directories represent different active branches.

The primary repository directory remains intact. Alongside it, an additional worktree directory: such as `zealous-jemison` (auto-generated by Claude Code) corresponds to another branch. Each parallel task operates within its own worktree context, which prevents interference between feature implementations.

In this example, three independent features were developed simultaneously: UI animations for the application, updates to the hook repository database, and a redesigned hero section. Each feature was implemented in a separate branch and later consolidated into a single branch.

Preparing to merge the artifacts

The remaining challenge is consolidating all the artifacts. You have three branches to bring together: a remote branch updated by the cloud agent, and two local worktree branches containing animation changes and database updates.

These changes must be merged into a single, coherent code base. Because one branch exists remotely and others exist locally through Git worktrees, the merge requires explicit coordination.

The next step is to instruct Claude Code to merge these branches so that all artifacts, including the animations, the updated hook repositories, and the redesigned hero section, are combined into a single unified branch, as shown in the following prompt.

```
Merge all the commits here to branch project/hookub
```

This transition from parallel execution to controlled integration completes the orchestration of local and cloud-based development workflows.

Understanding Git Worktrees in Claude Code

Before moving on to merging, we need to understand how Git Worktrees function under the hood and how version control behaves in this setup. The goal is to have the right intuition for what is happening when Claude Code creates isolated working copies.

When Claude Code creates a Worktree, it creates a separate working directory that is linked to the repository but checked out to a different branch.

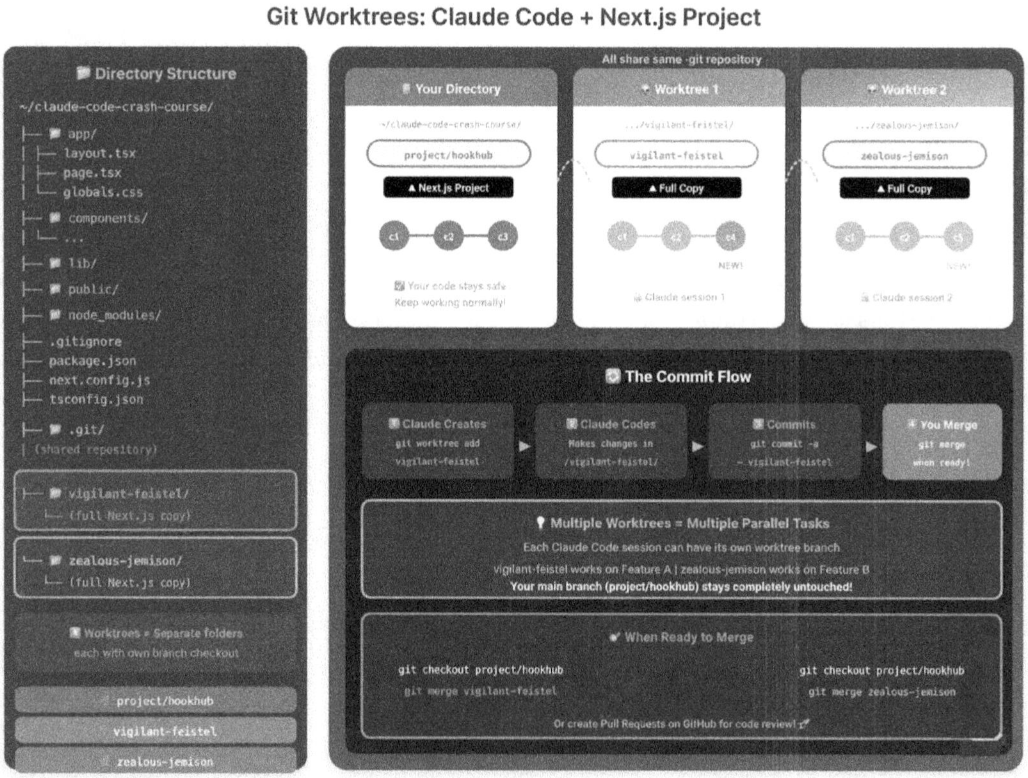

Figure 10.20 – Git Worktrees architecture used by Claude Code for parallel development

How Claude Code uses a Worktree

The flow is easier to understand when we look at it step by step. What follows is the exact sequence of actions that take place when Claude Code creates and begins working inside a Worktree:

1. Claude Code creates a Worktree with a new branch. For example, we can name the Worktree `vigilant feistel` (auto-generated by Claude Code).
2. All code and all changes happen inside the Worktree directory.
3. When we commit the code, the commit lives in the `vigilant feistel` branch.
4. The original branch, `project/hookhub`, remains completely untouched.
5. If we like what Claude Code built, we merge it.
6. If we do not like it, we delete the Worktree and the branch and leave no mess.

Multiple Worktrees in parallel

In *Figure 10.20*, there were two Worktrees—`vigilant feistel` and `zealous jemison`:

1. We open the editor and see the regular `hookhub` directory structure.
2. We also see two additional directories, where each directory contains an exact copy of the original branch's code base.
3. Even though the directory structures match, the Git branches are separate; `vigilant feistel` and `zealous jemison` are separate GitHub branches, distinct from `project/hookhub`.
4. This allows multiple parallel tasks, with each Claude instance working in a totally different branch and using a completely fresh copy of the original code.

Working with multiple agents requires orchestration, meaning developers must coordinate multiple working contexts, branches, and tasks. Git Worktrees provide a convenient mechanism for managing this coordination.

Merging parallel feature branches

The local Claude Code instance implemented the animation inside the `vigilant feistel` directory. That directory is a Git Worktree linked to the main repository but checked out to a different branch.

Even though the target branch is `project/hookhub`, all the actual work happened inside the `vigilant feistel` directory. This is exactly how Git Worktrees operate. They allow development in isolated directories while still pointing to the same repository.

Now we want to take the code generated there and commit it. Instruct Claude to create a commit and explicitly state in the message that the changes were generated via Claude Code Desktop.

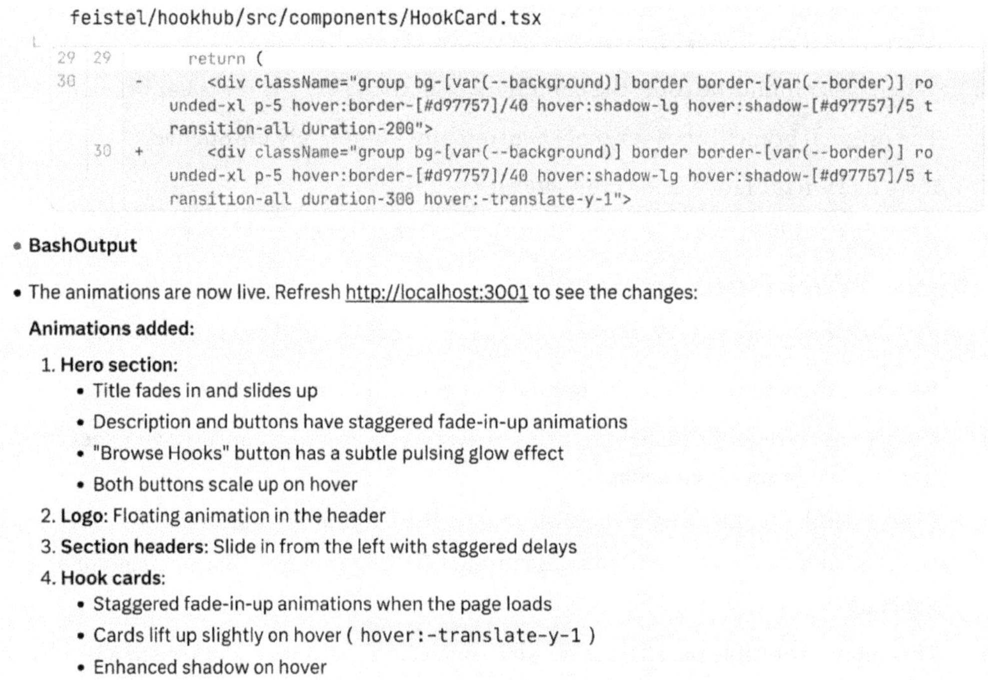

Figure 10.21 – Reviewing animation feature changes generated in the vigilant_fiestal worktree

While that process (`vigilant fiestal`) was running, another local Claude instance was working on updating GitHub URLs using a JSON file in a separate Worktree named `zealous jemison`. Both instances were operating independently. Claude prepares the staging command.

The following screenshot shows Claude Code preparing the commit and presenting it for approval.

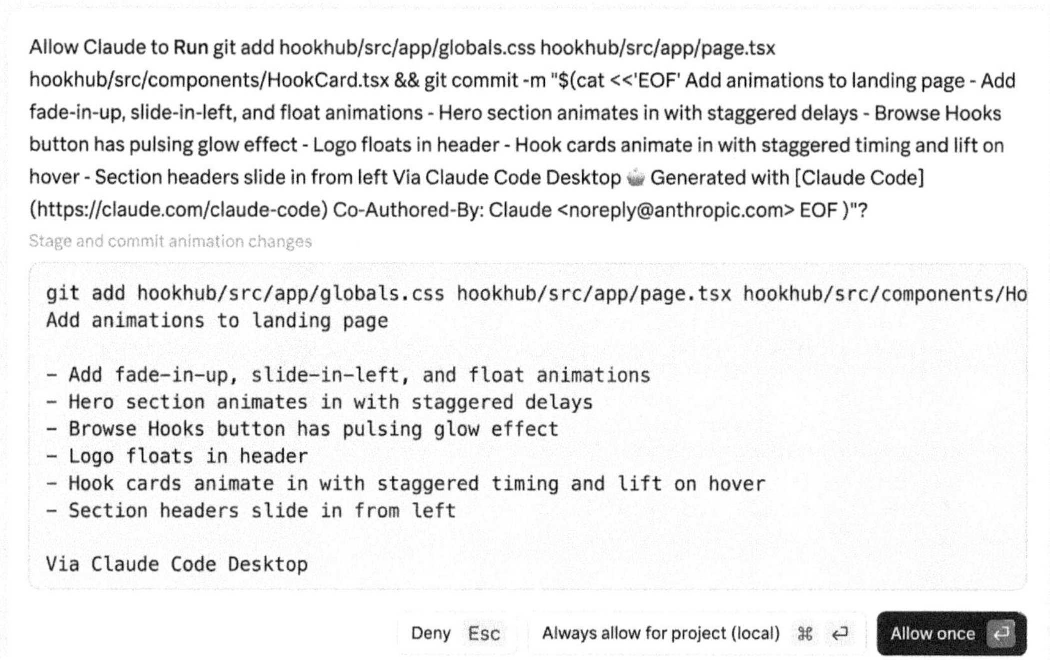

Figure 10.22 – Claude Code preparing a commit for the animation feature changes

Approve it. The commit message clearly indicates that the changes were generated with Claude Desktop. After approving, something important becomes visible. The active branch is not `project/hookhub`. It is `vigilant-fiestel`.

```
● Bash git diff
  └       <div className="flex items-start justify-between gap-3 mb-3">
            <h3 className="text-base font-semibold text-[var(--foreground)] leading-
    snug">...
    ... +180 lines

● Bash git log --oneline -5
  └ 16a2531 initial project
    fa598ec 1-start-here
    1f4813c first commit
    ... +2 lines

● Bash git add hookhub/src/app/globals.css hookhub/src/app/page.tsx
       hookhub/src/components/HookCard.tsx && git commit -m "$(cat <<'EOF' Add animations
       to landing page - Add fade-in-up, slide-in-left, and float animations - Hero
       section animates in with staggered delays - Browse Hooks button has pulsing glow
       effect - Logo floats in header - Hook cards animate in with staggered timing and
       lift on hover - Section headers slide in from left Via Claude Code Desktop 🌐
       Generated with [Claude Code](https://claude.com/claude-code) Co-Authored-By:
       Claude <noreply@anthropic.com> EOF )"
  └ [vigilant-feistel b438f44] Add animations to landing page
     3 files changed, 100 insertions(+), 13 deletions(-)

✻ Musing...
```

Figure 10.23 – Commit applied to the vigilant-fiestel Git worktree branch

This confirms how Worktrees behave. When a commit is created inside a Worktree, it is applied to that Worktree's branch—not to the original branch. The commit is successfully added to `vigilant-fiestel`.

Pushing Worktree branches

Now we push the changes. Switch to the `zealous jemison` Worktree. That branch already contains its commit. Push it as well.

Claude will request permission to push. The following screenshot shows what it looks like for `zealous-jemison:`, which implements the database update that adds the new Claude Code repository entries to `hooks.json`.

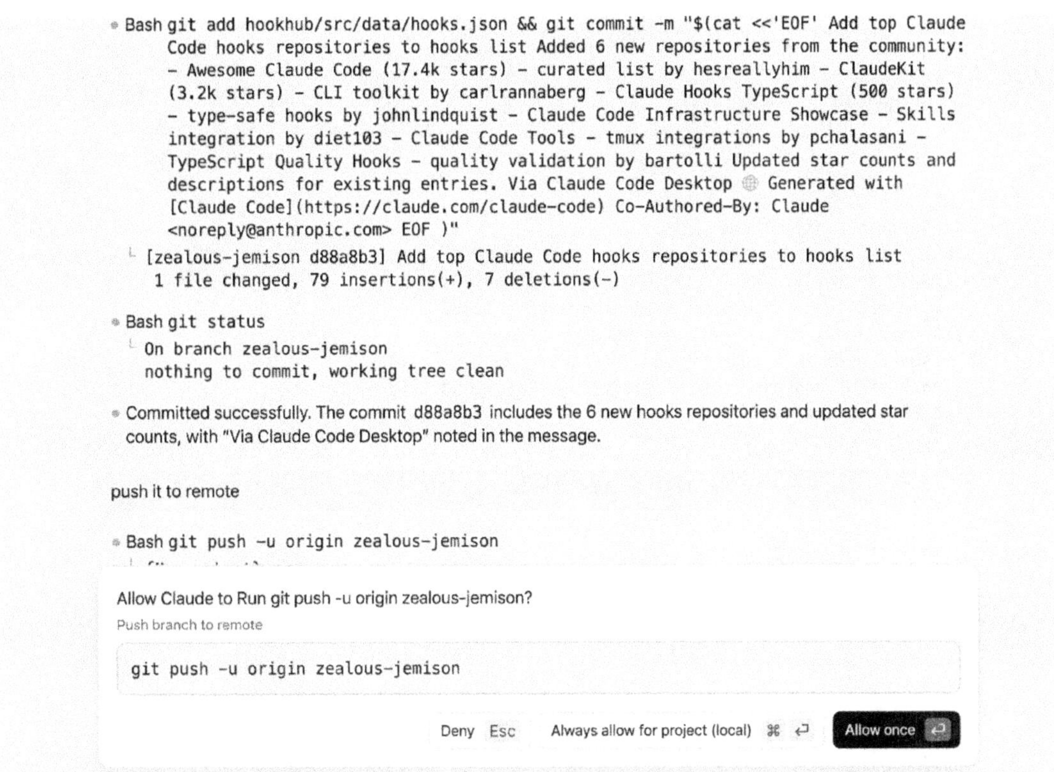

Figure 10.24 – Pushing the zealous-jemison worktree branch to the remote repository

This is what it looks like for `vigilant-fiestel`: implements the UI animation feature for the landing page hero section.

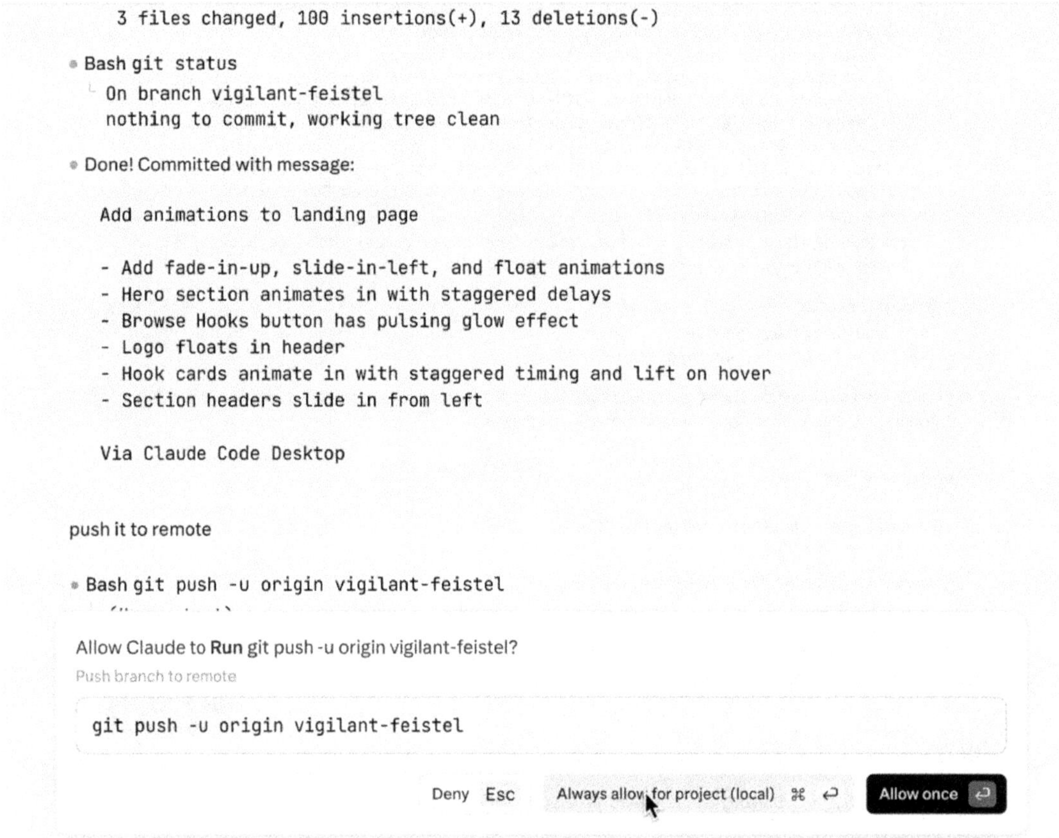

Figure 10.25 – Pushing the vigilant-fiestel worktree branch to the remote repository

Approve both. The `project/hookhub` branch still does not show new commits. That is expected. Each Worktree maintains its own branch.

There is also a third branch created by a remote Claude Code instance, called `claude/anthropic-hero-design/<id>`.

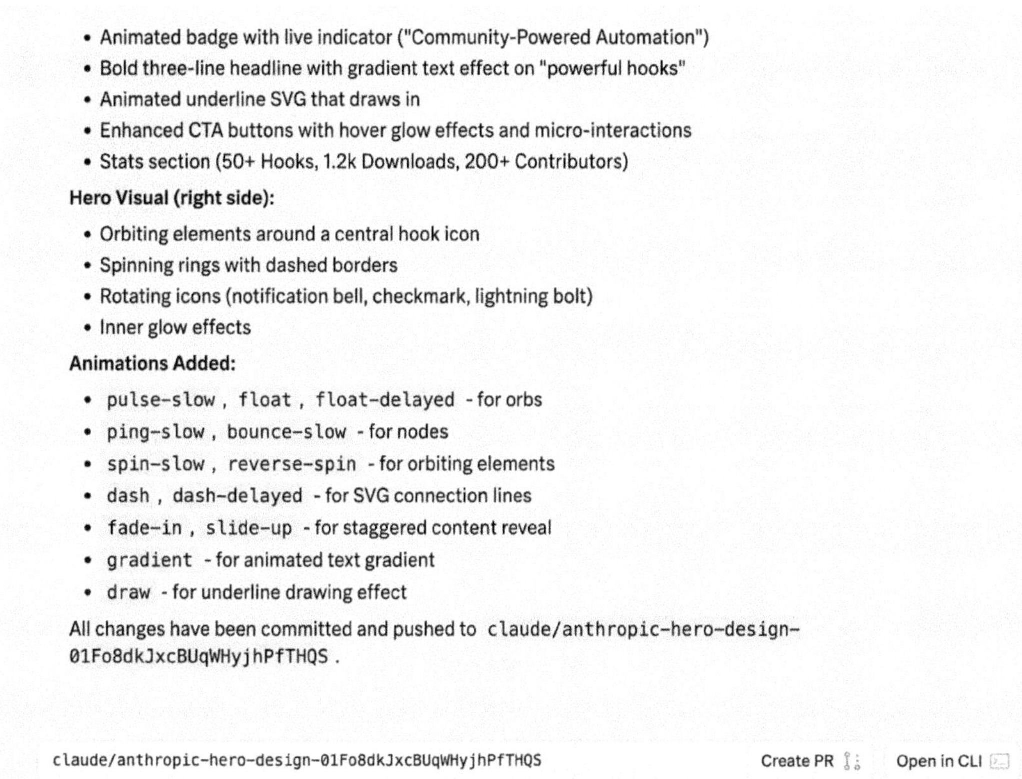

Figure 10.26 – Remote Claude Code agent completing the hero section redesign

All changes in that branch have already been committed and pushed remotely.

Refreshing the repository confirms three new branches:

- `vigilant fiestel`
- `zealous jemison`
- `Anthropic Hero Design`

The following screenshot shows the repository view where these newly created branches are visible.

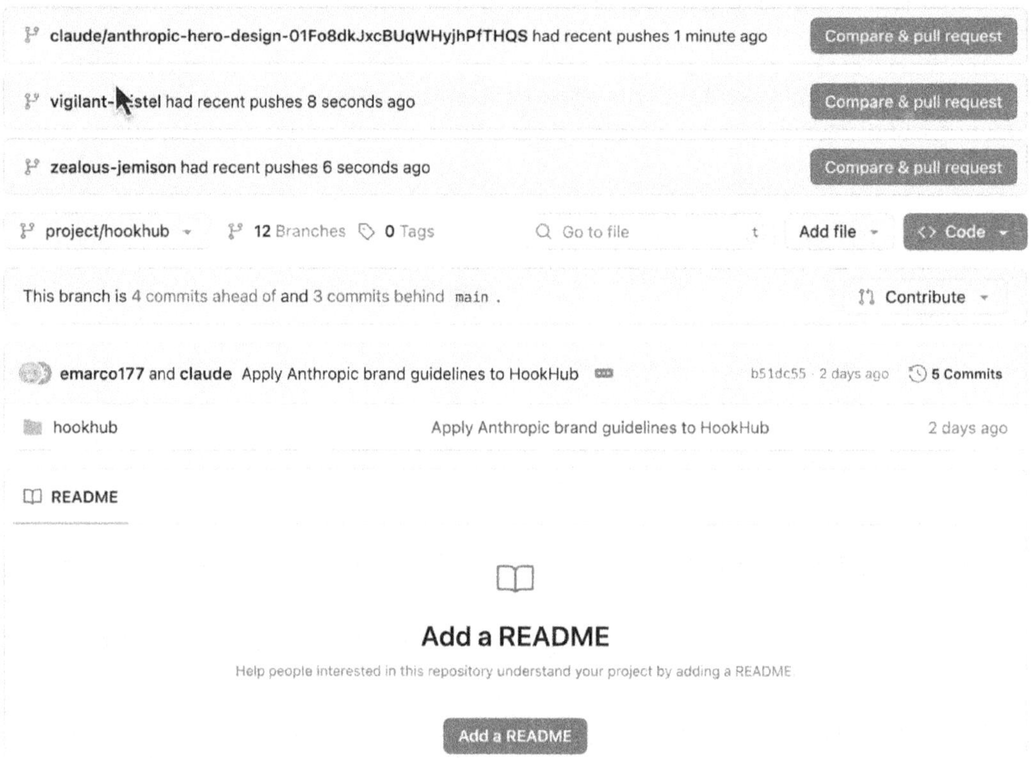

Figure 10.27 – GitHub repository view showing newly created feature branches

Each branch represents a feature developed independently.

Merging everything into project/hookhub

Now we want to bring all these implementations together into `project/hookhub`.

Instead of manually checking out and merging each branch, we delegate the task to Claude Code.

We provide the branch names and instruct Claude to merge all commits into `project/hookhub`.

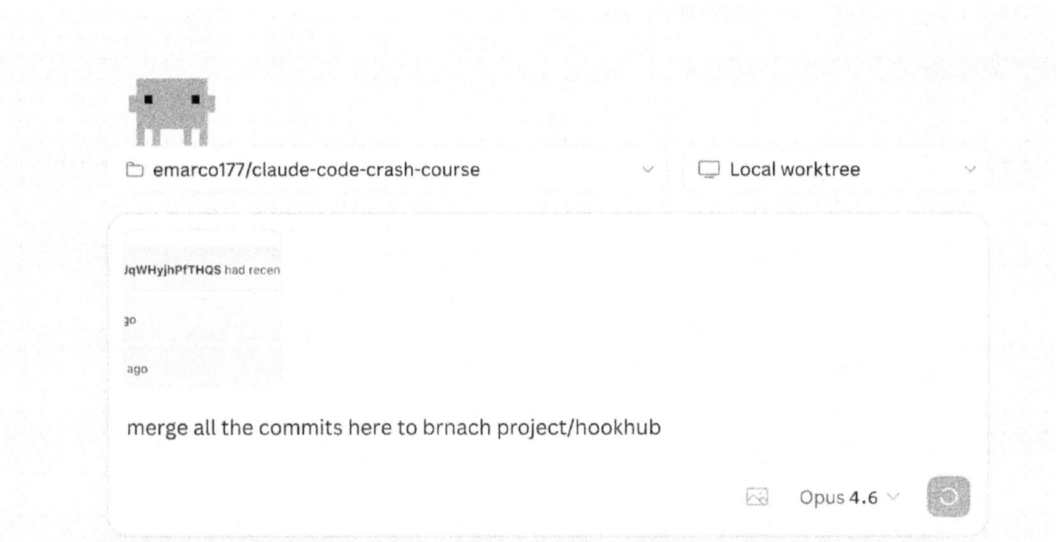

Figure 10.28 – Prompting Claude Code to merge all feature branches into project/hookhub

Claude starts working locally and creates another Worktree named `suspicious-bassi`.

Rather than merging directly into `project/hookhub`, it creates a temporary integration branch, `project/hookhub-merge`.

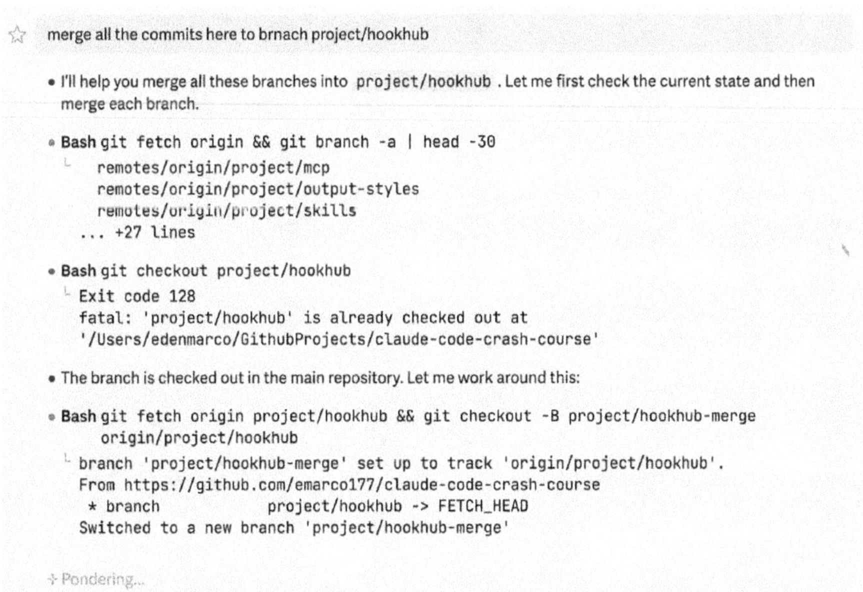

Figure 10.29 – Creating the temporary project/hookhub-merge integration branch

This allows consolidation before touching the main development branch.

Performing the merge

Claude Code begins the merge process. During the operation, a merge conflict appears.

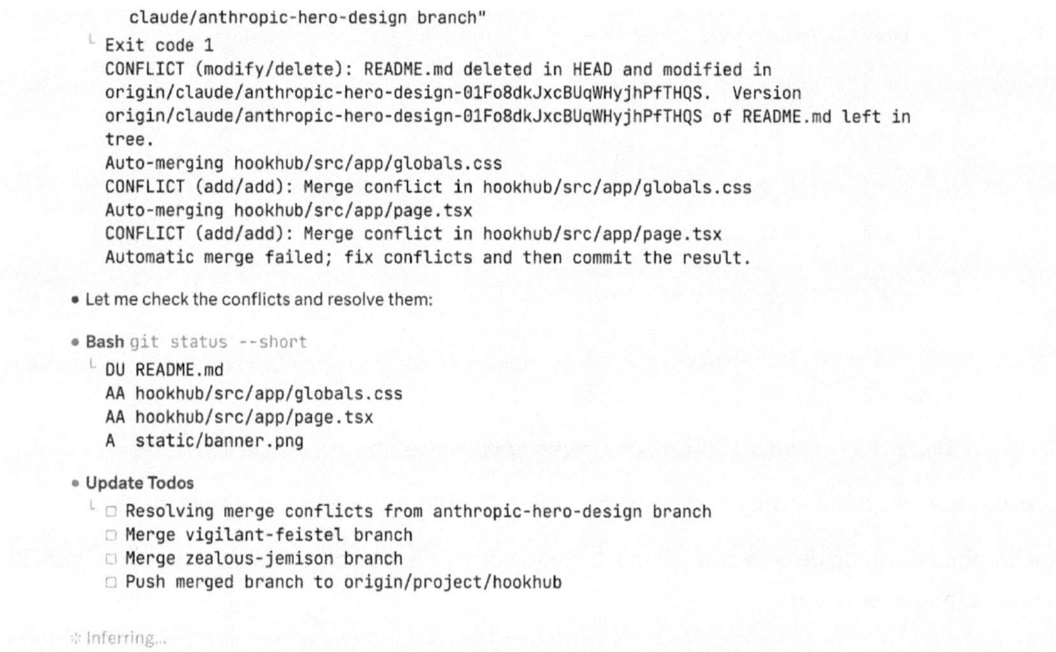

Figure 10.30 – Merge conflict detected during branch consolidation

Claude prepares a resolution plan:

1. Resolve conflicts from `anthropic-hero-design`.
2. Merge `vigilant-fiestel`.
3. Merge `zealous-jemison`.
4. Push everything to `project/hookhub`.
5. The conflict involves the global CSS file.
6. Claude proposes edits. We approve them.
7. The merge commit is created.

8. Claude continues:

```
git merge vigilant-fiestel
```

9. Then run the followng:

```
git merge zealous-jemison
```

The following screenshot shows Claude Code performing the merge and presenting the merge commit for approval.

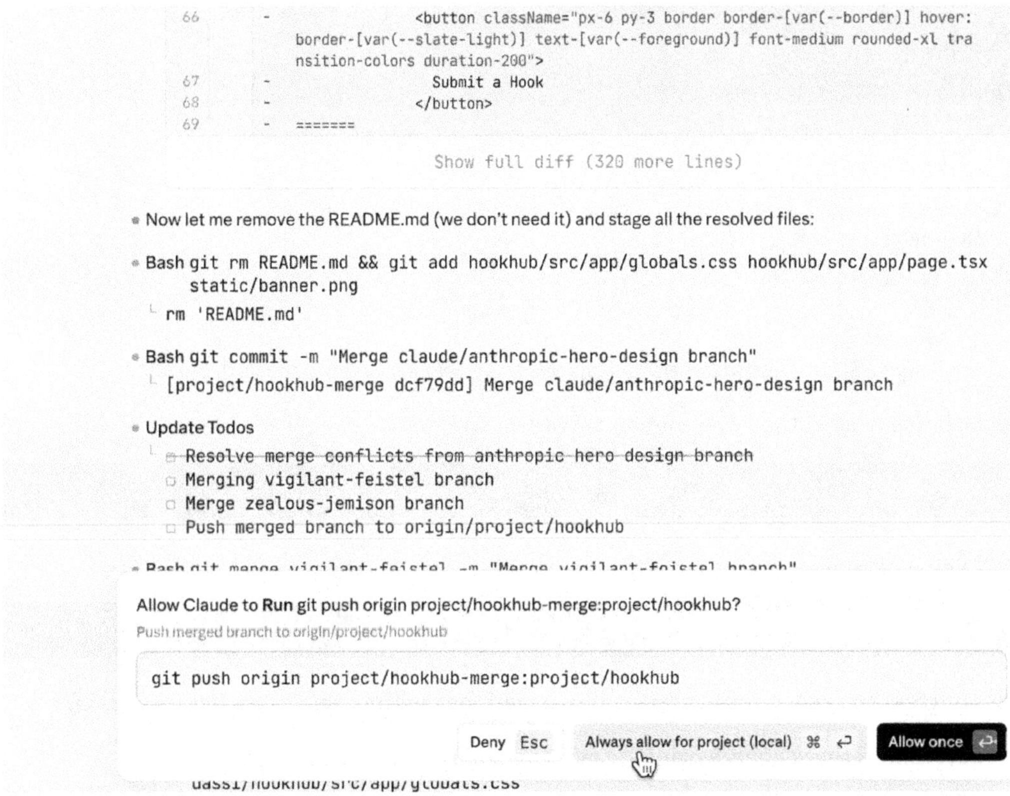

Figure 10.31 – Claude Code presenting the final merge commit for approval

At this point, all feature branches are consolidated into `project/hookhub-merge`.

Testing before pushing to project/hookhub

Claude requests permission to push the merged result into `project/hookhub`.

Do not approve it yet. Before pushing, test locally.

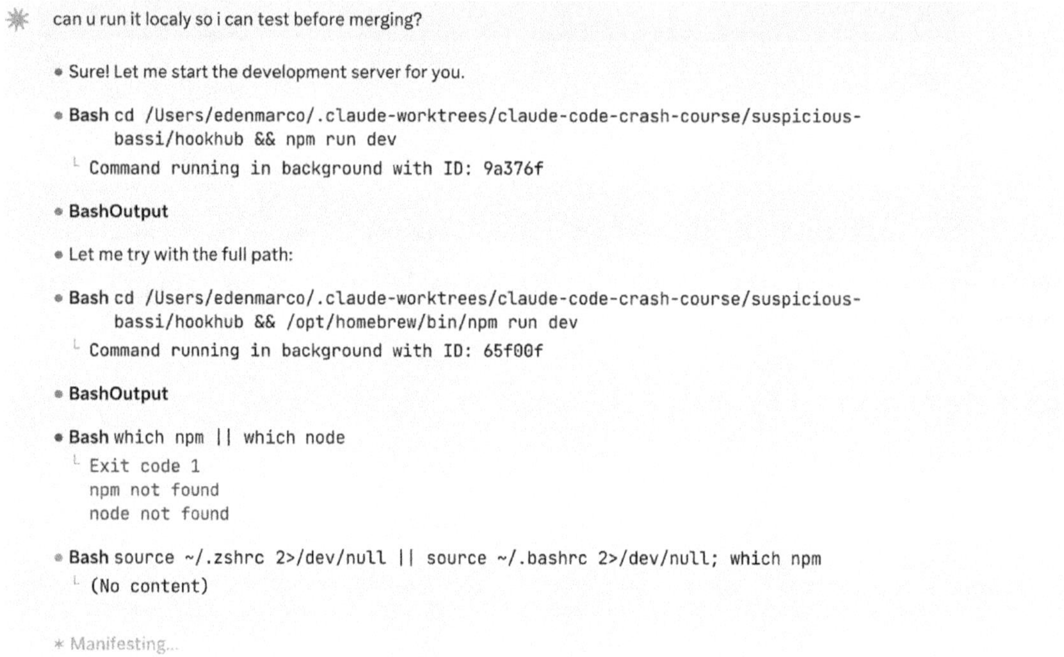

Figure 10.32 – Testing the merged project locally before pushing to the main branch

Instruct Claude to start the development server:

```
npm run dev
```

An error can appears:

```
npm is not found
```

Claude sources the `.zshrc` configuration file to load the environment and attempts again.

It then determines that dependencies are missing and runs the following:

```
npm install
```

Now, two processes are running:

- `npm install`
- `npm run dev`

Once dependency installation finishes, the development server successfully starts on port `3002`. The merged implementation is now running locally.

Validating the integrated result

Open the application running on port `3002` and compare it with the original implementation.

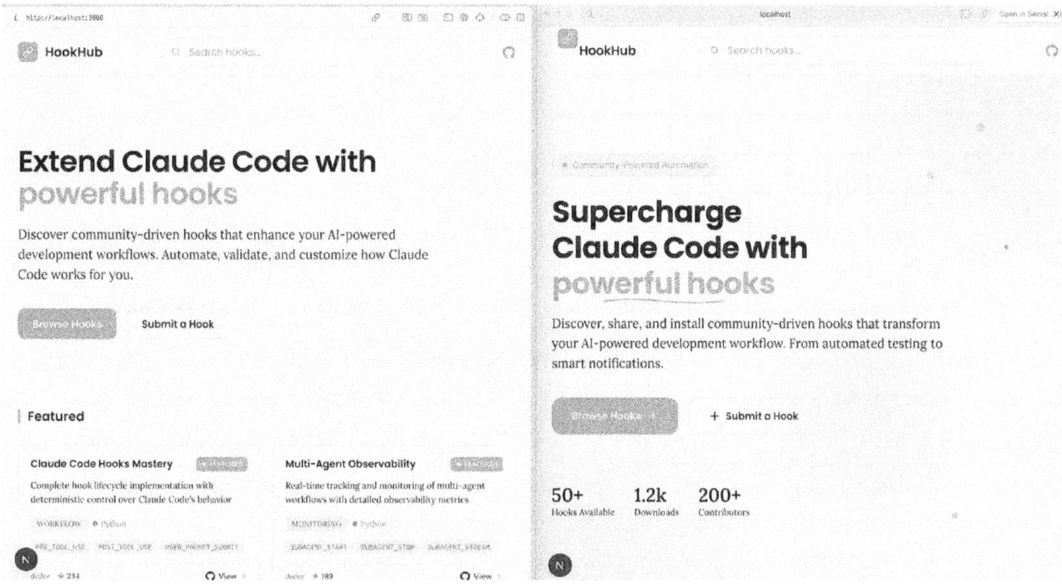

Figure 10.33 – Comparing the original and enhanced HookHub hero section

The differences are immediately visible. The new hero section now includes the following:

- A grid background
- A banner element
- A squiggly line
- Repository statistics
- Animated effects

The repository list contains more entries than before. These were researched and added by Claude Code. Animations are present throughout the entire website, not just in isolated components. The experience feels dynamic compared to the original static version.

All three independently developed features coexist correctly.

Finalizing the merge

With validation complete, we approve the push. Claude merges `project/hookhub-merge` into `project/hookhub`.

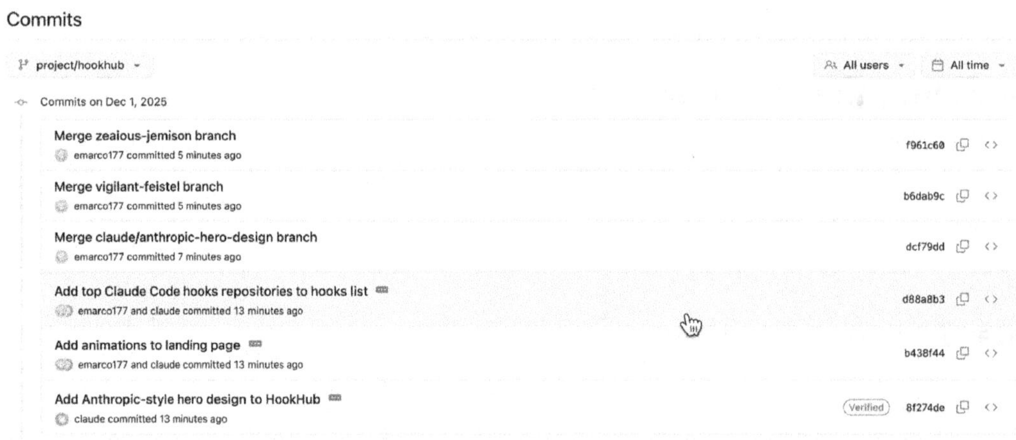

Figure 10.34 – Final commit history after merging all feature branches into project/hookhub

Refreshing the repository confirms the result. The branch now contains three commits. Each commit merges a different branch originating from a separate Worktree created by Claude Code. Each of those branches represents a feature that was implemented independently.

This setup highlights an important shift in how development can scale. Three separate features were developed in parallel by different Claude Code instances, operating at the same time. In addition to the two local instances, another Claude Code instance was running remotely.

Seeing these three independent lines of development converge into a single branch makes the implications clear. We are effectively scaling ourselves as developers by delegating parallel feature implementation.

It is also worth noting that there is limited frontend experience involved in this process. The Claude Code model powering these implementations handled the frontend work and proved capable of producing the required code.

Running Claude Code in the cloud via mobile

Claude Code is now integrated into the mobile application. The same workflow used on the desktop can be initiated directly from a phone. In this case, the `claude-code-crash-course` repository is selected from the mobile interface, and the session begins from there.

Because the mobile environment does not execute code locally, all operations run in the Anthropic cloud. There is no dependency on a local machine. The repository is cloned remotely, branches are checked out remotely, and changes are committed remotely.

We begin by instructing Claude to switch to the `project/hookhub` branch and implement an Anthropic-style footer.

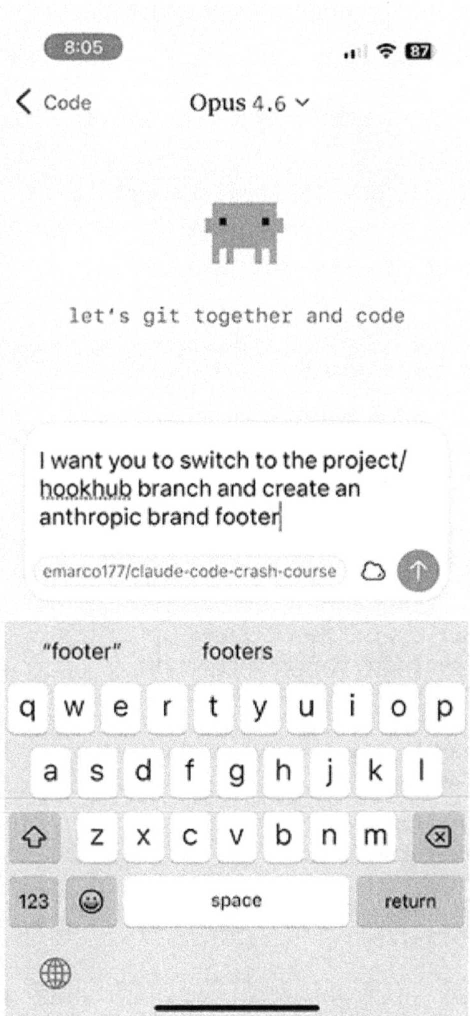

Figure 10.35 – Running Claude Code from the mobile application interface

The workflow mirrors the desktop experience: Claude clones the repository, checks out the target branch, inspects the project structure, implements the feature, commits the changes, and prepares a pull request.

The process unfolds step by step. The repository is fetched. The branch is switched. Files are examined. The system instruction confirms the branch change to `project/hookhub`.

Figure 10.36 – Claude Code analyzing the repository from the mobile session

Once the project context is understood, Claude identifies that the repository is a Next.js application with Anthropic-style branding and proceeds accordingly.

It is worth noting that the default cloud configuration does not include MCPs, custom hooks, or output styles. The environment runs with default settings. Custom configurations can be added separately, but this session operates without them.

Implementing the footer component

Claude generates a new `footer.tsx` file under the `components` directory.

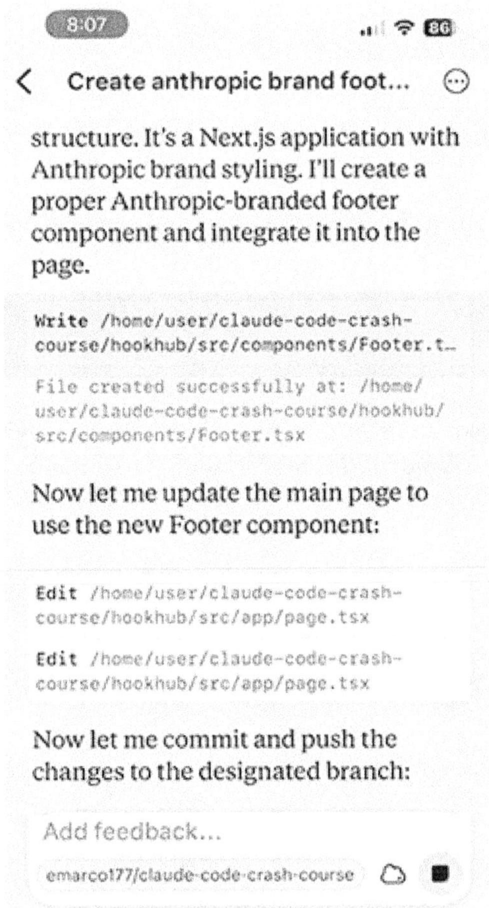

Figure 10.37 – Creating and integrating the footer component from the mobile Claude Code session

The footer component reflects the Anthropic visual style. After creating the component, Claude integrates it into `page.tsx` by importing and rendering it within the main page.

Version control operations follow automatically. The changes are staged and committed. Because the request specified pushing changes to `project/hookhub`, and Claude Code uses Git worktrees internally, additional Git operations occur behind the scenes to merge the worktree commit into the correct branch.

The Git log confirms previous merges and commits from earlier work. The new footer component and page modifications are now part of the branch history.

Reviewing the pull request

Opening the repository on GitHub reveals the newly created pull request. Initially, the pull request targets `main`, which is not the intended base. The base branch is corrected to `project/hookhub`.

With the branch adjusted, the pull request reflects two modified files:

- `page.tsx`
- `footer.tsx`

The diff shows the footer component integration as expected.

At this stage, Claude can also be tagged directly within GitHub to review the pull request. Since no GitHub workflow is configured for this branch, automated checks are not triggered.

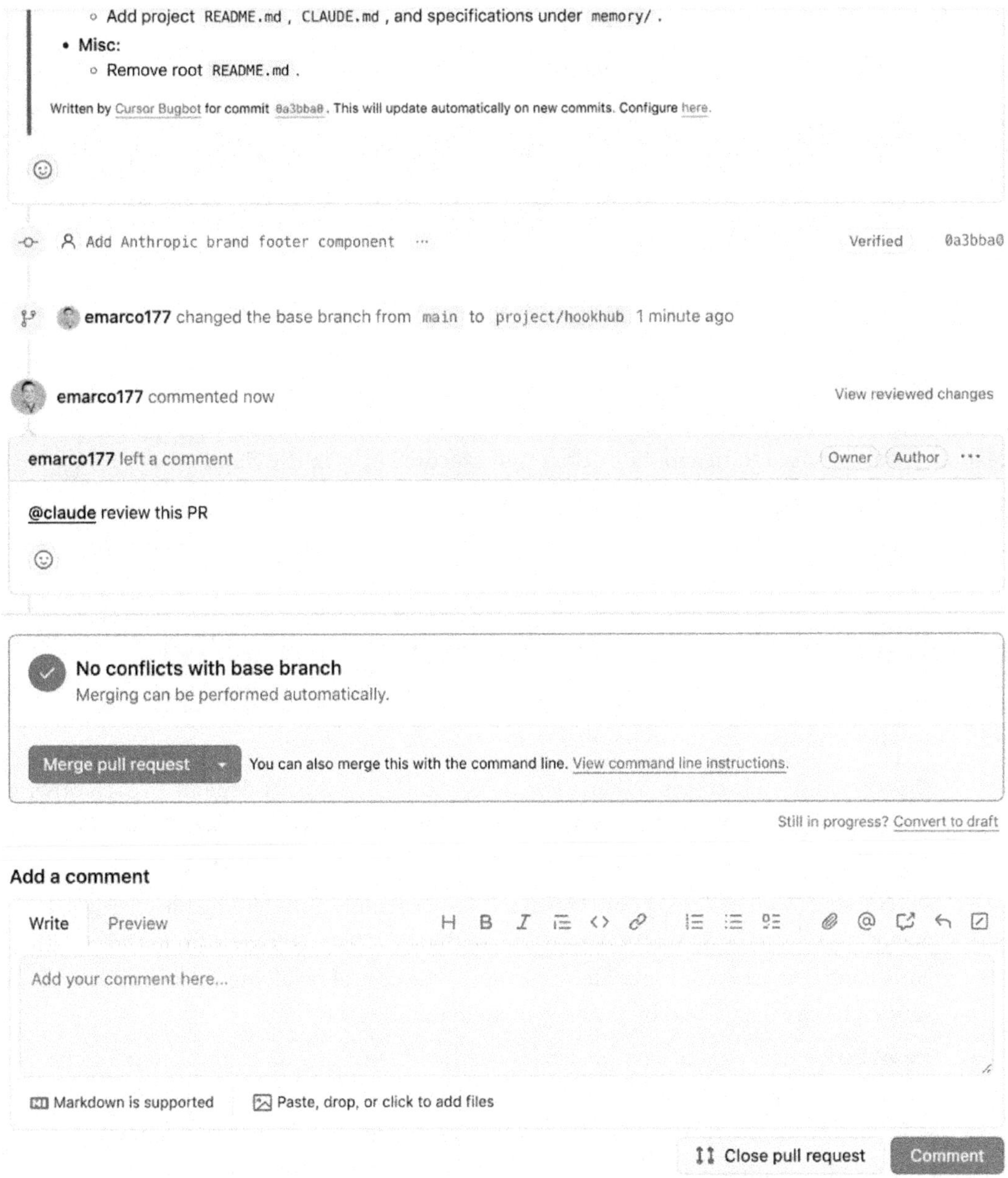

Figure 10.38 – Reviewing the pull request created by Claude Code on GitHub

The review remains manual.

Verifying the changes locally

To verify the integration, run the following:

```
git fetch
git pull
npm run dev
```

After starting the development server, the application loads with the new footer rendered on the page. The branding line **Built with love for Claude Code powered by Anthropic** appears at the bottom.

The layout requires a minor adjustment, which can be delegated back to Claude Code for refinement. The important outcome is that the entire workflow—from cloning to pull request creation—was initiated from a mobile device and executed fully in the cloud.

The engineering model remains consistent: specify intent, allow Claude to reason through the repository, review the output, and iterate. The interface changes, but the underlying development process does not.

When Parallel Agents Are Counterproductive

Parallel coding agents are useful, but they are not always the right choice. Here are the situations where running agents in parallel tends to work against you.

- **Tightly coupled features**: When tasks modify the same files or depend on each other's output, parallel agents will produce merge conflicts or silently overwrite each other's work. If feature B needs feature A's interface to exist first, run them sequentially.
- **Shared state and ordering constraints**: Database migrations, config file changes, and shared type definitions create implicit dependencies. Two agents adding entries to the same config, schema, or route file will collide. The cost of resolving those conflicts often outweighs the time saved by running them in parallel.
- **Small tasks**: Every agent session carries overhead: spinning up context, reading the codebase, and planning the work. For a task that takes two minutes to complete sequentially, splitting it across agents and then reviewing and merging the results can actually take longer. If a task fits comfortably in a single session, keep it there.

- **High coordination cost**: If you find yourself writing detailed, unambiguous specs just to keep agents from stepping on each other, that is a signal. The more time you spend defining boundaries, the less you are gaining from parallelism.
- **Exploratory or uncertain work**: When you do not yet know the right approach, such as debugging a tricky issue or prototyping an unclear design, parallel agents just multiply the uncertainty. One focused session that iterates is more effective than several agents exploring dead ends at the same time.

Note

Protip:

The mental model: parallel agents work best when tasks are independent, well-scoped, and touch different parts of the codebase. When in doubt, start sequential and parallelize only after you've confirmed the tasks don't interact.

Parallel Development Checklist:

1. Ensure each task operates on independent files/components
2. Verify the correct starting branch in each agent's prompt
3. Test the merged result before pushing to the target branch
4. Clean up worktree directories after merging

Summary

In this chapter, you learned how to use Claude Code within the desktop application, switch between **Local worktree** and cloud modes, and run multiple coding agents in parallel. You saw how Git Worktrees isolate feature development, how background agents operate in the cloud, and how independently developed branches can be merged, tested, and consolidated into a single working code base. You also explored how the same workflow extends to mobile, where all execution happens in the cloud.

This information is useful because it demonstrates how to move from sequential development to orchestrated, multi-agent workflows. By understanding how to manage parallel branches, coordinate local and remote agents, and safely merge their outputs, you can significantly increase development throughput while maintaining control over your code base.

In the next chapter, we examine deep agents and their role in long-horizon task execution. We define the characteristics of deep agents and analyze the LangChain deep agents harness, including its architecture and execution model.

Get this book's PDF copy, code bundle, and more

Scan the QR code (or go to `packtpub.com/unlock`). Search for this book by name, confirm the edition, and then follow the steps on the page.

Note: Have your invoice handy. Purchases made directly from the Packt website don't require an invoice.

11

Understanding Deep Agents

In this chapter, we dive into Deep Agents. Deep Agents are agents that are capable, useful, and designed to perform a variety of tasks, specifically long-horizon tasks that require sustained reasoning and action over multiple steps. Coding agents such as Claude Code, Cursor CLI, and the LangChain Deep Agents fall into this category. These systems are not limited to single-step tool usage; they operate across extended workflows, making decisions, adapting their plans, and acting iteratively until a broader objective is achieved.

We begin by taxonomizing Deep Agents, establishing what qualifies an agent as "deep" and identifying the defining characteristics that distinguish them from simpler agent patterns. From there, we define at a high level what makes an agent a deep agent and examine the properties that enable long-horizon execution.

This provides a practical glimpse into how state-of-the-art coding agents such as Claude Code are implemented, grounding our understanding in real engineering.

The following topics will be covered in this chapter:

- Agent taxonomy in production systems
- What makes an agent deep

Agent taxonomy in production systems

Before discussing Deep Agents, we first need to establish a taxonomy and clarify what kinds of agents are currently used in production across the industry. I will simplify this and describe how I view the landscape.

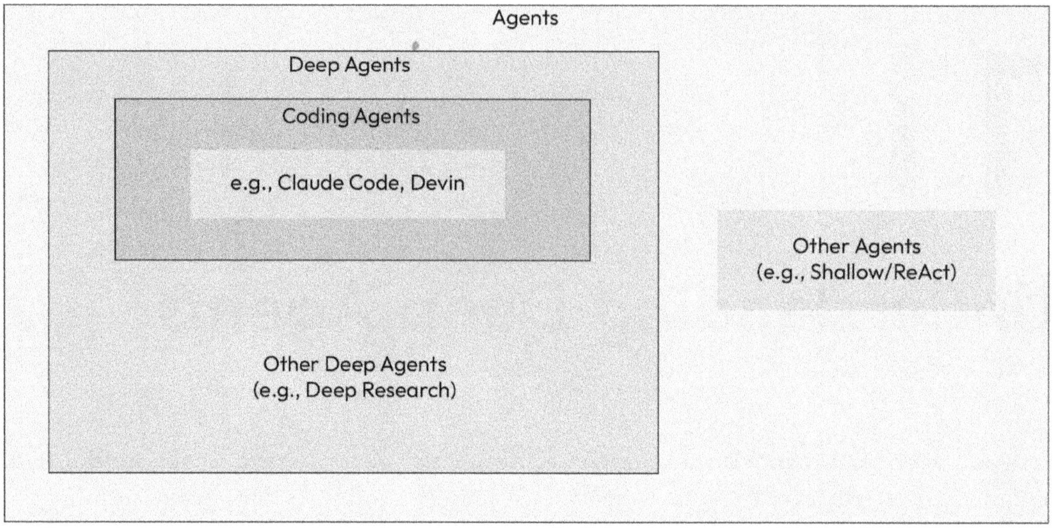

Figure 11.1 – Agent taxonomy showing coding agents within Deep Agents

At the broadest level, we have the domain of agents. This domain includes all types of agents currently deployed in real systems. These can be fully autonomous agents or agentic applications. A common example is a hybrid RAG architecture in which an LLM decides which step to execute next.

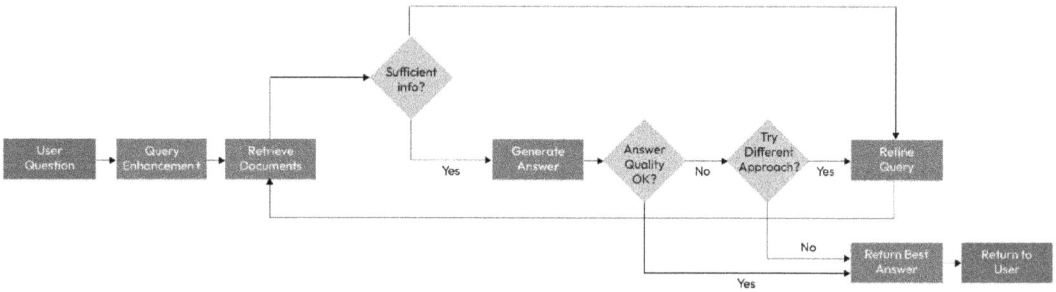

Figure 11.2 – Hybrid RAG workflow orchestrated by an LLM

The model may decide whether to perform a search, whether to rephrase a query before retrieval, or whether to execute another operation. The LLM is effectively orchestrating the next action in the predefined workflow.

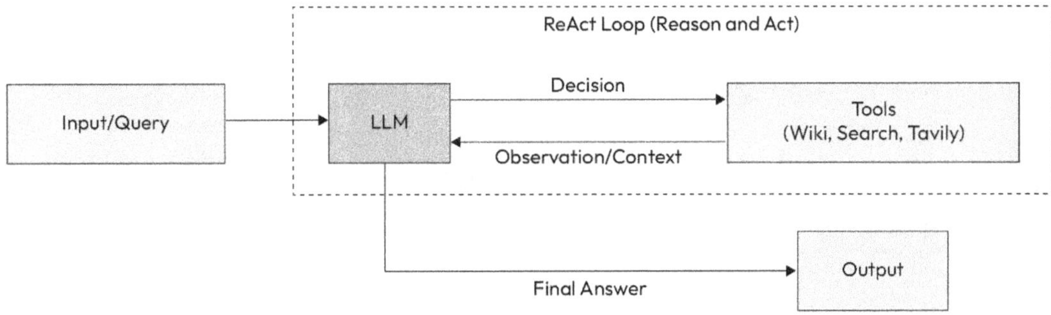

Figure 11.3 – ReAct loop connecting the LLM to external tools

Within this umbrella, we find the ReAct (Reason and Act) agent. In a ReAct agent, an LLM decides whether to use a tool. If a tool is selected, the system executes it and returns the result as an observation. The LLM then decides whether it has sufficient information to return a final response. If not, it continues the loop: selecting another tool, receiving another observation, and iterating until it reaches an answer.

This ReAct loop is what initiated the broader agent paradigm. The majority of modern agent architectures trace back to this algorithmic structure. The approach was introduced in the paper "*ReAct: Synergizing Reasoning and Acting in Language Models*" (`https://arxiv.org/abs/2210.03629`).

Shallow agents and their limitations

In this taxonomy, I am categorizing the ReAct agent as a shallow agent. The reason is not that it lacks utility, but that it lacks the capability to go deep. Consider a task that requires thorough and extended research. Even if the agent has access to a search tool, a wiki tool, or a Tavily tool, it is unlikely to perform sufficiently deep research. The limitation is rooted both in architectural design and in the realities of modern LLMs.

This agent relies on function calling. At each decision point, the LLM makes a function call to select the tool to execute. There is nothing inherently wrong with function calling, although it has trade-offs. The core limitation, however, is the context window.

Every iteration in this loop adds more information to the context. The LLM decides, a tool is executed, the result is injected back into the prompt, and the cycle repeats. With one or two iterations, this remains manageable. As the number of iterations increases, the context grows larger and larger.

This growth leads to context rot. We begin to see context confusion, context contradiction, and context pollution. Over time, performance degrades and the agent may go off the rails.

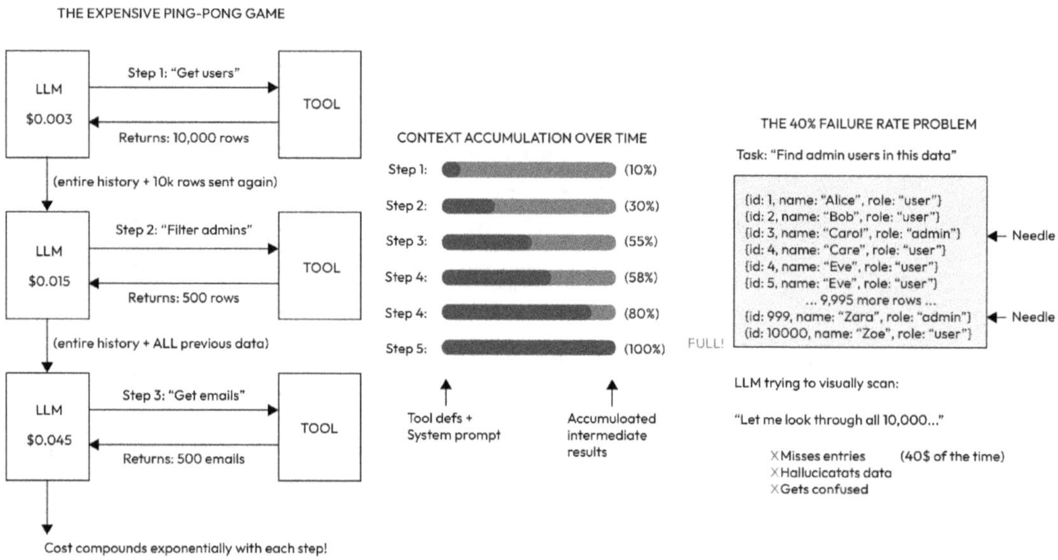

Figure 11.4 – Context accumulation in iterative tool-calling workflows

This limitation becomes critical when dealing with complex, long-running tasks, such as implementing a feature, conducting deep research on a topic, or performing a multi-stage workflow that requires continuous reasoning and information gathering. These are fundamentally different from simple requests, such as booking a flight.

In addition to degraded quality, the cost increases. Each LLM call becomes heavier because it includes more tokens. More tokens increase latency and expense. While the ReAct architecture is foundational and powerful, it is not well-suited for complex, long-horizon tasks.

That said, shallow agents are highly effective for tasks that require only a few iterations. Many production systems use this architecture successfully. In numerous real-world use cases, this pattern is sufficient and does not require additional complexity.

Deep Agents

Returning to the taxonomy, we now move from shallow agents to Deep Agents.

Deep Agents are designed to perform long-horizon tasks. These tasks are complex, require many iterations, and involve significant reasoning and processing. Deep Agents are long-running systems. They may run for minutes, hours, or even days. They can pause execution, request user input, and resume after receiving that input.

Deep research agents are a common example. Systems such as Perplexity expose deep research features that trigger a deep agent run. Many vendors now provide similar research capabilities.

Claude Code includes a research option. ChatGPT includes a research option. Each of these triggers a deep agent implementation, though the internal design differs across vendors.

There are also open source deep research agents. GPT Researcher (`https://github.com/assafelovic/gpt-researcher`) is one of the most popular open source projects in this category. I have created a course for this. You can find it here: `https://www.udemy.com/course/langchain/?srsltid=AfmBOopb6uyyf5oNvX1gvDus-Nqdln5B-bwZtJAW1NLsv7z7ggPJLX9A`.

Coding agents as Deep Agents

Another major subset of Deep Agents is **coding agents**. Examples include Claude Code, Devin, Cursor, and Gemini CLI. Coding agents are one of the strongest demonstrations of how Deep Agents can be effective and widely adopted in the industry. Millions of developers use them.

As you can see, for this book, I have mainly focused on Claude Code, which, at the time of writing this book, is one of the most popular coding agents. Claude Code is highly capable and can handle a wide range of long-running tasks that require depth and scale.

We can ask such an agent to implement an application or a feature. It does not merely generate code. It can run tests, execute the application, open a browser, take screenshots, and perform many of the same steps a software engineer would perform manually.

Coding agents are, therefore, a specialized subset of Deep Agents, tailored specifically for software development workflows.

Innovation at the application layer

Deep Agents currently drive much of the innovation in this space. LLMs continue to improve, but those improvements are gradual. Reasoning quality increases. Capabilities expand. However, the progress is incremental rather than exponential.

At the same time, the application layer built on top of LLMs is advancing rapidly. By layering abstractions on top of agents and composing agents within systems, we can build highly capable machines that automate complex human reasoning tasks. This application layer is often referred to as an Agent Harness.

> **Note**
>
> An **Agent Harness** is a ready-to-use environment for building AI agents. It sits on top of the tools and systems that run agents, and comes pre-configured with everything you need: default prompts, tool handling, planning, file access, and more. Frameworks give you raw building blocks. Runtimes manage execution. A harness does the heavy lifting so you can start building without setting everything up from scratch.

Five years ago, the idea that an AI system could create a functional and visually polished application from scratch without human intervention would have seemed unrealistic. Today, this capability exists.

The key driver is not only the improvement of the base models, but also how we, as developers, harness them (harness engineering). The innovation is happening in the application layer, in how we implement and orchestrate Deep Agents.

What makes an agent deep?

There is no strict formal definition of a deep agent. In practice, I consider an agent deep if it can perform complex, long-running tasks with quality and reliability.

To achieve this, Deep Agents require capabilities that address context bloat and accumulation. The core challenge becomes context engineering and smart context management. Without it, long-horizon execution breaks down.

Most Deep Agents implement several common ideas:

- **A planning tool**: The agent plans what it is going to do before executing steps
- **Sub-agent capabilities**: The system spawns specialized workers that operate in isolated contexts. This allows concurrent execution without bloating a single shared context.
- **A filesystem for intermediate state**: Intermediate results and shared state are written to disk rather than retained entirely in the LLM context. This prevents uncontrolled context growth.
- **A large system prompt**: Deep Agents typically rely on a comprehensive system prompt that encodes instructions, constraints, and operational guidance

If we examine modern deep agent implementations, we typically see these four ideas reflected in some form. In the next section, we will dive into each of these components and examine concrete implementations.

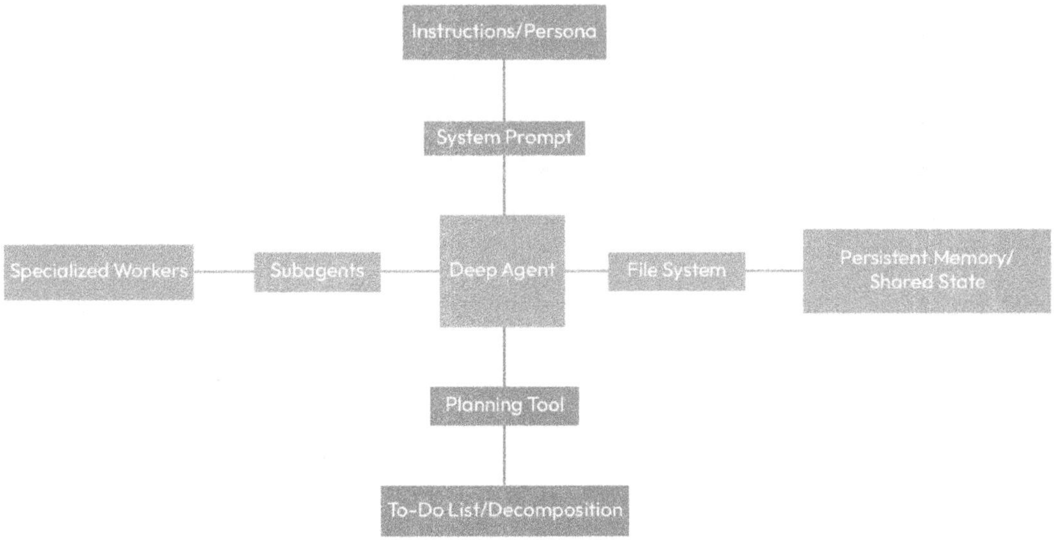

Figure 11.5 – Core components of a deep agent architecture. Adapted from: LangChain Blog, Deep Agents, https://blog.langchain.com/deep-agents/

Planning tool in Deep Agents

Although "Deep Agents" is a general term, the LangChain team articulated it clearly after analyzing multiple deep agent implementations. Every deep agent includes a planning tool.

When we run the tool, we see a list of tasks: some are already completed, one may currently be in progress, and others are queued for execution. What we observe is not implicit planning through chain-of-thought reasoning inside the model. Instead, Deep Agents rely on explicit planning tools.

This planning mechanism is usually implemented as a **to-do list** in Markdown format. Between execution steps, the agent actively reviews and updates this plan. The plan is dynamic. Tasks are marked as *pending*, *in progress*, or *completed*. If a task fails, the agent does not blindly retry it as in the original ReAct agent loop. Instead, the planning tool helps steer execution in a more controlled manner.

The plan is continuously updated, and users can influence the task list. In Claude Code, the planning tool itself is internal and its implementation is not directly accessible. In practice, `TodoWrite` and `TodoRead` actions are invoked. The `TodoWrite` tool creates and updates the to-do list, taking a `{todos: Todo[]}` parameter. The `TodoRead` tool reads the current list. This call updates the to-do list, reflecting changes in the execution plan. Even though the internal reasoning is not directly visible, actions such as `TodoWrite` and `TodoRead` provide insight into how the agent dynamically adjusts its plan while working through a task.

The deep agent continuously updates this to-do list, which improves reliability and increases the likelihood of successfully completing complex tasks. Conceptually, this is intuitive. When handling complex work, we break it down into smaller tasks and track progress over time. The planning tool formalizes that same pattern inside the agent architecture.

Subagents and hierarchical delegation

We discussed the planning tool, or the to-do list tool. Another defining characteristic of Deep Agents is the subagent capability.

Deep Agents employ subagents to enable hierarchical delegation. The main agent can spawn new instances of itself, but those instances are specialized for focused tasks. Each subagent operates with its own system prompt, its own description, and its own set of tools, as shown in the following diagram:

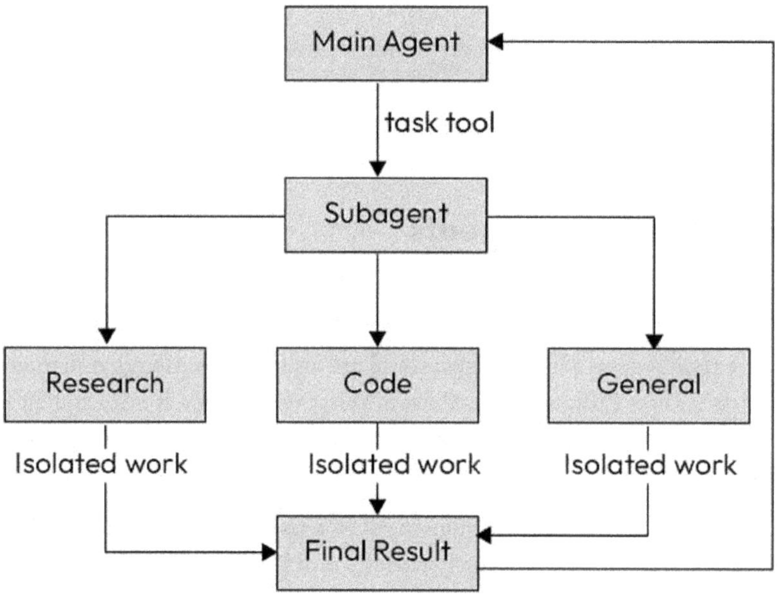

Figure 11.6 – Hierarchical delegation using subagents

This design mirrors how delegation works in real life. When delegating a task, it is not enough to assign the work. The delegated party must have the correct skills and the correct tools. It is also necessary to communicate clearly what needs to be done.

Consider a practical example. Suppose there is a task that requires specific craftsmanship skills, such as fixing a structural issue in a house. If the required expertise is missing, the task must be delegated to someone who has the appropriate skills and tools. That person arrives with their own equipment, performs the work independently, and delivers the final result. The details of the intermediate steps remain isolated from the original requester. What matters is the final outcome.

This is a useful analogy for subagents. The main agent delegates a task by providing a clear description. The subagent operates with its own tools and internal instructions, executes the work independently, and returns the result. During execution, the subagent works in isolation. The main agent does not see every intermediate reasoning step. It only receives the final output.

From a systems perspective, this means subagents run in their own context window. They do not pollute the main agent's context. Each subagent can have a different system prompt and a different set of tools tailored to its specialization. This enables scaling and improves quality by assigning focused responsibilities to specialized agents.

Internally, subagents execute their own tool-calling loops, including their own ReAct-style cycles. When finished, they return only the final response, not the full chain of intermediate observations. This delegation pattern achieves context isolation, prevents specialized work from bloating the main agent's context, and allows parallel execution of tasks. As a result, both efficiency and depth improve.

In practice, we can observe this pattern in systems such as Claude Code. Consider the following example:

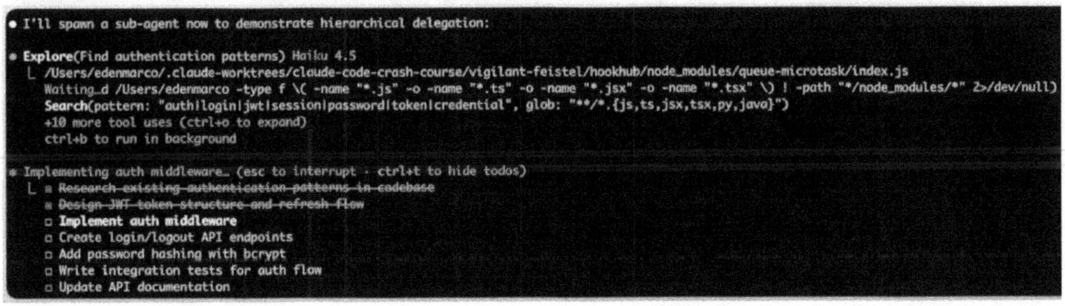

Figure 11.7 – Claude Code spawning a subagent to explore authentication patterns

In this example, Claude Code spawns an exploration agent to search for authentication patterns. That exploration agent runs concurrently, performs its own searches, and operates independently while the main agent continues its execution. This demonstrates built-in support for subagents and hierarchical delegation.

Up to this point, the discussion has focused on concepts and architectural reasoning rather than implementation details. The goal here is to make the conceptual structure clear and to connect these capabilities to the tools used in everyday workflows.

This builds directly on the discussion in *Chapter 7*, where we examined how subagents prevent context bloat, enforce context isolation, and ultimately lead to better results.

Filesystem access in Deep Agents

Another key characteristic of Deep Agents is access to a filesystem. Deep Agents are equipped with tools to search for files, read files, update files, delete files, and generally maintain full control over a filesystem. This capability plays a central role in managing context for long-horizon tasks.

In Claude Code, this manifests through a set of file operation tools.

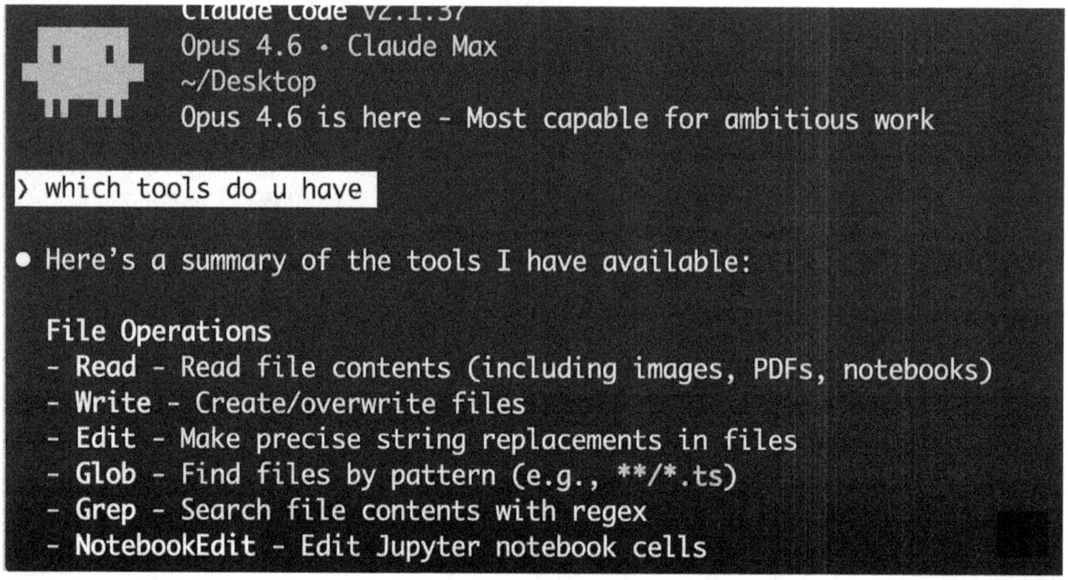

Figure 11.8 – Claude Code file operation tools available to the agent

As you can see, there is a `Read` tool to read file content, a `Write` tool to create or overwrite files, and an `Edit` tool to perform precise string replacements. In addition, Claude Code provides `Glob` and `Grep` tools to search for files and search within files.

If we examine LangChain's Deep Agents documentation, we see a similar filesystem interface: `ls`, `read_file`, `write_file`, `edit_file`, `glob`, and `grep`. Deep Agents expose an interface rather than a specific implementation. This means the underlying storage can vary. For example, the filesystem could be backed by Firestore on Google Cloud or DynamoDB on AWS. The interface remains the same, while the implementation is flexible.

Why filesystems matter for long-horizon tasks

As discussed earlier, as a conversation grows, the context window grows with it. This leads to a range of problems that ultimately result in context rot. Context rot produces degraded responses from the LLM. The degradation may stem from context contradictions, context confusion, or excessive noise in the prompt.

In one of LangChain's blog posts, there is an illustration that captures the core challenge of context engineering for agents. The diagram shown here is inspired by that explanation.

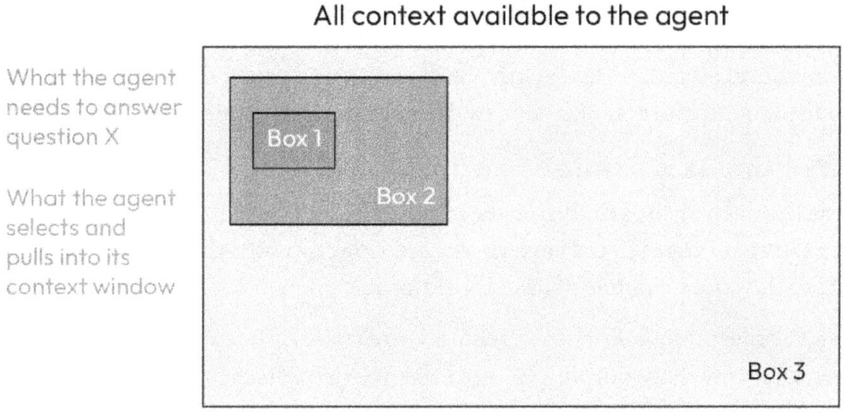

Figure 11.9 – Available context vs. selected context vs. required information. Source: LangChain Blog, How agents can use filesystems for context engineering, https://blog.langchain.com/how-agents-can-use-filesystems-for-context-engineering/

Imagine a large blue rectangle (Box 1) representing all available context: code bases, documents, web search results, files, and databases. This space is potentially large and messy.

Within that, a Box 2 represents the subset of information the agent selects and pulls into the context window for a given step. This is what the agent chooses to read or search. Finally, Box 3 represents the information the agent actually needs to complete the task.

Whenever the red circle does not properly align with the green circle, several failure modes emerge:

- **Under-retrieval**: The agent retrieves only part of Box 2 and misses the necessary information.
- **Over-retrieval**: **Box 2** becomes too large, pulling in excessive noise and diluting the signal.

- **Misaligned retrieval**: The agent searches in the wrong place, and **Box 1** does not overlap with the **Box 2** at all.
- **Context window limits**: The purple box is finite. It cannot contain everything, and if it becomes too large, performance degrades.

The goal of context engineering is to make the red circle as small as possible while fully covering the green circle. This selection process can occur at almost every iteration of the agent. Each step requires optimizing what to include in the context window.

For this reason, how information is structured, retrieved, and prioritized often matters more than the prompt itself. The agent's quality is bound by whether the right information is present in the context window. Even with a strong reasoning model, incorrect or incomplete context can lead to incorrect results or an inability to complete the task.

The filesystem as a context engine

This is where the deep agent's filesystem becomes critical. The filesystem acts as the engine that enables the agent to reach the correct context. Conceptually, the entire filesystem corresponds to the blue rectangle of available information:

1. First, the filesystem allows the agent to write context to persistent storage. Temporary results, intermediate outputs, or retrieved information can be written to files. Instead of bloating the context window, these artifacts are stored externally.
2. Second, the filesystem provides mechanisms for selecting relevant context. Tools such as `glob` allow the agent to find files by pattern, and `grep` allows it to search file contents using regular expressions. These tools enable the agent to retrieve precisely what is needed for the next step.

In this way, the filesystem implements two core principles of context engineering (*Chapter 1*): writing context to persistent storage and selectively retrieving relevant context. It is the mechanism that enables both, and it is fundamental to how Deep Agents manage long-horizon tasks without suffering from context bloat.

System prompt

In AI engineering, it has become somewhat of a cliché to state that "*system prompts are important.*" However, observing the actual practices of industry leaders reveals just how critical this component is. We see system prompts that span hundreds of lines, heavily augmented with massive, injected tool descriptions.

Companies dedicate immense engineering resources to iteratively curating, refining, and updating these prompts as LLMs evolve. For a deep agent, the system prompt is the fundamental architecture of its reasoning, identity, and boundaries.

A highly effective system prompt leverages what state-of-the-art LLMs naturally excel at: pattern recognition and applying general rules to specific, novel situations. A well-crafted system prompt achieves the following:

- **Establishes clear identity and scope**: By clearly defining what the agent is (e.g., "customer support for basic orders") and what it is not (e.g., "not sales or marketing"), the prompt immediately establishes operational boundaries
- **Empowers rather than constrains**: Instead of dictating exactly which tool to use at what time, a great prompt establishes the end goal (e.g., "efficient resolution") and empowers the agent to select the appropriate tools autonomously.
- **Provides a reasoning framework, not a flowchart**: Instead of rigid "If/Then" branching logic, the prompt gives a repeatable framework (e.g., 1. Identify the core issue, 2. Gather context, 3. Provide resolution, 4. Confirm satisfaction). This teaches the model how to approach problems, allowing it to succeed even when it encounters entirely novel situations.
- **Utilizes heuristic boundaries**: It relies on compressed principles rather than exhaustive lists. For example, instructing the model to "always choose the simplest solution" acts as a greedy algorithm heuristic, guiding behavior across thousands of potential edge cases without wasting token space.
- **Maintains language efficiency**: A good prompt does not waste words. It avoids repetition and overlapping instructions that could confuse the LLM or cause contradictory behavior.

The following is LangChain's Deep Agents built-in system prompt. The prompt can be found in the official repository (`https://github.com/langchain-ai/deepagents/blob/main/libs/deepagents/deepagents/base_prompt.md`) and is available under the MIT License.

```
You are a Deep Agent, an AI assistant that helps users accomplish tasks using
tools. You respond with text and tool calls. The user can see your responses and
tool outputs in real time.

## Core Behavior

- Be concise and direct. Don't over-explain unless asked.
- NEVER add unnecessary preamble ("Sure!", "Great question!", "I'll now...").
- Don't say "I'll now do X" — just do it.
- If the request is ambiguous, ask questions before acting.
- If asked how to approach something, explain first, then act.
```

```
## Professional Objectivity

- Prioritize accuracy over validating the user's beliefs
- Disagree respectfully when the user is incorrect
- Avoid unnecessary superlatives, praise, or emotional validation

## Following Conventions

- Read files before editing — understand existing content before making changes
- Mimic existing style, naming conventions, and patterns

## Doing Tasks

When the user asks you to do something:

1. **Understand first** — read relevant files, check existing patterns. Quick but
thorough — gather enough evidence to start, then iterate.
2. **Act** — implement the solution. Work quickly but accurately.
3. **Verify** — check your work against what was asked, not against your own
output. Your first attempt is rarely correct — iterate.

Keep working until the task is fully complete. Don't stop partway and explain what
you would do — just do it. Only yield back to the user when the task is done or
you're genuinely blocked.

**When things go wrong:**
- If something fails repeatedly, stop and analyze *why* — don't keep retrying the
same approach.
- If you're blocked, tell the user what's wrong and ask for guidance.

## Tool Usage

- Use specialized tools over shell equivalents when available (e.g., `read_file`
over `cat`, `edit_file` over `sed`)
- When performing multiple independent operations, make all tool calls in a single
response — don't make sequential calls when parallel is possible.

## File Reading Best Practices

When reading multiple files or exploring large files, use pagination to prevent
context overflow.
```

```
- Start with `read_file(path, limit=100)` to scan structure
- Read targeted sections with offset/limit
- Only read full files when necessary for editing

## Progress Updates

For longer tasks, provide brief progress updates at reasonable intervals – a
concise sentence recapping what you've done and what's next.
```

You can see that the system prompt is the cognitive baseline. Relying on overly specific hardcoding breaks the model's ability to reason, while relying on vague instructions results in chaotic inconsistency.

Summary

In this chapter, we established a practical taxonomy of agents in production, identified the limitations of shallow agents in the face of context bloat and long-running workflows, and defined what makes an agent "deep." We then analyzed the core building blocks that enable deep execution: explicit planning through a dynamic to-do list, hierarchical delegation through specialized subagents operating in isolated contexts, and filesystem access as a mechanism for persistent state and precise context selection. By connecting these components to real systems such as Claude Code and the LangChain DeepAgents' harness, we grounded the discussion in concrete implementations.

Get this book's PDF copy, code bundle, and more

Scan the QR code (or go to `packtpub.com/unlock`). Search for this book by name, confirm the edition, and then follow the steps on the page.

UNLOCK NOW

Note: Have your invoice handy. Purchases made directly from the Packt website don't require an invoice.

12

Unlock Your Exclusive Benefits

Your copy of this book includes the following exclusive benefits:

Follow the guide below to unlock them. The process takes only a few minutes and needs to be completed once.

Unlock this Book's Free Benefits in 3 Easy Steps

Step 1

Keep your purchase invoice ready for *Step 3*. If you have a physical copy, scan it using your phone and save it as a PDF, JPG, or PNG.

For more help on finding your invoice, visit `https://www.packtpub.com/en-us/unlock?step=1`.

> Note
>
> **Note**: If you bought this book directly from Packt, no invoice is required. After *Step 2*, you can access your exclusive content right away.

Step 2

Scan the QR code or go to `packtpub.com/unlock`.

On the page that opens (similar to *Figure 12.1* on desktop), search for this book by name and select the correct edition.

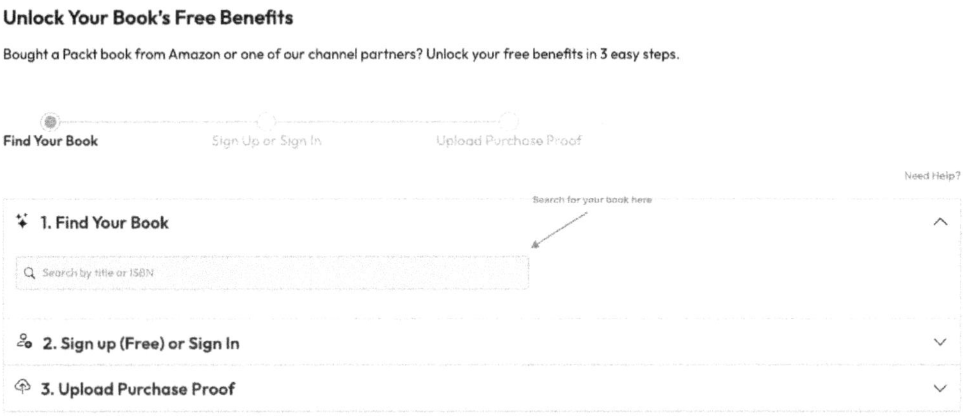

Figure 12.1: Packt unlock landing page on desktop

Step 3

After selecting your book, sign in to your Packt account or create one for free. Then upload your invoice (PDF, PNG, or JPG, up to 10 MB). Follow the on-screen instructions to finish the process.

Need Help

If you get stuck and need help, visit `https://www.packtpub.com/unlock-benefits/help` for a detailed FAQ on how to find your invoices and more. This QR code will take you to the help page.

> **Note**
>
> If you are still facing issues, reach out to `customercare@packt.com`.

Other Books You May Enjoy

If you enjoyed this book, you may be interested in these other books by Packt:

Learn Model Context Protocol with TypeScript

Christoffer Noring

ISBN: 9781806661398

- Understand the MCP protocol and its core components
- Build MCP servers that expose tools and resources to a variety of clients
- Test and debug servers using the interactive inspector tools
- Consume servers using Claude for desktop and Visual Studio Code agents
- Secure MCP apps, as well as managing and mitigating common threats
- Build and deploy MCP apps using cloud-based strategies

Learn Model Context Protocol with Python

Christoffer Noring

ISBN: 9781806103232

- Understand the MCP protocol and its core components
- Build MCP servers that expose tools and resources to a variety of clients
- Test and debug servers using the interactive inspector tools
- Consume servers using Claude Desktop and Visual Studio Code Agents
- Secure MCP apps, as well as managing and mitigating common threats
- Build and deploy MCP apps using cloud-based strategies

Packt is searching for authors like you

If you're interested in becoming an author for Packt, please visit `authors.packtpub.com` and apply today. We have worked with thousands of developers and tech professionals, just like you, to help them share their insight with the global tech community. You can make a general application, apply for a specific hot topic that we are recruiting an author for, or submit your own idea.

Share your thoughts

Now you've finished *Agentic Coding with Claude Code*, we'd love to hear your thoughts! Scan the QR code below to go straight to the Amazon review page for this book and share your feedback or leave a review on the site that you purchased it from.

`https://packt.link/r/1806022591`

Your review is important to us and the tech community and will help us make sure we're delivering excellent quality content.

Index

D

P

R

S

www.ingramcontent.com/pod-product-compliance
Lightning Source LLC
Chambersburg PA
CBHW081126180926
51611CB00005B/68
9781806022595